CULT POP CULTURE

CULT POP CULTURE

How the Fringe Became Mainstream

Volume 1: Film and Television

Bob Batchelor, Editor

 PRAEGER

AN IMPRINT OF ABC-CLIO, LLC
Santa Barbara, California • Denver, Colorado • Oxford, England

Library of Congress Cataloging-in-Publication Data

Cult pop culture : how the fringe became mainstream / Bob Batchelor, editor.
  p. cm.
Includes bibliographical references and index.
  ISBN 978–0–313–35780–0 (set : alk. paper) — ISBN 978–0–313–35781–7 (set : ebook) — ISBN 978–0–313–35782–4 (v. 1 : alk. paper) — ISBN 978–0–313–35783–1 (v. 1 : ebook) — ISBN 978–0–313–35784–8 (v. 2 : alk. paper) — ISBN 978–0–313–35785–5 (v. 2 : ebook) — ISBN 978–0–313–35804–3 (v. 3 : alk. paper) — ISBN 978–0–313–35805–0 (v. 3 : ebook)
1. Popular culture—United States. 2. Subculture—United States 3. United States—Civilization. 4. National characteristics, American. I. Batchelor, Bob.
E169.12.C766   2012
306.0973—dc23   2011027591

ISBN: 978–0–313–35780–0
EISBN: 978–0–313–35781–7

16 15 14 13 12   1 2 3 4 5

This book is also available on the World Wide Web as an eBook.
Visit www.abc-clio.com for details.

Praeger
An Imprint of ABC-CLIO, LLC

ABC-CLIO, LLC
130 Cremona Drive, P.O. Box 1911
Santa Barbara, California 93116-1911

This book is printed on acid-free paper ∞

Manufactured in the United States of America

To Ray B. Browne, a mentor and guiding spirit for all popular culture enthusiasts, and with all my love to my wife Kathy and our daughter, Kassandra Dylan. Without them, nothing is possible.

CONTENTS

INTRODUCTION

Bob Batchelor

The word *cult* carries two distinct meanings in the United States. The first is destructive, most often associated with extreme religious groups and messianic individuals, such as Charles Manson or Jim Jones. A mere mention of the word in this context and one's mind immediately conjures up grainy television footage of some psychotic and often includes extreme violence. Given that many cult movements have ended in total destruction, perhaps television, movie, or documentary images of that person or clan pop into view. I would bet, for example, that the image of Powers Boothe playing Jim Jones in the 1980s miniseries *Guyana Tragedy* is more recognizable than actual photos of Jones.

Thankfully, however, the second definition is less scary. When one refers to cults under this guise, the word means that a topic or individual possesses a kind of compulsive, rampant, or enduring popularity, usually slightly or overtly outside the mainstream. We see this when a figure or object is said to have a "cult of personality," or a "cult following."

What the two meanings of *cult* have in common is the idea that in each case, followers hold belief in the person or object deep in their souls, in most cases, willing to do battle to defend those thoughts or perhaps even die for them. Examining the dark form of cult based on fear, hatred, domination, and obsession, we see that the differences with the second definition are much greater. As a matter of fact, cult pop culture is built on ideas at the opposite end of the spectrum from the evil version: humor, charisma, mystery, and love.

In contemporary America, the Internet Age and sophisticated technological innovations are spinning the notion of cult and cult popular culture on its head. Due to the spread of mass communication channels, the definition and subsequent use of *cult* is changing significantly. For example, the widespread use of the word is in some ways clouding its meaning. One finds that anything, anyone, or any group that is slightly off kilter is dubbed a cult, just as is an item in these categories that gains quick or unexplained popularity.

Some products and corporate leaders are given the "cult of" label. Apple and its late charismatic chief executive Steve Jobs are a case study here. Although there are untold millions of Apple users (this essay is, in fact, being written and copyedited on a MacBook Pro), which might lead one to dismiss it as a cult phenomenon, there are also intensely devoted Apple consumers—the kind that will wait outside its retail stores for days on end to be the first to possess a new product, such as the iPad or latest iteration of the iPhone. Indeed, Jobs himself was said to be a kind of cult leader, maybe based on his Svengali-like ability to lead the company through the introduction of so many now-essential consumer goods. Jobs's success, despite the ongoing health challenges that eventually took his life and the gloomy economic picture, add to the cult-like implications. As the word has transformed over time, Jobs's version of it seemed to also entail traits such as secrecy, success, admiration, jealousy, and the general impression that someone so powerful must be doing something nefarious to achieve such heights.

Another interesting change occurring is that for the first time in history, any boundaries that walled off cult topics based on access or control over content are now virtually nonexistent. The Web, YouTube, file sharing, and global electronic communities have destroyed the demarcation between cult and noncult entities. The ability to access information on just about any topic under the sun is only a few keystrokes away. Perhaps most dramatically, there are images and video on niche subjects of every variety. The 2003 film *The Room*, for example, is now considered part of the cult industry, inspiring zany devotees to obsess about the movie in any number of ways. However, the notion of *The Room* as a cult topic must include that typing "The Room movie" into Google produces 381 million hits. In this way, the idea of cult popular culture has been put through the democratic mass media wringer, emerging on the other side outside the fringes that made it a cult topic in the first place.

With Google and YouTube, in particular, the amount of material one can now find on any cult topic both exemplifies and defies the label itself. On one hand, many (possibly millions) of search results reveal how deeply loved or obsessed over a cult topic might be. Its fans create new meaning by erecting virtual altars to it on the Web. Yet, on the other hand, the watering-down factor must by definition pull it toward the mainstream.

For example, if one's cult fetish happened to be the original Speed Racer cartoons that originally aired in the United States in 1967 and 1968, then in reruns over various later periods, it would have been difficult (if not impossible) and costly to find videotapes of the series or even a great deal of information about the show. Fast-forward to 2011, however, and a simple Google search returns more than 2.1 million hits, websites devoted to the series, places to buy all the episodes on DVD, and all the minute details that would set the cultist's heart aflutter.

This collection, then, examines and interrogates the idea of what makes a cult topic in contemporary America. A word of caution, though, is that in no way is it meant to be exhaustive or all encompassing. If one accepts my idea about the democratization of cult popular culture outlined above, then it is clear that no collection, regardless of rigor, could keep up with the number of new cult topics emerging quietly or blared from the faux news desk of a nightly celebutainment program.

Fittingly, the first volume in the *Cult Pop Culture* collection focuses on cult topics related to film and television. People are quick to tack the label on movies and television shows. The second volume travels through cult topics in literature and music. These essays reveal the profound attachment listeners and readers feel for their favorite artists, particularly when discovered prior to mainstream acceptance. This volume also addresses how fans (often with the help/promotion of the media) generate cult icons. The third set of essays grapples with cult topics across a series of interesting areas, including particular industries, events, places, sports, and the Internet. While this volume purposely offers snapshots of many topics that comprise contemporary cult pop culture, readers will find numerous threads that run through the sections. For example, Volume 3 examines several topics that are not based on a single person, group, or entity but instead take on broad subjects that engage larger numbers of people, such as poker/gambling, car collectors, and online virtual environments.

I did not force the *Cult Pop Culture* contributors to abide by a specific definition of what is or is not cult. Actually, I deliberately chose to not force my notions of cult popular culture on them so they would have the intellectual freedom to roam widely over the idea. What I think readers will enjoy about this collection is the ability to read it in a non-linear fashion. As a matter of fact, each book, similar to the way people surf the Web, begs to be tackled based on interest. If Russ Meyer is your cult thing, feel free to start in the film section and see where the journey takes you.

The beauty and value of popular culture is its ability to let people explore the ideas, topics, people, and influences that matter to them most. This exercise actually forces people to engage in higher-order critical thinking skills involved in the formation of new ideas and impulses. As we wrestle with our own thoughts, dreams, and aspirations through popular culture exploration, we obtain, strengthen, and evolve our personal worldviews or core guiding ideologies.

Cult pop culture, then, opens up and allows others into the darker recesses of our obsessions. It swirls somewhere in our minds and comes alive at the intersection of the mass communication industries that developed to support and disseminate culture. And, just like non-cult popular culture, its cult cousin requires a nearly endless supply of fact, fiction, gossip, illusion, and misinformation. Based on the amount of information available, we are actually training ourselves to think amid this cacophony. The result of these countless pop culture impressions over the course of a lifetime is a permanently heightened sense of sensationalism, chased with healthy doses of societal angst.

The technology foundation is blurring the lines between cult and noncult, actually drawing the former into the mainstream. It is not possible to distinguish where one or the other stops or starts. At what point, for instance, does a film or person magically transform from something interesting to a phenomenon that creates obsessive, loving followers? A simple definition does not exist, so people are forced to draw their own conclusions.

What is clear, however, is that the ability to covet a cult topic individually is both shrinking and expanding as technology becomes more omnipresent. These contrasting forces enable one to be as completely obsessive as he or she wishes while simultaneously allowing that person to be fully public or private about it. A person can build an online shrine to his or her cult icons, potentially drawing an audience of many millions, or ferret out information alone with nothing but the ideas and a glowing computer screen in front of him or her.

Connections

The power of cult popular culture is in the way it connects people. One could reasonably argue, as a matter of fact, that it is in the connections with and between objects and people that the definition of broader popular culture resides. In essence, then, popular culture is not a kind of thing, as most definitions attempt to explain, like the antithesis of high art or culture. Rather, popular culture resides in the various impulses that draw members of the global community to a person, thing, topic, or issue that arise out of the juncture of mass communications, technology, political systems, and economic institutions.

In other words, I am proposing that we view popular culture not as an object, say Andy Warhol's famous Campbell's Soup can painting, but as the interface itself that draws viewers to or repels them from that artwork. Examining Warhol's piece, it is not that I say to myself, "wow, that is popular culture." Instead, it is the confluence of seeing that paining; interacting with it based on my life experiences; adding context, history, experience, and personality; and then creating a new meaning of it for me personally that defines popular culture.

The late Ray B. Browne explained popular culture, saying, "It is the everyday world around us: the mass media, entertainments, diversions, heroes, icons, rituals, psychology, religion—our total life picture." In addition, my definition asks that the consumer recognize that it is more than just the world around us; it also includes the exchange between a popular culture object and one's assimilation of the thing—the thoughts, emotions, and manner in which one consumes it. For me, the meaning of popular culture exists in that absorption rather than in attempting to define a tangible object as low-, high-, or middlebrow on a fabricated scale of hierarchies. In this respect, *popular culture* is a verb, not a noun, the total mental and physical interaction with a topic and the new synthesis or creation that occurs as a result of that fusion.[1]

It is no wonder that film and television are central facets when discussing cult topics. They define our national dialogue, essentially providing Americans with basic talking points across race, political ties, gender differences, or any other demographic features that separate people. The narratives, regardless of the reason they attract or repel us, give context and a way of interpreting society and culture.

As millions of Americans interact with mass media, whether watching the same movies and television shows or listening to radio programs, a common language develops that opens new lines of communications. The downside, however, is that the fascination with popular culture diverts attention from important challenges the nation confronts. In this light, popular culture serves as a kind of placebo. The obsessive, loving nature of cult objects intensifies this diversion critique of popular culture because the focus on a specific cult influence distracts people and, at the same time, enables them to feel good about the world without really forcing them to directly confront critical issues.

In terms of cult topics, the connection between people may be deeper and stronger, based on a sense that enthusiasts share some tightly held meaning or feeling of ownership regarding the object. In some cases, such as fan fiction or cover bands, people are so intricately wrapped up in the meaning of a cult topic that they will participate in the creation of new or alternative meanings.

How the Fringe Became Mainstream

Perhaps in an earlier era—one not so media saturated—cult popular culture objects could remain small, special, or maybe even hidden away. Looking back, individuals appeared to have greater control over their interaction with popular culture. A person could wade in and out of mass communication channels at will. More importantly, people possessed the ability and power to turn off the culture clatter.

In contemporary America, however, popular culture is omnipresent. This fundamental transformation has broad consequences because of its complete totality. Today, like Neo when he decides to enter the Matrix, there is no escape or turning back. As a result, the fringiest subcultures and most "out there" parts of the pop culture universe are within easy reach—often no further than a mouse click away.

At the heart of this transformation is our collective wanderlust regarding technology. The nation is in the midst of a technology mania, which is used as an excuse and tool to map out every inch of our cultural beings, from cravings and fascinations to depravities and fears. Now, entire industries are created on the whims and secret longings of people simultaneously tethered to their computers and set free to roam the broad infinity of the Internet. In an environment where most people accept the idea that popular culture is as pervasive as the air around us, the distance between cult and mainstream is stripped away.

At its heart, cult popular culture is not outside America or conventional society—it *is* America. Cult topics and objects are now part of mainstream culture, pretty much as accessible as any other cultural influence. In an earlier era, one's dedication to a cult notion might have served as a way of differentiating from traditional norms or values. This is no longer the case due to the ease in accessing information across mass media channels. By definition, when a person searches out information and finds it on a website, for example, he or she is interacting with others, since the searcher realizes that someone or group created the site itself. The Internet serves as a tether between cult enthusiasts, whether it is actively monitoring a Wikipedia entry on given object or watching a YouTube clip.

More importantly, perhaps, is that the enthusiast's commitment to a cult topic embodies the general fascination with popular culture in contemporary society. Given the way I have redefined popular culture as an action rather than an object, my view is that popular culture is not only central to what people believe but also crucial in how they understand and interpret the world. The challenge, whether dealing with a topic within or outside traditional culture, is that many people willingly allow themselves to be distracted by popular culture to the detriment of other critical aspects of contemporary life.

If a person is consumed by the latest film, television, or celebrity gossip, it is easier to put off thoughts of war, economic disparity, and melancholy. Thus, popular culture—literally the study of what influences people as they conduct their daily lives—can be a force for reinterpreting and changing the world. Or it can mask reality in favor of a Hollywood version of life that emphasizes happy endings and rainbows. Wake up or tune out—the choice is yours.

***

Creating a collection like *Cult Pop Culture* might seem like a solitary task, but actually this series would not exist without a strong team behind it. First, I would like to thank and congratulate the contributors, a group of scholars, professional writers, enthusiasts, and graduate students whose analysis and insight illuminated the idea of cult popular culture in new and engaging ways. I am really pleased that we were able to pull together such a phenomenal group of contributors drawn not only from several nations around the world but also from some of the finest popular culture scholars working today. In addition, young scholars and graduate students from some of America's finest schools, including Penn State University, Kent State University, Michigan State

University, and the University of South Florida, brought energy and enthusiasm to the project. I hope this brief note will accentuate how much I truly appreciate this group's work.

Cult Pop Culture would not have seen the light of day without the steady, enthusiastic support of our editor Dan Harmon. Dan and I have enjoyed a long history of work together across many projects. He is a true professional and good friend. Other friends offered support and help along the way, including Chris Burtch, Larry Z. Leslie, Kelli Burns, Tom Heinrich, Brian Cogan, and Tom and Kristine Brown. I have been lucky to have many fantastic mentors, including Lawrence S. Kaplan, James A. Kehl, Sydney Snyder, Richard Immerman, Peter Magnani, and Anne Beirne. A special note of thanks goes to Phillip Sipiora, who taught me so much at the University of South Florida and continues to be a role model for my own work as a scholar. So much of my career success resulted from my relationship with Ray B. Browne (1922–2009). This collection is dedicated to him, not only out of respect for his guidance, but also for all of us who are deeply interested in popular culture.

In addition, I would like to thank my colleagues at Kent State University for their support and encouragement, particularly Stanley T. Wearden, Dean of the College of Communication and Information, and Jeff Fruit, Director of the School of Journalism and Mass Communication. Their vision and leadership have been inspirational. Bill Sledzik, Danielle Coombs, Tim Smith, and Gene Sasso helped guide me as well. Financial support from JMC also enabled me to have two fine graduate research assistants and editors on the project: Sonali Kudva and Jodee Hammond. Both improved the collection immeasurably.

On a personal note, nothing I do is possible without the support of my family. Kathy and Kassie brought immeasurable joy into my life on a moment-by-moment basis. I cherish every instant we spend together—thank you.

Note

1. Ray B. Browne, "Popular Culture as the New Humanities," in *Popular Culture Theory and Methodology: A Basic Introduction*, edited by Harold E. Hinds, Jr., et al. (Madison: University of Wisconsin Press, 2006), 75.

TIMELINE

1900 to Present

1900   November 3–10, The Automobile Club of America sponsors the first automobile show in Madison Square Garden.

Kodak introduces the $1.00 Brownie Box Camera.

The College Entrance Examination Board is established by representatives from 13 colleges and preparatory schools.

"A Bird in a Gilded Cage," written by Arthur J. Lamb and Harry Von Tilzer, becomes a hit song.

1901   President Theodore Roosevelt causes a national controversy when he dines with Black leader Booker T. Washington at the White House.

General Electric develops the first corporate research laboratory.

United States Steel is formed and is the nation's first billion-dollar corporation.

The United States declares the war in the Philippines is over.

1902   Owen Wister publishes *The Virginian*.

Dr. Charles Wardell Stiles discovers hookworm, a parasite affecting countless poor Whites in the South.

Michigan defeats Stanford 49–0 in the first Tournament of Roses Association football game.

1903   May 23–July 26, Dr. Horatio Nelson Jackson and Sewall K. Crocker complete the first cross-country automobile trip.

The Boston Red Sox defeat the Pittsburgh Pirates in the inaugural baseball World Series.

The 23-story, steel-framed Fuller Building is completed in New York City; because of its unique shape, it becomes known as the Flatiron Building.

The Great Train Robbery, directed by Edwin S. Porter, is the nation's first action movie.

1904   The first organized automobile race, dubbed the Vanderbilt Cup race after William K. Vanderbilt, a wealthy auto enthusiast, takes place on Long Island.

The first Olympic Games held in the United States take place as part of the St. Louis World's Fair.

The first segment of the New York City subway, from the Brooklyn Bridge to 145th Street, opens.

1905   First nickelodeon (nickel theater) opens in Pittsburgh.

May G. Sutton becomes the first U.S. player to win a Wimbledon singles title.

The Rotary Club, the first business-oriented service organization, is founded in Chicago.

1906   Upton Sinclair publishes *The Jungle*, a novel that reveals impure food-processing standards in Chicago.

Devil's Tower in Wyoming is declared the first national monument by Theodore Roosevelt.

1907   As a result of the Immigration Act of 1907, Japanese laborers are excluded from immigrating to the continental United States by presidential order.

Ziegfeld's Follies opens on Broadway.

The *Lusitania*, the world's largest steamship, sets a new speed record, crossing the Atlantic from Ireland to New York in five days.

1908   Henry Ford introduces the first Model T, which sells for $850.

New York City passes the Sullivan Ordinance, which bans women from smoking cigarettes in public.

The first airplane fatality occurs when Lieutenant Thomas W. Selfridge dies in the crash of a plane piloted by Orville Wright, who is also seriously injured.

1909   George Bellows paints *Both Members of the Club.*

The Federal Bureau of Investigation (FBI) is established.

Football is banned from the New York City public schools due to its injury and even death rate.

Alice Huyler Ramsey is the first woman to drive across the United States—from New York to San Francisco.

Scribner's pays former president Theodore Roosevelt $500,000 for an account of his hunting trip to Africa.

The Pittsburgh Pirates win the World Series by beating the Detroit Tigers four games to three.

1910   Jack Johnson becomes the first Black heavyweight champion of the modern era with a fifteenth-round knockout of Jim Jeffries.

The Boy Scouts of America is chartered by William D. Boyce.

The Camp Fire Girls is chartered by Dr. & Mrs. L. H. Gulick.

Florence Lawrence is declared the first genuine movie star as the "Vitagraph Girl."

Architect Frank Lloyd Wright completes work on the Robie House, Chicago, Illinois.

The National City Planning Association is founded to help designers better coordinate architectural and landscape designs into American cities.

Morris and Rose Michtom found the Ideal Novelty & Toy Company.

1911   Edith Wharton publishes *Ethan Frome.*

The magazine *Masses* is rechristened with Max Eastman as editor.

Walter Dill Scott publishes *Influencing Men in Business,* which defines the methods of modern advertising.

Irving Berlin publishes hit song "Alexander's Ragtime Band."

The Kewpie doll, created by Rose O'Neill, appears.

Frank Lloyd Wright completes Taliesin, his home, studio, and retreat, near Spring Green, Wisconsin.

The Gideon Organization of Christian Commercial Travelers begins placing more than 60,000 Bibles in hotel rooms.

1912   The ocean liner *Titanic* strikes an iceberg and sinks (April 14–15), killing 1,523 passengers and crew.

The Girl Scouts of America is founded by Daisy Gordon.

Maria Montessori publishes *The Montessori Childhood Education Method,* describing new techniques in preschool education.

Mack Sennett founds the Keystone Company to produce comedy motion pictures.

Carl Laemmle forms Universal Pictures.

Novella *Tarzan of the Apes* is published by Edgar Rice Burroughs.

1913   The Armory Show of Modern Art is staged in New York City.

Congress designates the second Sunday in May as Mother's Day (May 10).

Horace Fletcher creates a national sensation through his "cure" for obesity and stomach ailment, called Fletcherism, which advocates chewing one's food at least 100 times before swallowing.

The Oreo cookie is introduced.

James Reese Europe becomes one of the first African Americans to secure a record deal, with Victor Records.

Clarence Crane introduces a hard candy called the Life Saver. His first flavor is Pep-O-Mint.

A. C. Gilbert begins marketing the Erector set.

George Herriman's cartoon strip "Krazy Kat" premieres in the *New York Journal.*

The Woolworth Building is completed in New York City.

1914   Tin Pan Alley songwriters organize the American Society of Composers, Authors, and Publishers (ASCAP) to protect their financial interests through royalty payments.

First transcontinental telephone service between New York City and San Francisco is successful.

Charlie Chaplin becomes a national star after the release of *Kid Auto Races at Venice*; "Charliemania" sweeps the country.

Tinkertoys are introduced.

W. C. Handy introduces America to the blues with the publication of the *St. Louis Blues.*

Construction begins on the Lincoln Memorial, Washington, D.C.

Mary Pickford becomes a national sensation after starring in D. W. Griffith's *Tess of Storm County.*

Margaret Sanger publishes *Family Limitation*, introducing many to the values of birth control.

The Harrison Drug Act is passed to restrict access to narcotics in the United States. The federal government estimates that 4.5 percent of the American public is addicted to drugs.

Gold is discovered in Alaska, leading to the last gold rush in American history.

1915   D. W. Griffith releases his landmark film *The Birth of a Nation.*

Carl Sandburg publishes *Chicago Poems.*

"Jelly Roll" Morton publishes the *Jelly Roll Blues.*

R. J. Reynolds creates one of the most successful brand-name advertising campaigns in modern history by introducing Camel cigarettes.

The Victor Talking Machine Company begins selling phonographs to the public.

Ford Motor Company produces its one-millionth Model T.

The state of Nevada passes the first no-fault divorce law, which requires six months of residency in the state.

1916   First permanent annual Rose Bowl football game is played.

Piggly-Wiggly, the first self-service grocery store, is founded by Clarence Saunders in Memphis, Tennessee.

D. W. Griffith films and releases the motion picture *Intolerance.*

Georgia O'Keeffe premieres at Alfred Stieglitz's New York Gallery, known as 291.

The Provincetown Players move from Cape Cod, Massachusetts, to Greenwich Village, New York, and become the most influential Little Theatre of the decade.

Norman Rockwell illustrates his first cover for the *Saturday Evening Post.*

Fortune cookies are introduced to the world by David Jung, a Los Angeles noodle maker.

1917   Ragtime pioneer Scott Joplin dies (April 1).

The Constitutional amendment prohibiting the manufacture, sale, and use of alcohol passes Congress and is sent to the states for ratification (December 18).

The National Birth Control League, later Planned Parenthood, is created by Margaret Sanger.

1918   The first installment of Irish writer James Joyce's *Ulysses* is banned by the U.S. Post Office.

The Raggedy Ann doll, created by Johnny Gruelle, is introduced.

1919   The Eighteenth Amendment, prohibiting the manufacture, sale, and consumption of alcohol, is ratified.

United Artists is founded by Charlie Chaplin, D. W. Griffith, Douglas Fairbanks, and Mary Pickford.

John Reed publishes *Ten Days That Shook the World.*

George "Babe" Ruth hits 29 home runs, shattering the old record. The next year Ruth will hit 54 homers, more than any other single *team* previously.

D. W. Griffith releases the movie *Broken Blossoms*.

Peter Paul Halajian of the Peter Paul Candy Company introduces the Konabar.

Lincoln Logs, a toy building set, are introduced.

1920   The Eighteenth Amendment, prohibiting the manufacture, transportation, and sale of alcohol, goes into effect (January 16).

The Negro National Baseball League is founded (February 12).

Grand Canyon National Park is dedicated (April 20).

The Nineteenth Amendment, granting women the right to vote, is ratified (August 26).

The American Professional Football Association (renamed the National Football League in 1922) is founded (September 17).

Station KDKA, East Pittsburgh, Pennsylvania, inaugurates regular radio broadcasting (November 2).

The Baby Ruth candy bar is introduced.

1921   Charlie Chaplin's first feature-length film, *The Kid*, premieres (February 6).

The first White Castle hamburger restaurant opens in Wichita, Kansas (March 10).

Margaret Gorman wins the first Miss American Pageant in Atlantic City, New Jersey (September 8).

The Sheik, starring Rudolph Valentino, premieres (October 31).

The Washburn-Crosby Company of Minneapolis creates Betty Crocker, a fictional model homemaker, to promote its Gold Medal brand flour.

Wonder Bread is introduced.

The Eskimo Pie ice cream bar sells more than one million units during its first year on the market.

1922   *Reader's Digest* publishes its first issue (February 5).

French fashion designer Coco Chanel introduces her signature perfume, Chanel No. 5 (May 5).

Abie's Irish Rose, the longest running Broadway play of the 1920s, opens (May 23).

The Lincoln Memorial is dedicated in Washington, D.C. (May 30).

Archaeologist Howard Carter and his excavation team discover King Tutankhamen's tomb in the Valley of the Kings near Luxor, Egypt (November 4).

Fruit, Garden and Home begins publication (renamed *Better Homes and Gardens* in 1924).

George Squier invents Muzak, first developed in order to calm anxious elevator riders.

Emily Post publishes *Etiquette in Society, in Business, in Politics and at Home*, which becomes a national best seller.

The Chinese tile game of mahjong becomes a fad in the United States.

The first A&W Root Beer stand opens in Sacramento, California.

The Klondike Bar is introduced.

1923   *Time*, the nation's first weekly news magazine, publishes its first issue.

Alma Cummings wins the first American dance marathon, held at the Audubon Ballroom in New York City.

Yankee Stadium opens (April 18).

Cecil B. DeMille's epic biblical film *The Ten Commandments* premieres on December 4.

Neon advertising signs are introduced.

Mars Candies markets its first candy bar, the Milky Way.

Jacob Schick receives a patent for the first electric razor.

Reese's Peanut Butter Cups are introduced.

The nonsensical "Yes! We Have No Bananas" becomes a major hit song, to the annoyance of countless Americans.

The Bell and Howell Company introduces a 16-mm camera, marking the advent of home movies.

1924   *Little Orphan Annie* comic strip debuts in the *New York Daily News* (August 5).

Macy's department store sponsors its first Thanksgiving Day parade.

The Kimberly-Clark Company introduces Kleenex, the first disposable facial tissue.

Flagpole sitting becomes a national fad.

Richard Simon and Max Schuster publish *The Cross Word Puzzle Book*, launching a major fad.

Wheaties breakfast cereal is introduced.

The Popsicle is invented.

1925   *The New Yorker* begins publication (February 21).

        The Gold Rush, starring Charlie Chaplin, premieres (June 26).

        Walter Chrysler incorporates the Maxwell Motor Car Company as the
        Chrysler Corporation (June 26).

        The *WSM Barn Dance* (renamed *The Grand Ole Opry* in 1927) begins its
        Saturday night broadcasts in Nashville, Tennessee (November 28).

        Bruce Barton publishes *The Man Nobody Knows*, a pseudo-biography of
        Jesus that becomes a national best seller.

        The Goodyear Tire and Rubber Company launches its first advertising
        blimp, *The Pilgrim*.

        F. Scott Fitzgerald publishes his most acclaimed novel, *The Great Gatsby*.

1926   Western Air Express, later renamed Trans-World Airlines (TWA),
        begins passenger service (May 23).

        Magician and escape artist Harry Houdini dies at the age of 52
        (October 31).

        The National Broadcasting Company (NBC), the nation's first radio net-
        work, premieres (November 15).

        The Book-of-the-Month Club is founded.

        The Butterfinger candy bar is introduced.

        Ernest Hemingway publishes *The Sun Also Rises*.

1927   The first demonstration of long-range television transmission, from a sig-
        nal in Washington, D.C., to a receiver in New York City, occurs (April 7).

        Aviator Charles Lindbergh completes the first solo, nonstop flight
        across the Atlantic Ocean (May 21).

        The Columbia Broadcasting System (CBS) begins broadcasting (Septem-
        ber 18).

        New York Yankees slugger Babe Ruth hits his 60th home run of the
        regular season, a major league record that will stand until 1961 (Septem-
        ber 30).

        Warner Brothers' *The Jazz Singer*, the first feature-length motion pic-
        ture with synchronized speech and music, premieres (October 6).

        The Ford Motor Company introduces its new Model A automobile
        (December 2).

        Kool-Aid (originally spelled Kool-Ade) is introduced.

1928   *Steamboat Willie*, Walt Disney's black-and-white animated cartoon
        featuring Mickey Mouse and synchronized sound, premieres (Novem-
        ber 18).

Peter Pan peanut butter is introduced.

Gerber baby food is introduced.

Dubble Bubble, the nation's first bubble gum, is introduced.

Kraft introduces Velveeta, a processed cheese food.

1929   The first science-fiction comic strip, *Buck Rogers in the 25th Century A.D.*, debuts (January 7).

Cartoonist Elzie C. Segar introduces a sailor character named Popeye in his *Thimble Theatre* comic strip (January 17).

The first Academy of Motion Pictures Arts and Sciences Awards ceremony is held in Hollywood, honoring films for the years 1927 and 1928 (May 16).

The comedy radio series *Amos 'n Andy* premieres on the NBC network (August 19).

The Museum of Modern Art opens in New York.

1930   The Chrysler Building opens on May 27 in New York City; it is briefly the world's tallest skyscraper.

Miniature golf becomes a fad, and dance marathons regain popularity.

Commercial air travel between New York and Los Angeles is initiated in October. United Airlines hires the first stewardesses.

The impact of the movies is felt in fashion: the cool, sophisticated looks of Greta Garbo, Joan Crawford, Jean Harlow, and Marlene Dietrich gain popularity.

1931   On May 1, the Empire State Building opens in New York City; it is the world's tallest skyscraper.

In October, Chester Gould's *Dick Tracy* makes its debut in newspaper comic strips.

Birds Eye frozen vegetables appear, along with Hostess Twinkies and Snickers candy bars.

Two new afternoon radio serials, based on popular comic strips, come on the air: *Buck Rogers* and *Little Orphan Annie*.

The movie *Dracula* reflects the growing popularity of horror films and makes Bela Lugosi a star. It is followed by *Frankenstein*, which establishes the fame of Boris Karloff.

1932   In February, the first Winter Olympics are held at Lake Placid, New York, sparking an interest in skiing.

In March, the infant son of Charles and Anne Lindbergh is kidnapped, setting off sensational press coverage. His body is found in May.

Despite the Depression, Radio City Music Hall, part of the unfinished Rockefeller Center, opens in New York City at Christmastime.

The Jack Benny Program and *The Fred Allen Show* premiere on network radio.

The first Big Little Book comes out; it features *Dick Tracy*.

Shirley Temple makes her film debut at three years old.

Walt Disney receives a special Academy Award for his creation of Mickey Mouse.

1933   In February, Congress votes to repeal Prohibition. By early December, enough states approve the measure, and the Twenty-first Amendment (Repeal) is passed.

In May, the Century of Progress Exposition opens in Chicago; architecturally, it features a mix of Modernism and traditional revival styles.

Bridge becomes the most popular card game; the sales of expert Ely Culbertson's *Contract Bridge Blue Book*, first published in 1931, soar.

42nd Street and *Gold Diggers of 1933* are the definitive Depression musicals; *King Kong* and *The Invisible Man* demonstrate how movie special effects can create great entertainment.

1934   On May 28, the Dionne quintuplets are born in Ontario; the event attracts unprecedented press coverage and public interest.

On September 18, Bruno Hauptmann is arrested for kidnapping Charles Lindbergh's infant son.

In December, Benny Goodman's *Let's Dance* show brings big-band swing to radio nightly.

John Dillinger, "Baby Face" Nelson, "Pretty Boy" Floyd, and Bonnie and Clyde are shot and killed by law officers, effectively ending the reign of colorful gangsters.

1935   On January 1, the trial of Bruno Hauptmann begins for the kidnapping and murder of the Lindbergh baby. He is convicted of all charges by mid-February.

In April, *Your Hit Parade* begins on NBC radio, tracking the most popular records of the week, and a new comedy series, *Fibber McGee and Molly*, also debuts on the network.

Bingo is allowed in movie theaters and becomes a craze, as do chain letters.

The board game Monopoly becomes an overnight sensation.

The Marx Brothers challenge high culture in *A Night at the Opera*.

1936   Girl Scouts inaugurate annual cookie sales.

On April 3, Bruno Hauptmann is executed for kidnapping and killing the infant son of Charles Lindbergh, ending one of the most sensational investigations and trials in U.S. history.

The Douglas DC-3 begins production in June. The airplane quickly sets the standards for luxury and safety in air travel.

Famed director Cecil B. DeMille begins hosting *Lux Radio Theater* in June; it becomes a major dramatic show, with scripts based on popular movies of the time.

Margaret Mitchell's *Gone with the Wind* sells more than a million copies by December and eclipses all competition.

More than 5,000 artists paint thousands of murals in post offices, train stations, courthouses, and other buildings across the country as part of the Federal Arts Program.

1937   In March, teenagers jitterbug in the aisles of New York's Paramount Theater to the swing of Benny Goodman.

On May 9, *The Chase and Sanborn Hour* introduces ventriloquist Edgar Bergen and Charlie McCarthy on NBC radio.

Aviatrix Amelia Earhart disappears over the Pacific Ocean on July 2.

Beginning in November, Arturo Toscanini and the NBC Symphony Orchestra bring classical music to a large radio audience.

Howard Johnson begins franchising restaurants, opening the market to chain eateries and fast food.

Walt Disney's *Snow White and the Seven Dwarfs*, all color and all animated, opens.

1938   The growing popularity of jazz and swing gives rise to a concert by Benny Goodman's band in New York's Carnegie Hall on January 16.

The June issue of *Action Comics* features the adventures of a brand-new character, Superman.

Orson Welles, as a Halloween prank, frightens many Americans with his radio adaptation of H. G. Wells's *War of the Worlds*.

Dale Carnegie's *How to Win Friends and Influence People* enters its second year as a leader among nonfiction books.

Singer Frank Sinatra makes his radio debut on small stations in the New York area.

1939   Swallowing goldfish becomes a campus fad in March.

On April 30, the New York World's Fair opens, despite depressing international news. Germany is excluded. The extravaganza is billed as

"The World of Tomorrow." The opening ceremonies are televised, and TV monitors are a big hit at the fairgrounds.

After a year of promotion, the film version of *Gone with the Wind* opens on December 15, overshadowing all other movie events.

Nylon stockings go on sale in the face of a silk shortage.

1940   Rockefeller Center opens in New York City.

The Pennsylvania Turnpike officially opens (October 1).

The Chicago Bears beat the Washington Redskins 73–0 in the NFL championship game, the first professional football game broadcast nationally on radio (December 8).

Novelist F. Scott Fitzgerald dies of a heart attack (December 21).

The first Dairy Queen opens in Joliet, Illinois.

The first McDonald's drive-in restaurant opens in San Bernardino, California.

John Ford's movie adaptation of *The Grapes of Wrath* is released.

Jukeboxes appear everywhere, including stores, bars, and gas stations. A nickel buys one song.

Eighty million people per week attend the movies.

Bugs Bunny debuts in the Warner Brothers cartoon *O'Hare.*

1941   M&M's, Cheerios, aerosol cans, and La Choy Canned Chinese Food are introduced.

Famed producer Hal Roach's *All American Co-Ed* released (directed by LeRoy Prinz), featuring hit songs in a comedic romp that promised "Three Cheers for the College where Everybody Majors in Fun!"

Orson Welles's *Citizen Kane* is released.

The phrases "Kilroy was here" and "Rosie the Riveter" first appear.

"Uncle Sam Wants You" posters appear everywhere.

Mount Rushmore is completed.

At a folk music festival in Seattle, the term "hootenanny" is coined.

1942   The U.S. Government War Production Board enacts Regulation L-85, which regulates all aspects of clothing production and inhibits the use of natural fibers.

The U.S. government orders production of all civilian autos halted (February 22).

President Roosevelt creates the Office of War Information and the War Advertising Council.

Janette Lowrey's *The Poky Little Puppy*, which goes on to become one of the best-selling children's hardcover books of all time, is published.

Dannon Yogurt and Kellogg's Raisin Bran are introduced.

Michael Curtiz's *Casablanca* is released.

Bing Crosby sings "White Christmas" in the film *Holiday Inn*.

1943 The term "pin-up girl" originates in the April 30, 1943, issue of *Yank*, an armed forces newspaper.

Rodgers and Hammerstein's *Oklahoma!* and Bernstein, Comden, and Green's *On the Town* debut.

The Jefferson Memorial in Washington, D.C., is completed.

1944 The Federal-Aid Interstate and Defense Highway Act is passed, creating the National System of Interstate Highways.

Frank Sinatra's concert appearances at the Paramount Theater in New York City cause bedlam.

Seventeen magazine debuts.

1945 In November, the Slinky is first sold in Philadelphia for $1.00 each.

1946 Tupperware is introduced.

Minute Maid Frozen Orange Juice, Maxwell House Instant Coffee, Ragu Spaghetti Sauce, Tide, and French's Instant Mashed Potatoes are introduced.

The first homes are sold in Levittown, New York.

The first televised soap opera (*Faraway Hill*, DuMont Network) debuts.

1947 Jackie Robinson debuts with the Brooklyn Dodgers, breaking baseball's color line.

Reynolds Wrap Aluminum Foil, Elmer's Glue, Redi Whip, and Ajax are introduced.

B. F. Goodrich introduces tubeless tires.

The term *Cold War* is first used.

CBS unveils the 33 1/3 rpm record (June 21).

President Truman becomes the first president to address the nation on television.

Tennessee Williams's *A Streetcar Named Desire* debuts on Broadway.

The Central Intelligence Agency is created.

The seven-game Dodgers versus Yankees World Series is the first to be televised.

The Howdy Doody Show debuts on NBC (December 27).

1948   The first Baskin-Robbins ice cream store opens; Cheetos, Nestlé's Quik, and V8 Juice are introduced.

The National Association for Stock Car Auto Racing (NASCAR) is founded by Bill France Sr. The family retains control over the sport as it grows into a multiseries sanctioning body and gradually becomes one of the most popular sports in the United States.

Milton Berle's Texaco Star Theater debuts (June 8).

Norman Mailer's *The Naked and the Dead* is published.

The transistor is invented.

1949   General Mills and Pillsbury begin selling instant cake mix.

KitchenAid introduces consumer electric dishwashers.

Gene Autry records "Rudolph the Red-Nosed Reindeer."

Silly Putty, Legos, Scrabble, Candyland, and Clue all debut.

These Are My Children, the first daytime TV soap opera, debuts on NBC.

The Goldbergs, the first TV sitcom, debuts on CBS.

1950   Sixty million Americans go to the movies each week.

The Colgate Comedy Hour, Your Show of Shows, and *The Steve Allen Show* all premiere on network television, and Bob Hope makes the jump from radio to television, one of the first major radio comedians to do so. Soon after, most other radio stars follow suit.

In a clever marketing move, Earl Tupper decides to sell his plastic kitchen containers directly to consumers by way of "Tupperware Parties."

DuPont introduces Orlon, a new miracle fiber, and Xerox produces its first copying machine.

1951   *The Catcher in the Rye* is published. Written by J. D. Salinger, the novel centers on the angst, teen rebellion, and confusion of its protagonist Holden Caulfield. Reportedly, the book has sold more than 65 million copies.

Remington Rand begins to manufacture the UNIVAC I, the first commercial business computer.

In June, CBS presents the first commercial color telecast.

Edward R. Murrow's *See It Now* premieres on TV, as does a new comedy series titled *I Love Lucy*.

The comedy team of Dean Martin and Jerry Lewis becomes a box office favorite.

Singers like Tony Bennett, Rosemary Clooney, Nat "King" Cole, Perry Como, Bing Crosby, Doris Day, and Frank Sinatra dominate record sales, effectively ending the reign of the big bands.

DuPont introduces Dacron, another new artificial fiber.

1952 The conservative "man in the gray flannel suit" comes to epitomize both the fashions and lifestyles of the era.

Fiberglass is introduced.

Dick Clark's *American Bandstand* debuts in January on Philadelphia television (it will become an ABC network offering in 1956). *Dragnet* premieres on TV after a successful radio run, and comedians Jackie Gleason and Ernie Kovacs introduce new shows.

RCA introduces tiny transistors that can replace bulky vacuum tubes; soon thereafter, the Sony Corporation brings out the first transistorized radios.

On college campuses across the nation, the first "panty raids" occur.

1953 In a bow to the new medium's success, the Academy Awards presentation is televised for the first time, with Bob Hope serving as host.

Starring Marlon Brando as gang leader Johnny Strabler, *The Wild One* is released. László Benedek directed the film and Stanley Kramer produced.

More than 300 television stations schedule regular broadcasting, triple the number from 1950.

CinemaScope, a projection technique employing a wider screen and stereophonic sound, is introduced; *The Robe*, a religious epic starring Richard Burton, becomes the first offering using the new system.

Big, string-filled orchestras have a momentary burst of popularity among music fans. Percy Faith, Hugo Winterhalter, Frank Chacksfield, and Mantovani are among the leaders.

IBM introduces its first computer, the Model 701.

1954 Elvis Presley's first commercial recordings are released by Sun Records.

"Serious" pictures, like *On the Waterfront, Rear Window, The Country Girl,* and *A Star is Born*, dominate the movies as producers search for films that will lure audiences away from television.

1955 In July, the first Disneyland opens in Anaheim, California.

"The Pill," an oral contraceptive for women in capsule form, is introduced. More effective than previous birth-control devices, it will help change sexual behavior throughout the country.

Smog, a combination of smoke and fog, enters the language as a means of describing polluted air. The condition becomes particularly noticeable in Los Angeles, where the exhausts from large numbers of vehicles mix with damp air and cause a thick haze over the city.

Rock 'n roll begins to attract a mass audience. The August release and success of Chuck Berry's "Maybelline" draws attention, and RCA Victor purchases Elvis Presley's contract with Sun Records.

In September, actor James Dean dies in an auto accident. A cult almost immediately forms around his memory.

1956   Grace Kelly, a popular movie actress, marries Prince Rainier of Monaco in April.

Billed as a "hillbilly singer," Elvis Presley makes his TV debut on a show called *Stage Door*. Noting the publicity the vocalist's appearance inspires, Ed Sullivan books him for his *Toast of the Town*. In the meantime, Presley's "Heartbreak Hotel" proves a tremendous hit.

Country singer Johnny Cash crosses over to the pop charts with "I Walk the Line" in October. The lines dividing popular music genres continue to blur.

Disposable diapers are invented.

1957   The Ford Motor Company introduces the much-heralded Edsel.

Popular music follows several avenues: traditional (Debbie Reynolds, Johnny Mathis), rock 'n roll (Elvis Presley, Bill Haley and His Comets), country (Elvis Presley, the Everly Brothers), rhythm and blues (The Platters, Sam Cooke), and mixtures of all of the above.

In September, *West Side Story* opens on Broadway.

1958   In October, the Boeing 707 jetliner begins regular New York–Paris flights.

Elvis Presley enters the U.S. Army in March.

In April, a young American pianist named Van Cliburn wins the International Tchaikovsky Competition held in Moscow, becoming a star overnight.

A love triangle involving singer Eddie Fisher and two women, his wife Debbie Reynolds and "homewrecker" Elizabeth Taylor, titillates the public for months and results in the divorce of Reynolds and Fisher.

Groups like Danny and the Juniors ("At the Hop"), the McGuire Sisters ("Sugartime"), the Silhouettes ("Get a Job"), and the Champs ("Tequila") begin to hold sway over individual vocalists.

Beatnik enters the language; it refers to people who do not conform to perceived proper behaviors. The *-nik* suffix comes from the publicity surrounding Russian successes with space satellites called Sputniks.

1959   The science fiction/horror cult classic *Plan 9 from Outer Space* hits film screens. Written and directed by Edward D. Wood, Jr., the low-budget movie is loved by audiences for its campiness and silly special effects.

The rush to build home bomb shelters accelerates.

The Immoral Mr. Teas is released. The film becomes Russ Meyer's first successful commercial movie and launches the career of "The King of the Nudies."

Congressional investigations into television quiz show scandals commence in November.

In November, Ford Motor Company ceases producing the Edsel, the costliest failure in automobile history.

1960   Elvis Presley is discharged from the U.S. Army on March 5.

Joan Baez and Pete Seeger play at the Newport Folk Festival in May.

John Kennedy and Richard Nixon engage in the first of their televised presidential debates on September 26.

Martin Milner and George Maharis take their first ride in their Corvette on the television series *Route 66*.

John Fitzgerald Kennedy is elected president, the first Roman Catholic and the youngest man (43) to hold the office.

1961   Bob Dylan begins to perform in Greenwich Village clubs.

Jacqueline Kennedy wears a pillbox hat to the presidential inauguration, setting off a pillbox craze among American women.

The first Hardee's fast-food restaurant opens, specializing in charcoal-broiled hamburgers and cheeseburgers.

Newton Minow labels television a "vast wasteland" before a gathering of the National Association of Broadcasters on May 9.

Ernest Hemingway kills himself in his Ketchum, Idaho, home on July 2.

Roger Maris of the New York Yankees breaks Babe Ruth's single-season home-run record by hitting his 61st on October 1.

1962   John Glenn becomes the first American to orbit Earth on February 20.

Wilt Chamberlain scores 100 points in a game, a National Basketball Association (NBA) record.

Jack Paar concludes his run as host of *The Tonight Show* (actually called *The Jack Paar Show* during his tenure); substitute hosts preside until Johnny Carson takes over on October 1.

Students for a Democratic Society (SDS) releases its Port Huron Statement.

Actress Marilyn Monroe dies after apparently taking a drug overdose on July 22.

The Beverly Hillbillies strike oil on television as one of the most popular television series ever.

Federal legislation is approved in October declaring LSD a hallucinogenic drug that must be regulated by law.

1963   Schlitz sells beer in new tab-opening aluminum cans.

Julia Child demonstrates on television how to prepare *bœuf bourguignon*, the first of a series of cooking lessons on educational television stations.

Sylvia Plath, author of *The Bell Jar*, commits suicide on February 11.

Joan Baez, Pete Seeger, and other artists perform at the first nonprofit Newport Folk Festival.

Little Stevie Wonder becomes the first performer to simultaneously top the American pop singles, pop albums, and rhythm and blues singles charts on August 24.

1964   The Beatles perform on *The Ed Sullivan Show* on February 9.

Cassius Clay (later Muhammad Ali) becomes heavyweight boxing champion by knocking out Sonny Liston on February 25.

Twelve Beatles records are on the top one hundred list in April.

Jim Ryun, a high school student, runs the mile in less than four minutes on June 5.

A San Francisco bar features topless go-go girls.

The first Arby's fast-food restaurant, specializing in roast beef sandwiches, opens on July 23.

Students initiate the Free Speech Movement in October at the University of California, Berkeley.

ABC, CBS, and NBC simultaneously broadcast in color for the first time on December 20.

1965   A teach-in to oppose the Vietnam War occurs at the University of Michigan March 2, beginning a new antiwar tactic.

The restaurant T.G.I. Friday's, which caters to young singles, opens in New York City in March.

The Astrodome, an indoor domed sports facility, opens in Houston on April 9.

In a rematch May 25, Muhammad Ali knocks out Sonny Liston in the first round with the famous "phantom punch."

Bob Dylan switches to an electric guitar at the Newport Folk Festival on July 25 and is roundly booed.

The Highway Beautification Act is enacted October 22 to improve the appearance of the nation's highways.

1966 Beginning January 1, cigarette packages contain a warning that "Cigarette smoking may be hazardous to your health."

Simon and Garfunkel's "The Sounds of Silence" is number one in *Billboard* for the week of January 1.

Truman Capote's novel *In Cold Blood* is published on January 17.

The Starship *USS Enterprise* makes its first flight as *Star Trek* launches on NBC. The short-lived show later becomes a stalwart of the cult industry, launching countless TV and film spin-offs, fan zines, fan fiction, and conventions, in addition to turning William Shatner ("Captain Kirk") and Leonard Nimoy ("Mr. Spock") into cult icons.

1967 The Rolling Stones perform the song "Let's Spend the Night Together" on *The Ed Sullivan Show*, but Sullivan requires them to revise it to "Let's Spend Some Time Together."

The Green Bay Packers defeat the Kansas City Chiefs 35–21 in the first Super Bowl on January 15.

Johnny Carson wears a Nehru jacket on *The Tonight Show* in February, creating an instant fashion craze.

The Smothers Brothers Comedy Hour premieres on CBS.

Muhammad Ali refuses induction into the Armed Services and is subsequently stripped of his championship and convicted on April 28 of violating Selective Service laws.

The Monterey International Pop Festival occurs in Monterey, California June 16–18, beginning "The Summer of Love."

The rock musical *Hair* opens on Broadway in December.

1968 On January 16, Abbie Hoffman and Jerry Rubin found the Youth International Party, a radical group better known as the Yippies.

In April, students for a Democratic Society (SDS) members occupy buildings at Columbia University to protest the Vietnam War.

The science-fiction film *2001: A Space Odyssey* opens in New York City.

The documentary *Hunger in America* airs on CBS.

Valerie Solanas shoots and seriously wounds pop artist Andy Warhol on June 3.

Tom Wolfe's *The Electric Kool-Aid Acid Test* appears from Farrar, Straus and Giroux, describing the 1964 LSD trip across the country by Ken Kesey and his Merry Pranksters.

Television viewers watch massive antiwar demonstrations at the Democratic National Convention in Chicago August 26–29.

Tommie Smith and John Carlos protest U.S. racial injustice and South African apartheid with a black-glove salute after winning medals at the Olympic Games in Mexico City October 16.

Elvis Presley returns from films to concert performances December 3 with a televised performance popularly known as "The 68 Comeback."

1969   The New York Jets deliver on quarterback Joe Namath's promise of victory by defeating the favored Baltimore Colts, 16–7, in Super Bowl III on January 12.

The first commercial Boeing 747 flight lands successfully on February 8.

The Doors' Jim Morrison is arrested and charged with obscene actions while performing in Miami.

The *Concorde* supersonic airliner makes its first flight on March 2.

The film *Midnight Cowboy* opens on May 25.

The play *Oh, Calcutta!*, featuring total nudity, opens Off-Broadway on June 17.

The film *Easy Rider*, starring Peter Fonda and Dennis Hopper, opens in July.

Members of Charles Manson's "family" commit multiple murders, including the murder of actress Sharon Tate in August.

Almost half a million people watch many of the country's most famous singers and musicians perform at a festival in Woodstock, New York, August 15–17.

Jack Kerouac, author of *On the Road*, dies of alcoholism on October 21.

1970   Two prominent rock singers—Janis Joplin and Jimi Hendrix—die of drug overdoses.

El Topo (The Mole), a 1970 Spanish-language cult western and underground film, is released. Alejandro Jodorowsky directed and starred in the movie.

Monday Night Football premieres on ABC.

Childproof safety caps are introduced.

California becomes the first no-fault divorce state.

Big Bird of *Sesame Street* appears on the cover of *Time* magazine.

1971   Stanley Kubrick directs *A Clockwork Orange*, a film adaptation of the 1962 novel by Anthony Burgess. A satire of modern youth culture, the movie stars Malcolm McDowell as a gang leader who leads a crew of "droogs" on a violent rampage.

Jim Morrison of the Doors dies of heart failure; drug overdose widely speculated.

Andrew Lloyd Webber and Tim Rice's musical, *Jesus Christ Superstar*, debuts on Broadway.

The first word processor, the Wang 1200, is invented.

Cigarette advertising is banned on radio and television.

All in the Family, starring Carroll O'Connor as Archie Bunker, debuts on television, changing the direction of programming dramatically.

Charles Manson and three female followers are convicted of murdering Sharon Tate and sentenced to death.

Congress passes the 26th Amendment, which lowers the voting age to 18.

1972   David Bowie's album, *Rise and Fall of Ziggy Stardust*, ushers in the era of glam rock.

Five burglars are arrested after breaking into the Democratic National Headquarters; this becomes known as the Watergate break-in.

The Godfather, starring Marlon Brando, receives 10 Academy Award nominations; it wins Best Picture, Best Actor, and Best Adapted Screenplay.

Nike shoes debut.

The Supreme Court declares the death penalty cruel and unusual punishment; sentences of Charles Manson, his followers, and others convicted are commuted to life in prison.

Atari's Pong begins the video game craze.

HBO launches its cable subscription service in New York.

1973   The Supreme Court hears *Roe v. Wade*; it overturns prohibitions on first-trimester abortions and eases restrictions on second-trimester ones.

The Exorcist, a horror film, receives five major Academy Award nominations.

1974   President Richard Nixon resigns because of the Watergate scandal and an impeachment threat; Gerald Ford becomes president and pardons Nixon for any Watergate crimes.

Hank Aaron hits his 715th home run, breaking Babe Ruth's record.

The first programmable pocket calculators become available for sale.

Eight former White House aides are indicted for conspiring in Watergate cover-up.

1975   The precursor to the home computer, the Altair, debuts; assembly required.

Lynette "Squeaky" Fromme, a Charles Manson follower, attempts to assassinate Gerald Ford.

The FBI captures Patty Hearst, who now goes by the name of Tania.

Joshua Reynolds invents and begins marketing the mood ring, a fad that sold millions.

Gary Dahl packages the pet rock and becomes a millionaire within a year.

After scoring a perfect 800 on his math SATs, William Gates drops out of Harvard University to write software programs for a small computer company, Micro-Soft.

Saturday Night Live debuts on late-night television and satirizes politicians and other social phenomena.

1976 On April Fool's Day, Apple Computer launches its first product, selling it for $666.66.

4.8 million people apply for a CB license; it is estimated that only half of CB users actually apply for licenses.

The first stand-alone Betamax VCRs are put on the market.

The United States celebrates its bicentennial; the U.S. Mint issues commemorative coins and President Gerald Ford gives a nationally televised speech.

Journalist Tom Wolfe gives the decade the nickname that sticks: "The 'Me' Decade and the Third Great Awakening."

1977 King of Rock and Roll Elvis Presley dies at age 42; heart disease is named as the cause.

John Travolta stars in *Saturday Night Fever*, furthering the popularity of disco.

Star Wars also debuts in theaters, with its phrase "May the force be with you."

ABC airs the hugely successful television miniseries, *Roots*, based on a book written by Alex Haley.

1978 American cult leader Jim Jones of the People's Temple persuades hundreds of his followers to commit suicide in Guyana, most by drinking poisoned Kool-Aid.

The first arcade game, Space Invaders, premieres in Japan.

Dallas, an evening soap opera starring Larry Hagman as J. R. Ewing, first airs on CBS.

1979 The Sony Walkman is introduced in Japan.

Francis Ford Coppola's movie about the Vietnam War, *Apocalypse Now*, wins the Academy Award for Best Picture.

1980   United States hockey team beats the U.S.S.R. at the Winter Olympics in Lake Placid, NY.

The "Who Shot J. R.?" episode of prime-time soap *Dallas* draws 83 million viewers.

John Lennon is murdered in front of his apartment building in Manhattan; a disturbed fan, Mark David Chapman, is tried for his murder.

Bruce Springsteen's *The River* is the number one album of the year.

The Empire Strikes Back opens in movie theaters, shattering box-office records.

On the best seller list: *The Official Preppy Handbook* edited by Lisa Birnbach.

On Television: *The Cable News Network* (CNN), ABC's *Nightline*, *Magnum, P. I.*, *Too Close for Comfort*, and *Bosom Buddies*.

In stores: 3M's Post-It Notes, cordless telephones, and Rollerblades.

1981   The *Columbia*, America's first space shuttle, makes its maiden voyage.

The Centers for Disease Control publishes a report naming a new disease Acquired Immune Deficiency Syndrome (AIDS).

Prince Charles, heir to the British throne, marries Lady Diana Spencer on July 29.

On television: *Music Television* (MTV), *Dynasty*, and *Hill Street Blues*.

In stores: IBM personal computers; Nutra-Sweet; Pac-Man.

1982   Disney's EPCOT Center opens in Orlando, Florida.

Pink Floyd The Wall, a hypnotic live action/animated film, is released. Based on the 1979 Pink Floyd album *The Wall*, it stars Bob Geldof as Pink and is directed by Alan Parker.

The Vietnam Veterans Memorial, designed by 21-year-old Yale student Maya Lin, is opened and dedicated in Washington, D.C.

Director Ridley Scott releases *Blade Runner*, a science fiction thriller starring Harrison Ford. Critically panned and earning less-than-stellar revenues, the movie ultimately grew into a cult classic and won acclaim as a work of art.

1983   Karen Carpenter, 32, dies of a heart attack, calling attention to eating disorders such as anorexia nervosa and bulimia.

Star Wars—the network news's term for the Strategic Defense Initiative—is unveiled by President Regan.

Sally K. Ride becomes the first woman in space when she blasts off with four crewmates aboard the space shuttle *Challenger*.

"Just Say No" drug campaign is launched by First Lady Nancy Reagan.

In stores: *Trivial Pursuit*; the compact disc; the contraceptive sponge.

1984 "Where's the Beef?" becomes the latest catch phrase when 83-year-old Clara Peller begins appearing in television spots for Wendy's restaurants.

William Gibson's science fiction thriller *Neuromancer* appears. The award-winning, dystopian novel about a computer hacker introduces the terms *virtual reality* and *cyberspace* into modern vernacular.

Alec Jeffreys develops "genetic fingerprinting," the ability to link an individual to a crime by tracing his or her DNA.

1985 "We Are The World" becomes an instant number one single after 45 rock stars get together to cut the record to raise money for famine victims in Africa.

New Coke is introduced, the first altering of the soft drink in its 99-year history; ten weeks later, the old Coke, now termed Coca-Cola Classic, is brought back in response to the millions of complaints against the new product.

Pete Rose makes hit number 4,192, breaking Ty Cobb's 57-year record for most hits during a career.

Willie Nelson organizes the first Farm Aid concert in Urbana, Illinois, to benefit farmers at risk of foreclosure.

A hole in the ozone layer is discovered in the atmosphere over Antarctica.

Rock Hudson dies of AIDS on October 2 at age 59—the first public figure to acknowledge that he was dying of the disease.

In stores: Microsoft Windows software; Nintendo entertainment systems; the Ford Taurus.

1986 The space shuttle *Challenger* explodes on January 29, 73 seconds after liftoff, killing all seven crewmembers, including Christa McAuliffe, the first teacher in space.

Microsoft, co-founded by Bill Gates, goes public.

1987 The California Raisins appear on television singing "I Heard It Through the Grapevine" to plug the raisin industry.

Featuring a title matchup between the popular Hulk Hogan and bad guy, 520-pound Andre the Giant, WrestleMania III too place at the Pontiac Silverdome in Pontiac, Michigan. The show scored the largest attendance for a live indoor sporting event in North America, reaching 93,173. Millions more watched via closed circuit TV or pay-per-view, the latter generating $10 million. WrestleMania III is considered the apex of professional wrestling's 1980s popularity.

1988   Theoretical physicist and cosmologist Stephen Hawking publishes *A Brief History of Time*, which becomes a bestselling book and launches a craze for space topics and issues.

Rain Man, directed by Barry Levinson, stars Dustin Hoffman as Raymond Babbitt, a man with autism who is led on a cross-country trek with his brother Charlie (Tom Cruise). The film introduces many people to autism and increases autism awareness nationwide. *Rain Man* later won Academy Awards for Best Picture, Best Actor in a Leading Role (Hoffman), Best Director, and Best Writing, Original Screenplay.

Rap group Public Enemy releases its second studio album, *It Takes a Nation of Millions to Hold Us Back* (Def Jam Recordings). The album later went platinum, selling more than 1 million units in the United States. Critics consider it one of the most important and influential rap albums in music history.

1989   Starring Patrick Swayze as an undersized bouncer battling corruption in small town Missouri, *Road House* hits the big screen. Directed by Rowdy Herrington, the film is not a box office hit, but becomes a cult classic when it becomes a staple of cable television.

Featuring the theme song "Bad Boys" by reggae group Inner Circle, the reality television show *COPS* premieres on Fox. The documentary-style program follows police and other law enforcement officers as they capture criminals by embedding camera crews with them on patrol. *COPS* began its 24th season in 2011 and is broadly reshown via syndication. The show is one of the inspirations for the reality TV boom that would later take place on world airwaves.

1990   On TV, *Seinfeld*, and *Twin Peaks* debut.

Henry and June becomes the first film released with the new NC-17 rating.

Luciano Pavarotti, Plácido Domingo, and José Carreras, as the Three Tenors, release the most successful classical recording in decades (43 on the pop music charts).

Science fiction flick *Total Recall*, starring movie superhero and future California governor Arnold Schwarzenegger, is released. The intricate plot—based on a Philip K. Dick short story—and striking visual effects make it a cult favorite.

1991   Nirvana's *Nevermind* is released.

The Silence of the Lambs released. Introduces audiences to debonair serial killer Hannibal Lecter (Anthony Hopkins) and FBI Agent Clarice Starling (Jodie Foster) and launches a franchise based on the Thomas Harris novel.

Street Fighter II arcade video game is introduced.

Coca-Cola advertising uses deceased stars resurrected through digital technology.

Written by Douglas Coupland, *Generation X: Tales for an Accelerated Culture* is published. The novel popularizes the term *Generation X*, which generally refers to people born between 1965 and 1980.

1992   Art Spiegelman's *Maus* becomes the first comic book to win a Pulitzer Prize.

America's largest shopping center, the Mall of America, opens in Minnesota.

Johnny Carson retires from *The Tonight Show*.

Fubu (which stands for "For Us, By Us") line of hip-hop clothing begins.

Image Comics begins publishing creator-owned books.

Superman dies and is reborn.

Id Software, creators of video games *Wolfenstein 3D* and *Doom*, begins business.

Entertainment Weekly begins publication.

The Real World debuts on MTV.

1993   The ATF (U.S. Bureau of Alcohol, Tobacco, and Firearms) and FBI conduct raids on the Branch Davidian compound in Waco, Texas; more than 80 members of the church group die.

The *X-Files* debuts on TV. The series finale of *Cheers* airs.

Chicago Bulls basketball player Michael Jordan announces his retirement but returns to the sport the next year.

Stereograms come to the United States with the publication *Magic Eye*.

Barnes and Noble booksellers forge an agreement to serve Starbucks coffee in their stores.

The first 32-bit video game console, 3DO Interactive Multiplayer, is introduced by Panasonic.

1994   *The Crow* is released and becomes an instant cult classic based on the accidental shooting death of star Brandon Lee, son of martial arts movie superhero Bruce Lee.

Kurt Cobain of Nirvana commits suicide.

O. J. Simpson is arrested on two counts of first-degree murder.

Friends debuts on TV.

Quentin Tarantino's *Pulp Fiction* is released in theaters.

1995   In July, online book retailer Amazon.com begins operations.

Cal Ripken breaks Lou Gehrig's record for most consecutive games played in Major League Baseball (September 6).

The O. J. Simpson trial ends with a verdict of not guilty for both murders for which Simpson was charged.

ESPN creates the Extreme Games (later called the X Games).

Toy Story, the first fully computer-animated feature film, is released.

eBay online auction house is founded.

1996   Directed by actor/comedian Ben Stiller, the black comedy *The Cable Guy* is released. It stars Jim Carrey and Matthew Broderick. Rather than his usual slapstick, Carrey plays cable television installer Chip Douglas with maniacal sadism.

Oprah Winfrey begins an on-air book club (September).

The NAMES Project Foundation's AIDS Quilt is exhibited in its entirety for the final time in Washington, D.C.'s National Mall.

Marvel Comics files for bankruptcy.

Tickle Me Elmo is introduced.

McDonald's restaurants and Walt Disney forge a 10-year licensing agreement.

The Daily Show premieres, with Craig Kilborn as host.

1997   An antitrust suit is brought against Microsoft.

Maxim men's magazine debuts in the United States.

Tiger Woods wins the Masters Golf Tournament.

Camel cigarettes retires its mascot, Joe Camel, in response to increasing public and political pressure.

The Volkswagen Beetle is reintroduced.

Heaven's Gate cult commits mass suicide (38 people die) on the event of the passing of the Hale-Bopp comet.

Child beauty queen JonBenet Ramsey is found murdered.

World chess champion Gary Kasparov is defeated by IBM's computer opponent, Deep Blue.

1998   The scandal involving Bill Clinton's affair with intern Monica Lewinsky erupts.

J. K. Rowling's *Harry Potter and the Sorcerer's Stone* is published in the United States. (September).

The 5,000th episode of the TV game show *The Price is Right* airs.

Eminem's *The Slim Shady LP* is released.

Seinfeld series finale is the most watched single episode of a television series.

Titanic becomes the most successful motion picture ever made.

Viagra sexual stimulant is marketed.

The Furby toy is introduced.

America Online buys out Netscape.

1999   *Fight Club* hits movie screens. Directed by David Fincher, the film stars Brad Pitt and Edward Norton. The violent, existential movie is adapted from Chuck Palahniuk's 1996 novel. The success of the film, particularly after its DVD release, propels the author's fame, while the film becomes a cult classic. Allegedly, real-life fight clubs sprout up around the world . . . but we can't talk about that.

The women's U.S. soccer team wins the World Cup.

John F. Kennedy Jr. dies in a plane crash.

Star Wars: Episode I: The Phantom Menace is released in theaters.

The Blair Witch Project, filmed on a budget of $35,000, becomes a box office smash hit.

Woodstock '99 music festival is marred by violence.

Comedy *Office Space* is released. Written and directed by Mike Judge, the creator of iconic animated characters Beavis and Butt-Head, the film is a satire on work life. Basically a box office flop, *Office Space*'s popularity grew on its DVD release and fans' word of mouth.

2000   The historical epic *Gladiator*, directed by Ridley Scott and starring Russell Crowe, opens with a $35 million weekend and surpasses $100 million within two weeks. The film's success launches a series of imitators and others hoping to cash in on the historical epic fad.

Stock market jitters turn more widespread, signaling the end of the dot.com boom.

Computers around the world are infected with the "I love you" virus attached to spam e-mail.

Boy band extraordinaire *NSYNC sells 2.4 million copies of its CD *No Strings Attached*, which sets the record for highest first-week sales. The CD went on to become the best-selling album of the decade and top-selling album of the year.

2001   *The Royal Tenenbaums*, written by director Wes Anderson and actor Owen Wilson, is released. The film features the lives of the Tenenbaum family, particularly the children, as they cope with severe dysfunction after achieving fame as child prodigies.

The award-winning television series *Six Feet Under*, created and produced by Alan Ball, debuts on HBO. The Fisher family and friends are at the heart of the show, a quirky group that runs a funeral home in Los Angeles.

Featuring an all-star cast, the odd thriller/comedy *Donnie Darko* is released. The independent film received praise from critics and developed a cult following, which increased after the director's cut DVD appeared in 2004.

24 debuts on the Fox Network. The series stars Kiefer Sutherland as superspy, counter-terrorist agent Jack Bauer. Each episode covers a 24-hour period in Bauer's life. Noted for its gritty style and over-the-top violence, the show gains a cult following and widespread notoriety.

The terrorist attacks on the World Trade Center in New York City and the Pentagon in Washington, DC, as well as the thwarted effort resulting in a downed plane in Shanksville, Pennsylvania, launches the nation into a patriotic fervor. The event captures the world's attention, later developing cult-like aspects, including conspiracy theories and alternative histories.

2002   Former president Jimmy Carter wins the Nobel Peace Prize.

Dave Thomas, founder of the fast food chain Wendy's, dies. He had gained widespread fame from starring in the company's television commercials.

The Homeland Security Advisory System is introduced in March. The color-coded scale links the threat against the United States based on a five-point range, from red ("severe") to green ("low"). In early 2011, Secretary of Homeland Security Janet Napolitano announced that the system would be replaced by a new two-level National Terrorism Advisory System in April.

At the 74th Academy Awards, actress Halle Berry becomes the first African American female to win the Best Actress award.

Baseball great Ted Williams dies. After his death, his family battles over his remains, with his son eventually having the body placed in cryonic suspension.

2003   Dixie Chicks lead singer Natalie Maines sets off a national controversy when at a London concert she exclaims that the group members feel "ashamed" that President George W. Bush is a fellow Texan.

The DaVinci Code, a novel by Dan Brown, reaches the top of the best-selling fiction lists and stays there for three years. (The movie version is released in 2006, starring Tom Hanks.)

Allied forces rescue Army Pfc. Jessica Lynch, a prisoner of war held at an Iraqi hospital, who becomes a patriotic symbol.

Federal and local authorities raid the BALCO offices owned by Victor Conte. The raid sets in motion the investigation of professional athletes with ties to BALCO.

2004   *Napoleon Dynamite* is released. Co-written and directed by Jared Hess and Jerusha Hess, the film stars Jon Heder. Similar to the John Hughes films of the 1980s, the movie depicts quirky high schoolers and the antics that fill their lives.

Former president Ronald Reagan dies in his Bel-Air, California, home at the age of 93.

The Boston Red Sox win the World Series. The victory breaks the supposed "Curse of the Bambino," said to haunt the franchise since it last won a title and then later sold the rights to Babe Ruth in 1918 to the New York Yankees.

After a long investigation and trial, a jury finds Scott Peterson guilty of the murder of his wife Laci and unborn son Conner. The case dominated the news after Peterson reported his wife missing on Christmas Eve in 2002.

2005   Jennifer Aniston and Brad Pitt announce their separation, setting off an entertainment news media frenzy.

The Office debuts on NBC as a midseason replacement.

Lifestyle celebrity Martha Stewart is released from a West Virginia prison after serving a five-month sentence for lying to federal investigators about the questionable sale of stocks.

The House Government Reform Committee holds hearings to investigate steroid use in baseball. Ten players, including Mark McGwire and Sammy Sosa, testify.

Pfc. Lynndie England pleads guilty to seven criminal counts related to her role in torturing Iraqi prisoners of war held in Abu Ghraib.

May, W. Mark Felt reveals that he is the famous "deep throat" informant who leaked information to Bob Woodward and Carl Bernstein regarding Watergate.

Pop singer Michael Jackson is acquitted of 10 charges, including molesting a child, conspiracy, and providing alcohol to minors, in a California courtroom.

Musicians in nine countries hold Live 8 concerts in July to raise money and awareness in the global fight against poverty in Africa.

The Colbert Report, a mock news show, debuts, satirizing right-wing news shows and general pomposity. It is a spin-off from another satirical news show, *The Daily Show with Jon Stewart*, and both are critical and popular successes, especially with young people.

Serenity, a space western written and directed by Joss Whedon, hits screens. The film continues the story of the cancelled television series *Firefly* that went off the air in 2002. Like many Whedon projects, the movie was critically acclaimed and won several awards.

2006 *Hannah Montana* debuts on the Disney Channel. The show is about a teenage girl (Miley Stewart) who lives a double life as a famous pop singer (Hannah Montana). Miley Cyrus (daughter of country singer Billy Ray Cyrus, who also stars on the show) plays both parts. Millions of girls around the world soon idolize Hannah Montana, a strange twist of fate for Cyrus, who soon leads a real double life with her TV persona.

MTV celebrates its 25th anniversary.

Bob Dylan's *Modern Times* album debuts at number one on the Billboard chart, his first work to hit the top spot since 1976's *Desire*.

Technorati, the first blog search engine, estimates that there are 28.4 million blogs online.

Directed by James McTeigue from a screenplay written by the Wachowski brothers (*The Matrix* trilogy), *V for Vendetta* opens. The dystopian thriller is adapted from the Alan Moore/David Lloyd comic book series and stars Natalie Portman and Hugo Weaving.

2007 Former vice president and senator Al Gore wins the Nobel Peace Prize for his work on global climate change.

The final episode of the HBO hit drama series *The Sopranos* airs. Fans and critics debate the open-ended finale.

Price Is Right host Bob Barker retires from the show at age 83 after 35 years of helming the show. Barker is replaced by comedian Drew Carey.

Apple Computer launches the iPhone, a high-tech cell phone with a sleek black design and virtual keyboard that enables users to easily surf the Web and download music as well as actually make a telephone call.

"I Got a Crush . . . on Obama," a YouTube video posted by "Obama Girl" Amber Lee Ettinger, gains wide popularity. Although Barack Obama criticizes the video, it gets more than 3 million viewings by the fall.

2008 Neil Diamond, age 67, becomes the oldest performer to reach number one on the *Billboard* album chart with *Home Before Dark*, produced by music impresario Rick Rubin.

The Office begins cable network syndication on TBS and Fox-owned stations in the United States.

Lady Gaga (Stefani Germanotta) releases her debut studio album *The Fame*. The disc propels her to national and international fame with hit singles, including "Just Dance" and "Poker Face."

The Hunger Games, the first book of the Hunger Games trilogy by Suzanne Collins, is published. It is a young-adult science fiction novel about a post-apocalyptic world featuring 16-year-old Katniss Everdeen.

2009   The longest-running drama in media history, the soap opera *Guiding Light*, is cancelled. In total, the show had been broadcast since 1937.

Celebrity pitchman Billy Mays (born 1958) dies. Mays gained fame as a home shopping and commercial spokesman for a variety of products including OxiClean and Mighty Putty.

The television series *Glee* debuts on Fox. Created by Ryan Murphy, Brad Falchuk, and Ian Brennan, it is a musical comedy-drama television series that centers on the exploits of an Ohio high school glee club, teachers, and their families.

2010   *Lost* (ABC) ends after six seasons on the air. The show inspired a dedicated fan following, sometimes dubbed "Losties," who supported the show, despite often-mediocre ratings. They created a separate Web-based universe for the show, ranging from a *Lost* encyclopedia to fan fiction.

Apple begins selling the iPad, a sleek computer tablet. In its first year, more than 15 million units are sold.

Comedians/talk show hosts Jon Stewart and Stephen Colbert of Comedy Central hold a "Rally for Sanity" movement in Washington, D.C., that attracts more than 200,000 people.

2011   Reality television personality Nicole (Snooki) Polizzi is paid $32,000 by Rutgers University to give a talk at the New Jersey college, which is $2,000 more than what it paid Nobel laureate Toni Morrison to speak at spring commencement.

The Hollywood Reporter's fourth annual Reality Power List concludes that producer, radio personality, and *American Idol* host Ryan Seacrest is the most powerful reality personality in the world.

After 11 years, the *Scream* franchise returns with the release of *Scream 4*. Also returning are the stars that turned the original *Scream* (1996) into a cult classic, including Courtney Cox, Neve Campbell, and David Arquette.

Market research firm comScore releases figures on online video engagement revealing that 176 million United States Internet users watched online video content in May (an average of 15.9 hours per viewer). The total audience had more than 5.6 billion viewing sessions during the month. In addition, some 83.3 percent of the United States Internet audience viewed online video.

Media company TechCrunch reports that Facebook has approximately 750 million regular users who log on to the social-networking site at least once per month.

FILM

CHAPTER 1

Sexploitation Cinema and the Rise and Fall of Russ Meyer

Adam G. Capitanio

Russ Meyer is the Eisenstein of sex films.

—John Waters[1]

Among the exploitation and independent filmmakers of his period, Russ Meyer remains a singular figure, someone who still commands serious critical attention and who has maintained a devoted following 30 years after the release of his last film. Although many of his contemporaries in the American exploitation film industry—Doris Wishman, Roger Corman, Herschell Gordon Lewis, Ted V. Mikels, and Radley Metzger, among others—are well known among cineastes, and especially cult film enthusiasts, none matches Meyer's continued success in both those circles and in mainstream recognition. Today, his best-known film, *Faster, Pussycat! Kill! Kill!* enjoys greater name recognition than any of the films produced or directed by the filmmakers mentioned above.[2] His name became more or less synonymous with the sexploitation feature in the 1960s and 1970s, and his career has been called a "virtual history of the development and maturation" of that subgenre.

Socially, Meyer's films were a driving force in the visual culture front of the sexual revolution.[3] His first narrative film, *The Immoral Mr. Teas*, was released in 1959, less than a year before the FDA approved the birth control pill; his final film, *Beneath the Valley of the Ultravixens*, a film that satirizes fundamentalist Christianity (among many other things), was released in 1979, a year before Ronald Reagan would be elected president due to his popular support among the religious right, a conservative coalition formed partly in response to loosening moral strictures regarding sexuality. During his 20-year career (and long afterward), Meyer has been singled out for the emphasis in his films on strong, active female characters and his thematic concern with the problem of female sexual fulfillment. However, these progressive claims about Meyer's films should be taken with a grain of salt, as they were usually coupled with a fair share of regressive attitudes embodied by what Meyer became famous for: a visual style that existed largely to display the naked, voluptuous female form.

Meyer's films mirrored the tensions and negotiations of the cultural moment and its tendency to reinscribe normativity just as often as it was liberatory. And even as Meyer contributed to a shift in the terms of culturally acceptable sexual expression, they just as soon passed him by as well. It is that tension in his films, a tension still with us today in the era post–sexual revolution, as well as the fact that they represent a bygone era in the sex film, that account for continued interest in his films today.

The Exploitation Film and Meyer's Early Career

Born in 1922, in Oakland, California, Meyer took an interest in photography at an early age, becoming accomplished enough as an amateur that he was assigned to the Signal Corps during World War II, shooting footage of combat operations that would later appear in newsreels. After the war ended, Meyer tried to get a job as a cameraman in Hollywood but failed because of the glut of union photographers returning from the front. He ended up working on industrial films, eventually shooting pictorials for *Playboy*, and helped make a burlesque film, *The French Peep Show*, in 1950.[4] As Meyer himself put it, "it was the marriage of industrial movies and shooting tits for magazines that brought all of this about."[5] Even in his early career, Meyer was part of a sex industry that was slowly becoming part of the mainstream during the early years of the sexual revolution. *Playboy*'s part in this process, for better or worse, is well documented (by Beth Bailey, among others),[6] and Meyer's contact with the world of the burlesque theater, the forerunner of the strip club, later helped him find actresses for his films, as most of them were in "the show-business world—premiere strippers."[7]

In 1959, Meyer made a narrative film, and the result was *The Immoral Mr. Teas*. As Roger Ebert describes it:

The premise of *The Immoral Mr. Teas* is simple: Teas is a harassed city man, cut off from the solace of nature and burdened by the pressures of modern life. He can find no rest, alas, because he has been cursed by a peculiar ability to undress girls mentally. At the most unsettling times (in a soda fountain, in a dentist's office) women suddenly appear nude. What's worse, Teas cannot control his strange power . . . as plots go, *Teas* was not terrifically subtle.[8]

As adolescent as *Teas* was, it ushered in an entirely new genre of filmmaking, the "nudie-cutie" that would become part of the sexploitation subgenre.

These films were qualitatively different from the earlier forms of exploitation filmmaking that had existed for decades to the chagrin of Hollywood and censorship boards across the country. As Meyer bibliographer David K. Frasier put it, "[i]n the late fifties, the narrow subgenre of sexploitation had degenerated from films exploiting social ills like teen pregnancy, prostitution, and incest to badly made nudist colony sagas."[9] Earlier exploitation films, explored in Eric Schaefer's excellent book-length study *"Bold! Daring! Shocking! True!,"* appealed to "prurient" interest in sex and violence while at the same time (hypocritically) justifying such representations with a "square-up" that claimed the film was made for the sake of education or improving public morality. This was the only way such films could bypass local censorship boards and avoid charges of indecency.[10] Beginning in the 1950s and 1960s, however, exploitation filmmakers no longer needed to include such moralizing to thinly justify their "prurience." *The Immoral Mr. Teas* "didn't pretend to be educational . . . it was about naked women. And it was about looking at naked women."[11] For some audience members, that alone may have been a learning experience.

Such a film could be exhibited widely, meaning it could be played in a greater number of movie houses than earlier exploitation films, for several reasons. With the sharp postwar decline in movie attendance—often attributed to some combination of television and suburbanization—theaters needed to coax audiences back into the seats. Many independent movie houses turned to films with taboo topics to generate interest. The famous 1948 antitrust decision in *U.S. v. Paramount Pictures et al.* forced the major film studios to divest themselves of the theaters they owned, enabling theater owners to book whatever films, studio produced or not, they wanted. This created a perfect situation for independent producers: the majors, faced with dwindling profits, closed down their B-units (the sections of the studios that produced cheap, quickly made genre films to turn rapid, though modest, profits), creating a vacuum in the industry that independents could step into. Theaters, in turn, could book those independently made films as a result of the *Paramount* decision.

In addition to those independent productions, theaters also filled their screens with imports from Europe, where films with nudity and sexual themes were being made in growing numbers during the 1950s. Audiences in urban areas were already becoming accustomed to films featuring unclothed European sex symbols such as Brigitte Bardot. Finally, court cases such as the 1952 decision in *Burstyn v. Wilson*, which protected films under the First Amendment, led to a decrease in the legal power of both national and local obscenity/decency boards.[12] These factors paved the way for films that openly displayed "nudity, sexual situations, and simulated (i.e., nonexplicit) sex acts, designed for titillation and entertainment" rather than mired in the mixed messages generated by the juxtaposition of visual sensation and sensuality with a moralistic, "redemptive" educational motivation as in the "classic" exploitation film.[13]

The integration of female nudity and sexual play into a comic narrative film in *Teas*—without the guilt trip—helped make Meyer's film a great (if relative) success. The comedy, in particular, helped eliminate feelings of "embarrassment or self-consciousness" for audiences seeing the film, many of whom might have been seeing nudity in a cinema for the first time.[14] However, the film was still rather juvenile, with a flimsy premise and largely nonexistent plot that operated mostly as pretexts for the nudity, which was largely for male viewing pleasure. In this sense, it anticipated hardcore pornographic features like *Deep Throat*, where sexually explicit spectacles were integrated into an unconvincing, (often unintentionally) comedic plot.

Major Themes and Periods

Roger Ebert, one of Meyer's collaborators[15] and his earliest critical defender, suggests that as Meyer's career progressed, his view of sexuality became more nuanced, particularly as it pertained to women. *Mondo Topless*, to use Ebert's example, is a film that mostly consists of San Francisco strippers performing in a series of unusual settings. However, the titillation of the visuals is in tension with the soundtrack, where the women being visually objectified gain subjectivity through audio interviews where they discuss the advantages and, significantly, the disadvantages, of having a prominent bust.[16] That tension, produced by contrasting the film's visual and audio tracks, plays out in different ways in the three periods of Meyer's career Ebert identifies: the "early voyeuristic comedies, always in color and with voice-over," which include *The Immoral Mr. Teas* and *Mondo Topless*; the "black and white, synch-sound, Gothic-sadomasochistic melodramas," including *Lorna* and his best-known film, *Faster, Pussycat! Kill! Kill!*; and the "color, synch-sound sexual dramas," the best of which is *Vixen*.[17] To those three, David K. Frasier adds a fourth: "the parody-satires," among which are Meyer's sole successful studio film, *Beyond the Valley of the Dolls*, and his final film, *Beneath the Valley of the Ultravixens*.[18]

Despite the differences in format and tone between Meyer's films, his characterizations, settings, and style have remained surprisingly consistent. Frasier has suggested that this consistency marks Meyer as an *auteur* as worthy of study as a Hitchcock or Ford, while Jonathan L. Crane argues that the technical and thematic strength of Meyer's films raises them to cult status above other sexploitation films that are "typically bereft of even the unintentional charms that knowing audiences find in the hapless enterprises of earnest but technically challenged film makers."[19] Both scholars agree on the elements of the films that mark them as unmistakably Meyer's.

The first and most obvious, of course, are the big-breasted, hourglass-figured women who populate Meyer's films and whose bodies are matched with "gargantuan appetites for all liminal desires."[20] Meyer's female characters are sexually aggressive and promiscuous—often unapologetically so. Meanwhile, the men in Meyer's films are often working-class squares: conventionally handsome and strong, but also traditional and mentally thick. As Crane notes, unlike the women, whose bodies are a "truthful and transparent signifier" in the films, the men, "however well-proportioned and muscularly defined, are not correlated with any set of innate virtues or intrinsic powers."[21] These characters usually find themselves in rural or at least decidedly nonurban settings. In part, shooting in such areas was a cost-cutting measure on Meyer's part, but the forests, bayous, meadows, farms, and cabins that appear in his films also suggest the copulation and nudity in his films as natural, an expression of the "fecundity of nature."[22]

Finally, Meyer's films might be termed fantasies grounded in a form of realism, produced through the use of, among other things, editing and color in his films. Frasier claims that the women in Meyer's films are essentially "pinups come to life" through

> lighting, photography, and editing . . . Firmly believing that editing is the single most important contribution a director can make to a film,

Meyer evolved an editing style that animated his pinups, and masked, as
much as possible, the acting deficiencies of performers . . . the actresses,
already anatomical exaggerations of "normally" constructed women,
are photographed from extreme angles that further accentuate their outrageous dimensions.[23]

Editing and camera angles produce idealized fantasy women out of
the bodies and performances of regular women, but the tension
between reality and fantasy is also present in Meyer's cinematography.
Crane notes how Meyer's use of color and tone "give these films a hal-
lucinatory air . . . [an opposition] between exquisite materiality and
appearing too good to be true, [which] gives Meyer's erotic fantasies
an extra charge that is not to be found in any other softcore film."[24] So
another way to understand Meyer's career is as a negotiation between
lively sex fantasies and their grounding in versions of reality: to crib
Ebert's periodization, moving from fantasy in *The Immoral Mr. Teas*
to the black-and-white aspirations to social realism in *Lorna* and natu-
ralistic color films like *Vixen*, and finally back to almost total fantasy
with a film like *Supervixens*. I would suggest that this friction is key
to understanding the continued popularity of Meyer's filmmaking,
something that will be returned to below. Now, it may be instructive
to turn to one of Meyer's films in an effort at understanding his importance to the shifting cultural mores concerning sexuality.

Lorna

Lorna is one of the films Meyer made, in Kristen Hatch's words,
"parallel to the nascence of second-wave feminism" that exhibited a
"dramatic shift in the popular understanding of normative sexuality
for women."[25] It serves as an example of the tensions around sexuality,
particularly female sexuality, that focus the plot and much of Meyer's
work in general. The film opens with Luther and Jonah, manual
laborers in a small Southern town, encountering a drunken woman
on their way home from a bar. After she refuses Luther's proposition-
ing, they follow her. As they trail her, the editing alternates between
close-up, tracking shots of the duo's leering faces and the woman's
backside. This shot/reverse-shot suggests rather obviously where
Luther and Jonah's interest lies, even while implicating the audience
in the uneven exchange of lustful glances through their own desire to
gaze at the woman's parts. This sequence of shots can be likened to a
"rapist's gaze" as Luther breaks into the woman's home and attempts
to force himself on her. She resists him and the attempted rape turns

into a beating. It's a complex moment, as the objectification of a woman results in an act of violence, while at the same time the film implicates the audience through its enjoyment of the earlier shots of her rear.

The main plot focuses on Jim's inability to please Lorna, his voluptuous and sexually dissatisfied wife, and this conflict is signaled in two contrasting scenes. The first is early in the film, where Jim and Lorna make love, and the second later on, when an escaped convict ravishes Lorna. In the first scene, the camera pans from the bed to the curtains by the window, a knowing play on the cliché representational substitution for an act of coitus. Off screen, Lorna asks, "Jim, could you, would you?" a clear entreaty for him to please her, but after he has finished, he asks, "what were you gonna say?" and she responds, "too late now." Her dissatisfaction is reemphasized the next morning, when she refuses to awaken before Jim leaves for work, forcing him to make his own lunch. Jim's failure to fulfill his conjugal duty (pleasing his wife sexually) is matched with Lorna's refusal to fulfill hers (the preparation of food for her husband). While the film acknowledges female sexual desire and the importance of female sexual satisfaction, it is figured in terms of a traditional marriage with typical gender roles.

Unlike the earlier scene between Luther and the unnamed woman, the interruption of Lorna's morning idyll by the convict turns into the ecstasy of ravishment. This sequence features a stylistic parallel with shots from the point of view of the convict, objectifying Lorna, manifesting once more the "rapist's gaze" and aligning the audience with the ravisher's perspective. However, it seems that in the film's logic, rape will become ravishment if the participants are sexually starved enough, and if the assailant is traditionally desirable—the convict is young, handsome, blond, and muscular, whereas Luther is middle-aged, haggard, dark, and thin. In this moment of profound contradiction, the film not only reveals its own confused concept of female sexual desire but also reinforces predominant beauty standards for men, as it has already done for women by demonstrating the desirability of the youthful, busty, and blonde Lorna. Seemingly made stupid by the pleasure the convict has given her, Lorna takes him back to her home, where she offers him food and drink, doting and beaming at him, even going as far as to make the bed when he wants to rest. The "womanly" duties she refused to perform for Jim now come as a joy to her in light of having found a satisfactory sexual partner.

The film concludes with Jim heading home after settling his differences with Luther, who has insinuated that Lorna is cheating on him, only to find the convict still at his home. Both Lorna and the convict die in the ensuing melee. The film's preacher appears at the conclusion with fire and brimstone rhetoric: "woe to the libertine . . . as ye sow, so shall ye reap," a condemnation of Lorna's adultery, although her "comeuppance" should be taken as much a result of her husband's weakness as it is her infidelity.

Although female desire is recognized in the film, it is still carefully circumscribed as "improper" and punishable if it disrupts the bonds of marriage. The gender roles in the film remain traditional as well, with Jim expected to labor while Lorna cooks and shops, and it is only the sexual tension between them that disrupts this order—as if the growing questions surrounding women's place in the social order would be solved if their mates could only learn to bring them to orgasm. This moralism is striking as it seems a strange backpedaling from the "no-strings" sexuality of *The Immoral Mr. Teas* and a resurrection to the "bad old days" of exploitation films justifying their content through claims of moral instruction.

Meyer's Middle Career and the Response to Hardcore

As Meyer's career continued, the mainstreaming of hardcore pornography had a profound effect on his filmmaking. In 1968, Meyer made *Vixen!*, which starred Erica Gavin as a sexually voracious woman whose behavior included incest, group sex, and lesbianism but who refused to engage in miscegenation. *Vixen!* became the first sexploitation film to play in mainstream theaters, and Meyer believed it was the first film of its kind to be viewed by couples together.[26] This comment was part of Meyer's attempt to construct his own persona as a sexual revolutionary, which is also apparent when, in an interview, he compared *The Immoral Mr. Teas* to *Deep Throat* on a continuum of increasingly permissive (and by implication, liberatory) possibilities for the visual representation of sexuality.[27] In some respects, this success as a sexploitation filmmaker produced the conditions that would undo Meyer's career. After making *Vixen!*, Meyer had a series of confrontations with antiporn feminists,[28] and Gavin later disassociated herself from Meyer's films,[29] condemning them (and Meyer) in no uncertain terms:

> *Vixen!* is really a put-down of women. It says that all women want is sex, that they're never satisfied and they'll go anywhere to find it. It shows that women have no loyalty, no sensitivity in sexual relationships . . . I think that some woman really fucked Russ up. He doesn't like women. He does but he doesn't . . . he portrays women as freaks. They're plastic.[30]

Despite the mutual animosity, Meyer would say years later, "I have gotten so little static from the feminists," and restate the argument (one that many of his critics have uncritically repeated as a defense) that in his films "women are the smart ones. The men are klutzy and muscular and willing, but the women call the shots."[31] I would suggest that, rather than being impressed by the characterization of women in Meyer's films, by the time feminists had turned their attention toward films, the rising visibility of hardcore pornography grabbed their interest as an easier and more controversial target.

Meyer's films were essentially seen as the least objectionable manifestations of an industry that degraded and exploited the image and labor of women. For Meyer, however, the situation was complex, as the emergence of hardcore pornography into the (relative) mainstream posed a threat to the brand of filmmaking he was engaged in. The rapidly growing hardcore industry, which affected the range of acceptable representations of sexuality in mainstream cinema, would lead to the increasing marginalization of his films.

The difference between Meyer's films and the most sexually explicit material available to audiences was already noticeable in 1969, when *New York Times* film critic Vincent Canby asked "is Russ Meyer archaic?" and observed that "the rapidly changing patterns of sexual behavior in conventional films are making decently intended, softcore pornographic films increasingly difficult to achieve."[32] Canby's remark is also revealing in that Meyer's films were considered "pornography," albeit "decently intended." Meyer would spend much of his later career trying to dispel that misconception.

Hardcore reached a new plateau of visibility and profitability with the release of *Deep Throat* in 1972, from which the pornography industry has never looked back. Simultaneously, Meyer was engaged in a brief foray into mainstream respectability, making two films for 20th Century Fox, both of which bombed: *Beyond the Valley of the Dolls* and *The Seven Minutes*. Returning to independent filmmaking, he found his niche in jeopardy, stating, "I think that the majors on one side have hacked away at the sexual freedom that I was able to express in my early films; and the porno bunch, the hardcore people, have chipped away at the audience from the other side."[33] In a filmmaking climate with *Deep Throat* on one side and *Last Tango in Paris* on the other, where would Meyer find himself?

One place he would not find himself would be in hardcore. Meyer's reasons were numerous: he claimed that the women he worked with wouldn't do it, he prided himself on his films playing in "first-class theaters," the comedy in his films wouldn't work in an explicit context, and he had a personal disinterest in hardcore films.[34] Ebert made a similar claim about his friend, claiming, "Meyer feels that complete explicitness is the enemy of erotic fantasy."[35] He continues by arguing that the women in Meyer's films are "often caricatures, broadly drawn, and their common denominator was insatiable sexual hunger."[36] Ebert essentially argues that the women in Meyer's films are part of a male pornographic imaginary, but the explicitness of hardcore would actually break down the pleasure gained from that imaginary. There is fetishistic desire at work, where the complete, explicit visualization afforded by hardcore pornography would destroy the fantasy engendered by a visualization that is never total, always left curtailed.

Despite the dime-store psychoanalytic reasoning employed by Meyer, Ebert, and myself, the reality of the situation was that sexploitation filmmakers did feel their livelihood was being threatened. Eric Schaefer reports that the *Technical Report of the Commission on Obscenity and Pornography* in 1969 determined there were approximately 600 venues that regularly played sexploitation films, but this was soon to change. Sexploitation was also being shown in mainstream theaters, but in 1970, MPAA chief Jack Valenti launched a campaign to discourage exhibitors from booking the (often independently made) films; at the same time, many of the theaters that specialized in showing exploitation films were looking for a cheaper product, and many eventually became porno theaters.[37] As film industry scholar Justin Wyatt straightforwardly states, "the hard core market did erode the soft core audience," to the point where, in 1969, soft-core filmmakers such as Radley Metzger and Jay Feinberg formed the Adult Film Association of America, designed to help protect sexploitation filmmakers from laws and censorship aimed at hardcore films.[38]

What, ultimately, was Meyer's response? His films could no longer sustain their success by being merely good-natured sexual comedies or "Gothic, sadomasochistic melodramas" like *Lorna*.[39] Instead, the films of the final phase of Meyer's career were more like sexual cartoons:[40] colorful, rapidly paced, often episodic films that thrived on comedy and ridiculous scenarios. They were also, however, often a good deal more explicit than his earlier films: for example, 1975's *Supervixens* contains simulated sex, as well as a few brief shots of male genitalia.

Meyer's final film, *Beneath the Valley of the Ultravixens*, betrayed the influence of hardcore pornography even more than *Supervixens*. A small town in Texas is the setting for the film, which centers around the sexual relationship of voracious Lavonia, played by Kitten Natividad, who would later become a pornographic actress, and dim-witted Lamar. The primary narrative problem of the film is not, as one might expect, Lavonia's rampant adultery, but rather Lamar's fixation on anal sex. While Lavonia seduces men all around town and takes a job at the local strip club, the film never condemns her for her actions—the film's narrator never suggests that she should be derided for her sexual appetite, she is not punished by the narrative for her transgressions, and Lamar does not seem bothered her actions. Lamar's "perversion," his "inability to look a good fuck in the eyes," as his buxom boss Sal puts it, is the main issue of the film. In a move typical of Meyer's filmmaking, the film reinforces a particular normative type of sexuality (heterosexual, nonsodomotical), even while deconstructing another (taboos against adultery and multiple sexual partners).

Aside from being the most explicit of Meyer's films—in addition to shots of male genitalia and endless simulated sex, one is surprised to see the trademark Meyer shot, a close-up of breasts shot from a low angle to accentuated their size, has largely been replaced by a waist-high shot of the female pubic area—*Beneath the Valley of the Ultravixens* is also structured like a hardcore feature. Like *Deep Throat* (among others), the film centers on the protagonist's bizarre sexual problem, which can only be solved through repeated intercourse. The sex problem, in the narrative equivalent of a self-fulfilling prophecy, creates a loose, episodic framework that acts as an excuse for the copious representation of sexual acts that follow.

Meyer's Retirement

Beneath the Valley of the Ultravixens would be Meyer's last film, assaulted as he was on both sides by the increasing popularity of hardcore pornography and the growing permissiveness toward nudity and simulated sex in mainstream films. He couldn't get much closer to the former than in *Beneath*, nor did he have a desire to, and he was refused access to the latter by the gatekeepers of culture. As if sensing that it would be his last film, Meyer appears in person at the film's finale to give a summation of the film's themes and those of his career. Once the film was released, Meyer took the chance in *Variety* to summarize his career as well. In the pages of the publication, he "claims never to have lost a dollar on any of the 23 feature films he has made."[41] He also took the opportunity to differentiate himself from hardcore pornographers:

I am really working in the movie mainstream . . . my principal competition is Streisand and Redford and others of that sort . . . I attract a
cross-section of the population . . . rednecks, college students, middle-
aged couples and a lot of film buffs. Thirty percent of the audiences at
my films are women and that isn't the case with most hardcore films.
My films have played opposite such product as "101 Dalmatians" in suburban multiplexes.[42]

It is difficult to take Meyer at his word here, as it is doubtful that star-
driven Hollywood films were ever his real competition. But the fact
that Meyer felt he needed to distance himself from hardcore is telling.
As his career was ending, the political assault on pornography had
only gotten worse, and Meyer did not have the respectability or clout
that the mainstream film industry had to protect his films from attack
and cultural disapproval. Perhaps sensing his cultural moment was
over, with the rise of the religious right, hardcore replacing sexploitation, and the mainstreaming of the feminist critique of sexual explicitness in the media, Meyer chose to retire after *Beneath the Valley of the
Ultravixens* was released.

Meyer as a Cult Filmmaker

Meyer's critical reputation has improved greatly since his last film
was made. Critics, perhaps hyperbolically, have written that "until
Bonnie and Clyde and *The Wild Bunch*, no American filmmaker equaled
Meyer's dexterity in creating exhilarating montage"[43] and, contrary
to the heyday of his career, that "today, his films are enthusiastically
embraced by feminists."[44] His film *Faster Pussycat! Kill! Kill!*, centering
on the murder and mayhem caused by an unapologetic girl gang, has
become a favorite with contemporary cult audiences. John Waters,
who called *Faster Pussycat!* the "best movie ever made," claims that
the appeal of Meyer's films lies in the fantasies they provide:

He is single-handedly responsible for more hard-ons in movie audiences
than any other director, despite the fact that he has refused ever to make
a hard-core feature. Married couples have flocked to his films for twenty
years because they know Russ delivers and feel that the erotic images he
is so famous for give them fodder for fantasies and actually add a little
zing to their dull sex lives.[45]

According to Waters and others who have since written about
Meyer, his continued appeal rests largely on the fundamental difference
between his and contemporary sex films. *Faster Pussycat!* in particular,

features very little nudity and no sex, yet still carries a substantial erotic charge due to the performances of its three "bad girl" leads. The film has fascinated both male and female audiences, as have Meyer's films in general.

In *Faster Pussycat!* the three leads are all attractive and sexually desirable women, but the narrative that encompasses them is driven by their actions and emphasizes both their physical and sexual power over men. In other words, the film complicates gendered stereotypes while playing on fantasies of dominance and submission, all through a tone that contemporary audiences interpret and enjoy as camp. And while the gang is punished with death at the end of the film, that punishment feels tacked on—like the classic gangster films of the 1930s, or the early exploitation films Schaefer writes about—the reassertion of moral authority at the end of *Faster Pussycat!* rings hollow, as if the audience is supposed to suddenly disavow its previous delight in watching Varla, Billie, and Rosie behaving badly.

Meyer's films not only paved the way for the increasing visualization of the naked (usually female) form in films, but his films were a site where new social ideas about sexuality were being negotiated during the 1960s and 1970s. The paradox of his films and the secret to their continued appeal lie in the fact that they combine progressive and retrograde ideas about acceptable sexuality. Ultimately, in a contemporary era where hardcore has taken over as the predominant filmic expression of sexuality, the tension in Meyer's films reminds us of the cultural anxieties that sparked the sexual revolution and are still with us today, as well as the paradoxical, sometimes politically problematic, nature of sexual fantasy itself.

Notes

1. John Waters, "Russ Meyer: Master," in *The Very Breast of Russ Meyer*, ed. Paul A. Woods (London: Plexus Publishing, 2004), 42.

2. An exception to this might be Corman's *Little Shop of Horrors*, but only because of Frank Oz's popular 1986 musical remake of the same name.

3. David K. Frasier, *Russ Meyer: The Life and Films* (Jefferson, NC: McFarland & Company, 1990), 1. The first section of this book, a brief biography of the filmmaker, occasionally discusses how Meyer's films contributed to the loosening of acceptable depictions of sexuality.

4. Legs McNeil and Jennifer Osborne, *The Other Hollywood: The Uncensored Oral History of the Porn Film Industry* (New York: Regan Books, 2005), 7–8.

5. Russ Meyer, "Interview," by Tom Teicholz. *Interview*, 16.1 (Jan. 1986): 71.

6. See Beth Bailey, "Sexual Revolution(s)," in *The Sixties: From Memory to History*, ed. David Farber (Chapel Hill: University of North Carolina Press, 1994), 235–62.

7. Russ Meyer, "Interview," by Jim Morton. *Re/Search* 10 (1986): 78.

8. Roger Ebert, "Russ Meyer: King of the Nudies," *Film Comment* 9.1 (Jan/Feb 1973): 36.

9. Frasier, 4.

10. Eric Schaefer. *"Bold! Daring! Shocking! True!": A History of Exploitation Film, 1919–1959.* (Durham, NC: Duke University Press), 69–72.

11. Eddie Muller and Daniel Faris, *Grindhouse: The Forbidden World of "Adults Only" Cinema* (New York: St. Martin's Griffin, 1996), 82.

12. Schaefer, 327–37.

13. Ibid., 338.

14. Ebert, 36.

15. Ebert co-wrote *Beyond the Valley of the Dolls* and, under a pseudonym, *Up!* and *Beneath the Valley of the Ultravixens.*

16. Ibid., 40.

17. Ibid., 37.

18. Frasier, 4.

19. Jonathan L. Crane, "A Lust for Life: the Cult Films of Russ Meyer," in *Unruly Pleasures: The Cult Film and Its Critics*, ed. Xavier Mendik and Graeme Harper (Surrey, UK: FAB Press, 2000), 90.

20. Ibid., 91.

21. Ibid., 92.

22. Ibid., 98.

23. Frasier, 12, 19.

24. Crane, 98.

25. Kristen Hatch, "The Sweeter the Kitten, the Sharper the Claws: Russ Meyer's Bad Girls," in *Bad: Infamy, Darkness, Evil and Slime on Screen*, ed. Murray Pomerance (Albany: SUNY Press, 2004), 149–50.

26. Ebert, 41.

27. Meyer, Interview with Morton, 83.

28. See, for example, "Meyer and 2 Feminists Exchange Barbs at Yale," *The New York Times* (Mar. 4, 1970): 38, or "Debate Whether Women Exploited by Russ Meyer," *Variety* (Oct. 20, 1976): 6.

29. Meyer, Interview with Teicholz, 72.

30. Erica Gavin, "From Vixen to Vindication: Interview," by Dannis Peary, *The Velvet Light Trap* 16 (Fall 1976): 24.

31. Meyer, Interview with Teicholz, 72.

32. Vincent Canby. "Screen: by Russ Meyer," *The New York Times* (Sept. 6, 1969): 21.

33. Russ Meyer. "Sex, Violence and Drugs, All in Good Fun: Interview," by Stan Berkowitz, *Film Comment* 9.1 (Jan/Feb 1973): 48.

34. Meyer, Interview with Teicholz, 71–72.

35. Ebert, 36.

36. Ibid., 37

37. Eric Schaefer, "Gauging a Revolution: 16mm Film and the Rise of the Pornographic Feature," *Cinema Journal* 41.3 (Spring 2002): 5–7.

38. Justin Wyatt, "Selling 'Atrocious Sexual Behavior': Revising Sexualities in the Marketplace for Adult Films of the 1960s," in *Swinging Single: Representing Sexuality in the 1960s*, ed. Hilary Radner and Moya Luckett (Minneapolis: University of Minnesota Press, 1999), 121.

39. Ebert, 37.

40. Muller and Faris, 129.

41. Lewis Lazare, "Russ Meyer Analyzes His Own Films, 'No Losers'." *Variety* (Sept. 26, 1979): 22.

42. Ibid., 22.

43. Muller and Faris, 100.

44. Hatch, 144.

45. Waters, 42.

Bibliography

Bailey, Beth. "Sexual Revolution(s)," in David Farber, ed. *The Sixties: From Memory to History*. Chapel Hill: University of North Carolina Press, 1994, pp. 235–62.

Canby, Vincent. "Screen: by Russ Meyer." *The New York Times* (Sept. 6, 1969): 21.

Crane, Jonathan L. "A Lust for Life: The Cult Films of Russ Meyer," in Xavier Mendik and Graeme Harper, eds. *Unruly Pleasures: The Cult Film and Its Critics*. Surrey, UK: FAB Press, 2000, pp. 87–101.

"Debate Whether Women Exploited by Russ Meyer." *Variety* (Oct. 20, 1976): 6.

Ebert, Roger. "Russ Meyer: King of the Nudies." *Film Comment* 9.1 (Jan/Feb 1973): 35–45.

Frasier, David K. *Russ Meyer: The Life and Films.* Jefferson, NC: McFarland, 1990.

Gavin, Erica. "From Vixen to Vindication: Interview." By Dannis Peary. *The Velvet Light Trap* 16 (Fall 1976): 22–27.

Hatch, Kristen. "The Sweeter the Kitten, the Sharper the Claws: Russ Meyer's Bad Girls." In Murray Pomerance, ed. *Bad: Infamy, Darkness, Evil and Slime On Screen*. Albany: SUNY Press, 2004, 143–55.

Lazare, Lewis. "Russ Meyer Analyzes His Own Films, 'No Losers.'" *Variety* (Sept. 26, 1979): 22.

McNeil, Legs and Jennifer Osborne. *The Other Hollywood: The Uncensored Oral History of the Porn Film Industry*. New York: Regan Books, 2005.

"Meyer and 2 Feminists Exchange Barbs at Yale." *The New York Times* (Mar. 4, 1970): 38.

Meyer, Russ. "Sex, Violence and Drugs, All in Good Fun: Interview." By Stan Berkowitz. *Film Comment* 9.1 (Jan/Feb 1973): 47–51.

Meyer, Russ. "Interview." By Jim Morton. *Re/Search* 10 (1986): 77–85.

Meyer, Russ. "Interview." By Tom Teicholz. *Interview* 16.1 (Jan. 1986): 70–73.

Muller, Eddie and Daniel Faris. *Grindhouse: The Forbidden World of "Adults Only" Cinema.* New York: St. Martin's Griffin, 1996.

Schaefer, Eric. *"Bold! Daring! Shocking! True!": A History of Exploitation Film, 1919–1959.* Durham, NC: Duke UP, 1999.

Schaefer, Eric. "Gauging a Revolution: 16mm Film and the Rise of the Pornographic Feature." *Cinema Journal* 41.3 (Spring 2002): 3–26.

Waters, John. "Russ Meyer: Master." In Paul A. Woods, ed. *The Very Breast of Russ Meyer.* London: Plexus Publishing, 2004, pp. 42–47.

Wyatt, Justin. "Selling 'Atrocious Sexual Behavior': Revising Sexualities in the Marketplace for Adult Films of the 1960s." In Hilary Radner and Moya Luckett, eds. *Swinging Single: Representing Sexuality in the 1960s.* Minneapolis: University of Minnesota Press, 1999, 105–31.

CHAPTER 2

SWAYZE IS AMERICA: *ROAD HOUSE*, *POINT BREAK*, AND THE CULT/CAMP MOVIE OF THE 1980S AND 1990S

Bob Batchelor

Watching *Road House* now, into the second decade of the twenty-first century, is an exercise in 1980s nostalgia—a critical component of contemporary popular culture, given the seemingly permanent popularity of the decade's actors, films, music, and fashions. The movie's opening scene is a virtual highlight reel of 1980s excesses: blazing neon, a hot red Lamborghini, strikingly high heels, short skirts, and packed crowds.

When Patrick Swayze finally appears on the screen—after a montage of $100 bills, poofy 1980s perms, and *Miami Vice*-inspired leisurewear—the first thing the viewer notices is Swayze's mane. Perfectly feathered and seemingly cemented into place, Swayze's hair is a central character in *Road House*; kind of like Superman's cape, it is a representation of his power and vitality. The viewer can gauge sequences in the film by simply looking at Swayze's locks: Flawless hair equals Dalton at the top of his game, while messy indicates either impending danger or emotion. When he first shows up at the Double Deuce, the rundown nightclub he is hired to clean up, his cowlick is particularly superhero-like.

A little later, after he endures his second knifing in the first 38 minutes of the movie, he emerges from the battle with plenty of blood spilled and a wild mane. Luckily, by the time he arrives at the hospital (for nine staples to sew up the slashing) to flirt with leggy, blond "Doc" (Kelly Lynch), his hair reverts to perfection; thus, the viewer knows Dalton is okay.

Road House also symbolizes the decade by reflecting the extremes of American life. On one hand, Dalton is educated at NYU and reflects the glitz and glamour of the "big city." However, he leaves all that behind for the wonders of the small town in Reagan's America (plus a $5,000 retainer and a $500 per week salary). The battle between big and small is a consistent theme in *Road House*. While Dalton represents the small business owners and townspeople who just want a safe place to drink, Brad Wesley (Ben Gazzara) typifies the evil of big-box invasion by the likes of JC Penney and other machinations that turn little towns into big, impersonal monoliths.

Reminiscent of Boss Hogg in the popular television show *The Dukes of Hazzard* (1979–1985), Gazzara's Wesley is strangely out of place in the little town. There are similarities: the quest for money, strange clothing (he wears an ascot for most of the flick), and bumbling henchmen. The idea that the evil villain has so many foibles is a mainstay in 1980s and 1990s movies, as if moviegoers expected as much but still felt that the battle between good and evil stood in question. Yet in the campy *Dukes*, small-town sheriff Roscoe P. Coltrane did not assault the boys, commit arson, or murder anyone. Certainly, 1980s films thrived on such simpleminded violence and gore. Over-the-top violence confronted the decade's filmgoers, whether in purposely aggressive films, such as the Steven Seagal vehicle *Hard to Kill*, or in critically acclaimed movies, like Spike Lee's *Do the Right Thing* or Oliver Stone's *Born on the Fourth of July*.

Another interesting character in *Road House* is Dalton's landlord, Emmet (Sunshine Parker), who looks like Santa Claus in overalls. A personification of a small town's interaction with new ideas, Emmet scratches his head often, gazing in wonder at the collision between old and new society and culture. The character reeks of the word *new-fangled*, itself a coded symbol of earlier (better) times. Everything about him represents a nostalgic vision of small-town America: the kindly old man, the rustic horse farm overlooking a pond, and a world-view built around fairness. Emmet's compassion and love for Dalton as a kind of father figure compels the younger man to stand up against Wesley and his henchmen, even though his better judgment reveals that it is a losing proposition.

When Wesley has Emmet's house blown up, Dalton pulls him out in his head-to-foot red pajamas. The anger is too much for Dalton, which results in the film's most famous scene—Dalton and Jimmy fighting, karate-style, to the death. Dalton wins the battle—pulling his foe's trachea out of his throat with his bare hands—but proves Doc's point that if Dalton doesn't change, the town will need to be saved from him. Battered, beaten, and bloody, Dalton floats the body across the pond toward Wesley's mansion.

"I Thought You'd Be Bigger"

Adding to Dalton's Superman persona is the running theme that his current and past actions will inevitably lead to his later demise. As they sit on the roof/balcony naked, Doc tells him that he will face a lot of pain later in life if he doesn't quit, yet Dalton faces the thought with a glib remark and a sigh. The viewer knows the remark sinks in, however, because Dalton's hair is out of place, thus revealing an existential crisis in the works. Doc tells him that he can stay (so they can be together), yet Dalton knows that his only commitment is to the next battle. All the while, Wesley watches from his darkened room, contemplating his next malicious plot.

Perhaps the most intriguing character in *Road House* (and a perennial fan favorite) is Wade Garrett (Sam Elliott), a legendary cooler and Dalton's mentor. Elliott, as fine a character actor as America has produced, plays Garrett as a crusty yet loveable character who spouts wisdom, such as "that gal has entirely too many brains to have an ass like that"[1] about Dalton's love interest.

Like Dalton, or perhaps a glimpse of the character's future, Garrett seems too small to be so tough, a virtual Jedi warrior in the heart of small-town America. When Dalton loses his cool and throws a wild, roundhouse punch at Garrett, the mentor catches the punch midair, serenely declaring, "No, we don't want to do this."[2]

After Dalton's death match with Jimmy, his hair is a dripping, sweaty mess, which reveals the depths of his newfound crisis. As a result, Wesley gives Dalton an ultimatum: choose between Doc and Garrett. When Dalton hesitates, Garrett finds himself on the Double Deuce bar with a knife sticking out of his chest.

Returning to another heroic trope of 1980s action films, Dalton seeks revenge. He invades Wesley's compound, despite being outnumbered and outgunned. A killing spree erupts in the palatial estate, and only the bumbling, 400-plus-pound henchman, Tinker, lives on, incapacitated when a life-size, stuffed polar bear falls on him. Wesley and Dalton battle with a variety of weapons, including an African spear, with Wesley actually holding his own (helped along since he shot Dalton in the shoulder earlier in the scene). Until, that is, Wesley thinks of shooting him while his back is turned.

Spurred on by Dalton's destruction of Wesley, the town elders finally have the guts to challenge him, each one shooting him up with a rifle. Detectives arrive on the scene and do nothing, leaving viewers to wonder where the police were for the most part during the film's timeline. Interestingly, the audience might also ask why it takes four men to kill Wesley off, each firing from about eight feet away, declaring, "This is our town. Don't you forget it!"[3]

The climatic, final death of Wesley symbolizes the victory of small-town America over the encroaching power of big-box stores and despots like Wesley who want to force the contemporary world onto areas where they are not wanted. Even though it is a violent, gory death, the viewer is asked to recognize the deeper moral necessity of guarding small towns against such invading forces, even if it calls for lethal force.

Bodhi and Johnny Utah: The Bromance

Jumping into the 1990s, arguably one of the world's top box office draws after the success of the romance *Ghost* with Demi Moore and Whoopi Goldberg, Swayze returned to the action genre in *Point Break*, playing bad guy bank robber Bodhi, up against Keanu Reeves's FBI Agent Johnny Utah. Similar to *Road House*, *Point Break* enjoyed initial success at the box office, taking in about $83 million on a $24 million budget. The revenues paled in comparison, however, with *Ghost*, which brought in a stunning $505 million. Surprisingly, though, while *Ghost* has been essentially forgotten among Swayze's films, *Point Break* also attained cult status.

Drawing some inferences from this juxtaposition, it seems as if Swayze's broad appeal in the 1980s and 1990s as a romantic lead actor enabled him to gain superstar status. However, the long-term popularity of his cult films—propelled by cable-watching male audiences—creates his lasting reputation. In his 2009 autobiography *The Time of My Life*, written with his wife Lisa Niemi, Swayze acknowledges his cult status, explaining, "*Road House* created a cult following for me among men. With its multiple bar-fight scenes and macho, tough-shit antagonists, it was a classic guys' film."[4] Yet cult status did not seem enough for him. Like other actors known for action-flick prowess and good looks, Swayze constantly wanted to be judged as an actor and writer rather than just a pretty face. Teaming with Keanu Reeves, another Hollywood pinup, however, would do more to solidify Swayze's cult hero standing.

Released in 1991, *Point Break* has a much different vibe than *Road House*. While the latter symbolized the battle between nostalgia and consumer culture, *Point Break* contains political overtones that ask the viewer to reconsider the sanctity of traditional institutions, particularly the presidency and banks. From a less academic perspective, though, the aspect of the film that jumps out at the viewer is the relationship between Bodhi and Johnny, a kind of boy meets boy, boy loses boy, boy gets boy in the end battle. The "bromance" overtones are quite evident, particularly in the loaded, double-entendre dialogue. Certainly the film's producers did not envision *Point Break* as a gay male love story, but it foreshadows that conclusion.

Although there is the typical 1980s/1990s gratuitous female nudity in *Point Break*, the amount of male skin is staggering. Like the rumors regarding Tom Cruise's sexual preferences during the release of *Top Gun* (1986), similar questions swirling about Reeves fueled further examination and interest. In addition, there is little or no chemistry between Reeves and the female lead Lori Petty, while Swayze and Reeves exhibit a strong bond.

For example, in the midst of one action scene, Bodhi tells Johnny, "You want me so bad, it's like acid in your mouth,"[5] right before he leaps from a plane. Later, after Bodhi escapes and Johnny chases him down in Australia, the FBI agent says, "You gotta go down. It's gotta be that way."[6] Such coded language runs rampant through the film.

Both in its initial release and the countless times the film has been on cable television, audiences were well aware of the plethora of sun-soaked male bodies and physicality of its actors, who are often aggressively touching one another. The movie's publicity poster, as a matter of fact, features Swayze with a full, blond mane, while Reeves sports slick, dark hair. A quick glance at the poster and the viewer might assume that *Point Break* is a love story . . . and in many respects it can be viewed that way.

Hair, Muscles, and Football

Before Bodhi realizes that Johnny is famous former Ohio State quarterback Johnny Utah, the surfing gang and various cronies play full-contact football on the beach at night, with headlights to light the way. The game results in an alpha-male battle between the surfer and FBI agent, each quarterbacking his respective team. The players—all heavily muscled and with antiestablishment long hair—take turns manhandling each other, but the ultimate fight takes place between the two protagonists.

At the moment of truth, Johnny tackles Bodhi into the water (even though no one else has gone anywhere near the drink in the game), forcing them to eye each other warily. As the gang assembles, assuming there will be a fight, Bodhi announces who it is and they all bond over Utah's exploits in the college ranks. The homage to football adds to the movie's cult following. Male viewers are attracted to films featuring sports or sports heroes like moths to fire. The added note that Utah had to leave the game due to a knee injury makes the character even more likable.

Later, when Johnny mistakenly targets a competing surfing gang (who knew, by the way, that there were so many surfing gangs in early 1990s America?), Bodhi comes to his rescue. Although they are outnumbered two to one, the Zen surfer (shirtless) and undercover agent break out martial arts moves to win the fight. Bodhi's Buddha personality is revealed after the fight, when he tells Johnny how the "Nazi" gang is "wired wrong," unable to "get the spiritual side of it [surfing/ocean]."[7] After joking about the meaning of surfing, Bodhi and Johnny swap loving looks and a firm handshake, and then the older man invites him to a party at his house.

According to Swayze, Bodhi represented a "once-in-a-blue-moon character, the bad guy who you love because you believe in what he believes in—until he believes in it too far and breaks the law and kills someone. I loved Bodhi because I identified with his quest for perfection and the ultimate adrenaline high."[8] As an actor, playing Bodhi enabled Swayze to again break out of the traditional romance stereotype.

Amidst the hard bodies and surfing scenes, some of *Point Break*'s most startling images come from the exploits of the Ex-Presidents, a gang of bank robbers who wear masks portraying former commanders-in-chief: Ronald Reagan, Jimmy Carter, Lyndon Johnson, and Richard Nixon. Swayze wears the Reagan guise and leads the crew through 27 heists over three years, ironically without shooting anyone. While a viewer could look at the choices of masks as simply the most popular ones available, it is also an indictment of those presidents—ones who have robbed the nation in a variety of ways. As the leader of the gang, Bodhi/Reagan casts derision on the Reagan/Bush years simply by being antirules and by being against traditional institutions. Nonconformist elements exist even in some of the cheesiest dialogue, such as when Bodhi asks Johnny as they prepare to rob their last bank, "Why be a servant to the law, when you can be its master?"[9]

At the end of the film, Bodhi and Johnny have largely switched places. Bodhi is clean cut, while Johnny sports long hair and denim.

In other words, the character that represents authority has been transformed by his experiences with the would-be villain, now repentant because his friends are all dead. The cat-and-mouse game ends after they nearly beat each other to death, but Johnny handcuffs himself to Bodhi, finally achieving his goal of capturing his prey. Rather than force the Zen master to rot in a jail cell, Johnny allows him to surf to his death among the 50-foot waves. As Johnny walks away, he tosses his badge into the surf—the ultimate way to disrespect the authority position he represents.

Swayze Is America

As big as the myth that symbolizes his Texas roots, Patrick Swayze represented a new breed of American hero in the 1980s and early 1990s. Now, closing in on a couple decades later, his brand of cult hero standing forces the conclusion that these ideas still resonate with viewers. In *Road House*, he is the nostalgic avenger, thwarting the twin evils of consumerism and tyranny. *Point Break*, on the other hand, enables Swayze to portray a villain, but one who embodies beliefs that the audience holds. Bodhi is a kind of modern-day Robin Hood, at least until the end of the movie, when seeking the ultimate thrill clouds his judgment and he is forced to kill an innocent bystander. Until that time, his carefree surfer mentality stands in opposition to his bank robber/gang leader persona but somehow sparks a note with viewers. At least the money is used to fund the Zen master's quest for the perfect wave.

At the heart of Swayze's appeal, which carries through to today's audiences, is a central reservoir of vulnerability despite the tough-guy characters he played. As it turns out, this feeling mimicked the actor's real-life emotions. He explained, "No matter how confidently I projected myself onstage and in everyday life, inside I was still a scared boy—afraid of rejection and willing to do whatever was necessary to stave it off."[10] Swayze's duality—portraying strength and grit with basic emotional openness—provides male viewers with a model that fulfills their need for toughness while at the same time nodding to the vulnerability that women admire.

At this point, *Road House* occupies a central role in cult circles versus *Point Break*, fueled by repeated showings on basic cable television stations. Sadly, while he recognized the film's following, Swayze did not seem to take much pleasure in its standing, only devoting about three pages of his autobiography to *Road House*. Perhaps if Swayze lived into old age (he was tragically struck down by pancreatic cancer in 2009), he might have appreciated his cult status more fully. Despite its campy moments, Swayze's performance reveals the power of image making. He embodies the role so well that one is at a loss to imagine an actor who could have done a better job in the movie.

Propelled by *Road House* and *Point Break*, Swayze transcended mere box office stardom to transform into a cult figure, thus remaining relevant long after more celebrated actors of his day drooped from the spotlight. According to writer Joe Queenan, "Somewhere along the line, much like John Wayne, Swayze became one of those stars whose acting skill ultimately became irrelevant to his appeal . . . like Wayne, he made a lot of movies that no one remembers and a handful of movies no one will ever forget."[11] The evolution from movie star to legend is a difficult one to undertake and often has a great deal to do with qualities an actor carries deep within his or her true self. Film audiences recognize this pull in Swayze and his portrayals of Dalton and Bodhi. The results are quintessentially American movie figures mixing action, romance, and (often unintentional) comedy that will continue to captivate and entertain viewers hoping to escape into the world of film.

Notes

1. *Road House*, DVD, directed by Rowdy Herrington (Culver City, CA: Sony Pictures Home Entertainment, 2006).

2. Ibid.

3. Ibid.

4. Patrick Swayze and Lisa Niemi, *The Time of My Life* (New York: Atria, 2010), 155.

5. *Point Break*, DVD, directed by Kathryn Bigelow (Beverly Hills, CA: Twentieth Century Fox Home Entertainment, 2000).

6. Ibid.

7. Ibid.

8. Swayze and Niemi, 173–74.

9. *Point Break*

10. Swayze and Niemi, *The Time of My Life*, 49.

11. Joe Queenan, "The Film that Made Patrick Swayze an Action Hero," *The Guardian* (London), September 16, 2009, http://www.guardian.co.uk/film/2009/sep/16/patrick-swayze-joe-queenan (accessed 18 August 2010).

CHAPTER 3

MIDNIGHT MOVIES AND THE PHENOMENON OF THE CULT FILM

Tomás F. Crowder-Taraborrelli

The phenomenon of the midnight movie took Hollywood by surprise. A small number of low-budget independent films caught the interest of counterculture hipsters who began to form long lines in New York to see heretical films such as George Romero's *Night of the Living Dead* (1968) and Alejandro Jodorowsky's *El Topo* (1970). Jodorowsky, Mexican in origin, lived in Paris, where he was part of a surrealist theater group.[1] Theater owners and distributors promptly realized that a niche market stood ready for exploitation and quickly searched for other films that might have similar appeal.

However, there is some indication that cult films date back to the earliest days of movies. Cult film historians Karl French and Philip French argue that characteristics of cult films appear in early silent films, the most notable being *The Cabinet of Dr. Caligari* (1919) and *Nosferatu (Eine Symphonie Des Garuens)* (1922).[2] That said, I argue that the cult film is mostly a phenomenon of the 1960s and 1970s, a period in which film going combined with recreational drug use for many.[3] The United States was the epicenter of spread of the midnight movie circuit, but soon other countries followed, such as Japan, Spain, and Germany.

A number of factors, both social and technical, contributed to the development of the midnight movie phenomenon in the 1960s and 1970s. The United States was creeping out of the fear of nuclear obliteration and launching a bloody war against its communist foes in Korea and Vietnam. Hollywood studios had a series of blockbusters underway which "recycled ideas and plots from B movies, and serials . . . "[4]

As a reaction to political and cultural conservatism, a small group of filmmakers broke onto the scene with movies that subverted film traditions and cultural mores. Cult directors felt that part of America's decadence was due to Hollywood's despotic influence on the evolution of cinema and, as a consequence, on the national character.[5] The cult films that kids began lining up to see in New York and Chicago in the 1960s introduced a set of characters, narrative strategies, and cinematography tactics that slowly grew into a staple of contemporary films. Although it is often surprising to see what film falls within the category of cult film or midnight movie, there is an undeniable consensus of what constitutes an example of the genre.

One of the most frequently quoted definitions of a cult movie comes from Italian cultural critic and semiologist Umberto Eco:

> The work . . . must provide a completely furnished world so that its fans can quote characters and episodes as if they were aspects of the fan's private sectarian world, a world about which one can make up quizzes and play trivia games so that the adepts of the sect recognize through each other a shared expertise.[6]

Taking Eco's definition even further, one finds that foremost, a cult film or a midnight movie blockbuster is defined by the fanaticism it generates among audiences. Traditionally, viewers may watch their favorite movies dozens of times, but with cult films, fans will get together to act out scenes, interject their own lines, and sometime even dress up as their favorite stars.

For many critics, *The Rocky Horror Picture Show* (1975) conjures the definition of a cult film. Most film directors would kill for a pinch of director Jim Sharman's success in involving audiences during screenings of the film. *The Rocky Horror Picture Show*, which began as a musical in England, blends glam rock's aesthetics with the B-horror flick. Scott Michaels recalls the days when he discovered the film:

> I grew up in Detroit, in a very blue-collar neighborhood. It never is cool to be different, but it was especially uncool in Detroit. Around 1978, well after *The Rocky Horror Picture Show* "cult" began elsewhere in the country, it finally hit my town. I never heard a word about this piece of celluloid until one evening it was used as a human-interest story on the local news station. I saw. I wanted. That was for me. The report showed scenes of mayhem in the movie house, with hundreds of people throwing food, dancing and singing in the aisles—it was something I wanted to belong to.[7]

As Ernest Mathijs and Xavier Mendik note in the introduction to their anthology on cult films, the most revealing research about cult films mixes qualitative analysis with ethnographic episodes, such as interviews, confessions, personal anecdotes, and behind-the-scenes gossip.[8] As interesting as these adventures may be, they also reveal the challenges cult producers and directors face when making independent films (most midnight movies and cult films fall within this category). Lloyd Kaufman and James Gunn, producers of the *Troma* cult favorite *The Toxic Avenger* (1984), have this to say about the cult movie's commitment to establishing an intimate relationship with audiences:

> By letting the audience see the seams on our makeshift latex-and-syrup, we are, in fact, allowing them to become a part of the imaginative process it takes in creating the film. I have long said that *Troma* movies were one of the first interactive mediums. Our intention is not to dazzle, but to create a true spiritual connection between the audience and the film . . . we have faith in the imagination and humanity of the audience.[9]

These films, then, are more than mere representations of a fictional world. They allow viewers to create new cultures within the confines of likeminded enthusiasts that extend the meaning of the film itself.

There is an implicit commitment with most cult films to turn the classic passive spectator into an active spectator, and with any luck, into a devotee for life. Directors employ narrative strategies that call for audiences to participate in the performance of the film. Of course, there are different degrees with which filmmakers are successful in breaking through the confines of the mundane life of spectators and the melodramatic reality of movies. According to Gillo Dorfles, the development of industrial societies, and particularly the omnipresent media, has contributed to the numbing of people's ability to create personal bonds with belongings.

> Unfortunately, mass-culture, being as it is at the root of the new distribution of time, has killed all ability to distinguish between art and life; all trace of a "rite" in the handing out of cultural and aesthetic nourishment by the mass media (radio, TV magazines, cinema) has been lost, and this lack of the ritual element has brought about an indifference in the onlooker when he is faced with the different kinds of transmissions and manifestations which are forced upon him.[10]

Dorfles is right to point out the ephemeral existence of cultural objects, more true today with our reliance on online realities, but cult films have been at the forefront of struggle to do away with the "indifference" of spectators who, if seduced, will cheerfully embrace the satirical versions of life often represented in midnight movies. The most representative characterization of Dorfles's "onlooker" in the 1970s was the zombie, a walking corpse who has been deprived of rationality by an overdose of commercialism, but who, like film spectators, longs to feel like a member of some sort of brotherhood. Always looking for creative ways to conquer new audiences and make a buck, filmmakers searched for creative ways to turn passive spectators into active ones, drawing from dramatic traditions such as Brechtian theater and anticipating some of the interactivity created in the video and electronic gaming industry.

In *Midnight Movies*, J. Hoberman and Jonathan Rosenbaum mentioned how important it is for a midnight movie theater to be located in a neighborhood with after-hours restaurants and bars. In his review of Jodorowsky's *El Topo* (1970), *Village Voice* critic Glenn O'Brien described such an urban atmosphere:

> It's midnight mass at the Elgin. Cocteau's *Blood of a Poet* has just ended, and the wait for *El Topo* is a brief grope for comfort before sinking back into fantastic stillness. The audience is young. They applauded Cocteau's sanguine dream as though he were in the theater, but as credits appear on the screen, they settle again into rapt attention. They've come to see the light—and the screen before them is illumined by an abstract landscape of desert and sky—and the ritual begins again.[11]

The type of ritualistic camaraderie that O'Brien describes was something that Americans craved during the dark years of the Vietnam War. A whole generation of young filmmakers came of age in this milieu, watching the carnage of war on TV.

The Transformation of Film to Cult Film

The reason a film becomes a cult phenomenon is left to the unpredictable tastes of audiences. Actually, some "serious" filmmakers are dismayed when their work becomes a sardonic treasure of cult enthusiasts. This mainly is because many cult films walk a fine line between counterculture subversion and bad taste.

In some cases, like John Waters's *Pink Flamingos* (1973), for instance, directors are resolved to turn mass-produced, low-quality cultural objects into objects of artistic contemplation (the modern sofa cover in plastic, polyester leisure suits, etc.). Generally, cult films tend to poke fun at suburban middle-class values that display cheap replicas of luxury objects connected with the elites. Some films go to the extreme of vindicating bad taste and the illicit. This is why some actions in cult films flirt with the grotesque and the surreal. A classic example of this can be found in an infamous scene in *Pink Flamingos* in which cult icon Divine eats dog excrement. The drag actor had this to say about the experience: "It was strictly done for shock value. I threw up afterward, and then I used mouth-wash and brushed my teeth. There was no after-taste of anything. I just forgot about it as quickly as I could."[12] One fan's surrealism is another's bad taste. However, it is the individual audience members that determine which, a kind of power that cult filmgoers grasp in the extended creative process.

Audiences are generally aware that when they buy a ticket to a low-budget film, they can anticipate that some of the Hollywood norms will be overhauled. In spite of this, cult films can shock and upset even the cultish insider. For example, David Lynch's *Eraserhead* (1977) established a conventional horror film mood, but spectators were unable to protect themselves from the uncanny revelations in this shocker.[13] In *Cult Movies: The Classics, the Sleepers, the Weird and the Wonderful*, Danny Peary begins his review of Lynch's first feature by invoking the revolting sensations that the film evoked in him:

> Ever had a dream while sleeping face down, with your mouth and nose buried in your pillow? In your discomfort you might have conjured up, something that approximates *Eraserhead*; but it seems to me that the only way you can expect to duplicate this nightmare is by somehow entering the dark, uneasy dream/subconscious world of the most paranoid, depressed individual in the universe on the day he or she will either commit suicide or roam the streets wearing a doomsday placard.[14]

Most cult films tend to be rewarding forms of entertainment. They are memorable in a way that a debauched party gets out of hand but stays in the mind long past a natural expiration date. A few directors, such as Lynch, are inducted into the cult hall of fame at the beginning of their careers. Their films are strangely familiar but horribly unsettling. Lynch seems to have his finger on American sensibilities or his fingers in an open wound, as he always seems to be able to shock and disturb but also to set off critics and the Hollywood establishment. In his review of Lynch's *Blue Velvet* (1986), Guy Maddin said that: " ... [Lynch's] surrealism seems more intuitive than programmatic. For him, the normal is a defense against the irrational rather than vice versa."[15] Allan Havis hits the nail on the head when describes *Blue Velvet*

as a sort of grenade to be thrown at "Ronald Reagan's nostalgic rein-
vention of America and at the Republican Party's idealization of small
towns and exurbia."[16]

The success of Lynch's films as midnight blockbusters persuaded
many filmmakers that achieving cult status could guarantee successful
distribution. Because cult films are perceived as being antiestablishment, they are often competitors for a smaller size of the consumer
pie. That said, cult film directors' disdain for the commercialism of
mainstream films has more to do with a scornful look at their parents'
possession and ambitions than a revolutionary mission to undermine
the structure of capitalism.

Cult Films and Technology

As it is difficult to assess the cultural value of a present-day film, it is
also difficult to gauge a film's cult potential. Not all critics can ascertain
the pulse of what a national audience wants to watch. When Stanley
Kubrick's *2001: A Space Odyssey* was released, film critic Annette
Michelson wanted to prove stilted critics wrong when she praised the
monumentality of the film, saying, " . . . here is a film like any other, like
all others, only more so . . . If one were concerned with an 'ontology' of
cinema, this film would be a place in which to look for it."[17]

Technology also plays a role in how a film is perceived. As a result,
midnight films shown on big screens remind viewers attuned to watching at home or on a computer of the power of cinema. For example,
many viewers first saw *2001* on a TV screen in DVD format. A few
years ago, it had a limited release on 70 mm. The experience of watching Kubrick's tour de force on the big screen complete with
primates achieving consciousness as they come to blows over a bone,
Technicolor landscapes, spaceships waltzing, a computer that believes
humans are morons, and so forth can only be compared to watching a
psychedelic circus act. Recent 3-D films, such as the off-the-wall *Cloudy
with a Chance of Meatballs* (2009), have come close to Kubrick's achievement. James Cameron, director of cultish hits like *The Terminator*
(1984) and *Avatar* (2009), foresees that technical innovations will
increase audience involvement: "You feel like you're bearing witness,
and that makes the journey more real."[18] Despite Cameron's enthusiasm for high-tech feats—as cult films have demonstrated since the
1970s—a movie's success continues to be its capacity to represent not
so much the fantastic but the commonly strange and the oddly familiar.

Shock and Awe

It is no surprise that horror movies hold a special place in the pantheon of cult films. The genre has always flirted with the subversive and its allegorical apparatus has always aimed at unmasking the grotesque hypocrisy of bourgeois culture. The chainsaw slayer in Tobe Hooper's *The Texas Chain Saw Massacre* (1974) stands for more than the manifestation of psychopathic behavior. He embodies the return of the repressed, the uncontrolled eruption of resentment of an underclass.

The audience cringes when he appears on screen and they should, since they could just as easily be the target of this cult killer's raving madness. Despite the possible rejection that horror films might arouse in mainstream audiences, there is something undeniably gratifying in witnessing a director bring cultural junk to the surface for all to see. Wes Craven, director of such chillers as *A Nightmare on Elm Street* (1984) and *Scream* (1996), refers to this particular act of directorial liberation as follows:

> ... gore stood for everything that was hidden in society. Guts stood for issues that were being repressed, so the sight of a body being eviscerated was exhilarating to the audience because they felt: "Thank god it's finally out in the open and slopping around on the floor."[19]

The American Nightmare (2000), an essential documentary on the origins of contemporary horror film, attests to the fact that the key figures of the horror genre had been soldiers in Vietnam, affected by their memories of the surreal forms of disemboweled bodies. In 1971, George Romero's low-budget zombie chiller *Night of the Living Dead* opened at the Waverly in New York to sold-out audiences. Peary argues that the film's success was due to people recommending it to each other.[20] According to Ben Hervey, the film set a new box office standard for cult films.[21] The zombies, despite their gruesome appearances and cannibalistic tendencies, awakened audiences' sympathies. They seemed desperate, animalistic in their desire to satisfy a hunger for body parts and entrails (actual entrails were provided by one of the film's producers, who was a butcher). Dressed like suburbanites, for the young audiences that packed the movie houses, the zombies probably acted a lot like their own parents and neighbors.

Due to budgetary reasons, Romero filmed *Night of the Living Dead* with an old Arriflex camera, which gives the film a grainy black-and-white look. The hand-held camera shots gave his work a newsreel feel.

The wide angles and deep focus distorted the spatial relationship between the characters and the objects that surrounded them.

Film historians have dwelled on Romero's decision to cast a Black actor as the heroic lead. Romero denies having cast Duane Jones to make a statement about the civil rights movement or racial politics.[22] Nevertheless, Jones's presence in the film challenges audiences' expectations about the role of heroes in classic horror films (normally White men fervent about saving their families, girlfriends, and communities). Despite its powerful political allegories, *Night of the Living Dead* is undeniably a campy, funny film. One of Romero's major accomplishments was to subvert some of the tropes of the classic Universal and Hammer studio films.

Antiheroes and Cult Icons

In order to establish the intellectual origins of the cult film, it is important to discuss the definition of *camp*. In her influential essay "Notes on 'Camp,'" cultural critic Susan Sontag argues that "the essence of Camp is its love—of the unnatural: of artifice and exaggeration. And Camp is esoteric—something of a private code, a badge of identity even, among small urban cliques."[23] Although Sontag is not particularly interested in establishing the difference between camp and cult, she associates the most salient characteristics of cult films with camp. As mentioned before, the most salient characteristic of cult films is their open invitation to spectators to construct a private code around the secret meanings found in the films.

Visibly, the difference between camp and cult, as Sontag cleverly observes, is that "the pure examples of Camp are unintentional; they are dead serious."[24] Camp, we can conclude, in its naiveté takes itself very seriously, while cult is ironical and comical, intended for those that get the joke. One of the reasons fans come back to watch the same cult movie again and again is to be able to laugh at the obscure humor lost on most audiences.

Cult films have to find their constituency, which sometimes entails having a successful run in an art theater. Cameron Mitchell's instant cult classic, *Hedwig and the Angry Inch* (2001), is a case in point. A bustling line curved around the block in the Castro District on the day of its San Francisco premier. For the first time in years, the upper balcony of this historic theater was packed with people in drag, hipsters, and local luminaries, all waiting for Mitchell to introduce the film that was based on his popular off-Broadway musical (itself based upon his drag performances in night clubs).

Traditionally, the narrative arc of a classic Hollywood film centers on the journey and trials of a hero. The hero typically undergoes a transformation, and in the end, either triumphs or fails, but not without teaching the audience an important moral lesson. Unlike this classic model, the cult film hero is, in reality, an antihero. Instead of displaying qualities to be emulated or being representative of the national character, cult heroes poke fun at our own weaknesses. Cult heroes, like Mitchell's fame-starved, intersex drag artist Hedwig, reflect our shortcomings and secret desires, which is why we feel sympathy for their tribulations.

These days, the quintessential cult hero *par excellence* is Jeffrey Lebowski, aka The Dude, from the Ethan and Joel Coen's *The Big Lebowski* (1998). *New York Times* critic Dwight Garner named *The Big Lebowski* the most established cult film of the 1990s. "It's got that elusive and addictive quality that a great midnight movie has to have: it blissfully widens and expands in your mind upon repeat viewings," he explains.[25] The film has spawned a subculture of urbanites who celebrate "Lebowski Fest: A Celebration of All Things Lebowski," organized by cult historians Will Russell and Scott Schuffitt, authors of *I'm a Lebowski, You're a Lebowski: Life—The Big Lebowski and What-Have-You.* At Lebowski Fest, devotees of the film gather in bars wearing the Dude's signature uniform of jellies sandals, Mexican sweaters, and Limpie pants.

Lebowski, an unemployed, urban beach bum, struggles to comprehend what his life is really about. The ultimate representative of the California loser, the Dude has only a few ambitions in life: to enjoy his white Russian cocktails, to perfect his bowling technique, and to raise enough dough to stay unemployed and buy weed. There are several legendary scenes in *The Big Lebowski*, like the scene in which the Dude drops a roach onto his lap while rocking out to a Credence song and slams his 1973 Ford Torino against a trash container.

Perhaps the Dude's appeal has something to do with the fact that he represents everything that the entrepreneurial ideology of his day does not promote. As in the case of the Dude, humor in cult films is frequently based on the naiveté of the protagonists. They seem to have faith in the most obviously corrupt institutions.

Although Jeff Bridges's impersonation of The Dude brought him critical acclaim, an actor's career can be ruined by the often dubious achievement of entering the cult pantheon with a midnight feature. One of the most notorious cases is that of David Carradine, who himself has admitted to struggling to find the working environment to be able to display his acting skills. He enjoyed his run as a cult hero when he played martial arts expert and peace activist Kwai Chang Caine in the series *Kung Fu* (Bruce Lee had conjured the character for himself, but ABC did not allow Asians to be lead actors on its television shows).[26]

There are a few soft-porn and fully pornographic films that have achieved cult status, have enjoyed wide distribution, and have been shown as midnight movie attractions in art house cinemas. For example, the notorious nudie club owners the Mitchell Brothers produced and directed a porno film that was shown at the Cannes Film Festival. In the last two decades, with the advent of video technology, the DVD format, and Internet sites, porn films have moved from the specialty theaters to the home. Most specialty theaters are now closed, and only a few titles from the 1970s, the golden days of midnight movies, have retained their cult status. *Behind the Green Door* (1972), *Deep Throat* (1972), and *Caligula* (1980) have seen short revivals in art house theaters.

Midnight movies and cult film flirt with mainstream Hollywood films. They are the black sheep of the family, the rebellious siblings, always looking for ways to deceive and make fun of familial authorities. Cult film directors are pranksters who are clearly infatuated by classic genre films but always searching for ways to undermine their visual and narrative stereotypical structures.

Notes

1. Allan Havis, *Cult Films: Taboo and Transgression* (Lanham, MD: University Press of America, 2008), 58.

2. Karl French and Philip French, *Cult Movies* (New York: Billboard Books, 2000), 6.

3. Havis, *Cult Films*, 3.

4. Michael Weldon, *The Psychotronic Video Guide* (New York: St. Martin's Griffin, 1996), viii.

5. Danny Peary, *Cult Movies: The Classics, the Sleepers, the Weird, and the Wonderful* (New York: A Delta Book, 1981), 9.

6. Paul Simpson, Helen Rodiss and Michaela Bushell, eds., *The Rough Guide to Cult Movies* (London: Rough Guides, 2004), 6.

7. Scott Michaels and David Evans, *Rocky Horror: From Concept to Cult* (London: Sanctuary, 2002), 324.

8. Ernest Mathijs and Xavier Mendik, eds., *The Cult Film Reader* (Berkshire: Open University Press, 2008), 164.

9. Lloyd Kaufman, *All I Need to Know About Filmmaking I Learned from the Toxic Avenger* (New York: Berkley Boulevard, 1998), 47.

10. Gillo Dorfles, *Kitsch: The World of Bad Taste* (New York: Universe Books, 1969), 30.

11. Dennis Lim, ed., *The Village Voice Film Guide: 50 Years of Movies from Classics to Cult Hits* (Hoboken, NJ: Wiley, 2007), 268.

12. Peary, *Cult Movies*, 264.

13. Steven Jay Schneider, "The Essential Evil in/of *Eraserhead* (or, Lynch to the contrary)," in *The Cult Film Reader*, ed. Ernest Mathijs and Xavier Mendik (Berkshire: Open University Press, 2007), 254.

14. Peary, *Cult Movies*, 86.

15. Lim, *The Village Voice Film Guide*, 55.

16. Havis, *Cult Films*, 76.

17. Greg Taylor, *Artists in the Audience: Cults, Camp, and American Film Criticism* (Princeton, NJ: Princeton University Press, 1999), 132.

18. Dana Goodyear, "Man of Extremes: The Return of James Cameron," *The New Yorker*, October, 2009, 55–67.

19. Ben Hervey, *Night of the Living Dead* (London: Palgrave Macmillan, 2008), 91.

20. Peary, 228.

21. Hervey, 120.

22. Hervey, 42.

23. Susan Sontag, "Notes on 'camp,'" in *The Cult Film Reader*, ed. Ernest Mathijs and Xavier Mendik (Berkshire: Open University Press, 2007), 42.

24. Sontag, 46.

25. Dwight Garner, "Dissertations on His Dudeness," *New York Times*, December 30, 2009, sec. E.

26. Louis Paul, *Tales from the Cult Film Trenches* (Jefferson, NC: McFarland, 2008), 41.

Bibliography

Dorfles, Gillo. *Kitsch: The World of Bad Taste*. New York: Bell Publishing, 1969.

French, Karl and Philip French. *Cult Movies*. London: Pavilion Books, Limited, 1999.

Garner, Dwight. "Dissertations on His Dudeness." *New York Times*, December 30, 2009, sec. E.

Goodyear, Dana. "Man of Extremes: The Return of James Cameron." *The New Yorker*, October, 2009, 55–67.

Havis, Allan. *Cult Films: Taboo and Transgression: A Select Survey over 9 Decades*. Lanham, MD: University Press of America, 2008.

Hervey, Ben. *Night of the Living Dead*. London: Palgrave Macmillan, 2008.

Kaufman, Lloyd and J. Gunn. *All I Need to Know About Filmmaking I Learned from the Toxic Avenger.* New York: Berkley Boulevard, 1998.

Lim, Dennis. *The Village Voice Film Guide: 50 Years of Movies from Classics to Cult Hits.* Hoboken, NJ: Wiley, 2007.

Mathijs, Ernest and Xavier Mendik. *The Cult Film Reader.* Berkshire: Open University Press, 2007.

Michaels, S. and D. Evans. *Rocky Horror: From Concept to Cult.* London: Sanctuary Publishing, 2002.

Paul, Louis. *Tales from the Cult Film Trenches: Interviews with 36 Actors from Horror, Science Fiction and Exploitation Cinema.* Jefferson, NC: McFarland, 2007.

Peary, Danny. *Cult Movies: The Classics, the Sleepers, the Weird, and the Wonderful.* New York: Delta Trade Paperbacks, 1981.

Schneider, Steven Jay, "The Essential Evil in/of *Eraserhead* (or, Lynch to the contrary)." In *The Cult Film Reader*, ed. Ernest Mathijs and Xavier Mendik. Berkshire: Open University Press, 2007.

Simpson, P., H. Rodiss, and M. Bushell. *The Rough Guide to Cult Movies.* London: Rough Guides, 2004.

Sontag, Susan. "Notes on 'Camp,' " in Ernest Mathijs and Xavier Mendik, eds. *The Cult Film Reader.* Berkshire: Open University Press, 2007.

Taylor, Greg. *Artists in the Audience: Cults, Camp, and American Film Criticism.* Princeton, NJ: Princeton University Press, 2001.

Weldon, Michael. *The Psychotronic Video Guide.* New York: St. Martin's Griffin, 1996.

CHAPTER 4

THE GODFATHER OF CULT: *THE ROCKY HORROR PICTURE SHOW*

Jeffrey C. Jackson

Should not enough come of that/Rocky Horror, son of Dread . . .
— *The Kalevala*[1]

The Rocky Horror Picture Show has been referred to variously as "the granddaddy of all midnight movies"[2] and "the mother of all midnight movies."[3] Although it flopped at the box office, it returned from the grave to become the most successful cult classic of all time. As of June 7, 2009, the movie's all-time box office gross is listed at $139,876,417.[4] *RHPS* has enjoyed the longest continually running theatrical release in history, has a fan club with more than 50,000 members, recently marked its 30-year anniversary, and is still going strong. As any of its millions of fans can attest, the movie has legs. And lips—giant disembodied ones that croon the title song and that an affronted studio flack called "lewd and lascivious."[5]

For such a famous film, though, the *RHPS* canon surprisingly lacks uniformity. Some of the urban legends about the film are merely apocryphal: Mick Jagger wanted to play Brad Majors; supporting actor Meat Loaf and director Jim Sharman attended a showing in the Midwest at which they were the only people in the audience.[6] (The former is most likely a conflation of the iconic lips from the opening credits with the Rolling Stones' famous lips-and-tongue logo.) Other bits of conventional wisdom contain a kernel of truth but have been widely exaggerated: leads Tim Curry, Barry Bostwick, and Susan

Sarandon absolutely refuse to discuss the movie. (It is true that all three have struggled to distance themselves from their seminal roles, but only Sarandon declines to reminisce, and even she admits to having been delighted to land the part, saying it "struck a chord with many kids.")[7] Still other details have simply been misreported. Those famous singing lips have been variously attributed to both the characters of Riff Raff, played by the movie's writer and creator, Richard O'Brien, and Magenta, played by Patricia Quinn. (Quinn is lip-synching O'Brien's vocals.) An epidemiologist could make a career of studying the mechanisms of *RHPS*'s transmission. Having spread to all corners of the globe, the movie's high-camp humor is not just infectious, it is pandemic: legions of researchers have put it under the microscope trying to identify the genetic markers of its virulence, while still others have attempted to sequence its DNA hoping to clone similar strains.

O'Brien's highly contagious brainchild began its life as a musical—call it Patient Zero—titled first *They Came from Denton High*, then *The Rock Horroar Show* [sic], and finally *The Rocky Horror Show*.[8] In creating Riff Raff, O'Brien no doubt drew on his own experiences, having a rock star's voice but a skinny physique and male-pattern baldness that consigned him to playing second bananas. In the early 1970s, O'Brien was a struggling actor and musician in London working odd jobs to make ends meet. He had recently been cast in *Jesus Christ Superstar* but had been let go after just one performance.[9] He references this disappointment in *RHPS*'s climax: an embittered Riff Raff turns on his master, lamenting "You never liked me!" He wrote the title song, "Science-Fiction Double Feature," to perform at an EMI Christmas party.[10] Frustrated by his lack of artistic success and inspired by the double-billed features he had seen as a child in New Zealand, O'Brien began writing a rock opera. He had always loved B-movies "because of the unconscious humor invested in them . . . [I]n those days, horror had just a little touch of irony and cynicism invested in the journey. The tongue was in the cheek."[11] O'Brien then brought the script to director Jim Sharman, who had worked with him on *Jesus Christ Superstar* and *Hair* and who shared his love of B-movies, having ". . . dabbled in sci-fi kitsch with a 16 mm film called *Shirley Thompson Versus the Aliens* . . ."[12] Next, O'Brien set about casting his labor of love.

Both the stage play and the movie owe a great deal of their success to an eclectic mixture of foresight and happenstance. On his way to the gym, O'Brien bumped into his friend and *Hair* co-star Curry, who just happened to be acting at Sloan Square, a small 60-seat theater decorated as a seedy movie house. Coincidentally, it was in this very theater space that the *Rocky Horror Show* would make its debut.[13]

The play premiered, appropriately enough, on a dark and stormy night. On June 16, 1973, the audience included such luminaries as Vincent Price.[14] After the initial six-week run of *RHS* sold out and won critical acclaim, " . . . the show transferred to a real run-down movie theatre, the 270-seat Classic Cinema,"[15] where diehard fans began returning to see it time and again. Fortuitously, these included actress Britt Ekland, who convinced her boyfriend Lou Adler, an American producer, to see the show. Adler then not only brought the show to L.A. in March of 1974 but also spearheaded the drive to make it into a motion picture. Stacking the house with *RHS* regulars, he invited 20th Century Fox studio head Gordon Stulberg to the American premiere at Adler's Roxy club.[16]

Green-lighted and given a modest $1 million budget, production on the project now titled *The Rocky Horror Picture Show* began in November of 1974 "at the old Hammer studios in Berkshire, in an old Victorian mansion that had been the site of such Hammer horror classics as *The Curse of Frankenstein* and *The Horror of Dracula*. Another very good omen."[17] Sharman signed on once more to direct and was able to strengthen the cast by keeping most of the London and L.A. companies, with a few crucial changes. O'Brien and Curry reprised the roles of Riff Raff and Frank-N-Furter, along with cast originals Quinn as Magenta and "Little" Nell Campbell as Columbia. Meat Loaf returned as the undead delivery boy Eddie. Campbell and Quinn had originally doubled as an Usherette, and Meat Loaf had also played a dual role as Dr. Scott, a role now taken over by Jonathan Adams, who had originally played the criminologist.[18] After this bout of (musical) musical chairs, Charles Gray stepped into the narrator's role, Peter Hinwood won the part of Rocky, and two newcomers, Bostwick and Sarandon, were hired as the movie's WASPish, inhibited protagonists. The concept of dual roles—good for plays with small casts and movies with limited budgets—remained. Curry, O'Brien, Quinn, and Campbell appear as townsfolk in the opening wedding scene. The rest, as they say, is history.

A funny thing happened on the way to boffo box office returns. The movie tanked. Actually, it failed twice, first in movie theaters and then again on Broadway. Curry, who won acclaim in Tom Stoppard's *Travesties*, recalls, "I was in the biggest flop and the biggest hit on Broadway in the same year."[19] Perhaps 20th Century Fox was unsure how to promote a movie about a "sweet transvestite from transsexual

Transylvania." The company never marketed *RHPS* as a first-run movie. Its opening at the Waverly Theatre in Greenwich Village was heralded by a paltry $400 promotional budget.[20]

Reviews—early ones and some later ones as well—were not kind. One called it "a 'somewhat pointless' story of what happens when Middle American morals 'come up against the ultimate decadence the '70s are heading for.'"[21] Another opined, *"The Rocky Horror Picture Show* is a far cry from *The Sound of Music* or *My Fair Lady.* It is not uplifting, pleasant, heart-warming, star-studded, or expensively made, but is a raunchy, vulgar, and jolting film."[22] However, as undead Eddie would tell you, it is hard to keep a good man (or a bad meatloaf) down.

The movie, however, found a devoted niche audience among college students and urban hipsters, who watched it repeatedly. Against all odds, the film even began to make a profit on the East and West coasts. The film's backers took note: "Sensing a cult in the making, the producers re-cut the film's ending to make it more upbeat and released it on the midnight screening circuit."[23] After repeated viewings, diehard fans learned the movie's lines by heart. It is not a big intellectual leap (to the left or the right) from there to fans calling out responses to the film. In his book *The Tipping Point,* epidemiologist Malcolm Gladwell describes three characteristics of fads, the first of which he calls The Law of the Few.[24] "Social epidemics," he explains, are "driven by the efforts of a handful of exceptional people."[25] In their book *Midnight Movies,* authors J. Hoberman and Jonathan Rosenbaum identify one of these extraordinary instigators. In attendance at the Waverly one night was Louis Farese Jr., a mild-mannered teacher by day. Farese "suddenly felt compelled to talk back to the movie, and his wisecrack[s] ... were soon picked up by other Waverly regulars." When Janet used a newspaper to shield herself from the rain, Farese yelled out "Buy an umbrella, you bitch," and by doing so inspired others to heckle, bring costumes and props, dance in the aisles, and mime the film's action.[26]

Small causes often lead to big results, and *RHPS* was no exception. "Within weeks," according to one source,

> the phenomenon of fans dressing up and "calling back" to the screen was born. Taking to heart the film's message—"Don't dream it, be it"—fans held the first Rocky Horror Revue in 1977 in Los Angeles, in which a costumed cast lip-synched along to the entire film.[27]

Like Dr. Frankenstein, O'Brien had successfully brought his creature to life; it just didn't behave as he expected it to.

The *Rocky Horror Picture Show* Experience

If you have read this far, you are probably not a virgin. That is to say, you have probably seen the movie, preferably in a theater full of devotees. If, however, you are new to the scene, let me describe the phenomenon in the hope of sparing you an atomic wedgie or other indignities often bestowed upon the uninitiated. "Expect harassment," one source warns. "[*RHPS*] 'Virgins' are marked by a red V on their forehead and publically initiated (read: humiliated) before the show. This might include having your bra passed around while you try to chase it down . . . ."[28]

Here are the basic "musts" for viewing *RHPS*. First, choose the character you would like to be (keeping in mind that these are not specific to a particular gender or sexual orientation). Next, bring some props: rice, water pistol, lighter or flashlight, rubber gloves, noisemaker, party hat, toast, bell, or toilet paper. (Some venues provide prop kits for those who show up empty-handed.) By following the crowd, you will know what to do when the time comes: throw the toast, for example, during Frank-N-Furter's dinnertime toast. Be prepared also to throw caution to the wind and thrust your pelvis like Elvis during the Time Warp. If you do not have a script of one-liners handy, worry not, for you will catch on quickly. Be ready to mock the criminologist for seemingly having no neck and to shout "Asshole!" and "Slut!" at Brad and Janet. Those of you with an exhibitionist bent: feel free to prance around in racy underwear.

RHPS and the Meaning of *Cult*

An article from 1978 noted prophetically and with charming understatement that "although most films lose ground after a while, *Rocky Horror* seems to be holding its own and may even be gaining ground over the past two and a half years."[29] The question is "Why?" Why did *Rocky Horror* succeed while others (some of which were conceived as cult classics to begin with) failed? What makes a work a cult classic? Where does one draw the line between "cult classic" and just plain "classic?" Which categorization is preferable? This last issue is, I believe, far from being a moot point.

Not long ago, lecturing a group of college freshmen on the difference between a word's connotations and its denotations, I explained that *famous* has a positive spin while *infamous* has a negative one. This was met with some skepticism by students who felt that being infamous held a certain cachet in today's society, and their point is well taken.

To understand why the film endures as a cult phenomenon, we must put the movie "on the slab," as Frank-N-Furter says, dissect it, and anatomize the different parts that make up O'Brien's creation. First, let me be frank about the movie's vices and virtues. In some ways it resembles warts-and-all Eddie, Frank-N-Furter's first, failed project. The production values are slightly subpar. Urban legend has it that the builders omitted a door prescribed in the set design, which is why Dr. Scott arrives bursting through the wall, literally crashing Frank-N-Furter's party.[30] In the B-movies of old, the plot was secondary to the special effects. In *RHPS*, the movie is tightly plotted at first—arrival, unveiling, undressing, seduction—but descends into mayhem somewhere between the second and third act. Magenta, who only gets four lines of dialogue, never becomes a fully realized character. Finally, the chorus line and pool party toward the end try to emulate a Busby Berkley extravaganza but have too few dancers for this and the choreography is pretty slapdash in execution.

On the other hand, much of the movie resembles Rocky, Frank-N-Furter's golden boy. O'Brien is a dab hand at songwriting. The movie is quite funny, too, and absolutely refuses to take itself seriously. The actors mug to the camera, flailing arms and pounding chests in a send-up of Hollywood melodramas. Campy hijinks and tongue-in-cheek comments abound, as when Eddie breaks out of his crypt to perform a 1950s-reminscent sha-la-la-la-la ditty, after which Frank-N-Furter quips, "That's one from the vaults!" The movie elicits both appreciative nods with references to *Forbidden Planet* and *The Day the Earth Stood Still* and bemused groans over dopey puns such as "Dana Andrews said prunes/gave him the runes."

Plus, it is just a hoot to watch the earnest squares Brad and Janet wince and squirm under the Transylvanians' ministrations. The irreverent humor, distinctive costuming, and catchy tunes make up what Gladwell identifies as the second ingredient in trends: The Stickiness Factor.[31] He writes, "Stickiness means that a message makes an impact. You can't get it out of your head. It sticks in your memory."[32] I defy any skeptics out there to listen to "Time Warp" and then deny that the tune is stuck in their heads.

Lots of flawed yet fun movies get released each year, though, so what makes *RHPS* so special? The first key to its success, one that cannot be underestimated, is the aforementioned audience participation, admittedly an element O'Brien never planned explicitly, but the seeds of which can be seen in how the background characters jeer at the leads. Many of the interactive elements are actually woven right into the fabric of the film. The criminologist, who is also watching the movie, frequently interrupts the action to comment on it. The lyrics to the rousing "Time Warp" number offer instructions on how to perform the dance. During "Dammit, Janet," the background characters respond to Janet and Brad's lines with a wiseacre chorus of "*Janets*" and "*Oh Brads*." Director Stuart Samuels, whose documentary *Midnight Movies: From the Margins to the Mainstream* looks at cult hits of the 1970s, believes that *RHPS* is the "the first cultural product where the audience completed the experience of the product."[33]

Alienated teens are drawn to experiences that let them feel like insiders. NPR commentator Laura Lorson remembers dragging her prim mother to the show. Her mother, though somewhat chagrined, was also pleasantly surprised, telling Lorson, "I heard your voice calling out lines and jokes and interacting with other people and I felt something unexpected . . . I realized that you could be fearless. I admired you."[34] The film's shock value may have worn off over time, but the festive, clubby atmosphere remains. "Maybe they return," one observer notes, "because week after week the movie stays the same, but the party changes all the time."[35] *RHPS* embodies the allure of another quintessential American tradition, the freak show, but lets the spectators become the main attraction.

Like all great works of art, *RHPS* works on many levels. Sure, it has flesh and flash. "One, it's cheap cheerful, trashy, joyous entertainment," O'Brien admits. "But if it were just that, it wouldn't have the longevity."[36] It also has gender-bending *savoir faire*, which gives the film "associations of louche times and infinite sexual possibilities."[37] These elements, O'Brien notes, make it "liberating; it gives hope and joy to people who are in a state of flux in their understanding of gender and their place in society. But that's not enough, because that would be just playing to special-interest groups." *RHPS* must therefore tap into something more archetypal. "It's the eternal fairy tale," O'Brien concludes. "It's a root myth, a re-telling of a story which is almost in the psyche by now. And I think that really is what gives it its ability to continue to entertain on a deeper level, on a subconscious level."[38] Scholars have long noted the psychological verities of both Greek and Shakespearean dramas, pointing to these elements as keys to the works' enduring popularity.

The film also draws on traditional theater in many ways. The story at the core of *RHPS* is a retelling of Mary Shelley's *Frankenstein*, which itself alludes to Greek mythology with its subtitle: *A Modern Prometheus.* We can also see echoes of Pygmalion in Frank-N-Furter's adoration of Rocky. A "Medusa ray" turns Brad, Janet, Rocky, and Columbia into statues. Amittai F. Aviram explores the link between Frank-N-Furter and Dionysus, "the god of wine and one of the gods of music . . . the god of epiphanies . . . the only one among the Greek immortals who . . . dies."[39] He also sees parallels between Riff Raff and Apollo, Magenta and Artemis, Eddie and Orpheus, and notes that the word *cult* "in its classical sense" means "the celebration of mystic rites pertaining to a divine being . . . and to the appropriate secret lore,"[40] which seems apropos of *RHPS* and its enthusiastic fans. A professor of Greek history at the University of Durham, Edith Hall, concurs. "We know," she explains, "that Dionysus, god of drama, had numerous rituals in his cult that weren't actually theatre but involved putting on women's clothes, rituals reaching back to the sixth century B.C." She explains, "transvestism has always been in the theatre, it's an aboriginal feature of the genre, so it's not surprising that it's never gone away."[41]

Transvestism also hearkens back to Elizabethan times, when women were prohibited from appearing on stage. The current artistic director of Shakespeare's Globe Theater, Mark Rylance, has played women's roles in *Twelfth Night* and *Anthony and Cleopatra.* He notes, "Cross-dressing is central to Shakespeare's work. It's one of the ways he shows that play-acting and disguise are very much a part of being human."[42] Female impersonation's popularity endures. "Some men just have a really deep desire to be in a frock," says Bette Bourne, a drag queen currently appearing in *Romeo and Juliet* as the nurse.[43] Whether one is a Shakespearian-trained actor or just enjoys donning a corset and fishnets for a midnight airing of *RHPS*, dressing in drag can help one make a statement of one's identity or simply offer an escape from humdrum reality. "Cross dressing in performance appeals to all of us," explains O'Brien, "not just the trannies, queens and hairy fairies."[44]

The movie features an international cast of American, British, Irish, New Zealander, and Australian actors. Similarly, the art direction, dialogue, and lyrics form a complex mélange of styles, settings, and allusions, mixing European classicism with pure Americana. The latter include homage to Grant Wood's *American Gothic* and Whistler's *Mother.* Greco-Roman statuary lines the walls of the laboratory; the bottom of the swimming pool sports a copy of Michelangelo's *Creation of Adam*; reproductions of the *Mona Lisa* hang on the mansion walls; a stained-glass window depicts Atlas shouldering the earth. The allusion to Atlas also ties in with ubiquitous nods to 1950s America: in

"(In Just Seven Days) I Can Make You a Man," Frank-N-Furter alludes to Charles Atlas's weight-training regimens. Other examples of mid-century Americana include a reference to "heavy petting," nods to Brando in *The Wild One*, and rock-and-roll songs in the vein of Chuck Berry. Decade nostalgia generally lags two decades behind (hence the 1980s nostalgia prevalent now in the 2000s). *Grease* and *Happy Days* are other products of the 1970s with 1950s settings. *RHPS* also makes references to "downers," Nixon's farewell radio address, rainbows, and geodesic domes. All of these give the movie the third key ingredient Gladwell identifies in trends: The Power of Context.[45] Fads and crazes, he explains, "are sensitive to the conditions and circumstances of the times and places in which they occur."[46] *RHPS*'s freewheeling collage of different places and times gives the movie an appeal that is universal and timeless.

Cult Films, Posers, and Wanna-bes

Whereas nine out of ten people probably have heard of *Rocky Horror*, and at least six out of ten have probably seen it, you will most likely find just one soul in ten who has actually seen the movie's forgotten—and forgettable—sequel. The writer, director, and producers no doubt hoped to catch lightning in a jar a second time with a sequel called *Shock Treatment* in 1979. This feeble follow-up is known to the faithful as *"Shocky,"* but *"Shlocky"* would be more accurate. Cult classics are unpredictable, unrepeatable rarities. Furthermore, sometimes even worthy contenders fly under the radar of public awareness.

Consider the wonderful yet virtually unknown *Forbidden Zone*. Released in 1980, this campy musical features offbeat peccadilloes (one character is attracted to chickens), Herve Villechaize as the King of the Underworld, and boisterous songs by Danny Elfman, who plays the Devil (Elfman's brother Richard wrote, produced, and directed). It has many of the elements that made *RHPS* a success, yet it never caught fire, in part due to the zeitgeist of trickle-down Reaganomics and Just Say No. (Many culture vultures prophesied *RHPS*'s demise during the Big Brother 1980s.) To this day, *Forbidden Zone* remains in the "obscure but noteworthy" category and can be best termed not a "cult" but an "occult" classic.

Not only is it unlikely for a cult classic to spawn a cult sequel, it is also problematic to deliberately set out to create one. Just ask the makers of the 2008 release, *Repo! The Genetic Opera*. The movie is set in a dystopian tomorrow in which plastic surgery is *de rigeur* and organ transplants are big business, but watch out: if you fall behind on payments for your new liver, you might lose (drum roll, please) an arm and a leg. Like *RHPS*, *Repo!* began onstage before making the transition to film, and director Darren Lynn Bousman reportedly hoped to achieve midnight movie fame. One reviewer notes, "This goth rock opera features buckets of gore, a campy score and melodrama galore in a calculated effort to become a 21st century *Rocky Horror Picture Show*. Its creative juices, however, are strictly anemic."[47] The movie lacks appeal, despite having the illustrious singer Sarah Brightman to add class and the ignominious Paris Hilton to provide notoriety. Another critic calls it an "...unfunny, unscary, preposterous bloodbath...," goes on to describe it as "a convoluted mess" featuring "the most banal songs imaginable," and hopes it will "be repossessed by its financiers."[48] Although only time will tell, it does not seem likely that *Repo!* is bound for cult classicdom. A great title goes a long way, but this one is clunky and a little too reminiscent of the much-admired *Repo Man*. Second, people tend to like rock operas, but *opera* operas? Not so much. A true cult classic aims for greatness but somehow achieves a backdoor type of fame.

Ironically, the movie that does seem bound for cult classicdom is the very one to which *RHPS* was often unfavorably compared. One source explains, "[S]tories started to arrive from England about a new phenomenon. A couple of times a week ... people dressed as nuns or wearing lederhosen" and "carrying brown paper packages tied up with strings cram into a small London cinema to see 'The Sound of Music.'"[49] The beloved Julie Andrews musical has made a strange metamorphosis from classic film to cult classic. The newly interactive *Sound of Music* lets audiences participate by holding up a piece of cardboard painted with a question mark during "How Do You Solve a Problem Like Maria?" and waving plastic edelweiss to distract the Nazis while the Von Trapps make their escape. One would think that the movie's limited costuming—nun's habits, Alpine knickers, play clothes sewn from floral curtains—would hamper fans' choices for attire, but a costume competition yields some creative efforts. One attendee explains, "I am the hills this evening. The hills are alive. I have a green AstroTurf skirt with cows and houses all around it. And then as you go up the bodice, [it] turns into mountain tops with snowcaps."[50]

Following in these footsteps, a sing-along version TV's *Buffy the Vampire Slayer*, based on the popular musical episode "Once More, With Feeling," is currently touring.[51] The most recent craze to hit

New York and L.A. is *The Room*, a bizarre movie that fans have decided is not just terrible, but terribly good fun. They are lining up around the block for a chance to echo dialogue, shout responses, and throw popcorn at the screen.[52]

Living Post-*RHPS*

Time and the tides of public opinion have been kind, in the long run, to *RHPS* and its stars. The movie's two most pivotal actors, O'Brien and Curry, have enjoyed lauded and long-running careers. O'Brien continued to write and act, frequently appearing with his *RHPS* costars. He was in a movie called *Jubilee* with Campbell and also worked with her in a play called *Mickey Mouse Now* by Sam Shepherd, in which he played the iconic cartoon character as a broken-down middle-aged drunk. He wrote another musical, *Disaster*, which featured *RHPS* alums Quinn and Adams in the cast.[53] O'Brien also appeared in the movies *Flash Gordon*, *Dark City*, and *Dungeons and Dragons*, just to name a few.

O'Brien has come to terms with the character roles he plays. "I'm an exceptionally skinny, strange-looking individual," he admits. "I know that nature didn't make me look like Pierce Brosnan—and as a result one does always get typecast, but ... to be miscast is a dreadful state of affairs for everybody."[54] In the 1990s, he even became a popular game show host. In 2004, New Zealand unveiled a bronze statue of Riff Raff on the site of the theater where B-movies had enthralled O'Brien as a child.[55]

Curry went on to record three pop albums, portray William Shakespeare for the BBC, and act in several films. Many fans saw shades of Frank in Curry's portrayal of the devil for Ridley Scott's *Legend*. He also has voiced numerous cartoon characters, including "a series of animated Bible stories, in which he played Judas ... and the Serpent, ... Captain Hook ..., an evil manta ray in 'The Little Mermaid,' Taurus Bulba in 'Darkwing Duck,' Hexus in 'Ferngully: The Last Rainforest,' and MAL in the series 'Capt. Planet and the Planeteers.'"[56] In 1981, he was nominated for a Tony Award for playing Amadeus on Broadway. More recently, he has returned to Broadway as King Arthur in *Monty Python's Spamalot* (the musical reworking of *Monty Python and the Holy Grail*). With a fitting appreciation for little-known gems, he names as his favorite role the part of Long John Silver in *Muppet Treasure Island*, which gave him the opportunity to ham it up alongside one of his idols, Miss Piggy.[57]

The *RHPS* ingénues, Bostwick and Sarandon, have prospered, too. Bostwick starred in the sitcom *Spin City* as a befuddled mayor not dissimilar to Brad Majors. He also "metamorphasized into a master of the TV miniseries, second only to Richard Chamberlain, including the title role in *George Washington* and no less than three minis based on Judith Krantz novels."[58]

Though Sarandon has tried to distance herself from Janet Weiss, some see parallels between that character and ones like "Sally in 'Atlantic City' and Reggie in 'The Client,'" characters who "in reaching out to connect [crash] through roadblocks [they] didn't even realize were there."[59] In 2006, the Philadelphia Film Festival honored her for artistic achievement. Most notably, Sarandon turned in an epic performance in *Thelma & Louise* and later won an Oscar for *Dead Man Walking*, working with her husband, Tim Robbins, who wrote and directed.

Campbell eventually dropped the nickname "Little" and opened Nell's, a trendy Manhattan nightclub, famous for once turning away Cher (but not, presumably, Cher impersonators in drag).[60] She continued working on stage and screen, as did Quinn, who appeared in a television production of *I, Claudius* and helped John Cleese sexually educate a group of British schoolboys in *Monty Python's The Meaning of Life*. Adams continued to work in theater and films, as did Gray, who as Blofeld once menaced James Bond. Hinwood appeared in *The Odyssey*, directed by Dino De Laurentis.[61]

Meat Loaf released his own rock opera, the record *Bat Out of Hell*, in 1977, which included "Paradise by the Dashboard Light" and "Two Out of Three Ain't Bad," singles that propelled sales of more than 35 million copies of the album.[62] He scored another hit with "I'd Do Anything for Love (but I Won't Do That)" on 1993's sequel, *Bat Out of Hell: Back Into Hell*. He has worked on television and starred in the movie *Roadie*. Meat Loaf also enjoyed stage success in *Rock-A-Bye Hamlet* on Broadway and Joseph Papp's *Shakespeare In the Park*.[63]

As for *RHPS* itself, the movie has a global following. As early as the 1980s, it had "productions touring Iceland, Germany and Japan. Russell Crowe cut his teeth in an Australian revival, while Gary Glitter starred in the New Zealand version."[64] In the new millennium, the movie still has some "snap left in its garters."[65] Beginning in 2002, fans began holding a festival dubbed "Rockypalooza."[66] A recent DVD release and 30th anniversary celebration breathed new life into O'Brien's monster hit, which "continues to play around the country to packed houses, where fans [still] dress as their favorite characters, act out scenes, and reach the fevered, ritualistic pitch of a tent revival meeting where everyone's saved and no one cares."[67] Some theaters do ask that you leave the Super Soakers and Zippos at home and throw the rice and toast up in the air, not at the screen. Even in the age of the cinema multiplex, nostalgia for all things retro ensures that *RHPS* faithful can still attend screenings at drive-ins, parks, and midnight matinees.[68]

Perhaps the largest *RHPS* mystery to remain unsolved is why the movie universally was deemed to have flopped in the first place. Is "flop" an accurate description for a movie that, 15 years after its release, was still pulling in $7 to $10 million dollars annually?[69] Is it accurate to tout the comeback of a movie that never really went away in the first place?

In today's global-village marketplace, and with DVDs' power to res- urrect arcane titles like *El Topo*, who knows which all-but-forgotten sleeper might awaken to become the Next Big Thing? *RHPS* has spread like an epidemic, one causing symptoms more delirious than deadly. It resembles the phenomenon Ishmael Reed describes in *Mumbo Jumbo* as a "Jes Grew" because it just keeps on growing. "A mighty influence," Reed writes, "Jes Grew infects all that it touches."[70]

Americans do have fleeting, 15-minutes-of-fame attention spans, so any work that does not become an overnight success, winning unal- loyed accolades from both critics and fans, risks being labeled a flop. But that is actually a good thing, because Americans also have a deeply ingrained sense of tolerance and fair play. This means that that we will always have a soft spot for the black sheep in the family, will always root for the underdog. It means that the term *cult* always will give an extra sheen to the word *classic*.

Notes

1. Elias Lonnrot, *The Kalevala* (Oxford: Oxford University Press, 1990), 529.

2. Dave Leon, "Classic Films, Midnight Shows and Outdoor Screenings— Offbeat Cinematic Pleasures for Long Summer Evenings," *San Jose Mercury News*, June 22 2006, *Academic Search Premiere*, EBSCOhost, http://www .ebscohost.com.

3. Terry Lawson, "Tim Curry Turns Camp into Cartoon Voices for TV and Movies," *Detroit Free Press*, December 17, 2002, *Academic Search Premiere*, EBSCOhost, http://www.ebscohost.com.

4. "All-Time Box Office Gross," in *Internet Movie Database*, http://www.imdb .com/boxoffice/alltimegross (accessed June 8, 2009).

5. Sophie Tedmanson, "Magenta's Lewd, Lascivious Lips do Time Warp Again," *The Australian*, February 21, 2001, *Academic Search Premiere*, EBSCOhost, http://www.ebscohost.com.

6. Niki Sullivan, "Let's Do the Time Warp: Rockypalooza Will Celebrate Cult Classic Rocky Horror Picture Show," *News Tribune*, June 4, 2006, *Academic Search Premiere*, EBSCOhost, http://www.ebscohost.com.

7. Simon Hattenstone, "Timeless Time Warp: Twenty-One Years On, The Rocky Horror Picture Show is Still the Greatest Cult Movie," *The Guardian*, April 8, 1996, *Academic Search Premiere*, EBSCOhost, http://www.ebscohost.com.

8. Rob Salem, "The Rocky Horror Picture Show from Stage to Screen to Your VCR: The Rocky Road to Cult Status," *Toronto Star*, November 4, 1990, *Academic Search Premiere*, EBSCOhost, http://www.ebscohost.com.

9. Salem.

10. Al Brumley, "Why Does 'Rocky Horror,' After 25 Years, Just Go On and On," *Dallas Morning News*, October 27, 2000, *Academic Search Premiere*, EBSCOhost, http://www.ebscohost.com.

11. Brumley.

12. Salem.

13. Ibid.

14. Ibid.

15. Ibid.

16. Ibid.

17. Ibid.

18. Ibid.

19. Ibid.

20. Hattenstone.

21. Debra Yeo, "Still a Sweet Transvestite," *Toronto Star*, October 1, 2005, *Academic Search Premiere*, EBSCOhost, http://www.ebscohost.com.

22. Mark Siegel, "The Rocky Horror Picture Show: More Than a Lip Service," *Science-Fiction Studies* Volume 7 (1980): 305. *Academic Search Premiere*, EBSCOhost, http://www.ebscohost.com.

23. Sean MacAulay, "Behind the Screen," *Times (UK)*, February 5, 2005, *Academic Search Premiere*, EBSCOhost, http://www.ebscohost.com.

24. Malcolm Gladwell, *The Tipping Point: How Little Things Can Make a Big Difference* (Boston: Little, Brown, 2002), 19.

25. Gladwell, 21.

26. Hattenstone.

27. MacAulay.

28. Sullivan.

29. Kathryn Esplin, "Rocky Horror Earns Cult," *Globe and Mail*, June 3, 1978, *Academic Search Premiere*, EBSCOhost, http://www.ebscohost.com.

30. Sullivan.

31. Gladwell, 19.

32. Ibid., 25.

33. Yeo.

34. Laura Lorson, "Mom, Meet Rocky Horror. Rocky Horror, Mom," *All Things Considered*, September 25, 2006, *Academic Search Premiere*, EBSCOhost, http://www.ebscohost.com.

35. Esplin.

36. Brumley.

37. Penny Wark, "Private—But Perfectly Frank," *Times (UK)*, October 9, 2006, *Academic Search Premiere*, EBSCOhost, http://www.ebscohost.com.

38. Brumley.

39. Amittai F. Aviram, "Postmodern Gay Dionysus: Dr. Frank N. Furter," *Journal of Popular Culture* 26, no. 3 (1992): 184. *Academic Search Premiere*, EBSCOhost, http://www.ebscohost.com.

40. Aviram, 183.

41. Jonty Claypole, "The Call of the Frock is As Strong As Ever For Male Actors. But Why, Wonders Jonty Claypole," *Times (UK)*, August 30, 2004, *Academic Search Premiere*, EBSCOhost, http://www.ebscohost.com.

42. Claypole.

43. Ibid.

44. Ibid.

45. Gladwell, 19.

46. Ibid., 139.

47. Colin Covert, "Movie Reviews: 'Repo! The Genetic Opera' 'A Thousand Years of Good Prayers,'" *Star Tribune*, 6 November 2008, *Academic Search Premiere*, EBSCOhost, http://www.ebscohost.com.

48. Claudia Puig, "See 'Repo!' At Your Own Risk," *USA Today*, November 7, 2008, *Academic Search Premiere*, EBSCOhost, http://www.ebscohost.com.

49. Melinda Penkava, "Profile: Premiere of Interactive Version of Sound of Music," *Weekend Edition Saturday*, September 3, 2000, *Academic Search Premiere*, EBSCOhost, http://www.ebscohost.com.

50. Penkava.

51. Neal Conan, "'Buffy: The Musical' Launches Sing-Along Tour," *Talk of the Nation*, July 17, 2007, *Academic Search Premiere*, EBSCOhost, http://www.ebscohost.com.

52. Alex Stone, "The Best 'Worst Movie' Ever Made," *ABC World News Webcast*, May 29, 2009, http://www.abcnews.com (accessed June 1, 2009).

53. Salem.

54. Brumley.

55. MacAulay.

56. Lawson.

57. Wark.

58. Salem.

59. Carrie Rickey, "Susan Sarandon's Secret? Seeing Past the Ingenue," *Philadelphia Inquirer*, March 24, 2006, *Academic Search Premiere*, EBSCOhost, http://www.ebscohost.com.

60. Salem.

61. Ibid.

62. Patrick Ferrucci, "Meat Loaf Releases His New 'Monster' 'Hell' Raiser," *New Haven Register*, 10 November 2006, *Academic Search Premiere*, EBSCOhost, http://www.ebscohost.com.

63. Salem.

64. MacAulay.

65. Yeo.

66. Sullivan.

67. Brumley.

68. Leon.

69. Salem.

70. Ishmael Reed, *Mumbo Jumbo* (New York: Simon & Schuster, 1996) 13.

Bibliography

"All-Time USA Box office," in *Internet Movie Database*, http://www.imdb.com /boxoffice/alltimegross (accessed June 8, 2009).

Aviram, Amittai F. "Postmodern Gay Dionysus: Dr. Frank N. Furter." *Journal of Popular Culture* 26, no. 3 (1992): 183–92. *Academic Search Premiere*, EBSCOhost, http://www.ebscohost.com.

Brumley, Al. "Why Does 'Rocky Horror,' After 25 Years, Just Go On and On." *Dallas Morning News*, October 27, 2000. *Academic Search Premiere*, EBSCOhost, http://www.ebscohost.com.

Claypole, Jonty. "The Call of the Frock is As Strong As Ever For Male Actors. But Why, Wonders Jonty Claypole." *Times (UK)*, August 30, 2004. *Academic Search Premiere*, EBSCOhost, http://www.ebscohost.com.

Conan, Neal. "'Buffy: The Musical' Launches Sing-Along Tour." *Talk of the Nation*, July 17, 2007. *Academic Search Premiere*, EBSCOhost, http:// www.ebscohost.com.

Covert, Colin. "Movie Reviews: 'Repo! The Genetic Opera' 'A Thousand Years of Good Prayers.'" *Star Tribune*, 6 November 2008. *Academic Search Premiere*, EBSCOhost, http://www.ebscohost.com.

Esplin, Kathryn. "Rocky Horror Earns Cult." *Globe and Mail*, June 3, 1978. *Academic Search Premiere*, EBSCOhost, http://www.ebscohost.com.

Ferrucci, Patrick. "Meat Loaf Releases His New 'Monster' 'Hell' Raiser." *New Haven Register*, 10 November 2006. *Academic Search Premiere*, EBSCOhost, http://www.ebscohost.com.

Gladwell, Malcolm. *The Tipping Point: How Little Things Can Make a Big Difference*. Boston: Little, Brown, 2002.

Hattenstone, Simon. "Timeless Time Warp: Twenty-One Years On, The Rocky Horror Picture Show is Still the Greatest Cult Movie." *The Guardian*, April 8, 1996. *Academic Search Premiere*, EBSCOhost, http://www .ebscohost.com.

Lawson, Terry. "Tim Curry Turns Camp into Cartoon Voices for TV and Movies." *Detroit Free Press*, December 17, 2002. *Academic Search Premiere*, EBSCOhost, http://www.ebscohost.com.

Leon, Dave. "Classic Films, Midnight Shows and Outdoor Screenings—Offbeat Cinematic Pleasures for Long Summer Evenings." *San Jose Mercury News*, June 22, 2006. *Academic Search Premiere*, EBSCOhost, http://www.ebscohost.com.

Lonnrot, Elias. *The Kalevala.* 1849. Translated by Keith Bosley. Oxford: Oxford University Press, 1990.

Lorson, Laura. "Mom, Meet Rocky Horror. Rocky Horror, Mom." *All Things Considered*, September 25, 2006. *Academic Search Premiere*, EBSCOhost, http://www.ebscohost.com.

MacAulay, Sean. "Behind the Screen." *Times (UK)*, February 5, 2005. *Academic Search Premiere*, EBSCOhost, http://www.ebscohost.com.

Penkava, Melinda. "Profile: Premiere of Interactive Version of Sound of Music." *Weekend Edition Saturday*, September 3, 2000. *Academic Search Premiere*, EBSCOhost, http://www.ebscohost.com.

Puig, Claudia. "See 'Repo!' At Your Own Risk." *USA Today*, November 7, 2008. *Academic Search Premiere*, EBSCOhost, http://www.ebscohost.com.

Reed, Ishmael. *Mumbo Jumbo.* New York: Simon & Schuster, 1996.

Rickey, Carrie. "Susan Sarandon's Secret? Seeing Past the Ingenue." *Philadelphia Inquirer*, March 24, 2006. *Academic Search Premiere*, EBSCOhost, http://www.ebscohost.com.

Salem, Rob. "The Rocky Horror Picture Show from Stage to Screen to Your VCR: The Rocky Road to Cult Status." *Toronto Star*, November 4, 1990. *Academic Search Premiere*, EBSCOhost, http://www.ebscohost.com.

Siegel, Mark. "The Rocky Horror Picture Show: More Than a Lip Service." *Science-Fiction Studies* Volume 7 (1980): 305–12. *Academic Search Premiere*, EBSCOhost, http://www.ebscohost.com.

Stone, Alex. "The Best 'Worst Movie' Ever Made." *ABC World News Webcast*, May 29, 2009. http://www.abcnews.com (accessed June 1, 2009).

Sullivan, Niki. "Let's Do the Time Warp: Rockypalooza Will Celebrate Cult Classic Rocky Horror Picture Show." *News Tribune*, June 4, 2006. *Academic Search Premiere*, EBSCOhost, http://www.ebscohost.com.

Tedmanson, Sophie. "Magenta's Lewd, Lascivious Lips do Time Warp Again." *The Australian*, February 21, 2001. *Academic Search Premiere*, EBSCOhost, http://www.ebscohost.com.

Wark, Penny. "Private—But Perfectly Frank." *Times (UK)*, October 9, 2006. *Academic Search Premiere*, EBSCOhost, http://www.ebscohost.com.

Yeo, Debra. "Still a Sweet Transvestite." *Toronto Star*, October 1, 2005. *Academic Search Premiere*, EBSCOhost, http://www.ebscohost.com.

CHAPTER 5

DEMAGOGUES IN DEATH AND NOTES FROM WAY UNDERGROUND: THE AMERICAN CULT POP CULTURE ICON

Kristi M. Wilson

> Landlady: There is something I should warn you of, Fyodor Mikhai-
> lovich. Pavel made a certain cult of his father—of Alexander Isaev, I
> mean.
> Dostoevsky: How does one romanticize a person like that?
> Landlady: By seeing him through a haze.
> —J. M. Coetzee, *The Master of Petersburg*[1]

The word *icon* or *ikon* comes from the Greek word *eikōn*, (*eikeni*) and means "to resemble." One could argue that icons are the earliest and most consistent forms of cult popular culture. Millennia-old iconic images of an Anatolian Mother Goddess filtered into the secret, ancient Greek mystery cults of Demeter and Dionysus.[2] The early-modern period saw the power of religious icons expand with the creation of the Emerald Buddha of Thailand and Virgin of Guadalupe in Mexico. Icons have traditionally straddled the line between image and divine presence. The unofficial, international cult of the Virgin Mary is founded upon the various locations in which she is said to have appeared (Lourdes, Lujan, Mexico City, etc.). Thus, the popularity and cultish quality of an icon is fueled by the desire to keep the dead living. Reproducibility of the icon was always a key component in its ritualistic popularity, functioning to establish religious continuity in some cases for millennia.

Fast-forward a thousand or so years, take into account Nietzsche's maxim that god is dead by our own hands, and what remains is but a new, ever more unique form of the icon: the celebrity who, even in death, does not die but sheds his or her mortal coil for the status of subcultural hero.[3] American celebrities, in general, come closest to emulating ancient Greek stories of select humans like Ganymede or Persephone, snatched too early from the living and given immortality by the gods' fancy. Or better yet, truly mythic celebrities like Madonna and Michael Jackson resemble gods like Dionysus who were said to have walked among the humans at will and to have entranced bands of frenzied followers. A 1958 mug shot of Elvis Presley, just before he had his hair cut to enter the military, makes a fitting cover for a recent translation of Euripides tragedy *The Bacchae*,[4] an ancient story that resonates with modern notions of celebrity worship. Some argue that processes of modernity and globalization have led to a flattening of "real" culture in exchange for a hyperreal model of culture in which visual image and simulation predominate.[5] Cultural icons thrive in such an environment of media-product saturation.

It goes without saying that icons, both ancient and modern, are subject to ritual use. Locations connected to them become shrines and, in some cases, ornamentation of the iconic images takes on epic proportions. The sixteenth-century statuette of the Virgin of Copacabana (or the Virgin de la Candelaria) in Bolivia is believed to work miracles. In fact, the icon has been so heavily endowed with gifts of jewels and wardrobe items from heads of state over the years that, on at least one occasion in 1879, the Bolivian government was able to help fund a war with the sale of some her riches. Millions travel to the Lake Titicaca region every year to see either the home of the Virgin de la Candelaria or the icon in procession.

The closest parallel to this sort of location-bound, full-scale icon worship in modern American popular culture consists in the phenomenon of Graceland, the former private home and current living memorial to Elvis. Graceland, which offers tours of Elvis's car collection, custom private planes, mansion, racquetball building, gold record collection and "mediation garden" where his body is buried, sees more than 600,000 visitors from all corners of the world and earns more than $150 million annually.[6] While it is safe to say that Elvis has transitioned from death to icon, his mainstream popularity throws his status as a cult pop culture icon into question. While replication is a key component of garnering undead icon status, too much replication threatens the cult pop culture community. In other words, overproduction weakens the potential rhetorical impact of a subcultural icon.

According to Hariman and Lucaites, icons are "capable of doing the heavy lifting required to change public opinion and motivate action on behalf of a public interest."[7] Elvis as an icon has pushed the boundaries of rock and roll. His legacy, which evokes large-scale revolutionary change in the history of rock and roll, exemplifies this type of heavy lifting, in spite of drug problems, eccentric wardrobe choices, and the mysterious nature of his death. If standard pop culture icons like Elvis ultimately tell stories about mainstream American values (achieving the American dream of superstardom from humble beginnings, respect for the military, etc.), to what extent do cult pop culture icons tell different types of stories or help us to interpret social eras differently?

If the standard cultural icon, reproduced *ad infinitum* by the forces of modern capitalism, is someone we can all identify with, cult pop culture icons like Marilyn Monroe, Judy Garland, James Dean, and John Belushi must resonate with more particular groups. Such cult pop culture icons in their deaths contrast with living icons like Madonna or Nelson Mandela, whose mythic status continues to grow, transform, and become more brand-like. While the cult pop culture icon has garnered exemplary status, this status comes at the moment of death, a rupture that can be said to exacerbate and elevate the conflicts and turmoil their lives represented. Thus, in their deaths, cult pop culture icons become especially seductive for particular subcultures whose values might lie outside of a mainstream American paradigm.

Marilyn Monroe

Marilyn Monroe, a.k.a. Norma Jean Mortenson, was born in Los Angeles, California, in 1926. Her birth marks the end of the silent film era, and her death at the age of 36 of a medication overdose remains shrouded in mystery. Even though she was married three times and struggled unsuccessfully to have children, she remains lodged in the collective memory as the world's "endless whore, the one that always came up smiling, no matter the way she was gossiped about."[8] Monroe emerged on the scene from nowhere special and when she died, with no family to call her own, she left her estate to Lee Strasberg. Her mother, Gladys, seems to have been mentally disturbed and abusive and her father out of the picture. She grew up in orphanages and foster homes and married her first husband, Jim Dougherty, to escape institutional life. In short, it is not a stretch to suggest that Marilyn Monroe may just be the ultimate victim of American society. Norman

Mailer suggests as much about the misunderstood starlet in his 1973 biography *Marilyn*:

> Marilyn is gone. She has slipped away from us. No force from outside, nor any pain, has finally proved stronger than her power to weigh down upon herself. If she has possibly been strangled once, then suffocated again in the life of the orphanage, and lived to be stifled by the studies and choked by the rages of marriage, she has kept in reaction a total control of her life, which is perhaps to say that she chooses to be in control of her death.[9]

Lisa Cohen suggests a more pointedly feminist reading of Monroe's iconic status, one that positions her as a powerful icon of 1950s *non* domesticity. Contrary to what her performed baby voice might have suggested about vulnerability, starting with her aircraft artillery factory work for the war effort in 1945, continuing with a strong focus on her acting career, and culminating in an overt affair with JFK, Marilyn Monroe seems to have raged against 1950s domesticity in her brief life.[10]

If Jackie Onassis represented everything well bred, proper, and classically beautiful about American values at the time, Marilyn Monroe (literally spilling out of her dress as she sang "Happy Birthday" to the president) could be seen as an ever-more seductive "economy of excess."[11] This reading is only possible postmortem, as during her life, Monroe's sexuality was "perceived and marketed as a force of nature."[12] Not that Monroe was unaware of or ambivalent about such marketing. At a 1955 press conference, she is reported to have said, "I didn't like a lot of my pictures. I'm tired of sex roles. I'm going to broaden my scope."[13] In spite of reservations about her career and a desire for change, she went on to make such sex-bomb classics as *The Seven Year Itch* (1955), *Bus Stop* (1956), *Some Like it Hot* (1959), and *The Misfits* (1961).

In additional to cult appeal for select feminists able to see beyond the bottle-blonde pinup persona (or perhaps able to revel in it), Marilyn Monroe is a drag icon. Jane Russell inaugurated Monroe's drag appeal by impersonating her in *Gentlemen Prefer Blondes*, and since then, she has figured prominently on drag stages. Wendy Lesser suggests that Monroe's acting career was based on impersonating actresses or showgirls, and others have flat-out called her a female impersonator who parodied femininity, "dumb-blondes," Whiteness, and innocence.[14]

Judy Garland

While Marilyn Monroe came in at number six, according to a recent poll of 5,000 gays and lesbians in the UK, Judy Garland, a.k.a. Dorothy in the *Wizard of Oz*, is the most important female gay icon of all time. Born Frances Ethel Gumm on June 10, 1922, in Grand Rapids, Minnesota, Garland has been referred to as an Elvis type of performer for homosexuals. Garland's iconic cult pop culture appeal did not begin with her suicide at the age of 47, but crystallized with it. Some argue that the combination of loneliness and superstardom that defined Garland's life resonated with the social oppression and prejudice felt by gays and lesbians of her generation. The practice of leading a double life and closeting one's true self seemed to bind Garland to the gay community. Garland is quoted as saying, "If I am a legend, then why am I so lonely?"

Since some films like *Some Like it Hot* are "recognized as masterworks by both the gay and mainstream underground," they help situate cult icons like Marilyn Monroe both inside and outside of gay culture. Judy Garland, however, does not posses such crossover appeal. She is understood squarely as a cult pop culture icon for the gay community largely because of her androgynous performance persona (use of boyish costumes and pantsuits) and her personal vulnerability associated with failed marriages and drug abuse.[15] Garland's appeal to the gay community stems from her history of close relationships with and acceptance of gay men as well. Her father, a theater owner, was rumored to be gay, as were two of her five husbands, her mentor at the studio, and many of her friends. According to Garland's official autobiographer, John Fricke, she was one of the hardest-working superstars in Hollywood:

> Judy Garland worked for nearly forty-five of her forty-seven years. She made thirty-two feature films, did voice-over work for two more, and appeared in at least a half dozen short subjects. She received a special Academy Award and was nominated for two others. She starred in thirty of her own television shows (the programs and Garland herself garnering a total of ten Emmy Award nominations) and appeared as a guest on nearly thirty more. Between 1951 and 1969, she fulfilled over eleven hundred theatre, nightclub and concert performances, winning a special Antoinette Perry (Tony) Award for the first of three record-breaking Broadway engagements at the Palace. She recorded nearly one hundred singles and over a dozen record albums; *Judy at Carnegie Hall* received an

unprecedented five Grammys in 1962 (including Album of the Year) and has never been out of print.[16]

Judy Garland started entertaining at an early age (some say 2½-years-old at her parents' theater in Michigan) and was signed on at MGM studios at the age of thirteen immediately after an audition in which she sang "Zing! Went the Strings of My Heart." Her early beginnings in a show business family continue even after her death, as her daughters Liza Minnelli and Lorna Luft are both performers. Liza Minnelli in particular has managed to follow in her mother's footsteps as an important American gay icon in her own right.

James Dean

If Judy Garland is overtly a cult gay pop culture icon, James Dean is subtly so. Born on February 8, 1931, in Marion, Indiana, Dean only began his acting career four years before his death in a car accident in 1955. In just a few years, Dean was able to create a powerful cult following based on his appeal as a hero for alienated, rebellious youth.

After two years of studying theater at the University of California, Los Angeles, Dean landed a role in a television commercial, which led to small roles in film and television. He also had roles in two Broadway productions, one as a gay houseboy.[17] Impressed by Dean's performance in *The Immoralist*, Elia Kazan cast him in one of his most famous roles, Cal Trask, in the film adaptation of John Steinbeck's *East of Eden* (1955). James Dean was nominated for an Academy Award for this performance. His reputation as a disenfranchised youth crystallized, however, with his portrayal as out-of-place high school student Jim Stark in *Rebel Without a Cause* (1955). Some say that the timing of this portrayal has a lot to do with Dean's ability to embody the angst of a young generation in conflict with their parents' values. Dean starred as farmer Jett Rink in George Stevens's film *Giant* (1956) but never lived to see the film's release. To this day, James Dean is the only actor to have been nominated for two Best Actor Academy Awards posthumously.

Dean's private life and sexuality have been the focus of much speculation. On the set, he was said to be a "challenge" to work with, as he continually pushed himself and other actors to redefine their roles. His sexuality is usually framed as ambiguous. Perhaps because of his willingness to take on a gay stage role in *The Immoralist*, not long after his death, Dean was firmly established as a cult gay icon in the "subtextual" realm. According to Michael DeAngelis, "[b]y the 1970s, however, gay cultural critics openly debate the matter of the star's sexuality among themselves as well as with mainstream writers, in a contestation whose stakes involve the open acknowledgement, recognition, and legitimization of homosexual identification and desire."[18] DeAngelis suggests further that Dean's persona as a teen rebel becomes pertinent to the homosexual rebellion in process at the time. Some trace Dean's popularity as a gay icon to Kenneth Anger's use of Dean's image in *Scorpio Rising* (1964), because his tortured image as an outsider contained some of gay subculture's self-image.

John Belushi

Like James Dean, the late John Belushi is a cult pop culture icon for rebellious, alienated, if drug-induced, youth. He is most famous for his work on the television comedy show *Saturday Night Live* and as the beer-guzzling college burnout Bluto in National Lampoon's *Animal House* (1978). But his rise to loud-mouthed, physical comedy superstardom had unlikely beginnings.

John Belushi was born in Chicago, Illinois, to Albanian immigrant parents in 1949. In high school he was co-captain of the football team, and at the end of senior year, he was elected homecoming king. Belushi also got his first taste of acting in high school, which eventually landed him summer theater roles. It wasn't until his first year at college that Belushi's persona changed from perfect student to the bad-boy, antiestablishment, party animal he later became famous for. After one year at the University of Wisconsin, Belushi returned home and went to junior college, where he founded an improv comedy group.

Belushi's cult iconic appeal is largely connected to the comedy subcultural appeal of *National Lampoon,* a "sick humor" magazine popular on college campuses in the 1970s that also produced theater, radio, television shows, and then films. Belushi was involved with *National Lampoon*'s theatrical rock musical *Lemmings* as an actor and as a writer for its syndicated Radio Hour. At the same time, he joined the cast of *Saturday Night Live,* which paved the way to stardom. The 1970s also saw the beginning of Belushi's infamous cocaine addiction, which would eventually take his life.

The 1980s saw the birth of his unforgettable role as soul man Jake Blues in *The Blues Brothers. The Blues Bothers,* costarring Dan Aykroyd, seemed to have integrated John Belushi's passions: acting, outrageous physical comedy, and blues music. Belushi was found dead in a hotel room at the Los Angeles Chateau Marmont hotel on March 5, 1982, at the age of 33. Police later sentenced his friend Cathy Smith to three years in jail for supplying Belushi with the injection of cocaine and heroin that ended his life.

As the examples of Marilyn Monroe, Judy Garland, James Dean, and John Belushi show, the celebrity-turned-cult-pop-culture icon usually represents, for the fans left behind, a life of contradiction in which the Olympian highs of success were more often than not leveled by everyday forms of suffering or misunderstanding. Ugly, untimely deaths by suicide, car accidents, or drug overdoses are quickly redeemed by subcultures of fans, iconicizers of memory who return cult pop culture icons to a more traditionally religious purpose by emphasizing and celebrating their legacies as social martyrdom.

Notes

1. J. M. Coetzee, *The Master of Petersburg* (London: Harvill Secker, 1994).

2. W. Burkert, *Greek Religion: Archaic and Classical* (New York: Wiley, 1899), 278.

3. F. Nietzsche, "The Gay Science, Trans," *Walter Kaufmann* (New York: Vintage, 1974) 111: 181–82.

4. P. Woodruff, *Euripides: Bacchae* (Indianapolis, IN: Hackett, 1998).

5. K. G. Tomaselli and D. Scott, *Cultural Icons* (Walnut Creek, CA: Left Coast, 2009), 11. Tomaselli and Scott draw upon the groundbreaking work of Jean Baudrillard in their discussion of simulation and hyperreality. See J. Baudrillard and S. F. Glaser, *Simulacra and Simulation* (Ann Arbor, MI: University of Michigan Press, 1994).

6. "Elvis.Com," www.elvis.com. Graceland as a destination for two wandering Japanese tourists features prominently in cult film director Jim Jarmusch's 1989 film *Mystery Train*.

7. L. C. Olson, C. A. Finnegan, and D. S. Hope, *Visual Rhetoric: A Reader in Communication and American Culture* (Thousand Oaks, CA: Sage, 2008), 177.

8. David Thompson, "Marilyn Monroe: An Icon at 80," http://www.independent.co.uk/news/people/profiles/marilyn-monroe-an-icon-at-80-477932.html.

9. N. Mailer, *Marilyn, a Biography* (New York: Putnam, 1981), 102.

10. Cohen notes that "In Hollywood ... movies and fan magazines glamourized the single working woman up until the mid-1940s, no matter how provisionally. After the war, however, '[f]emale film celebrities began to offer a new maternal model for identification,' as their publicity increasingly included images of their families and accounts of the types of housework they did." L. Cohen, "The Horizontal Walk: Marilyn Monroe, Cinemascope, and Sexuality," *Yale Journal of Criticism* 11 (1998): 266.

11. Ibid., 259.

12. Cohen citing Richard Dyer, R. Dyer, *Heavenly Bodies: Film Stars and Society* (London: Routledge, 2004).

13. A. Summers, *Goddess, the Secret Lives of Marilyn Monroe* (New York: Simon & Schuster, 1985), 124.

14. W. Lesser, *His Other Half: Men Looking at Women through Art* (Cambridge, MA: Harvard University Press, 1992). For an extended discussion of Marilyn Monroe and Whiteness, see L. W. Banner, "The Creature from the Black Lagoon: Marilyn Monroe and Whiteness," *Cinema Journal* 47, 4 (2008).

15. P. Roen, *High Camp: A Gay Guide to Camp and Cult Films* (San Francisco: Leyland Publications, 1993), 12.

16. J. Fricke, *Judy Garland: World's Greatest Entertainer* (New York: Henry Holt, 1992). Cited on the official Judy Garland website: www.jgdb.com.

17. The gay houseboy role was for the Broadway production of Andre Gide's book *The Immoralist*.

18. M. DeAngelis, *Gay Fandom and Crossover Stardom: James Dean, Mel Gibson, and Keanu Reeves* (Durham, NC: Duke University Press, 2001), 104.

Bibliography

Banner, L. W. "The Creature from the Black Lagoon: Marilyn Monroe and Whiteness." *Cinema Journal* 47, 4 (2008): 4–29.

Baudrillard, J. and S. F. Glaser. *Simulacra and Simulation.* Ann Arbor, MI: University of Michigan Press, 1994.

Burkert, W. *Greek Religion: Archaic and Classical.* New York: John Wiley Trade, 1899.

Cohen, L. "The Horizontal Walk: Marilyn Monroe, Cinemascope, and Sexuality." *Yale Journal of Criticism* 11 (1998): 259–88.

DeAngelis, M. *Gay Fandom and Crossover Stardom: James Dean, Mel Gibson, and Keanu Reeves.* Durham, NC: Duke University Press, 2001.

Dyer, R. *Heavenly Bodies: Film Stars and Society.* London: Routledge, 2004.

"Elvis.Com." www.elvis.com.

Fricke, J. *Judy Garland: World's Greatest Entertainer.* New York: Henry Holt, 1992.

Lesser, W. *His Other Half: Men Looking at Women through Art.* Cambridge, MA: Harvard University Press, 1992.

Mailer, N. *Marilyn, a Biography.* New York: Putnam Publishing Group, 1981.

Nietzsche, F. "The Gay Science, Trans." *Walter Kaufmann* (New York: Vintage, 1974), 111: 171.

Olson, L. C., C. A. Finnegan, and D. S. Hope. *Visual Rhetoric: A Reader in Communication and American Culture.* Thousand Oaks, CA: Sage, 2008.

Roen, P. *High Camp: A Gay Guide to Camp and Cult Films.* San Francisco: Leyland Publications, 1993.

Summers, A. *Goddess, the Secret Lives of Marilyn Monroe.* New York: Simon & Schuster, 1985.

Thompson, David. "Marilyn Monroe: An Icon at 80." http://www.independent
  .co.uk/news/people/profiles/marilyn-monroe-an-icon-at-80-477932.html.
Tomaselli, K. G., and D. Scott. *Cultural Icons.* Walnut Creek, CA: Left Coast,
  2009.
Woodruff, P. *Euripides: Bacchae.* Indianapolis, IN: Hackett Publishing Company,
  1998.

CHAPTER 6

BUILDING A GALAXY: GEORGE LUCAS AND THE *STAR WARS* EMPIRE

Lincoln Geraghty

Star Wars is cult. It is the world's biggest film franchise and has arguably the world's biggest cult fan following (although I'm sure *Star Trek* fans would have something to say about that). However, *Star Wars* is also mainstream. It has become part of international popular culture—from the cinema screen to global merchandising to American politics. From its inception, George Lucas's creation has challenged the very nature of cult within popular culture. One of the reasons for that success is that the universe, which informs the text, is so expansive and malleable that all fans, no matter what their cultural background or technical skill, can access it.

Although levels of fan devotion to the *Star Wars* franchise might vary, people cannot escape its influence given its reach across all forms of media, commerce, and culture (film, TV, Internet, books, conventions, toy stores, and comics, to name just a few). At the heart of this, I would argue, is a solid foundation from which the *Star Wars* narrative has emerged. Myth—Lucas's bread and butter—has been central to the story of its success. Whether it be the myth of the Hero with a Thousand Faces, first discussed by Joseph Campbell in 1949, which posits that all myths from around the world share a similar structure of a hero that ventures out into the world, undertakes tasks, and returns with certain powers and gifts; or whether the myth is personal, connected to how fans become fans, remembering that life-changing moment when they first watched *Star Wars* and were hooked; the function of myth in *Star Wars* is to pull viewers in and keep them entertained.

Myth

For J. P. Telotte, one method of analyzing myth in science fiction film is the Jungian psychoanalytical approach. This approach "treats film as a primary myth and thus a key reflection of cultural identity." For Jung, the individual was central, whose personal journey on the path of individuation—"an initiation into the demands of the human environment, combined with the gaining of a deep self-knowledge"— leads to a realization and formation of the self.[1] For characters such as the cowboy or superhero who act primarily on their own, there is a point in a film when the self is activated, perhaps triggered by scenes of personal disaster such as losing a loved one or assuming their superpowers for the first time, after which they embark on their own personal mission to attain individuation.

This definitive moment in *Star Wars* is perhaps one of the most remembered in cinema history, when Luke Skywalker decides to go with Ben Kenobi and learn to become a Jedi after he sees his aunt and uncle killed at the hands of the Empire.[2] Telotte points out that Jungian analysis "remains attractive for the way it manages to explain the compelling and apparently mythic power of film."[3]

In 1977, George Lucas's *Star Wars* used myth to bring back hope to a nation when it seemed in short supply. His vision was to resurrect the myths and legends that had once defined society but had since been forgotten because people had more pressing social problems to deal with. The problems at the time seemed insurmountable—the American economy stagnated, the Vietnam War ended with no clear victor, and Watergate stood as a scandal of epic proportions, causing further erosion of public confidence among those who had little faith left in government. America was in definite need of a cultural tonic that would inspire people and speak to their concerns and at the same time "offer some timeless wisdom."[4]

Into this rather negative environment entered *Star Wars*, which the filmmaker viewed as his prescription for America. It stood in stark contrast with Lucas' previous science fiction film *THX 1138* (1971), which depicted a futuristic dystopian world where humans were reduced to bottom-line budgetary numbers and America was wracked by racial, class, and economic tensions indicative of late-twentieth-century industrial society. However, as we see in *Star Wars*, where "a new hope" was literally reborn to save a way of life, the eponymous hero THX provided some optimism with his climb to freedom outside of his underground prison.

These two science fiction films appear to have the same basic creative foundations. Both were designed to speak to Americans in need of social and moral guidance. In creating these works, Lucas responded to his own social times and acted upon the contemporary issues that faced America in the 1970s. *Star Wars* is a hopeful story in which Jedi faith in the Force offers those battling the evil Empire the possibility of redemption. For David Wilkinson, Lucas gave America "hope that all things will be good in the end" and that hope was "located in the transcendent, that is, the Force, working through the response of people."[5]

Up until the 1990s, *Star Wars* had been largely restricted to the cinema, with only *Episode I: The Phantom Menace* (1999), *Episode II: Attack of the Clones* (2002) and *Episode III: Revenge of the Sith* (2005) showing the increased possibilities of the brand being extended across other platforms, such as TV and the Internet. Yet *Star Wars* relies upon the mediation of ancient myth to address American problems rather than being linked with newsworthy topics of the present day.

Lucas devoured the great themes: epic struggles between good and evil, heroes and villains, magical princes and ogres, heroines and evil princesses, the transmission from fathers to sons, and the power of both good and evil. What the myths revealed to Lucas, among other things, was the capacity of the human imagination to conceive alternate realities to cope with reality: figures, places, and events that were before now or beyond now but were rich with meaning for the present.[6]

Star Wars has taken history and Joseph Campbell's mythic structure and transformed them into a new package, quite literally taking a post-modern approach to looking back at the past to learn about the present. This commodification of the past indicates a cultural engagement with nostalgia so intimate and impervious that as Fredric Jameson has pointed out, "we are unable today to focus on our own present, as though we have become incapable of achieving aesthetic representations of our current experience."[7]

Jameson explains that *Star Wars*' use of nostalgia to convey the past metonymically is indicative of an America yearning to return to more innocent times: the films and Saturday-afternoon TV serials such as *Buck Rogers* (1939, 1950) and *Flash Gordon* (1936, 1959).[8] Adam Roberts links this yearning in *Star Wars* to a particular period of science fiction literary history: the pulps of the Golden Age. As well as eulogizing its sci-fi heritage, *Star Wars* "translates it into something larger-scale, bigger-budget, more sophisticated and glossy," acting as an "intertextual force" looking backwards "over the history of the genre itself."[9] Telotte goes further and describes *Star Wars* as "homage to a great number of films and film types—the western, war films, Japanese samurai films—all of which have contributed to Lucas's vision." This trend is not unique to *Star Wars* but marks "the stirrings of a postmodern pastiche influence that has increasingly characterized our science fiction films."[10]

Where *Star Trek* (1966–present) took myth and "clothed [it]," according to William B. Tyrrell, "in the garb of science fiction" in order to present a possible and positive future, *Star Wars* has taken ancient myth and created an "alternate reality" admittedly set in the past. Within this new and, at the same time, ancient reality, technological advancement and things of the future are set "a long time ago in a galaxy far, far away."[11] Steven Galipeau identifies it as a "mythic time" created by the "interweaving myths of technology and religion occurring in some other galaxy."[12] For *Star Trek*, again acting as an interesting comparison, mythology is a narrative tool with which it can illustrate and correct historical indiscretions, frame many of its episodes and plotlines, and create hope for the future. At the same time, it makes fans believe whole-heartedly that *Star Trek*'s reality has existed, still exists, and will continue to exist far beyond their lifetimes. For *Star Wars*, mythology is a historically based series of symbols and characters that connect with human society and tell us how things were done in the past—perhaps this is why some fans of *Star Wars* say it is not science fiction but rather science fantasy. Or, as Jay Goulding puts it more simply, "*Star Trek* as science fiction is overtly anti-mythic in its attempt to rationalize, systematize and package reality, while *Star Wars*, as fantasy, is overtly myth-affirming, with its reliance on unseen magical forces which bring order to the personality and to the universe."[13]

To further argue this point, Jon Wagner and Jan Lundeen emphasize that "while fantasy may bear a superficial resemblance to traditional myth in its rustic and magical character"—for example, the *Star Wars* battle between good and evil, young heroes, and ancient sorcery— science fiction like *Star Trek* "has a stronger functional parallel with older myths, because its futuristic setting entails a more serious kind of truth claim."[14] Nevertheless, both have acquired mythic status in the present, and with that go the hearts and imaginations of millions of fans.

What is striking about *Star Trek* and *Star Wars* is the enormous amount these films tell us about society. How much they represent contemporary trends and tastes is just as significant as what histories and myths they use to create their own versions of an alternate reality. Both franchises have turned to their own historical narratives to resurrect new and exciting stories to keep their fans involved and interested: *Star Trek* was rebooted on the big screen by J. J. Abrams in 2009, altering the history of the *Enterprise* through a slight tweak in its cataloged history. In the *Star Wars* universe, George Lucas has concentrated on fleshing out and substantiating his original trilogy by investing millions in making the three prequels that he hoped would recapture the imagination of cinemagoers.

These acts of self-examination not only highlight science fiction's trend of looking to its forebears, but they also show how much American society has become disgruntled with its own time; to all intents and purposes, the present is having a knock-on effect on what science fiction audiences want to see on their screens. As a result, the mythic and futuristic times offered by the *Star Wars* universe offer a way out of dealing with contemporary life; it is not because audiences want to live in a mythic past but rather because history and myth offer a better template to fantasize about and to create the future. Brooks Landon's claim that science fiction is not about "what the future might hold, but the inevitable hold of the present over the future" makes clear that it is the present that determines what constitutes our science fiction.[15] Therefore, *Star Wars* uses myth as a means to counteract the turmoil and uncertainty of that present American and perhaps global society.

Culture

For Kevin J. Wetmore, *Star Wars* as a franchise is the "embodiment of key American political and cultural concerns" but also "the films themselves have become the embodiment of American culture."[16] To see this for ourselves, we need not look any further than the multibillion-dollar industry that was spawned after 1977: the merchandise. The impact that the *Star Wars* toy action figures had on the toy industry was phenomenal, as evidenced by the fact that "in 1978 Kenner sold over 26 million figures; by 1985, 250 million." Profits from the toys, figures, lunchboxes, and video games eventually totaled $2.5 billion by the end of the first three films.[17] This was in addition to the huge takings at the box office, where *A New Hope* would follow Steven Spielberg's lead with *Jaws* (1975) and *Close*

Encounters of the Third Kind (1977) and achieve blockbuster status. *A New Hope*, which only cost $11 million to make, "began as a summer movie, ran continuously into 1978, and was re-released in 1979." It earned "over $190 million in U.S. rentals and about $250 million worldwide, on total ticket sales of over $500 million."[18] It is no secret that Lucas kept the rights to the merchandise in order to recover the investment in the film, and no doubt he has been smiling ever since. Yet the first movie's importance is that it helped to cement the summer blockbuster as part of American film culture and make merchandising an integral part of the Hollywood production plan.

Justin Wyatt sees *Star Wars* as a high-concept franchise, the first to really approach toy merchandising with vigor and, as a result, increase its market appeal. For Wyatt, the "high-concept" movie was an important part of the New Hollywood film industry. High-concept films are those that are conceived as highly marketable and therefore highly profitable, as well as being visually striking and stylistically innovative. Such films, for example *A New Hope*, are different through their "emphasis on style in production and through the integration of the film with its marketing."[19] In terms of the *Star Wars* features, we can describe them as high concept because they are comprised of what Wyatt labels "the look, the hook, and the book": "The look of the images, the marketing hooks, and the reduced narratives."[20] The fictional world of *Star Wars* that kept children engrossed for two hours also had underlying marketing advantages: "The film's novel environment and characters have been so striking that Kenner Toys has been able to go beyond the figures in the film by adding new characters to the *Star Wars* line in keeping with the film's mythological world."[21] The infinite potential for expansion kept the figures popular through the 1980s, as children continued to watch and rewatch the movies and play with their own make-believe worlds. Now there is diversification within diversification—a fictional universe within a fictional universe—as the animated series *Star Wars: The Clone Wars* (2003–2005) and film (2008) have produced their own brand image and tie-in products (*Clone Wars* action figures, DVDs, and books).

While *Star Wars* was influencing children playing, it was also having a profound effect on American politics. *Star Wars* has always held close links with contemporary American politics, and, as Peter Krämer points out, we can thank Ronald Reagan's March 23, 1983, televised speech asking for support for the proposed increase in the defense budget for prompting people to associate the two. However, despite the misperception regarding Reagan's use of the term, it was not

Reagan who first used *Star Wars* to paint a picture of America's Strategic Defense Initiative (SDI): "When Senator Edward Kennedy first attached the 'Star Wars' label to the President's vision in comments made on the floor of the Senate the day after the speech, it was to accuse Reagan of 'misleading Red Scare tactics and reckless *Star Wars* schemes.'"[22] Right-wing Cold War politics were indelibly etched onto the characters and backstory that informed the *Star Wars* universe: heroic rebels versus the evil empire became the United States against the Soviet Union. Intriguingly, for those opposed to the SDI, the rebellion in *Star Wars* could be seen as a metaphor for the left's struggle against Reaganism and the politics of big business.

Tom Engelhardt recognizes this yearning in the creation and development of the Kenner action figures of 1978 and argues that Lucas reconstituted "war play as a feel-good activity for children."[23] His new franchise reversed the feeling of loss after Vietnam and literally replaced it with *A New Hope*. The concerns over national politics, overpopulation, and energy shortages that had once weighed heavily on the films of the early 1970s were forgotten as George Lucas and Steven Spielberg took moviegoers to a faraway place.

Their films rejected the pessimism of the earlier period and suggested that the social problems of the decade could be solved. Many conveyed a vision of hope in which the future became a technological paradise complete with world peace. As a result, while *Star Wars* has been criticized for its affirmative visions, which have often been associated with a conservative shift to Reaganite cinema, it is possible to view the film differently.

The science fiction films of the early 1970s were unable to imagine the possibility of redemption and viewed humanity as simply doomed. Thus, while they have been seen as radical, they were also profoundly nihilistic with no alternative to the decadent order of things. In contrast, *Star Wars* was concerned with the exact opposite—becoming an attempt to imagine an alternative and establish a sense of hope. Kenner's decision to make the figurines pocket size meant that children could carry these representations of a fictional, future universe around and create their own make-believe world wherever they played. As we have seen, throughout American history, technology has stood as a symbol of progress. For example, as America became more industrialized in the eighteenth century, the notion of technological improvement became important to national identity.[24] Therefore, the futuristic-looking aliens, creatures, and humans with a superior command of technology, both on screen and in toy form, reassured adults and children alike that America was on the right track.

Some academics and film critics saw this nostalgic return to established genres as part of a conservative backlash to the political radicalism of the 1970s.[25] Andrew Britton, in his 1986 seminal article "Blissing Out: The Politics of Reaganite Entertainment," stated that "the banality of the films derives from the undialectical conception of Good and Evil and the reduction to the level of routine of the contest between them."[26] However, it should be stressed that many of the key examples of cinematic radicalism in the late 1960s and early 1970s were themselves examples of the nostalgic film: *The Wild Bunch* (1969), *Bonnie and Clyde* (1967), *Chinatown* (1974), *The Godfather* (1972), and even *2001: A Space Odyssey* (1968) were revisionist interpretations of the Hollywood western, film noir, gangster, and science fiction film. In addition, so-called nostalgic films shared much of the political paranoia of the early 1970s: the Empire in *Star Wars* represents bureaucratic, ruthless imperialism. Another interesting case study is Spielberg's *Close Encounters of the Third Kind*, which clearly plays on anxieties about the relationship between the state and the individual citizen.

Fans

Fan audiences have been and will always be eager to express their devotion to the objects of their affection. Of course, the *Star Wars* audience is no different. Henry Jenkins describes audiences as "active, critically aware and discriminating."[27] *Star Wars* fans are no strangers to intense critical debate as they advertise and defend their appropriation of George Lucas's strictly rigid fictional narrative canon on blogs, on websites, and at conventions. Often friendly in nature, these debates revolve around notions of story accuracy and characterization.[28] Remembering the thousands of characters, plot points, aliens, ships, planets, and weapons and collecting every piece of merchandise imaginable gives fans a certain level of esteem within the community.[29]

However, in one particular case, regarding the new character of Jar Jar Binks from *Phantom Menace*, conflict within the community arose and came together over whether Lucas was right to include such a "childish" and childlike main character. The fans' universal hatred of the new addition to the canon was a "tactic aimed at preserving the fans' 'good' objective of *Star Wars* as 'serious' and 'culturally significant.'"[30] This concern for seriousness and cultural significance is an important part of fan practice. It is reflective of their personal investment in the franchise and represents the film's value in terms of their accumulation of cultural capital. When we look at the enormity and impact of *Star Wars* fandom in popular culture, attention is drawn away from the perceived notion that a film's cultural value and worth is simply allied to box office receipts and its critical reception and is instead focused on fan discourse that drives debates concerning the valuing of film itself. Such vociferous fan activity intimates a deeply hierarchical and systematized structure of subcultural taste and political discourse Mark Jancovich terms "cult distinction."[31] As he explains in his article "Cult Fictions":

> The cult movie has much to tell us about the politics of cultural consumption and its relation to issues of economic and educational capital . . . and the ways in which its inconsistent and contradictory uses arise from its function as the Other, the construction of which allows for the production of distinctions and sense of cultural superiority.[32]

The negative reaction toward Lucas's first prequel was ubiquitous. The UK cult fan sitcom *Spaced* (1999–2001) routinely referenced the franchise, and the main character Tim can clearly be identified as a super-fan through his job working in a comic book store. *Spaced* is on the one hand a traditional sitcom, yet its positioning of science fiction fandom, particularly *Star Wars* fandom, lends it a certain intertextuality that references both the Lucas text and the strident fanbase surrounding it.

Will Brooker discusses Simon Pegg's role as Tim, the archetypal middle-aged *Star Wars* fan, in conjunction with the release of *The Phantom Menace* and the mass backlash against the film from those fans who saw it as childish and hollow. Scenes between Tim and his flatmate Daisy, in which they talk about how bad the film was, are interwoven with fantasy scenes that depict Tim dressed up as Luke Skywalker burning his *Star Wars* collectibles in a form of silent protest against Lucas. Brooker calls this an example of the series' "dual address," whereby it speaks to the popular audience of the time and offers a more subversive reading to those fans who are able to understand the reference within the joke and sympathize with Tim.[33]

The vehement criticism of the later films by hardcore fans signals an increasing disconnect between the producers of popular culture and its consumers. Mark McDermott's essay on fan-made videos that lampooned the prequels highlights this shift in fan productivity. Some fans followed traditional lines of criticism by writing about their reasons for hating *Phantom Menace*, others made videos, and a third group used desktop technology to re-edit the DVD release of the film to eliminate everything they despised about it.[34] *Star Wars* as a text had gone from mega franchise to object of intense scrutiny, with the fans claiming a sense of ownership over it that perhaps outstripped its creator, George Lucas.

With the use of new media such as the Internet and popular platforms such as blogs and YouTube, fans are able to immediately post and upload their thoughts and reactions to their favorite films or TV shows as they air and continue this interaction well after the initial thrill wore off. *Star Wars*, almost above all other cult texts, has motivated fans to pick up a camera, shoot some footage, and upload the result on the Web. As already highlighted, degrees of cult fandom and subcultural capital can be gauged through levels of consumption, knowledge, and esteem within a particular fan community. However, it is important to consider the impact that new media technologies and convergence have had on definitions of *Star Wars* fandom and to what extent those fans now use the Internet and new media as the primary means through which to consume and produce their own versions of the films. For some, the influence of new media has been to make physical places less important for fans when communications through websites, social networking sites, and video sharing allow for better distribution and diffusion of materials.[35]

Indeed, media audiences are becoming increasingly fractured as they spread out across a variety of popular and new media. From blogging to posting homemade videos, the *Star Wars* audience can no longer be seen as just one homogenous group. What is more, as new technologies influence the way we consume, use, and produce media texts such as *Star Wars*, audience tastes and value judgments tend to shift wildly as consumer choice increases. The fragmentation of media audiences has occurred due to the continually evolving "relationship between technologies, industries, markets, genres, and audiences." This convergence of media and technology, according to Henry Jenkins, "alters the logic by which media industries operate and by which media consumers process news and entertainment."[36] Consumers of *Star Wars* are now also producers of new versions of *Star Wars* as the established industry-made product is disseminated across multimedia platforms and chopped up and mixed with a multiplicity of differing images and texts. Once, Hollywood could never assume the film audience understood or watched a movie in the same way; now, even more, Hollywood has had to recognize that its diverse audiences are learning how to use new technologies to "bring the flow of media more fully under their control and interact with other consumers."[37] Those consumers who use existing media to produce new texts have been called "produsers": "Produsage exists within a wider context of new and emerging concepts for describing the social, technological, and economic environment of user-led content creation."[38]

As cult fandom continues to evolve with developing media technologies, *Star Wars* is sure to follow. The Internet now only exists to drive on the search for more content, and Lucas is eager to supply it. Of course, as more *Star Wars*-related ephemera are produced, the more fans want to consume it, use it, change it, and redistribute it. A popular culture phenomenon such as this will not die unless the desire to remediate it dies, and since the Internet has become the social glue through which global culture is held together, that cannot happen. The Force is strong with this one.

Notes

1. J. P. Telotte, *Science Fiction Film* (New York: Cambridge University Press, 2001), 48.

2. Steven A. Galipeau, *The Journey of Luke Skywalker: An Analysis of Modern Myth and Symbol* (Chicago and La Salle, IL: Open Court, 2001), 33–34.

3. Telotte, *Science Fiction Film*, 49.

4. Mary Henderson, *Star Wars: The Magic of Myth* (New York: Bantam Books, 1997), 6.

5. David Wilkinson, *The Power of the Force: The Spirituality of the Star Wars Films* (Oxford: Lion Publishing, 2000), 96.

6. Charles Champlin, *George Lucas: The Creative Impulse* (New York: Harry N. Abrams, Inc., 1992), 41.

7. Fredric Jameson, "Postmodernism and Consumer Society," in Hal Foster, ed., *The Anti-Aesthetic: Essays on Postmodern Culture* (Port Townsend, WA: Bay Press, 1983), 117.

8. Ibid., 116.

9. Adam Roberts, *Science Fiction: The New Critical Idiom* (London: Routledge, 2000), 85, 90.

10. Telotte, *Science Fiction Film*, 105.

11. William Blake Tyrrell, "*Star Trek* as Myth and Television as Mythmaker," *Journal of Popular Culture* 10.4 (1977): 712.

12. Galipeau, *The Journey of Luke Skywalker*, 60.

13. Jay Goulding, *Empire, Aliens, and Conquest: A Critique of American Ideology in Star Trek and Other Science Fiction Adventures* (Toronto, OT: Sisyphus Press, 1985), 67.

14. Jon Wagner and Jan Lundeen, *Deep Space and Sacred Time: Star Trek in the American Mythos* (Westport, CT: Praeger, 1998), 6.

15. Brooks Landon, "Bet On It: Cyber/video/punk/performance," in Larry McCaffery, ed., *Storming the Reality Studio* (Durham, NC: Duke University Press, 1991), 239.

16. Kevin J. Wetmore, Jr., *The Empire Triumphant: Race, Religion and Rebellion in the Star Wars Films* (Jefferson, NC: McFarland, 2005), 3.

17. Tom Engelhardt, *The End of Victory Culture: Cold War America and the Disillusioning of a Generation* (Amherst: University of Massachusetts Press, 1998), 269.

18. Kristin Thompson and David Bordwell, *Film History: An Introduction,* 2nd ed. (Boston: McGraw Hill, 2003), 522.

19. Justin Wyatt, *High Concept: Movies and Marketing in Hollywood* (Austin: University of Texas Press, 1994), 20.

20. Ibid., 22.

21. Ibid., 153.

22. Peter Krämer, "*Star Wars,*" in David W. Ellwood, ed., *The Movies as History: Visions of the Twentieth Century* (Stroud: Sutton Publishing, 2000), 46.

23. Engelhardt, *The End of Victory Culture,* 268.

24. Leo Marx, *The Machine in the Garden: Technology and the Pastoral Ideal in America* (New York: Oxford University Press, 1964), 197.

25. See Michael Ryan and Douglas Kellner, *Camera Politica: The Politics and Ideology of Contemporary Hollywood Film* (Bloomington: Indiana University Press, 1988).

26. Andrew Britton, "Blissing Out: The Politics of Reaganite Entertainment (1986)," in Barry Keith Grant, ed., *Britton on Film: The Complete Film Criticism of Andrew Britton* (Detroit, MI: Wayne State University Press, 2009), 113.

27. Henry Jenkins, "Interactive Audiences?" in Dan Harries, ed., *The New Media Book* (London: BFI, 2002), 157.

28. See Will Brooker, "Internet Fandom and the Continuing Narratives of *Star Wars, Blade Runner* and *Alien,*" in Annette Kuhn, ed., *Alien Zone II: The Spaces of Science Fiction Cinema* (London: Verso, 1999), 50–72.

29. See Nathan Hunt, "The Importance of Trivia: Ownership, Exclusion and Authority in Science Fiction Fandom," in Mark Jancovich, Antonio Lázaro Reboll, Julian Stringer, and Andy Willis, eds., *Defining Cult Movies: The Cultural Politics of Oppositional Taste* (Manchester: Manchester University Press, 2003), 185–201.

30. Matt Hills, "Putting Away Childish Things: Jar Jar Binks and the 'Virtual Star' as an Object of Fan Loathing," in Thomas Austin and Martin Barker, eds., *Contemporary Hollywood Stardom* (London: Arnold, 2003), 89; for more on *Star Wars* fans' attempts at establishing cultural status, see also Matt Hills, "*Star Wars* in Fandom, Film Theory, and the Museum," in Julian Stringer, ed., *Movie Blockbusters* (London: Routledge, 2003), 178–89.

31. Mark Jancovich, "Cult Fictions: Cult Movies, Subcultural Capital and the Production of Cultural Distinctions," *Cultural Studies* 16.2 (2002): 306–7.

32. Ibid., 320–21.

33. Will Brooker, *Using the Force: Creativity, Community and Star Wars Fans* (New York: Continuum, 2002), 79–85.

34. Mark McDermott, "The Menace of the Fans to the Franchise," in Matthew Wilhelm Kapell and John Shelton Lawrence, eds., *Finding the Force of the Star Wars Franchise: Fans, Merchandise, & Critics* (New York: Peter Lang, 2006), 243–44.

35. Mark Jancovich, Antonio Lázaro Reboll, Julian Stringer, and Andy Willis, "Introduction," in Mark Jancovich, Antonio Lázaro Reboll, Julian Stringer, and Andy Willis, eds., *Defining Cult Movies: The Cultural Politics of Oppositional Taste* (Manchester: Manchester University Press, 2003), 4.

36. Henry Jenkins, *Convergence Culture: Where Old and New Media Collide* (New York: New York University Press, 2006), 15–16.

37. Ibid., 18.

38. Axel Bruns, *Blogs, Wikipedia, Second Life, and Beyond: From Production to Produsage* (New York: Peter Lang, 2008), 2.

Bibliography

Britton, Andrew. "Blissing Out: The Politics of Reaganite Entertainment (1986)." In Barry Keith Grant, ed. *Britton on Film: The Complete Film Criticism of Andrew Britton*. Detroit, MI: Wayne State University Press, 2009, pp. 97–154.

Brooker, Will. "Internet Fandom and the Continuing Narratives of *Star Wars, Blade Runner* and *Alien*." In Annette Kuhn, ed. *Alien Zone II: The Spaces of Science Fiction Cinema*. London: Verso, 1999, pp. 50–72.

Brooker, Will. *Using the Force: Creativity, Community and Star Wars Fans*. London: Continuum, 2002.

Bruns, Axel. *Blogs, Wikipedia, Second Life, and Beyond: From Production to Produsage*. New York: Peter Lang, 2008.

Champlin, Charles. *George Lucas: The Creative Impulse*. New York: Harry N. Abrams, 1992.

Engelhardt, Tom. *The End of Victory Culture: Cold War America and the Disillusioning of a Generation*. Amherst: University of Massachusetts Press, 1998.

Galipeau, Steven A. *The Journey of Luke Skywalker: An Analysis of Modern Myth and Symbol*. Chicago and La Salle, IL: Open Court, 2001.

Goulding, Jay. *Empire, Aliens, and Conquest: A Critique of American Ideology in Star Trek and Other Science Fiction Adventures*. Toronto: Sisyphus Press, 1985.

Henderson, Mary. *Star Wars: The Magic of Myth*. New York: Bantam Books, 1997.

Hills, Matt. "Putting Away Childish Things: Jar Jar Binks and the 'Virtual Star' as an Object of Fan Loathing." In Thomas Austin and Martin Barker, eds., *Contemporary Hollywood Stardom*. London: Arnold, 2003, pp. 74–89.

Hills, Matt. "*Star Wars* in Fandom, Film Theory, and the Museum." In Julian Stringer, ed. *Movie Blockbusters.* London: Routledge, 2003, pp. 178–89.

Hunt, Nathan. "The Importance of Trivia: Ownership, Exclusion and Authority in Science Fiction Fandom." In Mark Jancovich, Antonio Lázaro Reboll, Julian Stringer, and Andy Willis, eds. *Defining Cult Movies: The Cultural Politics of Oppositional Taste.* Manchester: Manchester University Press, 2003, pp. 185–201.

Jameson, Fredric. "Postmodernism and Consumer Society." In Hal Foster, ed. *The Anti-Aesthetic: Essays on Postmodern Culture.* Port Townsend, WA: Bay Press, 1983, pp. 111–125.

Jancovich, Mark. "Cult Fictions: Cult Movies, Subcultural Capital and the Production of Cultural Distinctions." *Cultural Studies* 16.2 (2002): 306–322.

Jancovich, Mark, Antonio Lázaro Reboll, Julian Stringer and Andy Willis. "Introduction." In Mark Jancovich, Antonio Lázaro Reboll, Julian Stringer and Andy Willis, eds. *Defining Cult Movies: The Cultural Politics of Oppositional Taste.* Manchester: Manchester University Press, 2003, pp. 1–13.

Jenkins, Henry. "Interactive Audiences?" In Dan Harries, ed. *The New Media Book.* London: BFI, 2002, pp. 157–70.

Jenkins, Henry. *Convergence Culture: Where Old and New Media Collide.* New York: New York University Press, 2006.

Krämer, Peter. "*Star Wars.*" In David W. Ellwood, ed. *The Movies as History: Visions of the Twentieth Century.* Stroud: Sutton Publishing, 2000, pp. 44–53.

Landon, Brooks. "Bet On It: Cyber/video/punk/performance." In Larry McCaffery, ed. *Storming the Reality Studio.* Durham, NC: Duke University Press, 1991, pp. 239–244.

Marx, Leo. *The Machine in the Garden: Technology and the Pastoral Ideal in America.* New York: Oxford University Press, 1964.

McDermott, Mark. "The Menace of the Fans to the Franchise." In Matthew Wilhelm Kapell and John Shelton Lawrence, eds. *Finding the Force of the Star Wars Franchise: Fans, Merchandise, & Critics.* New York: Peter Lang, 2006, pp. 243–63.

Roberts, Adam. *Science Fiction: The New Critical Idiom.* London: Routledge, 2000.

Ryan, Michael and Douglas Kellner. *Camera Politica: The Politics and Ideology of Contemporary Hollywood Film.* Bloomington: Indiana University Press, 1988.

Telotte, J. P. *Science Fiction Film.* New York: Cambridge University Press, 2001.

Thompson, Kristin and David Bordwell. *Film History: An Introduction.* 2nd ed. Boston: McGraw Hill, 2003.

Tyrrell, William Blake. "*Star Trek* as Myth and Television as Mythmaker." *Journal of Popular Culture* 10.4 (1977): 711–19.

Wagner, Jon and Jan Lundeen. *Deep Space and Sacred Time: Star Trek in the American Mythos.* Westport, CT: Praeger, 1998.

Wetmore, Jr., Kevin J. *The Empire Triumphant: Race, Religion and Rebellion in the Star Wars Films.* Jefferson, NC: McFarland, 2005.

Wilkinson, David. *The Power of the Force: The Spirituality of the Star Wars Films.* Oxford: Lion Publishing, 2000.

Wyatt, Justin. *High Concept: Movies and Marketing in Hollywood.* Austin: University of Texas Press, 1994.

CHAPTER 7

LECTER FOR PRESIDENT...OR, WHY WE WORSHIP SERIAL KILLERS

Philip L. Simpson

Dr. Hannibal "the Cannibal" Lecter, as created by writer Thomas Harris and immortalized on the silver screen by actor Anthony Hopkins, is a bona fide celebrity. His fame brings him the kind of instant name recognition usually reserved for movie stars or U.S. presidents. Certainly the most famous fictional serial killer ever, Lecter exerts a continuing fascination upon the popular imagination as a sleek, elegant symbol of evil.

In the post–9/11 era, when we fear the quiet next-door neighbor may be a terrorist, a serial killer seems almost quaint as the basis of a cultural boogeyman. Yet Lecter remains one of popular culture's most recognizable personifications of evil. By turns charming and savage, he represents the best and the worst of human behavior. He is a brilliant psychiatrist and man of refined cultural taste who also happens to be a cannibalistic serial killer. At first an inexplicably evil character, Lecter has evolved over the course of four novels and five films to become more humanized, even sympathetic, in his portrayal. He has been rehabilitated into a lovable rogue, a vigilante who inflicts poetic justice upon those who do him harm, and a romantic leading man worthy of winning the hand of FBI Agent Clarice Starling.

He evokes many contrary emotions in us, as do serial killers in fact and fiction. David Schmid argues the serial killer inspires "feelings of attraction and repulsion, admiration and condemnation" in a fashion quite similar to the love/hate relationship between more conventional celebrities (such as film stars) and the public.[1] America is endlessly fascinated by its outlaws, elevating them to iconic, even folkloric status. Lecter's image makeover should not be that surprising given the celebrity status accorded to spectacularly violent criminals, especially serial killers, in America.

Though Lecter is fictitious, he nevertheless stands as the *ne plus ultra* of the celebrity serial killer in the American popular imagination. The conflation between real murderers and a fictitious character like Lecter is integral to the cultural construction of serial murder. After all, the serial killer's sequence of crime is played out in an episodic form roughly analogous to the progression and development of a story told in the longer serial format, a fact not lost upon former FBI agent Robert Ressler, who claims to have coined the term "serial killer" during the 1970s in part because of his childhood memory of serial adventure movies.[2]

Popular culture has always played a crucial role in the cultural creation of serial murder, back to at least the Jack the Ripper murders in London in 1888. Those crimes were framed, reported, and understood through the "Jekyll and Hyde" metaphor popular at the time as a result of Robert Louis Stevenson's novel, *Dr. Jekyll and Mr. Hyde* (1886). Why else were there so many theories and accounts of the Ripper as a doctor or some other professional man who had somehow given himself over to murderous savagery? Ever since, real-life serial killers have drawn upon real-life, literary, and cinematic precedents to conceive of and implement their crimes; the journalistic media have constructed their stories about these crimes on the basis of these same precedents; law enforcement has addressed the phenomenon through the romantic framework of detective and adventure fiction; and popular culture recycles its past narratives and the new material generated by new crimes to create new popular stories of serial murder. It has been a colossal feedback loop in which fact and fiction become indeterminate and, in a real sense, irrelevant. The narrative itself, of the lone mad genius killing victims in a rising crescendo of atrocity over a span of time, is what rules. And standing at the apex of it, shaping the perception of serial murder itself forever after, is Hannibal Lecter.

He represents what we dread and what we are drawn to in the phenomenon of serial murder, though the phenomenon itself bears little relation to him.[3] Whereas the vast majority of serial killers past and present are rather unremarkable men in every way (appearance, intellect, level of professional achievement), Lecter is an extraordinary individual, gifted in every way. Even before his arrest for murder, no one would call him "normal," simply because of the power of his intellect. His psychological insights, though completely divorced from sympathy or pity, are piercing.[4] Assisted by a formidable memory, he is observant of minute details to an extent rivaled only by the detective character of Sherlock Holmes, as created by Arthur Conan Doyle, or Holmes's literary predecessor, C. Auguste Dupin, as created by Edgar Allan Poe. His physical senses are as heightened as his mental acuity, especially his sense of smell. The only outward markers of his unique mentality are his oddly maroon eyes and an extra finger.

None of this, in and of itself, marks him as monstrous. What makes him a true monster is his amorality. This quality above any other allows him to take pleasure in the killing of his fellow human beings. At times, he resembles the cultural notion of the vampire (especially the Bela Lugosi portrayal of Dracula in the 1931 Universal film) as a cruel aristocrat who feeds off the life force of others. Freed of the constraints of conscience, he exercises his creative wit through murder. By doing so, he rebels against both conventional morality and Christian morality, which he finds particularly hypocritical.

Lecter's cultural ascendancy spans five novels, each published several years apart from the preceding one. His character evolves dramatically with each novel. He makes his first appearance in Thomas Harris's second novel, *Red Dragon* (1981), as a supporting character practically radiating predatory menace, though cannibalism is never mentioned. Lecter assumes a larger and, in spite of his newly established "cannibal killer" status, slightly more sympathetic role in Harris's third novel, *The Silence of the Lambs* (1988). As a mentor, he provides critical information in a serial murder case to FBI trainee Clarice Starling and, in the process, forces her to confront her own traumatic past. With the publication of Harris's next novel, *Hannibal* (1999), Lecter takes one of two starring roles, opposite FBI Special Agent Starling. The character's rehabilitation is well underway at this point, casting him as suffering from the shock of losing his sister to a cannibal gang on the Eastern Front of World War II. Harris's fifth (and to date final) novel is *Hannibal Rising* (2006), which details Lecter's traumatic boyhood and his subsequent revenge upon the men who killed and ate his sister. In each of these novels, Lecter transforms from a caged but untamable monster of incomprehensible motives into a domesticated, even sympathetic figure with motives clearly rooted in the traumatic loss of his sister.

Lecter's Biography

Based on these five novels, a fragmentary biography of Lecter emerges. He is born in the late 1930s in Lithuania, the eldest son of a wealthy mother and father. He has a younger sister, Mischa. Early on, Lecter demonstrates precocious intellectual ability, which is further cultivated by a private tutor. During the German invasion of Russia in World War II, Lecter's parents are killed and he and Mischa taken prisoner by a group of starving Lithuanian Hiwis, or militiamen. Under the leadership of a man named Grutas, the group kills and eats Mischa. Lecter survives but represses the traumatic memory of the manner of his sister's death. Enduring the privation of a Soviet state orphanage, he finally finds safe harbor in the home of his uncle, Robert Lecter, in France. Robert is married to a beautiful Japanese woman named Lady Murasaki. When a local butcher utters a sexual crudity to his aunt, Lecter kills the man, thus establishing his characteristic *modus operandi* of murdering the rude. Lecter then becomes a medical student in Paris a few years later. Recovering his memory, he seeks revenge against his sister's killers, systematically killing them one by one in progressively more savage ways. Grutas, now a ruthless human trafficker, proves to be a most formidable opponent, but he too is finally killed by Lecter. Eventually jailed for his crimes in Paris but freed because of a groundswell of public sympathy, Lecter comes to the United States as a medical student.

In the next phase of his life, Lecter becomes a successful psychiatrist and man about town in Baltimore during the 1960s and early 1970s. However, he leads a secret double life as a serial killer, consuming selected body parts of his victims in ritual re-enactment of the murder of his sister. Whenever possible, he later tells one of his jailers, he eats people who are rude to others in some way. His nine known victims during this time include a Princeton student, a musician named Benjamin Raspail, and a census taker. In an act of perverse whimsy, he feeds Raspail's sweetbreads to the board of his symphony orchestra in a gourmet meal. In another whimsical act, Lecter positions one victim to resemble the figure depicted in the medieval illustration *The Wound Man*. Two of his victims survive, including Mason Verger, a child molester and the wealthy son of a meatpacking magnate. Verger, having been persuaded under the influence of drugs by Lecter to peel off his own face with a mirror shard and feed the pieces to dogs, is left paralyzed and faceless. Lecter's reign of terror ends in the mid 1970s when Will Graham, a criminal profiler working for the FBI, identifies him. Graham is nearly killed when Lecter slashes him open with a linoleum knife. Found criminally insane during his highly publicized trial, Lecter is confined to a Baltimore mental hospital.

When he nearly kills one of his nurses in captivity, the security safeguards around him are tightened. He comes to despise the hospital administrator, Dr. Chilton, but forms an intellectual bond with his orderly, Barney. The years of his captivity pass by uneventfully until Graham consults him in the early 1980s on an active serial murder case, the so-called "Tooth Fairy" killings of two separate families in Birmingham and Atlanta. Lecter provides Graham with psychological insights about the kind of man whose specific madness drives him to slaughter entire families when the moon is full. However, in an act of revenge against the man who jailed him, Lecter secretly provides Graham's home address to the killer, Francis Dolarhyde. Dolarhyde does not kill Graham but does leave him disfigured.

Several years later, FBI Special Agent Jack Crawford sends a young female FBI trainee, Clarice Starling, to interview Lecter about another active serial killer, known by the tabloid name of Buffalo Bill. Lecter bonds with Clarice to the extent he gives her the information she needs to rescue the killer's latest female prisoner and kill Buffalo Bill, a man named Jame Gumb. Then Lecter escapes police custody, leaving a number of bodies behind. He obtains plastic surgery to alter his features and flees the United States.

Seven years after his escape, Lecter is living peacefully in Florence, Italy, until Starling's professional jeopardy following a botched drug raid catches his attention. Simultaneously, Mason Verger discovers the doctor's whereabouts and launches a plot to capture and torture him to death by feeding him to pigs (an act even more whimsically bizarre than what Lecter did to him). Starling ultimately foils the plot and rescues Lecter from Verger's henchmen. Wounded in the rescue, she is tended to by Lecter. He turns her into his lover (and fellow cannibal) through a combination of hypnosis, drugs, and intensive therapy sessions; however, through her strong will, she is able to cure him of his obsession with his dead sister. The couple ends up living in a blissful lovers' exile in Buenos Aires.

Lecter's Transformation: The Superhero of Serial Killers

Lecter's cultural evolution can be traced through each novel. In his first appearance in *Red Dragon*, the primary emotion Lecter evokes is fear. He frightens through the cruel fashion in which he toys with Will

Graham and then sets another monster loose on Graham's family. The next time we meet Lecter in *The Silence of the Lambs*, he is even more unabashedly evil. Solely to amuse himself, he holds back critical information in a new serial murder case and a time-sensitive abduction just so he can play at being mentor and therapist to Clarice Starling. As Linda J. Holland-Toll memorably puts it, "Hannibal Lecter finds pleasure in dissecting the innermost being of Clarice Starling."[5] Additionally, he exploits the situation to garner some privileges for himself and toy with the representatives of the society that put him into confinement.

Clearly, Lecter enjoys killing for the sheer transgressive sport of it. We learn secondhand that he eats the organs of his victims and stages their sadly violated corpses in grotesquely humorous tableaux. Even when he can't physically kill, he vicariously indulges in it through the case files brought to him by Graham and Starling. What could we possibly find to like, let alone admire, in such a despicable man? Yet the grandiosity of his evil compels our attention, and there is no denying Starling sparks some vestigial human feeling in him. Starling is the instrument of Lecter's eventual rehabilitation as a character.

In the next two novels, Lecter moves away from a straightforward boogeyman to become what David Sexton describes as a "lifestyle fiend . . . bedecked too with a dizzying plurality of historical, genealogical and mythological attributes."[6] In fact, he starts to look like a hero, albeit a tragically fallen one. He is articulate, witty, intelligent, and even idealistic in his own inestimable way. In spite of ourselves, we are drawn to him for his rogue's charm, devil's sense of humor, and tragic past. He infects us with his evil charm, seducing us like he does Starling as he plays to our vulnerabilities. Though we know better, we may even come to respect Lecter's strength because, even though he's been held captive in an asylum for years, he retains his sense of self-possession, even dignity. We marvel at his fearlessness when threatened with a hideous fate by his nemesis, Mason Verger. We approve of him when we realize he doesn't want to eat Starling—instead, he wants to help her. He is caring mentor, father figure, and passionate lover to her, all in one package. Maybe we even learn to sympathize with him when we find out how he lost his sister Mischa to a gang of starving cannibals on the Eastern Front in World War II. This devil is not evil incarnate after all; he's as human as the rest of us, in spite of his exceptional abilities.

Harris's Lecter terrifies with his ability to persuade us to lower our guard just before attacking us to rip off and eat our tongues, as he did to the hapless nurse in Chilton's hospital. He terrifies us because he directs his considerable charm and talents into the service of murder. Though his motives and hidden traumas may be all too human, he exhibits self-control to an inhuman extent. He can master fear and pain simply by retreating into himself, deep within what he calls his "memory palace," where everything he ever learned or felt is stored. His mental resources are so formidable as to seem impossible to match by those of us with anything less than a photographic memory. Against such an intellect, what chance do dullards like Inspector Pazzi or Paul Krendler stand, or even more formidable foes, such as Mason Verger? Lecter is truly the superhero of serial killers.

Screen Icon

If Lecter lived only in the pages of Harris's thrillers, however, it seems likely he would not be the icon he is today. It took his existence on the big screen to accomplish that. Lecter has thus far been portrayed by four separate actors: Brian Cox in *Manhunter* (dir. Michael Mann, 1986), the first screen adaptation of *Red Dragon*; Anthony Hopkins in *The Silence of the Lambs* (dir. Jonathan Demme, 1991), *Hannibal* (dir. Ridley Scott, 2001), and *Red Dragon* (dir. Brett Ratner, 2002); and Aaran Thomas and Gaspard Ulliel in *Hannibal Rising* (dir. Peter Webber, 2007). Since much of Lecter's cultural deification is owed to his film incarnations, it is instructive to examine each in some detail.

Brian Cox is a Scottish actor, known for his roles in *Braveheart* (1995) and *Rushmore* (1998). His breakthrough part, Hannibal Lecter, was one of his earliest screen performances. Cox's performance was little noted at the time, since Mann's film suffered a quick death at the box office. *Manhunter* lived on in video, however, to become a cult and critical favorite. It's a movie that seems better in retrospect, although admittedly dated by its sometimes garish and mannered *Miami Vice*-noir mise-en-scène. Preferring Cox's interpretation of the good doctor over Hopkins's has, in fact, become quite *de rigueur* among film critics and other self-appointed champions of the cinematically downtrodden and unjustly forgotten.

As played by Cox, Lecter is a brutish, dark, glowering psychopath whose civility clearly is a thin veneer over a raging mass of insanity. The widow's peak, the stout build, and the elegant British accent are the same between Cox's Lecter and Hopkins's, but there the similarities end. In the scene where Graham first faces down Lecter in the asylum cell, Cox radiates genuine menace. This Lecter (actually spelled "Lektor" in a newspaper headline glimpsed later in the film) is not a helpful mentor, dark oracle, foppish sophisticate, or discriminating connoisseur snacking on the vitals of rude people best expunged from the earth anyway. In a fashion much truer to typical serial killer behavior, this misogynistic Lecter kills college women "in bad ways," as Graham ominously hints to his son later. Though an intellectual, Cox's Lecter shows an animalistic hatred that comes across much more viscerally than Hopkins's.

A couple of underplayed but eerily effective scenes in the film capture Lecter's inner madness as well, or even better, than any amount of Hopkins's more mannered performance. In the first scene between Graham and Lecter in the asylum, Lecter regards Graham with an alternating parade of sullen hostility, keen appraisal, outright hatred, and mocking superiority playing subtly but unmistakably across his dark, blunt features. Through his verbal needles and indirect allusions to his own crimes, Lecter is clearly sniffing at Graham to sense his vulnerabilities, to test the firmness of his sanity. A few scenes later, after Lecter has used his phone privileges to con a hapless secretary into giving him Graham's home address, the camera holds on Lecter's face as he tries, not too successfully, to contain his smug sense of superiority and his anticipation at striking back at Graham.

In Mann's film, Lecter does not seem to be a supervillain of any kind. Rather, he comes across as a cunning and opportunistic psychopath, intent on using a turn of fortune to exact vengeance from his cell on the man who jailed him. Cox also plays Lecter as an extraordinarily intelligent man who has become rather stuporous from the boredom of captivity. He is depicted as lying down much of the time, bleary-eyed, and barely awake. Played in relatively low-key realistic fashion by Cox, this Lecter had little chance of capturing widespread audience attention, let alone altering the national zeitgeist forever.

No, it took Anthony Hopkins to make that happen. His Academy Award-winning performance in *The Silence of the Lambs* established the character's iconic status. Hopkins plays his part with slyly humorous, reptilian menace as the villainous foil to Jodie Foster's portrayal of earnest young Clarice Starling. The character is given a suitably ominous off-screen build-up during the first few scenes of the film, so that when Starling finally catches sight of him standing in waiting for her in his cell, all audience expectations are fulfilled. Though occupying the screen for only 20 minutes or so, in that short time, Hopkins's Lecter hissed memorable lines such as "I ate his liver with some fava beans and a nice Chianti" and "I'm having an old friend for dinner." Hopkins clearly relishes the opportunity to play such a malevolent character.

Before his superstar turn in *Silence*, Hopkins had achieved a solid reputation with parts in films like *The Elephant Man* (1980) and *The Bounty* (1984). He proved he was capable of playing a sympathetic character like Dr. Frederick Treves in the former film and a villain like Captain Bligh in the latter. Playing up and down this acting range in *Silence of the Lambs*, Hopkins portrays Lecter with courtly European manners, an unblinking crocodilian stare, an otherworldly distance, and a cultured British accent that occasionally slides into hisses calculated to induce pleasurable shudders in his American audience. Hopkins's voice makes the character as much as his physical presence. Modeling his enunciation after the precise voice of Hal 9000 in the film *2001: A Space Odyssey* (1968), Hopkins conveys a sense of cold menace that belies his courteous manners. The character's mocking intellectualism poses a shocking contrast to his over-the-top gleeful violence in the character's Memphis jailbreak, when he clubs a policeman to death and tears into the face of another like a rabid terrier. In doing so, Hopkins created an instant screen legend, which still consistently polls among critics and viewers as one of the top villains in film history.[7] At first sight, audiences loved Lecter, as proven by the film's eventual box office domestic gross of over $130 million.

The Academy of Motion Picture Arts and Sciences played a pivotal part in the cultural enshrinement of Lecter by first nominating and then giving Hopkins the Academy Award for Best Actor at its annual ceremony on March 30, 1992. Although Hopkins's screen time was short (about 17 minutes), the entire Oscar ceremony was essentially one long love note to Hopkins and, by extension, Hannibal Lecter.

The show began with host Billy Crystal's grand entrance. He was wheeled onstage on a handtruck while wearing a straitjacket and hockey mask, the same garb Lecter wore in a key scene in *Silence*. Then Crystal worked into his musical opening number a humorous line about Lecter's taste for "bouillabaisse of cheeks and necks and arms." Unable to resist Crystal's lead, many of the celebrities also made affectionate jokes from the stage about cannibalism, surely one of the most macabre running jokes in the history of the Academy.

In between jokes, the awards began to pile up. When all was said and done, *Silence* won Best Picture, Best Director (Jonathan Demme), Best Adapted Screenplay (Ted Tally), Best Actress (Jodie Foster), and Best Actor. It was the first film to sweep all five major award categories since *One Flew over the Cuckoo's Nest* did so in 1975, and no film has done so since. While *Silence*'s success is due to the talent of many individuals, there is little doubt Hopkins's portrayal of Lecter stole the movie, endeared the character to a vast audience, and ensured the Academy win that gave the film its stamp of mainstream cultural approval.

Serial Killer Popularity Skyrockets

Audiences clamored for more. So, after that . . . nothing. For 10 more years, people waited for Thomas Harris to take his serial-killer saga further, so that a sequel with Lecter and Starling could be filmed. In the void left by Harris's ongoing silence, scores of serial-killer/profiler crime melodramas proliferated in bookstores, most notably in the series of novels penned by Patricia Cornwell. Serial killers trolled for victims across the small screen in series such as *The X-Files* (1993–2002) and the big screen in films such as Oliver Stone's *Natural Born Killers* (1994), Jon Amiel's *Copycat* (1995), and David Fincher's *Seven* (1995). Each entry further diluted the freshness and resonance of Harris's approach to the material.

In the endless self-referential loop of modern popular culture, Lecter was parodied repeatedly in movies and television shows. Just to give one example, F. Murray Abraham played a Lecter-esque character named Harold Leacher in *National Lampoon's Loaded Weapon* (dir. Gene Quintano, 1993). Demme's film even inspired an award-winning off-Broadway musical called *Silence!* (1992), featuring nine different songs (music and lyrics by Jon and Al Kaplan), in which Lecter sings lines such as "Don't get cute/Else we're done/I can make you eat your tongue" to Starling.[8] When Harris did publish the controversial follow-up novel, *Hannibal*, Hopkins agreed to reprise his most famous role for the screen adaptation, even if the other important figures (star Jodie Foster and director Jonathan Demme in particular) from *Silence* declined to participate.

The Lecter in the film *Hannibal* shares the same mannerisms beloved by audiences in *Silence*. He hisses, smiles, winks, and puns his way through the part, as he did before. But he's different, too. Physically, he is older and heavier. Harris's "imperially slim" doctor would never let himself go like this. In spite of this middle-age bloat, the escape from confinement has served the screen Lecter well. Now free to indulge his expensive tastes and pursue his intellectual interests in the cultural heart of Europe, he has a certain joyful gleam in his eye. Far removed from the wild-eyed madman we see in a brief flashback to a scene in the asylum, he is the definition of cosmopolitan urbanity. Dispatching would-be assassins with savage glee and facing death by torture with an eerie sanguinity, Lecter is a man at peace with himself.

Yet he is driven to risk all of this in order to win Starling's heart, if he can. For his love of her, he crosses half the world and risks the vengeance of Verger. He offers her up her chief professional nemesis, Paul Krendler, as the main course in a gourmet meal. Unlike the novel, Starling does not partake. In fact, in a new ending endorsed by Harris, Starling rejects Lecter rather decisively by handcuffing him to her as the police are closing in. Forced to choose between cutting off his lady's hand or his own to escape, Lecter sacrifices his own and flees the country, this time to Asia. Although Hopkins drew some criticism from those who saw his performance as campy and overblown, the larger-than-life portrayal fits a character who revels in his freedom but risks it all for the love of a woman.

Since *Hannibal* scored a bonanza at the box office and *Manhunter* had done so poorly years before, it was inevitable that producer Dino de Laurentiis would greenlight a remake of *Red Dragon*. So Hopkins eagerly slicked his hair back and toned up a bit for his next outing as the good doctor in director Bret Ratner's "reimagining" of Harris's second novel. This time out, in a bit of visual incongruity best glossed over by faith, Hopkins plays Lecter several years before the events of *Silence*. Critics complained that producer de Laurentiis was trying to bury the memory of Mann's film through this remake and milk a few more dollars from the franchise. Be that as it may, Hopkins's portrayal this time dispenses somewhat with the over-the-top camp of *Hannibal* to return the character to his brutal roots.

In a precredit sequence, Hopkins portrays Lecter, at the height of his serial-killer career in Baltimore in 1980, nearly gutting Graham when the FBI agent comes calling late one night for help on a profile the two are working on. Lecter slashes Graham with shocking unexpectedness, the memory of which haunts every scene between the two of them later in the asylum. We particularly feel Graham's anticipation of another attack when he meets Lecter in the exercise yard. Lecter is tethered to a chain that prevents him from reaching Graham, but that doesn't stop Lecter from lunging at him to underscore a point he is making about the power of fear.

Hopkins makes the most of his few scenes, no doubt knowing this is probably the last time he will play the role. It's fitting, perhaps, that *Red Dragon* ends literally moments before the events of *Silence* begin. Lecter hears from his jailhouse tormentor, Dr. Chilton, that a pretty young FBI agent has come to interview him. Lecter considers this for a moment, seems on the verge of freezing Chilton out, and then almost in spite of himself asks, "What's her name?" At that moment,

12 years after he donned the institutional blue jumpsuit for the role, Hopkins has literally brought the character he enshrined forever in pop-culture mythology to full circle.

The other two actors who portray Lecter, Aaran Thomas and Gaspard Ulliel, have a thankless job to do in the prequel, *Hannibal Rising*. Thomas's sole function is to show us boyhood innocence before the fall, while Ulliel works hard to convince he is the teenage incarnation of the man we've seen in the other films. The perceived failure of both to do so, at least in the eyes of most critics, has little to do with their thespian skills. It has a lot to do with the material itself. Harris's source novel has a desultory, by-the-numbers air to it, obviously rushed in its composition for reasons far too potentially litigious to speculate on here. The screenplay adaptation Harris writes (marking the first time he has officially crossed over into playing an active role for one of the Lecter films) fares little better.

But there's an even bigger problem than the quality of writing. The Lecter we see here, no matter how skillfully performed by Ulliel, seems to have almost nothing to do with the character in the other films. On the most superficial level, this Lecter doesn't look anything like the older one, though Ulliel does credibly enough mimicking some of his most recognizable mannerisms (the wink, for example). More problematically, the events happening to this Lecter do not seem at all likely to result in the man we see in *Manhunter/Red Dragon, Silence,* and *Hannibal.* Other than the obvious cannibalism template created by the trauma of watching his sister killed and eaten by starving Lithuanian militiamen on the Eastern front in World War II, this Lecter engages in an all-too-familiar vendetta to kill those who victimized his family. He has none of the hallmarks of the kind of psychopathology we might expect in a boy who grows up to be a serial killer. Where's the bed-wetting? The fire starting? The cruelty to animals? Rather, we are asked to believe a single childhood trauma, combined with the brutal privations of wartime Europe, did the damage to Lecter's soul.

This Lecter is a killer, but is he a serial killer as we understand the term? Why would he continue to kill once the last of the men who ate his sister is dead? Perhaps his wartime suffering unleashed a monster that already existed within. Or maybe we just want to believe that no matter how much Lecter is explained away in terms of past history, he still defies any kind of cookie-cutter psychological explanations. Maybe we want to believe his evil is metaphysical in origin, that he consciously embraced evil for evil's sake, and not because genetics and environment made him so against his will.

In the final analysis, one of the most frightening aspects of Lecter, both in the novels and the movies, is his civilized veneer. Though there are those who come to know his evil well, especially the policemen and the women who pursue his secrets, they are struck by the stark contradiction between the considerable charms of the man and the depravity of the monster living within him. He is an evil paradox, a man/monster moving through the highest strata of society before his incarceration, with no one being the wiser to his murders. Before he is captured, his evil is hidden. He masquerades as a respected professional and a member of high society, an eligible bachelor and man about town who knows just when to give a card and when to give a gift. No one can see the monster.

When Lecter is captured and his mask is removed, he is free to be himself. His only real fear in captivity is boredom, so he retreats into his head for years at a time and emerges only when someone entertains him. Yet even unmasked for the monster he is, he looks the same. His monstrosity and his humanity exist behind the same features that fooled everyone for so long. His acts titillate, even inspire, the countless others who can only dream of doing what he has done and the deadly few who attempt to emulate him. In monstrosity, he achieves a transcendent superstardom that a mere Dr. Hannibal Lecter, M.D., would never have achieved.

Lecter boasts instant name recognition by millions of Americans. Though foreign born, he *is* American in spirit because he speaks to one of our grandest, most cherished national narratives. He is the European immigrant who comes to America, the land of opportunity, to succeed in his chosen trade—which happens to be murder. This national grand narrative is cited as an argument for American exceptionality by every person running for president of the United States. Now, it would be absurd to maintain that Lecter himself could ever run for president of the United States. (After all, he was born in Lithuania.) But in that his story reflects the disquieting marriage between westward expansion and violence that has characterized the American historical experience—Lecter *is* America.

Notes

1. David Schmid, *Natural Born Celebrities: Serial Killers in American Culture* (Chicago: University of Chicago Press, 2005), 6.

2. Robert Ressler and Tom Shachtman, *Whoever Fights Monsters* (New York: St. Martin's, 1993), 33.

3. David Sexton writes: "In truth, the Hannibal Lecter stories have about the same connection to social reality as, say, the stories of Bluebeard or Dracula. Like those stories, they still have, of course, an acute psychological reality." *The Strange World of Thomas Harris* (London: Short Books, 2001), 82.

4. Daniel O'Brien writes that "Lecter plays on common fears and suspicions of psychiatry—the probing and manipulation of the human mind which, normally based on trust, provokes terror when used for ruthless, systematic abuse." *The Hannibal Files* (London: Reynolds and Hearn, 2001), 8.

5. Linda J. Holland-Toll, *As American as Mom, Baseball, and Apple Pie: Constructing Community in Contemporary American Horror Fiction* (Bowling Green, OH: Bowling Green State University Popular Press, 2001), 68.

6. *Strange World*, 88.

7. To cite only one example among many, the American Film Institute in 2003 unveiled its list of the 100 greatest screen heroes and villains. Topping the "villains" list was, of course, Dr. Hannibal Lecter. Clarice Starling made the "heroes" list at position #6. The film itself made AFI's list of the 100 greatest movies at #65 in 1998.

8. The songs are available online at http://www.jonandal.com/silence .html.

CHAPTER 8

"Oh, Hi Humanity!": A Kaleidoscopic Account of Life in *The Room*

Daniel Harmon

Art is the most intense mode of individualism that the world has ever known.[1]

—Oscar Wilde

Anytime I see something screech across a room and latch onto someone's neck, and the guy screams and tries to get it off, I have to laugh, because what is that thing?[2]

—Jack Handey

Introduction

For several months last year, I was stalked by a minor celebrity.

It started at a dinner party, when a friend approached me with a DVD case in her hand. The cover consisted of a black-and-white portrait of one Tommy Wiseau and two words: *The Room*. Wiseau's expression was menacing. My friend's expression was giddy. "This is it!" she said. "This is what I was telling you about!"

For the next half an hour, I attended to this friend—let's call her Claudette—as she tried to tell me exactly what it was she had previously been telling me about. The subsequent monologue represented a sort of immersion into the culture of *The Room*, and it was a thoroughly irritating experience.

"It's horrible," Claudette said (among other things), "but there's a kind of genius in it. It will change your life! Thank me later. Thank

me now. Don't watch it alone; you'll hate it. . . . It's actually pretty boring, in a way. Let's watch it now. Let's buy tickets . . . 'Oh hi Mark' . . .
He's a genius . . . 'Lisa you are tearing me apart!'"

Finally I gave up, grabbed the box, and read through the copy on
the back. When I looked up again, Claudette was still in the throes of
her impressionistic explanation: "No, no, it's unique! Totally unique!"
I was confused.

Between Claudette's grand claims and convoluted exclamations,
I had gathered certain words and phrases—*a billboard . . . tuxes . . .
seven million dollars . . . soft-core . . . scotchka . . . football . . . spoons*—but
I couldn't at all distinguish between what was supposed to be in the
movie and what was supposed to be background information. In fact,
that distinction didn't seem to matter overmuch; meanwhile, whenever
I asked a straightforward question, I received contradictions ("It's a
perfect failure; it's *the* perfect failure") or strangely absurd analogies
in reply.

At one point Claudette, offered the following as a means of clarifi-
cation: "It's like if an alien came to Earth and opened up a diner, and
all the alien diner owner wanted to do was make you, his first cus-
tomer, the perfect hot dog. But when he serves you the hot dog, he
brings you an actual (yapping) dog; and *then, then* the guy just pours
some water into your coffee when you say you didn't want it black,
and then when you leave he asks 'Was it good!?' . . . and even though
you can't tell whether he's talking about the dog or the pet, you know
he means the question seriously! That's *The Room!*"

Eventually, after several other friends delivered similarly mystifying
speeches about the life-changing power of *The Room*, I gave up and
decided that where animate beings generated so much confusion, an
inanimate object might be more reliable. Thus, instead of trying to follow their testimony any longer, I began to use a sort of proxy to at
least keep my bearings in these hysterical conversations: I began to
use that face (that *face!*) as a stand-in for whatever it was I was supposed to understand. When people said *The Room*, I imagined Tommy
Wiseau's face on the DVD case; and, as a result, that was the face that
haunted me—cornering me at parties, e-mailing me at work, and generally bullying and importuning me—for the next eight weeks, until
I finally saw the movie myself, and of course became converted.

My intention here is to provide an account of *The Room* that can
benefit both the initiates and the uninitiated alike. However—for reasons that I'll attempt to outline in the next section—there are many
aspects of the movie that are paradoxical, and many aspects of the

way we experience the movie that border on the ineffable. As a result, I've tried to address each of the many elements that, together, have made *The Room* a cult success: the movie itself; its birth and burgeoning visibility in Los Angeles; the cult experience; Tommy Wiseau; and *The Room*'s second life on YouTube and in other media. Wherever a strict, objective history isn't possible, I've decided to speak of my own experience, because the audience for *The Room* is constituted entirely of individuals (in a way that audiences for summer blockbusters are not) and, as Tommy Wiseau has put it: "The Room was done intentionally to provoke the audience . . . But what is your next question?"[3]

So . . . What Is That Thing?

In Susan Sontag's landmark essay on the nature of camp, she adopted an aphoristic style because, in her words, "one must be tentative and nimble" in order to "snare a sensibility in words, especially one that is alive and powerful."[4] *The Room* is possessed of many of the traits that Sontag attributes to camp (including sincerity, failed seriousness, and "awfulness"), but Sontag's definition of a sensibility—as opposed to an idea—is even more important here. For whether we define *The Room* as a camp phenomenon or a cult phenomenon or both, we have to admit that those who revel in it do share a sensibility; they share something that cannot "be crammed in to the mold of a system, or handled with the rough tools of proof." Like great art and good jokes, a sensibility cannot be taken apart and reconstructed without losing its essential spirit.

Similarly, any attempt to circumscribe or define *The Room* will necessarily miss the point. Or, to put it another way, talking about *The Room* is like dancing the salsa with a dog: you can do it, but no matter how accomplished your movements may be, the dog will always look more natural than you do alongside it, dancing with a dog.

One way to avoid embarrassment would be to direct my comments exclusively to those who have already seen the film. In that way, I would avoid having to paraphrase something that, in its particulars as well as in its overall effect, seems to evade all analogies and explanations. But *The Room* is broadly relevant, and it would be a shame to abandon readers interested in Z-movies, self-exposure, American comedy, or even cult economics simply for fear of looking silly. (Also, nothing could be further from the spirit of Tommy Wiseau.) As a result, I shall try to speak plain truths about a plain movie, so that even those who haven't seen the film can ask with those of us who have: "How did this begin? Where will it end?" and of course, "What is going on?"

Let us go then, you and I. Let us dance with the dog.

I should begin by saying what the movie is not: *The Room* is not about a room. There are rooms, but none are held in special focus (focus is, in general, a problem), and spoons appear to play a larger thematic role in the course of the film. The title has no relevance. *The Room* was also not shot in single format or in a consistent style: some scenes are shot in 35 mm, others with a high-definition digital camera. And although the movie has clearly been shot in Los Angeles, the setting is San Francisco (as framing shots of the Golden Gate Bridge and the iconic painted ladies of *Full House* consistently inform the audience).

Most of the scenes—which vary in terms of genre from melodrama to slapstick to soft-core pornography, tragedy, and romance—center around the characters of Johnny, his fiancée Lisa, and his "best friend" (one of several oft-repeated phrases) Mark. These three also constitute a bizarre love triangle, which occasionally morphs into a rhombus through the intrusions of Johnny's young protégé, Denny. Every element of the movie appears to have been intended as "realistic," but the overall effect is . . . not.

The male characters repeatedly taunt one another with cries of "Chicken!" and "Cheep cheep, cheep cheep!" Characters suddenly disappear; several plotlines are abruptly dropped; a bitter strain of misogyny rises up between tender scenes of lovemaking (supplemented with R&B jams and rose petals) and impish moments of happiness (signified by rough-housing and sexual hijinks); almost every new conversation begins with an explicit greeting ("Oh, hi, Mark," "Hey, Johnny," "Hi, Lisa," etc.); and despite the domestic nature of the film as a whole, green-screen technology and dubbing are not at all uncommon. The plot, meanwhile, is shockingly trite and straightforward. It runs roughly as follows.

Despite an early glimpse into their apparently happy domestic life and a love scene in which both participants seem fully committed to each other, Lisa (Johnny's "future wife") is bored with Johnny. Thus, in an act that is as much about hurting Johnny as it is about her own desires, Lisa seduces Johnny's best friend, Mark, and the affair continues despite Mark's apparent reluctance and Lisa's own engagement. As this confusing dynamic endures, Lisa becomes increasingly egotistical and ever more determined to retain Mark's affection along with the security that Johnny provides through his very ambiguous work at a very ambiguous "bank." To some friends, Lisa alleges that Johnny has hit her, while to others she, remains adamant about Johnny's virtues.

As Lisa and Johnny's relationship deteriorates, several other sub-plots receive varying levels of attention. Denny has a run-in with an apparently dangerous drug dealer on Johnny's roof, Lisa's mother Claudette develops breast cancer and battles family members for control of shared property, and Lisa's friend Michelle gets caught having sex with her boyfriend Mike inside Johnny's apartment.

After these asides, the main plot resumes with a surprise birthday party for Johnny. There, Lisa's destructive behavior continues as she, in short order, is caught making out with Mark, announces (falsely) that she's pregnant, confesses her lie to Michelle and one "Steven" (a character who before this scene was never discussed nor seen), and provokes a blow-out fight between Mark and Johnny.

After the party, Johnny locks himself in his bathroom, and Lisa calls Mark to announce her intentions to drop Johnny and move out. Unfortunately, Johnny has recorded the phone call, and after hearing the truth, he destroys his apartment and shoots himself in the head. When faced with the body, Mark and Denny denounce Lisa for her role in the suicide, but all three stay with the body as ambulance sirens move in.

Although things change quickly in the course of *The Room*, viewers can rely, at least in the short term, on what the characters tell us. More generally, it could even be said that, in the context of the film itself, saying it makes it so: Lisa, in addition to being Johnny's future wife, is repeatedly referred to as "beautiful"—and therefore she is; Johnny is adamant that Mark is his "best friend"—and therefore he is; and Johnny (as we are informed in one choice scene) saved his bank "bundles," has lots of friends, and doesn't drink—and therefore it must be so (until the scotchka arrives, at least). But that level of candor belies the movie's enduring strangeness.

Although Tommy Wiseau may see Lisa as beautiful and although he may envision Mark as Tommy's best friend, the audience's understanding doesn't have to end there. Those descriptions amount to artistic propaganda. The leap from broad outlines to more specific meaning, from portrayal to poignancy, is the substance out of which most narrative art is formed. And while art may be profoundly lacking in *The Room* itself, something like it is provided in the strange dynamic that subsists among the movie, the audience, and the strange middle term that is Tommy Wiseau.

To understand this art, you have to turn to the movie's high priests: the community, the audience, the fans . . .

The Initiation Process

The Room, like any number of actual cults, requires that its adherents undergo a standard rite of initiation before it grants them access to its spiritual community, and it's worth orienting ourselves along that spectrum of understanding before we go any further.

There are generally three distinct stages to this education, and despite the preceding section, none of those stages traditionally involves an explicit account of the movie's plot—not because plot summaries are unavailable, but because, again, they add so little to an understanding of the film.

The first stage is thus one of almost total ignorance. If you have not seen the film, you too are presumably still rooted in this place, and I, in the role of friend, apologize for this (and for having subjected you to a summary). The more one hears about *The Room*, the less one knows, until the second stage, which begins when you, as the aspirant, throw up your hands and say: "How were *you* ever convinced to go in the first place?"

Only the poorest of evangelists will fail to provide the obvious answer to this question. For whether it was the spoons or the scotchka or the footballs or the tuxedoes, or the tuxedo-tees, if someone is telling you that you have to see *The Room*, then that person has surely participated in a screening at some point. And however difficult it may be to say what *The Room* really is[5], it is fairly easy to explain what it's like to participate in a screening.

Placing myself once more in the role of friend, I can tell you that after having read through the literature[6] in the course of Stage 2, I had learned that any screening was going to be loud, absurd, and possibly funny. People would dress up, scream, throw things, sing, quote, chant, and dance. This was not necessarily my idea of a good time (more on that later), but it was worthwhile to know that everyone who attended the screening at least expected to have a great time. So it was definitive: despite its foreboding title and the foreboding cover art, *The Room* was not a horror movie.

Once I understood how I was supposed to react, I felt much more comfortable about the whole idea. The movie was beginning to lose some of its mysterious aura, and I found myself proportionately less unnerved by Tommy Wiseau's face. When my discomfort was sufficiently reduced, I was even able to buy a ticket and thus move on to Stage 3 in my own personal education, wherein, almost simultaneously, I saw the movie, knew it, and began to convert others. (NB: I was also hit by spoons.)

If you've been to a screening, then you know about the spoons, the games of catch, the tuxes, the scotchka, "Hi Denny," and when it's appropriate to break into the *Full House* theme or bellow "focus/unfocus!" and "Go! Go! Go! Go!" (You also know that, unlike with other similar camp events, none of these acts was prescribed by the film itself.) If you haven't been to a screening, you should know that it all ends in a purity of elation that it is hard to overestimate.

Although everyone experiences *The Room* as a sort of personal revelation, that experience is only possible collectively. The revelation of strangeness doesn't happen without the audience's collective insistence that the strangeness is enduring and, in a way, meaningful. And that same necessity for the shared experience, for a single, unified point of revelation, also ensures that no one's experience of *The Room* is really that unique.

I've never been very excited by the idea of audience involvement. I prefer to watch movies alone, in some fair degree of darkness. It bothers me when anything distracts me from what I'm watching. Also, on a related note, most of the movies that provoke audience involvement—*Rocky Horror Picture Show*; the *Buffy the Vampire Slayer* sing-along episode; *The Sound of Music*—have a strong camp element that sends me, for one, hurtling back to the horrifying alternate universe that was *Pee-Wee's Playhouse* circa 1988. As a child, I would avoid all of the cartoons after 11:30 for fear of accidentally stumbling into Pee-Wee's antic asylum, and as an adult I still compulsively avoid anything that connotes Pee-Wee and his playhouse of terrors.

Nevertheless, at the end of my first screening, I was of course completely seduced. After that, I was the one insisting that *The Room* was perfect, was beyond speech, beyond sense—that no matter how confused I sounded, I was right, and the movie was amazing, and you had to go see it. In the end, I reduced my endorsement to two brief sentences: "Trust me. Just go." And whether one takes it on faith or probes deeper with articles, essays, testimonies, and YouTube clips, eventually everyone has to go to the theater. You just have to be there.

This third state, the point of nirvana, communion, rapture, and chaos, is an enduring state; and escape, if it is possible, only arrives intermittently (as, for example, in an extended written analysis of the situation).

Although these three stages may of course vary in their particulars, the fact that everyone has to overcome the same set of obstacles lays the groundwork for an especially devoted sort of community—the sort of community that we call identify as "cult." And although every

cult relies upon a strong sense of connection between each of its individual members and the given art object, it's also true that, over time,
all of the members in a given cult also come to share a single history,
and over time, that shared origin story also comes, in turn, to inform
the identity of its members.

An Armchair History of *The Room*

My experience of *The Room*—begun in confusion, concluded in elation (and sponsored throughout by the opaque portrait of Tommy
Wiseau)—was telling, but it was certainly not unique. From the time
of *The Room's* release in 2003 until the fall of 2008, an enormous, solitary billboard advertised the film to commuters on the Los Angeles
highway. Like the DVD case, the billboard contained the film's title
in blocky, shadowed type, along with the glaring face of Tommy
Wiseau[7]—the film's writer, director, producer, and star. Other promotional items claimed that it was "a film with the passion of Tennessee
Williams," but the billboard offered no further information or clues.
(It did, however, include the number for an RSVP line.) Thus, after
the film's short-lived run at two Laemmle theaters and a profoundly
negative *Variety* review, the people of Los Angeles weren't very likely
to encounter the film anywhere else.

The initial release had generated only a handful of reviews[8] (all negative) and less than $2,000 in revenue, but some of the curious early
viewers had, after some initial shock, fallen in love with it. One early
adopter, Michael Rousselet, claimed that at the final showing, he had
convinced another 100 people to attend. For the rest of Los Angeles,
however, *The Room* was just a billboard, and the billboard itself was
just a face.

From *The Great Gatsby* to Wall Drug, roadside billboards are a fix-
ture in American art and culture, and the lunar landscape of Tommy
Wiseau's face holds its own in this tradition. The billboard was out-
sized and seemed to speak of money and promise, but the movie, if it
was a movie (was it a brand? was it art? was it a joke?), remained
almost completely unknown. Unlike most billboard advertisements,
which stand like turrets within a larger edifice (which is itself a small
part of a larger campaign), this seemed more like the banner of a lone
soldier fighting in an endless, hopeless crusade.

It is very difficult to describe *The Room* without resorting to solip-
sisms or a kind of impressionistic chaos. These impressions (of seriousness and comedy; of transparency and opacity; of normalcy and

peculiarity) are as strong as they are contradictory, and so the question always remains: "what is that thing?"

This question also provides a quick and easy explanation of the movie's cult success. There was no watershed moment. People saw the billboard and they asked "what is that thing?" Then some of those people saw the movie and they asked their friends "what was that thing?" Then some comedians and performers—including Patton Oswalt, Kristen Bell, David Cross (and several other members of the *Arrested Development* team), Paul Rudd, and Tim Heidecker and Eric Wareheim (of *Tim and Eric Awesome Show, Great Job!* fame)—saw it and turned around and asked their audiences "what was that thing?" and then it started all over again.

Almost all of the truly iconic cult movies have a personality at their core who seems to transcend the film itself. The Dude's manner of being informs contemporary philosophy texts; Captain James T. Kirk is still working today, selling discounted flights and hotel rates; and David Carradine and Susan Sarandon have, with varying success, fought to maintain a professional identity apart from their roles in such hallowed films as *Kung Fu* and *Rocky Horror Picture Show*, respectively.

When commuters saw that billboard, they saw Tommy Wiseau; when I first encountered *The Room*, I encountered Tommy Wiseau; and when people talk about *The Room*, they talk about Tommy Wiseau. The identity between Wiseau's movie and his personality is one of the primary reasons people find *The Room* so compelling and why they have such a hard time describing it to people who haven't already experienced it themselves.

Tommy and Johnny

Little is known about Tommy Wiseau's past or point of origin, and the same can be said for his movie. Funding for the film exceeded $6 million, but his hint about the import and sale of leather jackets from Korea remains the most substantial piece of information about the source of those funds. As for Wiseau himself, his most personal revelation in last year's *Harper's* essay confirmed only a past marriage and some time spent in San Francisco. His age varies according to the article and the source. His native country remains unknown. "I speak French . . . another language, and English," he told Tom Bissell. In that same interview, he refused to provide the names of friends for background information and declined to say whether he had ever been in contact with any of his celebrity admirers.

Despite this veil of mystery, there has never been any doubt about Wiseau's authenticity—which is strange considering the fairly cynical reactions of late to Joaquin Phoenix's rap career or Charlie Sheen's meltdown. It's fair to say that wherever the schadenfreude seems too good to be true, we expect the worst—or, rather, we expect that we received the worst because it was exactly what we wanted.

The sense of doubt and uncertainty that Joaquin Phoenix engendered through his Letterman appearances and YouTube concert clips provoked conversation and stoked interest in his film; and Charlie Sheen has, at the point of writing, compelled American attention not only through his incredible hubris but also because everyone is wondering how much of the current Sheen is the result of drugs, how much stems from a mental imbalance, and how much is simply a put-on.

That sense of doubt and uncertainty is exactly what this sort of performance art usually thrives upon. In Wiseau's case, however, even a casual first viewing of the film (if such a thing exists) is sufficient proof of the film's seriousness. It turns out, then, that just as there is something compelling in the tension between contrivance and authenticity, there is also something cathartic in the release of this same tension, in diving wholeheartedly into an almost miraculous earnestness. There's something about the experience that I am even tempted to call "pure."

Wiseau's embargo against any factual accounting of his own life has been surprisingly successful; but it has also been fundamentally undermined by his character in the film: Johnny. In the movie's last scene, Denny even mourns his mentor and friend as "Tommy!" Wiseau has created a dream version of himself, and one of the reasons this iteration remains so compelling (despite repeated viewings) is because, as the product of other people's views, he has no real substance. There is no getting to the bottom of Johnny.

His core characteristics in the film aren't even characteristics so much as adjectives: Johnny is admired; he is good; he is well liked, and, in the end, he is of course betrayed. Betrayed, but also betraying, for while Johnny remains profoundly vague as a character, he simultaneously provides endless insights into the psyche of Tommy Wiseau. We are certain that Tommy feels undervalued and remains bitter about an apparent betrayal; his self-confidence is unflappable, although it can be punctured; he strives to be a typical American; hot chocolate is his signature drink; he is somewhat paranoid in his outlook and defensive in his bearing; he has a strong moral sense; he wants to be admired by men and loved by women; he is very concerned about how others view him.

As a supplement to these impressions (which have been served up to Wiseau for comment in various interviews), we also have Wiseau's own reflections: "You're right on the money. I don't know if it's my signature drink, because I have other drinks, but I like hot chocolate." "People don't realize that actually girls do more harm than guys. By my take, of course." "I always encourage people to see [The Room] several times, so they can grasp, maybe, what is behind it."[9] "Next question!"[10] "I am thirty-something."[11] And, of course, the ultimate goal: "I want 90% of Americans to see The Room."[12]

Tommy Wiseau may not want to talk about Tommy Wiseau, but Johnny certainly does, and both characters become more vivid as a result of this conversation. Ultimately, however, there is very little interest in uncovering the truth behind Wiseau Films and its highest-grossing project. When Wiseau speaks, he certainly affects our overall perception of Johnny, but nothing Wiseau says can put an end to our interest in Johnny (or in Tommy). The mystery abides.

The Room's Second Life

Tommy/Johnny's level of transparency is something almost without precedent in American culture (the closest analogies, from Kanye West to Tao Lin, are all contemporary)—but it takes more than transparency to make something understandable. The raw materials that Wiseau has provided are startling and precious, but they are also scattered wildly about, and it has been left to the audience to piece them all together. The results to date have included, among other things: a Flash video game; a Patton Oswalt parody; an April 1 screening on Adult Swim; and innumerable YouTube remixes and mashups. I don't think it's an exaggeration to say that almost all of these developments offer new insights into The Room's meaning and impact (in part because The Room's meaning is so directly tied to the audience's experience of it), but there are two instances in particular that I'd like to focus on here—one on behalf of those who have already seen the film and one for those who haven't.

For the novices, there is no better two-minute introduction to the film than the "oh, hi" montage[13]—a collection of every stock greeting that occurs in the course of the film. Although each superfluous introduction is comic in its own right, no amount of exaggeration can capture how surreal the sheer mass of hellos really is. This is an endless, rapid-fire experience of everything that is uncanny about the movie. Nothing could be more prosaic than a hello, and yet, in The Room's hand, nothing could be more alien. There are other individual scenes (including the flower shop scene, the rooftop scene, and the coffee shop scene) that give a similarly eerie sense, but only a montage can provide a clear idea of *The Room*'s thoroughgoing weirdness.

For the initiates, however, an even more profound pleasure is in store. In 2007, Brandon Hardesty[14] began reenacting scenes from various movies and posting the results to YouTube. The videos are generally impressive due to Hardesty's precise imitations, but nothing else in his oeuvre quite attains the heights that he achieved with his reenactment of *The Room*'s cult climax[15], when Johnny exclaims "You are tearing me *apart*, Lisa!" To see Hardesty so exactly replicate Johnny's voice and intonation (in his living room, opposite himself as an equally well-rendered Lisa) is at once to be torn away from *The Room*'s crazy logic and thrust right back into it. In a strange way, it offers a means of accepting that *The Room* really exists—that it really happened.

Every vocal stress and tic is perfectly recreated, but there is little attempt to mimic the overall appearance of the scene or the characters. Hardesty wears a red t-shirt as Lisa and a ridiculous wig as Johnny, but it's hard to say which experience is truly stranger: the one that is intended as comedy, or the one that isn't. In his interview with the A.V. Club, Wiseau alleged that his film was designed to provoke people and, in some cases (as in the sex scenes), to make them uncomfortable. Even if this argument arose to counter the audience's response, I think he may still have a point. The Hardesty scene is easier to laugh at, but what's funny isn't Hardesty exactly; it's the fact that there was an original scene to imitate in the first place.

In "Notes on 'Camp,'" Sontag writes: "Camp sees everything in quotation marks. It's not a lamp, but a 'lamp'; not a woman, but a 'woman.' To perceive Camp in objects and persons is to understand Being-as-Playing-a-Role."[16] The strain that *The Room* evinces through its "realism" raises everything in the film to the level of performance despite all of the individual failures to perform. We know we're supposed to be seeing a dramatic scene here, but what we have isn't even "drama." (It is not a "spoon," but a "[throws a plastic spoon] SPOON!") Reality is constantly strived for but never achieved. By placing Wiseau's entire scene in quotation marks, Hardesty manages to show how far away Wiseau's film is from anything that we could identify as an actual "source."

That being said, nothing comes of nothing, and therefore we have to ask again: "what is this thing?"

Metaphors and Bogus Trends

As a rule, cult phenomena have to burn out in relative obscurity (and even ignominy) before they can rise from the ashes and learn to thrive in a new age or with a new audience or in a new format. Thus, without a technological advancement or a technical loophole in copyright laws, many of our most revered cult hits would have remained admirable failures, remembered fondly by a few but completely forgotten by everyone else. In order to return to the market, there has to be some kind of renewed potential for profits, and from *It's a Wonderful Life* to *El Topo* to *Family Guy*, American's cult successes have all managed to cash in on this potential.

In this context, *The Room* appears to be more of a vanity project than a cult hit. As noted above, the film cost some $6 million to make—and that was before accounting for any of the publicity costs (including the iconic Los Angeles billboard, which at roughly $3,000 to $5,000 per month could probably have run up to $250,000). The film took in $1,900 during its first run, and although it has of course garnered tremendous support over the past seven years, it remains a once-a-week affair at best, and the financial arrangements of these screenings often involve some outlay on Wiseau's part as well.

The profits would then seem to be of the spiritual rather than the financial variety, or, as Wiseau has put it, "as long as [audiences] laugh or enjoy themselves, I enjoy with them . . . I wish I could attend all the screening in the world."[17]

In spirit, he does. Tommy Wiseau cannot be extracted from *The Room*. His is the face on the billboard; his dreams and his pretensions inform the script at every point; and when people describe the movie as strange, hilarious, profound, misguided, erratic, revelatory, or life-changing, they are of course talking about Tommy Wiseau as well.

The identities are so immediate, and Wiseau's own character appears to be so singularly pure, that it's hard not to view Wiseau as a kind of walking metaphor; but in order to keep *The Room*'s core personality alive and vital before us—in order to keep from corrupting the sensibility that binds his cult together—we have to fight against the impulse to say that Tommy Wiseau *means* this, or *is* that. He has to remain "fugitive."[18]

We are *not* all Tommy Wiseau (although at times, especially in adolescence, we certainly are). Neither is Tommy Wiseau an especially *novel* type of celebrity. He achieved his fame through a kind of negative revelry, but he joins a long list of celebrities (including Henry James and D. W. Griffith) whose ambition outstripped their ability at some point; and although it may be true that Wiseau is *only* famous for his failure, fame has certainly been had for less—and for worse.

Let us heed the warnings: can we really extract messages for a digital age from a movie that also employs 35 mm and that relies for its plot twists upon an answering machine?

If we love the movie, at some point we have to stop asking questions, lest we accidentally contrive some sort of an answer and denature the project entirely. Tommy Wiseau is compelling and unique and strange, and there *is* something coherent in the force of his ambition and personality; but in order to retain that unified sense—in order to maintain the well of hysteria into which we hope to plunge again—we have to allow the movie and the man to speak to us, the audience. Let us listen, then, to Tommy, to Johnny, and to *The Room* itself, when they tell us: "Love is blind" . . . and also when they say "Oh, hi, doggie."

Notes

1. Oscar Wilde, *De Profundis, and Other Writings* (Penguin, 1954), 34.

2. Jack Handey, *What I'd Say to the Martians: And Other Veiled Threats* (Hyperion, 2008), 36.

3. Elina Shatkin, "LAist Interviews Tommy Wiseau, The Face Behind The Billboard," *The LAist,* http://laist.com/2007/04/27/laist_interviews _tommy_wiseau_the_face_behind_the_billboard.php, April 27, 2007.

4. Susan Sontag, "Notes on 'camp,'" in *The Cult Film Reader,* ed. Ernest Mathijs and Xavier Mendik (Berkshire: Open University Press, 2007), 42.

5. The best overall history and description of the film is provided in Tom Bissell's piece for the August 2010 issue of *Harper's Magazine.*

6. I would recommend checking out the A.V. club's "Viewer's Guide to *The Room,*" available at http://www.avclub.com/articles/a-viewers-guide-to-the -room,25721/.

7. Wiseau referred to the image on the billboard as the "Evil Man" option in his interview with the A.V. Club.

8. Scott Foundas, "The Room," *Variety,* http://www.variety.com/review/ VE1117921325/, July, 18, 2003

9. Elina Shatkin, "LAist Interviews Tommy Wiseau, The Face Behind The Billboard," *The LAist,* http://laist.com/2007/04/27/laist_interviews _ tommy_wiseau_the_face_behind_the_billboard.php, April 27, 2007.

10. Kate Ward, "The Room: On the Scene at the Sold-Out Ziegfeld Theatre Screening of Tommy Wiseau's Masterpiece," *PopWatch,* http://popwatch .ew.com/2010/05/01/the-room-ziegfeld-on-the-scene/ May 1, 2010.

11. Tom Bissell, "Cinema crudité: The mysterious appeal of the post-camp cult film," *Harper's,* August, 2010, 63.

12. Tom Bissell, "Cinema crudité: The mysterious appeal of the post-camp cult film," *Harper's*, August, 2010, 65.

13. Oh, hi "The Room," http://www.youtube.com/watch?v=Cci3U5pv QkI (accessed March 28, 2011).

14. April Witt, "Going Viral: Brandon Hardesty discovered that in the age of YouTube, if you can make it in the family rec room, you can make it anywhere," *The Washington Post Magazine*, http://www.washingtonpost.com/wp-srv/special/artsandliving/brandon-hardesty/article.html, May 31, 2009.

15. Brandon Hardesty Presents . . . , "Recreation #52: The Room," http://www.brandonhardesty.com/videos/?action=view&id=Z1yJWUf9 (added Dec 21, 2009).

16. Susan Sontag, "Notes on 'camp,'" in *The Cult Film Reader*, ed. Ernest Mathijs and Xavier Mendik (Berkshire: Open University Press, 2007), 42.

17. Steve Heisler, "Interview: Tommy Wiseau," *The Onion* A.V. Club, June 24, 2009 http://laist.com/2007/04/27/laist_interviews_tommy_wiseau_the_face_behind_the_billboard.php, April 27, 2007.

18. Susan Sontag, "Notes on 'camp,'" in *The Cult Film Reader*, ed. Ernest Mathijs and Xavier Mendik (Berkshire: Open University Press, 2007), 42.

CHAPTER 9

Wes Anderson and the Cult of Hipster Aesthetics

Bob Batchelor

I'm not talking about dance lessons. I'm talking about putting a brick through the other guy's windshield. I'm talking about taking it out and chopping it up.
—Royal Tenenbaum (Gene Hackman) in *The Royal Tenenbaums*

What is cult pop culture? Well, contrary to what people typically consider it, cult pop culture is not necessarily a thing or tangible object that one could hold, taste, feel, or carry. Rather, in my mind, cult pop culture is an action, impression, or feeling. One's attraction to *The Rocky Horror Picture Show* as a cult object, for example, is not to the film itself—the actual celluloid reel or plastic DVD—or the typical facets that usually draw one to a movie, such as the lead actors, story-line, or director. Instead, people are drawn to *Rocky Horror* based on the sensation they get from watching the film in the company of like-minded people who engage in collective mayhem as a result. It is the sensory expression of interpreting the film through singing, dancing, chanting, reciting, dressing up, and engaging with other audience members that turns a piece of film into a cult pop culture experience. With a group or in the quiet of one's own home, it is the euphoria a person receives from the emotional connection that transforms the experience.

The power of cult popular culture is in this affecting connection. One could reasonably argue, as a matter of fact, that it is in the connections with and between objects and people that the definition of broader popular culture resides. In essence, then, popular culture is not a kind of thing, as most definitions attempt to explain, like the antithesis of high art or culture. Rather, popular culture resides in the various impulses that draw members of the global community to a person, thing, topic, or issue that arise out of the juncture of mass communications, technology, political systems, and economic institutions.

Ray B. Browne—the dean of pop culture scholars—provided his definition of popular culture, saying, "It is the everyday world around us: the mass media, entertainments, diversions, heroes, icons, rituals, psychology, religion—our total life picture." What I am including in my own theory regarding popular culture is that we add to Browne's "total life picture" how a person identifies, interprets, and interrogates that set of images. In addition, my definition asks that the consumer recognize that it is more than just the world around us; it also includes the exchange between a popular culture object and one's assimilation of the thing—the thoughts, emotions, and manner in which one consumes it. For me, the meaning of popular culture exists in that absorption rather than in attempting to define a tangible object as low-, high-, or middlebrow on a fabricated scale of hierarchies. In this respect, *popular culture* is a verb, not a noun, the total mental and physical interaction with a topic and the new synthesis or creation that occurs as a result of that fusion.[1]

In terms of cult topics, the connection between people may be deeper and stronger based on a sense that enthusiasts share some tightly held meaning or feeling of ownership regarding the object. In some cases, such as fan fiction or cover bands, people are so intricately wrapped up in the meaning of a cult topic that they will participate in the creation of new or alternative meanings.

For filmmaker/writer Wes Anderson, there are several aspects of film and filmmaking that merge to create his distinctive style, ranging from the mix of colors that seem more akin to paintings to the precise yet odd dialogue his characters employ. Individually, these pieces and the many others one could draw on as examples establish Anderson's method. Collectively, however, his work transforms from unique to cult when one takes into account what the mixing of these different parts creates for and within the viewer and audience. In Anderson's work, the notion of "hipster aesthetic" springs to life, revealing significant consequences in how viewers perceive, internalize, and consume his films. His ability to seamlessly blend quirky and surreal with emotion and bliss, all wrapped in a unique, multicolored world, provides a foundation for the cult label.

This essay examines Wes Anderson's work as a writer/filmmaker and grapples with his place as a cult artist in contemporary America.

Given space limitations, this piece cannot be exhaustive or encompass the director's entire oeuvre. Instead, I will focus primarily on *The Royal Tenenbaums* (2001), which I consider Anderson's preeminent work and the film that best symbolizes him as a cult figure, even though observers and critics first attached that label to him when his indie classic *Bottle Rocket* (1996) gained widespread critical acclaim.

Generation X Artistry

Some large part of what I have labeled "hipster aesthetic" could alternatively be dubbed "Generation X artistry." Gen X is considered to encompass those people born roughly between 1965 and 1980. Anderson (born 1969) undoubtedly embodies the traits and worldview of many people of his generational cohort, such as Paul Thomas Anderson (1970) and Spike Jonze (1969). Some of the other film-makers linked to this group are slightly older, kind of generational tweeners, but share artistic worldviews, including Richard Linklater (1960), Michel Gondry (1963), and screenwriter Charlie Kaufman (1958).

In some respects, Anderson the filmmaker might be the real-world manifestation of what Ferris Bueller might have become on reaching adulthood, at least with several pinches of sophistication sprinkled on top. Take Ferris out of the Chicago suburban public school system and transplant him to a Houston prep school, and suddenly the comparison seems realistic. Furthermore, to carry the analogy a little longer, like *Ferris Bueller's Day Off,* filled with episodes that collectively create the best high school skip day ever, Anderson's films are noted for whimsy and life-affirming messages. Ferris and his existential, angst-ridden best friend Cameron represent the high school version of yin and yang that Anderson explores so well in young adults and dysfunctional families.

By any measure, though, there is certainly a vibe that grows out of Generation X's cultural influences and current impulses that is foundational in Anderson's work. Without doubt, there is an air of erudition—a "Europeaness"—that sets Anderson apart from John Hughes's intensely American/suburban work, yet that sniff of upper-classness can be seen in the Gen X novels published in the early and mid-1980s, most notably books by Jay McInerney and Bret Easton Ellis. Or, perhaps, if the rich clique from *Pretty in Pink* actually mellowed out and became cool and quirky as adults, rather than the tools they were in high school, one might find them populating an Anderson film.

Writer Derek Hill sees a generation of American filmmakers emerging from this notion of hipster aesthetic, each adapting the vibe to fit his or her own specific artistic visions. He explains:

> Highly idiosyncratic yet intricately realized, accessible yet willing to overthrow the constraints of formal storytelling, surreal yet always grounded in human emotions, this new breed of American film captures the angst of its characters and the times in which we live, but with a wryness, imagination, earnestness, irony, and stylish wit that makes the slide into existential despair a little more amusing than it should be.[2]

The common thread running through these young directors is a disposition or ambiance that grows from and symbolizes their lives. Much of this work elevates character development over plot. In addition, style or artistry serves almost like a character in its own right. The look of their films is important and significant in the way audiences experience them.

Looking outside filmmaking for Gen Xers with similar worldviews, literature provides many examples. Novelists who seem to dip from a similar creative well as Anderson and his filmmaking brethren include David Foster Wallace, Michael Chabon, Aimee Bender, and Jonathan Lethem. Chabon, for example, might be most similar to Anderson—if one can make the comparison come alive across genres. As with the filmmaker, Chabon's fans fall in love with his luxurious prose and detailed characterizations.

Anderson, however, shares some of the same kind of criticism that is often leveled against novelists who are considered stylists rather than storytellers. Detractors have viewed his filmmaking as "style over substance," perhaps even—in biting terms—as "precocious" (interestingly, this is the same kind of general criticism leveled at John Updike when he is censured for the beauty of his prose, which stands in contrast to the confines of telling stories about suburban America, which some critics found narrow or limiting).

Writing in the *New Yorker* (historically an ally of stylistic artists) after the release of *The Darjeeling Limited* (2007), Anthony Lane employs fairly typical language in describing Anderson and his work: "daft awkwardness;" "mood ... blithe, and its coloration peacock-bright;" "cheap doodle, masking ... inability to sustain a strong emotion."[3] When one encounters criticism of Anderson's films, the recurring themes center on these ideas, from being too European influenced or hipster influenced to being considered too stylized or even superficial.

Drawing on their work, both Anderson and Chabon hold a kind of magical optimism at the center of their work, which some Anderson observers have labeled "whimsy." While Chabon creates masterpieces by inventing fantastic worlds with words, Anderson puts them on film, showing what a Chabon novel might look like sprung to candy-colored life. One could easily imagine Chabon's celebrated first novel *The Mysteries of Pittsburgh* given the Anderson treatment, just as *The Royal Tenenbaums* could be conceived as Chabon's fiction. There is an artistic sensibility that seems drawn from the same fountain, perhaps originating from the director's fooling around with a movie camera as a youngster while half a continent away, the novelist immersed himself in the world of comic books and pulp science fiction novels.

An obvious link connecting Generation X artists is the central role of popular culture in helping them create a worldview. In specifically discussing writers like Wallace and Dave Eggers, scholar Daniel Grassian explains, "Like it or not, popular culture has become the dominant culture and dominant history of the most recent generation of American fiction writers, and literature must make sense of it."[4] Similarly, many of today's Gen X directors are replacing historical context with popular culture.

As a result, time periods or eras are not identified by major world events or who served as president. Instead, as in *The Royal Tenenbaums*, the marker might be a closet full of board games, creating a historical feel by playing "Hey Jude" to evoke the late 1960s, or having a main character appear in a 1970s-style bright red running warm-up suit, replete with three white stripes down the sleeves. Certainly Gen Xers are not the first to use popular culture objects to replace or fill in for actual historical events or circumstances, but this generation of artists fully employs the tactic as a means of creating an atmosphere that appeals to fans of the hipster aesthetic.

One cannot be so bold as to claim that the majority of Anderson's fans or audiences are Gen Xers (though it may be true), but it is not a stretch to assert that this group is filled with hipsters or prohipster individuals, whether or not they actually fall into the Gen X era. The popularity of the 1980s plays a role here, without a doubt drawing in younger audiences who are interested in or adapted a kind of Gen X mentality.

One rationale for Anderson's success with this demographic is that his movies have provided filmgoers with milestones to engage with adulthood and the broader culture. As he explained to Richard Brody of the *New Yorker*: "In the course of doing these first few movies, I found a way that felt instinctively right for me, and I didn't feel constrained. The end result is that they're very personal movies in a way that some people really connect with."[5] In a very real way, Anderson is a Gen X filmmaker creating movies for his own generation while they are young enough to grow with him.

Bottle Rocket and *Rushmore* (1998) are released when he is 27 and 29 years old, precisely in the midst of the postcollege, early career phase in which viewers might be searching for films that can help them makes sense of their own lives. By the time *The Royal Tenenbaums* appears three years later, Anderson is 32, while the film's younger stars are about the same age: Luke Wilson (30), Owen Wilson (33), Gwyneth Paltrow (29), and Ben Stiller (36).

A magazine profile on Anderson written during the filming of his animated movie *The Fantastic Mr. Fox* (2009) reveals the genesis of his synergy with others in his generation. Foremost, he is the product of a split family (his parents divorced when he was eight). As a youngster, he loved movies, including *Star Wars* and Hitchcock films. The writer claims, "Already as a youth, Anderson was an aesthete," which he determines by the boy's extensive record collection and that he covered his bedroom walls in "his own graphic art and collages." I can attest, however, that things like this were not an oddity in 1980s America, nor were Anderson's love of reading (attracted to Fitzgerald) or his athletic endeavors (soccer, tennis, and track). What these experiences actually seem to expose is that the funny kid with his dad's Super-8 movie camera developed base influences similar to his peer group. Yet he used these foundations to fuel a vision that simultaneously presents his worldview and accentuates his audiences' connection.[6]

At the heart of *The Royal Tenenbaums* is Anderson's vision of how a family can be turned upside down by a wrecking ball father and the subsequent fallout that destruction has on children throughout their lives. Clearly, given that Gen X is alternately known as the "latchkey generation," because of high divorce rates, and the prevalence of single-parent homes, this is a subject that audiences have experienced either firsthand or through friends. The cult vibe in Anderson's films draws on this intensely familiar yet completely unique examination of what it is like to be a Gen Xer, hipster, aesthete, or any other label one might apply to his fan base. Here is a film for Xers and about Xers that explores the damages family triggers and how love can persist despite that pain.

Creating Cult Films

Anderson excels at pulling together the threads of what transforms a film into an object of cult affection. First, as a writer/director, he creates a narrative that appeals to the audience's intelligence and aesthetic sensibility. In the case of *The Royal Tenenbaums*, he and cowriter/actor Owen Wilson craft a story that engages the viewer on a more intellectual level than the shoot-'em-up-blow-'em-up flicks that dominate Hollywood. By its very nature, then, the film attracts a different kind of audience. Second, Anderson creates a visual world that not only brings the story to life but also enhances it. In this sense, Anderson is creating a worldview typical of great directors but doing it by marrying the disparate pieces. This equation falls in line with what directing legend Martin Scorsese views as the goal of creating a film. He sees the director as storyteller, but the role also consists of much more. "To implement his vision," Scorsese explains, "he has to be a technician and even an illusionist. This means controlling and mastering the technical process."[7]

The Royal Tenenbaums charts this course from the very beginning, for example, using Alex Baldwin's steady, deep voice to narrate the backstory of the family and the exceptional early lives of the children, and then showing the pretend book about their exploits—*Family of Geniuses* by Etheline Tenenbaum. This follows on the heels of the montage playing under the opening credits, another book that an unseen patron is checking out of the library. The movie title appears as the book title. The focus on books here heightens the viewer's receptivity, since one can assume that the kind of person who sees this kind of film is most likely probooks. Right away, Anderson is asking the audience to pay attention; this is a story about the kind of people that books are written about.

According to Brody, the stylishness and artistry of Anderson's films attracted "hipsters," described as "A generation born of a paradox, its members recognized themselves in the romantic ironies of Anderson's movies, as well as in his embrace of the expressive power of luxury objects."[8] Brody points to numerous publications and observers who crowned the director the king of the hipsters. Anderson's influence is sizeable on a number of ensuing movies, from *Juno* to *Napoleon Dynamite*. Brody notes one observer calling these Anderson disciples "Wes Wannabes."[9]

Part of "mastering the technical process" that Scorsese discusses is the way Anderson casts his films, using many of the same actors across different films, including Bill Murray, Owen Wilson, Jason Schwartzman, and Anjelica Huston. This familiarity adds to the cult feeling of an Anderson film, primarily due to the performance he is able to get from his cast. It is as if the director's quirkiness and worldview are consumed by the actors and spit back at the audience in a splash of sea foam and bright pink.

For example, Gene Hackman, an acclaimed actor given to playing presidents and powerful men like generals and commanders in the late 1990s and early 2000s, turns in a dazzling performance as Royal Tenenbaum. Hackman portrays the hedonistic, erstwhile patriarch with sinister charm and the right dollop of humanity underneath. These features shine in the scene where Royal goes to Margot's eleventh birthday party and watches the children act out her first play—involving them dressed in costumes as a bear, tiger, and zebra.

Chas (Stiller) asks Royal, "Whatja think, Dad?" Wearing dark sunglasses and taking a drag on his cigarette, he frowns, saying, "It didn't seem believable to me." When pushed further about the characters, he throws up his hands and says, "What characters, it was just a bunch of little kids dressed up in animal costumes." Royal's earnestness, which he sees in himself as a positive attribute, causes Margot to excuse herself from her own party. He responds, "Sweetie, don't be mad at me, that's just one man's opinion." Margot walks past her mother and the brightly lit cake, down the steps as the guests—led by Royal—begin to sing "Happy Birthday." They peter out as she descends. Baldwin speaks to the outcome, revealing, "He had not been invited to any of their parties since." The hurt on Margot's face as she turned and scowled at Royal remains for the majority of the movie, until it seems her natural guise. At the same time, she wants to be accepted by Royal, yet she despises him for the person he actually is. The consequences of this tattered relationship impact Margot's entire life and nearly all the decisions she makes over the next 22 years. As an adult, Baldwin notes, Margot is ultrasecretive, hiding that she smokes from her family, as well as the events of her journey into adulthood, such as her marriage to a Jamaican singer.

The mix of story and visuals is employed throughout the film to give it a kind of otherworldly aura that slips between dreamscapes and harsh reality. In this sense, it exemplifies life for many thirty-somethings in modern society. What Anderson does so well is capture the range of emotion that makes life more interesting, confusing, and even scary. He does all this through the combination of story, aesthetic, and music to create a world that audiences recognize as flawed yet cannot resist. In a film like *The Royal Tenenbaums*, the viewer is then awash in a sea of emotions that personify life, from perhaps wanting to help the family regain its footing to warning them of potential dangers ahead. Anderson, as guide, delivers this raw feeling like a shot, directly into the bloodstream.

Early in the film, after Royal launches his cancer scheme to foil Henry's (Danny Glover) attempt to marry Etheline (Anjelica Huston) and get back in his family's good graces, each child returns home. Richie (Luke Wilson) requests that his adopted sister pick him up at the station by way of the Green Line bus. As she descends the steps, Anderson slows the film, giving it an effervescent aura. The camera not only slows the pace but also gives the viewer the opportunity to really capture the look on Margot's face. For the first time in the movie, she is lively, clearly eager and slightly anxious about seeing him, and her hair tussles in the breeze, which is a visual clue regarding her happiness. While "These Days" by Nico plays hauntingly in the background, the frame cuts to Richie, who obviously loves her. They talk without him saying anything, with Margot providing the one-sided dialogue. Their embrace is filled with pathos. In this brief exchange, the director allows the viewer to enter the characters' innermost worlds and then to actually feel the pain in their secret, though unrequited, love.

The positive emotion Anderson generates there stands in stark contrast to Richie's suicide scene later in the film. As "Needle in the Hay" by Elliott Smith provides the pulsing background, the young man frantically chops at his hair and full beard with old-fashioned scissors. Then, as he looks directly at the audience, he says, "I'm going to kill myself tomorrow." As flashes of Margot pulse across the scene, he shaves and then cuts his wrists with the razorblade. Although Richie lives, the vision of near-death and the ensuing fallout for the family add layers to the film, revealing Anderson's ability to move into heavy, dark emotional territory.

When Richie and Margot reunite at the Tenenbaum homestead, the camera pans around the room, revealing the many portraits he drew of her over the years, including an unfinished one in oil of the adult Margot that he never finished. She is inside his tent, listening to records and smoking. Richie shows her his scars, which are gruesome. In the Criterion Collection film commentary, Anderson explains that the realism of the scene is necessary; "if we don't have that, we don't have enough."[10] Yet, the director balances the physical truth of a suicide attempt with having each finally admit loving the other. They decide to be secretly in love with each other as "Ruby Tuesday" by the Rolling Stones closes the scene and then carries over into the next.

One Man, One Film

The only realistic and enduring Hollywood theme might focus on the rise and fall of those who go there in search of fame and fortune.

Another consistency, though, seems to be in the role of "name" directors who are given the resources to make films. Though it might be
logical to think that directors were always at the center of the filmmaking process, studios used to farm out movies without too much
concern about who would direct, because the executives in the offices
would retain control.

In earlier eras, according to Scorsese, "To survive, to master the creative process, each filmmaker had to develop his own strategy." As a
result, famed leaders such as Frank Capra and Alfred Hitchcock
"carved a nice for themselves by excelling in a certain type of story
and being identified with it."[11] Their talent and vision led to getting
first billing—above the title—on films. More importantly, as Capra
believed, they gained artistic control over their work. "I couldn't
accept art as a committee," he explained. "I could only accept art as
an extension of an individual."[12]

Today's directors lavish in the results of this early work done by
Hollywood's iconic filmmakers. Scorsese and his generation of directors,
like Steven Spielberg, George Lucas, and Stanley Kubrick, took up the
reins of their predecessors. Over the last several decades, as the older
generation continues to make successful, award-winning films, another
wave of directors is stepping up to assume the mantle, such as Christopher Nolan, Quentin Tarantino, and Paul Thomas Anderson.

For Wes Anderson, the strategy for artistic survival hinges on remaining true to the hipster aesthetic. The challenge is that more and more of
his Gen X audience is morphing to a different lifestyle, based on families,
the suburbs, McMansions, and minivans. The director has already experienced some of this backlash, with both *The Life Aquatic with Steve Zissou*
(2004) and *The Darjeeling Limited* (2007) alienating many fans, even ones
who would place themselves at the center of his cult.

Despite these attempts at broad mainstream success that met with
audience apathy, Anderson remains intensely watched and followed.
Film critic Kent Jones explains the obsessive connection fans have to
his work:

> Anderson is a filmmaker whose work you either "get" or you don't. For
> someone like me, who connected directly with his sensibility from the
> first frame of *Bottle Rocket*, it's difficult to comprehend how anyone could
> NOT get the work of such an exquisite storyteller, such a devastating
> entertainer, such a deft manipulator of emotions.[13]

The notion that one either is an Anderson fan or not, with no middle
ground, reminds me of a discussion my wife Kathy and I had about

The Royal Tenenbaums after watching it on cable in early 2004. We devised a party game built around the movie that we decided almost instantly determined compatibility. Imagine, an easy way to know if the person across from you is compatible.

The test is simple: at a party or when meeting someone for the first time, movies are an inevitable topic of conversation. By bringing up *The Royal Tenenbaums,* the person who slips it into conversation can instantly tell if he or she will get along with the person he or she is talking with: if the other person loves *The Royal Tenenbaums* and cannot stop talking about the characters, the aesthetics, or the music, then automatic "thumbs up." If not, then give that person the boot. No matter the effort, the budding friendship or relationship is doomed. Come to think of it, this test would also work great for people on dates, assessing coworkers and colleagues, and even finding out a little something about mom and dad and friends and relatives. Online dating sites could make a killing by adding this one easy question to their surveys.

Seriously, though, if we return to my definition of cult pop culture and popular culture as a whole as not primarily the artifact itself but the feeling, action, or impression a person gets when interacting with the object alone or with other like-minded people, then the link between Anderson and his cult followers is palpable. Based on the features that permeate his work, such as whimsy, mischievousness, striking colors, thoughtful music, and compelling narrative, the cultist has an unlimited supply of Anderson to consume.

Notes

1. Ray B. Browne, "Popular Culture as the New Humanities," in *Popular Culture Theory and Methodology: A Basic Introduction,* ed. Harold E. Hinds, Jr., et al. (Madison: University of Wisconsin Press, 2006), 75.

2. Derek Hill, *Charlie Kaufman and Hollywood's Merry Band of Pranksters, Fabulists and Dreamers: An Excursion into the American New Wave* (Harpenden, UK: Kamera Books, 2008), 35.

3. Anthony Lane, "Leaving It All Behind." *New Yorker* 83, no. 31 (October 15, 2007): 104–5. *Academic Search Complete, EBSCOhost* (accessed April 3, 2010).

4. Daniel Grassian, *Hybrid Fiction: American Literature and Generation X* (Jefferson, NC: McFarland, 2003), 16.

5. Quoted in Richard Brody, "Wild, Wild Wes." *New Yorker* 85, no. 35 (November 2, 2009): 48–57. *Academic Search Complete, EBSCOhost* (accessed April 3, 2010).

6. Brody.

7. Martin Scorsese and Michael Henry Wilson, *A Personal Journey with Martin Scorsese Through American Movies* (New York: Hyperion, 1997), 68.

8. Brody.

9. Quoted in ibid.

10. Wes Anderson, "Commentary: *The Royal Tenenbaums*," The Criterion Collection DVD, 2002.

11. Scorsese and Wilson, 29.

12. Ibid.

13. Kent Jones, "Film Essay: *The Royal Tenenbaums*," The Criterion Collection DVD, 2002.

TELEVISION

CHAPTER 10

Omnipotent, Omnipresent, Omniscient: Oprah Winfrey's Cult Status

Carol-Ann Farkas

If I had been working on *Battlestar Galactica* or *Buffy the Vampire Slayer*, I would have been working alone—most of my colleagues, students, and friends are not fans of these shows and have only a vague idea of what they might be missing. But if I mention to people that I am writing about Oprah Winfrey's cult status within popular culture, there is immediate recognition and engagement. A student says she and her friends like Oprah (and we are all on a first-name basis with her) because she has had to deal with the same kind of struggles and challenges that we all do. My father says the older people he knows like Oprah for her open demonstration (especially crying) of compassion and empathy. Other friends debate the advice dispensed by Oprah's chosen experts: "Did you hear what Dr. Oz said about omental fat?" "Suze Orman says buy low, sell high!" A colleague admires Oprah's achievement but thinks she's so socio-economically and psychologically removed from the lives of ordinary people that she sometimes forgets how powerful her influence is, tipping people's fortunes into the black or the red with the most fleeting mention on her show.

That so many people in so many different life situations are able to comment knowledgeably about Oprah makes my task here less isolated—but it also underscores the major challenge in trying to explain Oprah as a cult figure in popular culture. Oprah is simply too well known, too popular, and her influence too pervasive to be considered a cult figure according to any *easy* definition. We might adore Buffy, but she tends not to drive philanthropy, the sale of beef, books, or soy milk, the passage of legislation, and the structure of print, broadcast, and online media the way Oprah has done for years.

How to account for Oprah? In this essay, I will explore Oprah's influence as an individual and as a complex system of cultural products that meet the needs of her vast audience (or seem to). Oprah *does* something *for* her audience and, arguably, *to* it, to the degree that almost everyone has some response to her, ranging from skepticism and impatience to respect and emulation to veneration. We might be able to explain how and why the Oprah phenomenon functions in our culture if we apply the full range of definitions associated with the term *cult*. Oprah, I will argue, does occupy the role of a cult figure in our popular culture, though for reasons less obvious than we might expect.

Many of our pop culture "icons" enjoy only fleeting attention; once their original media run is over, they slip from the forefront of public awareness to become the special concerns of devoted fans and graduate students (and some of their professors). Oprah, however, has been actively evolving within popular culture for more than 20 years. Unlike many of the phenomena we might classify as cult, Oprah has come to depend less on us than we on her. Her ability to generate interest from and influence over her vast audiences provides her a degree of autonomous power unusual in *cult figures* as we most often define them. In fact, the Oprah phenomenon has an effect or function most like that of a *cult* not because people venerate her (though some might) but rather because so many of her audience do what she says from matters spiritual to material.

Who or What Is Oprah?

When we talk about Oprah as a cult pop culture figure, we often talk interchangeably about both the woman and her vast industry, since the histories and functions of both are so intertwined. The basic facts of Oprah's biography are fairly well known.[1] Oprah Gail Winfrey was born in 1954; as a child, she was cared for in turns by her mother, grandmother, and the man her mother identified as Oprah's father. The periods spent with her mother seem to have been unstable. While in her mother's care, she was raped by male relatives, became—briefly—a wild adolescent, and ended up pregnant at 14 (the baby, a boy, died soon after birth). When living with her grandmother, and later with her father, she was active in her school and community, a star student, a popular speaker at church, even a beauty pageant contestant. Her talent and obvious affinity for public speaking led her into television, where by the early 1980s she made steady progress toward hosting her own show. The *Oprah Winfrey Show* began in 1986 and soon became one of the top two daytime talk shows, alongside, and often ahead of, the *Phil Donahue Show*.

In regard to her business strategy over the years, Oprah has said, "I haven't planned one thing—ever. I have just been led by a strong instinct, and I have made choices based on what was right for me at the time."[2] With a business savvy she denies has been conscious or deliberate, Oprah has maintained creative and financial control over all of her media products. In 1988, Oprah bought the rights to syndicate her show and has built steadily, one might say relentlessly, on that foundation, adapting to changing audience interests and concerns and using her growing influence to explore her own. In the mid-1990s, she gave her show a radical overhaul, prompted by criticism that she was no better than the worst of the then-popular trash-TV hosts, a decline in ratings, and, by her own account, a desire to do something more positive.[3] She began to include more explicit instruction on her show, mixing a kind of nondenominational spirituality with advice about all aspects of the modern woman's lifestyle: work, money, relationships, emotional/psychological development, and health.

In 1996, Oprah started her Book Club with a deliberate choice of works designed to inspire her readers. Though some authors have resisted the way she reads their work, they do not resist the effect her endorsements have had on book sales. Selection for Oprah's Book Club can take a work from obscurity to best-seller list, pushing sales into the millions.[4] Author Bret Lott felt a mixture of shock and dismay at the experience he had in 1999 when his book, *Jewel*, was "anointed by a celebrity talk show host. Not a celebrity but an icon. Not an icon, but a Force. A person so powerful and influential that simply by announcing the name of your book a month ago, your book has been born again."[5] The morning Oprah chose *Jewel*, the book had been number 1,069,713 in Amazon's sales; by the end of the day it was ranked number one.[6]

Also at this time, Oprah started to include more investigative reports on social issues, with a particular focus on women and children, the environment, and health. Many of us remember, as one example, the controversy Oprah became embroiled in as a result of a 1996 program on mad cow disease; Oprah swore off beef on the air, leading many viewers to do the same. The Texas Cattlemen's Association took her to court for defamation; Oprah emerged victorious and vindicated.[7]

Now, in 2011, when we talk about "Oprah," we might mean the individual woman—or her show; her magazine; her radio programs; Harpo entertainment, which produces films, TV programs, and Broadway plays; the Oprah Winfrey Network (OWN) which debuted in 2011 in partnership with the Discovery network; or Oprah.com, which serves as the online hub for all of these media, and the point of contact and "community" for Oprah's fans. In 2009, her personal net worth stood at an estimated $2.5 billion, while Harpo Inc. grossed $345 million two years earlier. At its height, her daytime talk show was broadcast in 144 countries, reaching a US audience of 44 million per week[8]. *O, The Oprah Magazine*, which launched in 2000, counted upwards of 16 million readers per month. In 2009, Oprah's website received 6.7 million visitors (96 million page views) per month.[9]

Oprah is also involved in politics, from spearheading legislation such as the National Child Protection Act (the "Oprah Bill") of 1993 to endorsing Barack Obama in the 2008 election. Perhaps more importantly, she is a known philanthropist, donating millions of dollars of her own fortune to her Angel Network, which in turn raised more than $80 million from its inception in 1998 until it ended in 2010 to support charitable causes ranging from relief efforts after Hurricane Katrina to scholarships to the Oprah Winfrey Leadership Academy for Girls in South Africa.[10]

Oprah represents her identity (no mere persona) as being dependent on the relationships she has built and maintained with others, most famously her long-time partner Stedman Graham and her best friend Gayle King. Nevertheless, despite her advocacy of family and community, her own life is unconventional in comparison to the average situation of her viewers and readers. Her audience is mostly female, White, lower- to upper-middle class, and married. The average annual household income of her online audience is $60,000 or below, and 40 percent do not have a college degree, while 59 percent do; her magazine audience tends to hold greater education and income. Her audience has aged a bit along with Oprah, and a large proportion of her audience are parents but have no children living at home.[11,12]

By contrast, Oprah herself, insofar as the public knows anything about her beyond what she reveals, has never married; her children are her adopted girls in South Africa. While Oprah certainly has a background of hardship and suffering, her life now—characterized by celebrity, power, and vast wealth—is almost completely removed from the everyday experiences of her viewers. She does not go to PTA meetings, she attends inaugural balls; she might do her own housework, but has not *had* to in decades; there are things her audience might have to do, or choose to do, that Oprah no longer can do easily because of who she is, including shop or go to regular church services.[13]

Oprah is as much an industry, a multimedia conglomeration, as a person; she is indeed a phenomenon in our culture. Can we consider her a cult figure? Individuals, groups, or products in popular culture can be said to have cult status when they have won a passionately devoted following. In particular, serious fans of a cult pop culture product commit themselves to *knowing* everything they can about the object of their devotion; a *lore* develops in relation to the cult item. Often, followers become so steeped in this narrative that it begins to infiltrate other aspects of their lives—they spend time reading, listening to, or viewing the item over and over, they collect other products associated with the item, they seek out the company of other devotees to exchange and share their experiences.

In this broader sense, Oprah might be said to be have a cult following, if not of the woman, then of the industry. There is no shortage of Oprah products to consume and no shortage of ways to incorporate "Oprah" into one's life—in addition to the media, the book club, and the Internet community, Oprah devotees can feel they are involved with Oprah through purchasing some of her "favorite things," taking part in the Angel Network, and following Oprah's exhortation to "live your best life" by making changes to their diet, exercise, medical care, relationships, and surroundings.

Nevertheless, there are several important differences between Oprah and the sorts of pop culture products that we think of as having cult status. First, figures with cult status typically are "admired by a [relatively] small group of fans and not by the general public, or at least not for the same reasons."[14] Take, for example, DC Comics's *The Watchmen*; millions of people happily watched *The Watchmen* film in March 2009, enjoying it as a fun but transient experience. However, while a major Hollywood film might popularize the comic book series for a few weeks, before and after the film's moment of celebrity, the comic's existence depends on the attention of serious *Watchmen* aficionados who have read, and possibly collected, all of the comics; who know the lore of the fictional world; and who go to events like Comic-Con to immerse themselves in *The Watchmen* milieu. Such devotees form a significant but relatively small subculture, and the difference between the serious and casual *Watchmen* fan is considerable, determined largely by the amount of time and effort required to *do The Watchmen* seriously.

Not so for Oprah: while she has some extremely serious fans, her cult status does not depend on them. Her audience is wide ranging, numbering in the millions, in countries around the world, all with comparably ready access to all facets of her industry. Indeed, unlike some cult products to which access is difficult—limited-edition designer handbags, import versions of albums or graphic novels, custom-built fixed-gear bikes sold in tiny shops by vendors who pride themselves on being initiates into the subculture and jealous guardians of its mysteries— Oprah's industry thrives *because* she makes her products widely available, nonexclusive, and meant for everyone. Her message is not *"some* of you can live your best life" but *"all* of you can live your best life."

Moreover, Oprah—the woman—is not as transparent as her industry likes to project and as some of her fans perceive her to be. Though there are many known details about her life, the story of Oprah is incomplete and unstable—there is much that we do not know about her personal life, either in her youth or now; and although she appeals to many as a guide who draws lessons from her own personal journey of self-discovery to share with us, the fact that those lessons and her chosen teachers change frequently over the years suggests that she may face challenges in her private life that we never see. As a result, though millions of people do look to Oprah's industry as a source of guidance and information, she herself is perhaps too frustratingly distant and closed a figure to be granted cult status.

Finally, the typical cult pop culture phenomenon appeals to its followers at least in part because it fits in with or helps define their identity as a sub- or counterculture. Members of subcultures tend to reject the values and social structures of mainstream culture.[15] Often, members of a subculture consider themselves as better—better informed, better enlightened—than the mainstream, perhaps subversive of it, or at least, ideally, more cool than it (or just: cool). People may affiliate themselves with a subculture because they do not find acceptance in the mainstream. A subculture's choice of symbols helps reinforce both positive and negative distinctions with the dominant culture; displaying an affinity for or expertise in an item with cult status is a way to declare allegiance and opposition.

If one common criterion for a cult figure, then, is its association with a sub- or counterculture, Oprah is not one. Oprah has certainly devoted attention to a variety of potentially subcultural subjects—veganism, assorted New Age teachings, alternative medical theories—but while her enthusiasm for these things can be intense—and very profitable for their spokespeople—it is usually temporary. Sooner or later, either because her attention is diverted elsewhere or because someone within the Oprah industry senses present risk or future opportunity, Oprah moves on to something new. The business of Oprah is too enmeshed in an economy of ad sales, media tie-ins, and business relationships, too resolutely capitalistic and materialistic, to be sub- or countercultural.

In fact, for the occasional "alternative" product or practice that Oprah takes up, it is as common, if not more so, for her to focus on things that are custom tailored to the relatively conventional socioeconomic profile of her revenue stream, her audience. Her audience, taken as a whole, is not remotely sub- or countercultural, made up of mostly working- and middle-class women, people who may be open minded enough to accept the "unusual" or marginalized but who, for the most part, are not marginalized themselves—and, importantly, do not *wish* to be.[16] As Illouz has found, Oprah's media reflect her audience's solidly middle-class beliefs in "the value of success, the necessity to adapt the self to social institutions, the intrinsic worthiness of marriage, the fear of marginality, the orientation of identity to production and reproduction."[17] For them, Oprah's various media products do not serve to subvert but, rather, "provide a sense of guidance in a difficult and chaotic social order."[18]

For example, Oprah regularly profiles individuals in potentially marginalized situations with the view to promoting awareness and education among her audience. Over the years, and especially since her shift to "change your life TV" in the mid-1990s, Oprah's audience has been taught to be more open minded and understanding about differences in religion, race, sexual orientation, and physical ability. Rather than portray such cases as bizarre or deviant, over the years, she has increasingly emphasized points of commonality—everyone wants to be the same, in stable, rewarding relationships, members of a community, socially and financially secure, and well dressed. Her interaction with subculture is one of integration or assimilation—making the "abnormal" normal, showing connections between individuals rather than emphasizing difference between groups. As Illouz observes, the most subversive thing Oprah does may be to blur the lines between the mainstream and the subcultural, "queering the ordinary, and normalizing the deviant." However, the intention does not seem to be to destabilize the authority of social institutions but rather to reconcile and assimilate the marginalized to/within them, a process that tends to reinforce existing power arrangements rather than challenge or defy them.

Interestingly, Oprah's show has become hugely popular among female viewers in countries like Iran or Saudi Arabia. On the one hand,

Oprah might be a subversive element in this cultural context, with her emphasis on individual empowerment and self-esteem, particularly for women. Although local authorities censor some content, Middle Eastern women are exposed to programs on everything from fitness to combating domestic violence, an education that may have lasting effects on their participation in their societies. At the same time, because Oprah's focus is on individual success and integration within stable social structures rather than challenging authority through rebellion or protest, her effect is inspiring rather than radicalizing and easily assimilable to local values. Oprah's compassion and sympathy and her focus on the domestic lives of women line up well with her Middle Eastern audience's conservative religious teachings.[19]

A New Kind of Cult

Thus, Oprah is not exactly a cult figure in the sense of being an important but obscure symbol for any sub- or countercultural cult group. However, we have not, by any means, exhausted the possible definitions of the term *cult* as applied to Oprah. If she is not rare, eccentric, or subversive enough in her appeal to be categorized as a cult figure, Oprah may very well have achieved status as an actual cult. I hasten to clarify: first, I am considering the *effect* Oprah has, separate from her or her audience's intentions or conscious beliefs; moreover, in applying the term *cult* to Oprah and the Oprah phenomenon, I have worked my way to the broadest sense of cult as a sect, a group of people unified around a set of beliefs and/or practices, often led by an individual venerated for her embodiment of her own teachings.[20]

Cults do appear in the form of sub- or countercultures, opposing mainstream values and regarded with suspicion and disapproval in return; when we use this definition of *cult*, we think immediately of bizarre, brainwashing, apocalyptic groups such as The Solar Temple or Aum Shinrikyo.[21] Though Oprah does inspire some considerable critique, few of her detractors would go so far as to place her in the same category as those fringe groups, if for no better reasons than that the Oprah industry is far larger and poses no threat of violence to either its members or society at large.[22] Moreover, Oprah herself does not, like many sect leaders, claim that hers is the only truth, nor does she demand or even ask for the devotion of her followers. In particular, as we have seen, her message is integrative not isolationist; our emulation of Oprah is meant to help us live more happily within our social groups, not separate us from them. Nevertheless, it is possible to draw parallels between the Oprah industry and other sects—cults—that blend into the mainstream, functioning in place of or as a complement to more established belief systems.

One characteristic of cults is that their leaders demonstrate what Weber described as charismatic authority. Charismatic leaders do not derive their authority from traditional social structures or specific expertise—their power is not that of a monarch or president nor that of a genius in some particular field of study. Rather, their authority depends on the power of their personal narrative and its perceived relevance to followers; charismatic leaders represent themselves as people who have demonstrated unique skills in overcoming adversity and have found a way to share their ability with others for their betterment.[23] As Illouz suggests,

> Oprah displays the qualities that help assert charismatic leadership and authority: endurance and self-control; spiritual or moral equality with those the charismatic leader wants to save or lead . . . ; the capacity to "care" for others and to stimulate them with the energy the leader has accumulated from "saving" himself. (45)

That is, Oprah has won the admiration and loyalty of her fans and has been accorded a high degree of authority by them by demonstrating moral, spiritual, and social qualities that her audience members value and aspire to but have not been able to easily access on their own. And she makes her audience feel cared for: Oprah intervenes in the lives of individuals on a regular and well-publicized basis. In addition to her charitable and philanthropic work, most of her shows involve her giving help: in the form of material goods such as makeovers or giveaways of her "favorite things;" of expert financial, psychological, or social advice; of exposure of shameful injustices or lamentable disasters with a view to raising social and financial support for their relief.

In addition to the power of her personal attention to individual or group problems, Oprah has put in place structures to involve others—by participating in the Angel Network, for example, her audience not only has the potential to be helped but is also given the power to help others. Thus Oprah blends a message of self-esteem (you deserve to be cared for) with one of self-efficacy (you have as much power to care for others as I do), a combination that her audience seems to find especially appealing.

***

If Oprah is a cult, it is one that has aroused a great deal of criticism and suspicion; some observers detect problematic elements in the Oprah

industry, leading them to apply the term *cult* not as a neutral descriptor
of function and structure but as accusation, even epithet. Both religious
and secular critics express similar concerns about the significance that
all things Oprah have come to have in the lives of her audience/fol-
lowers: they argue that Oprah's "teachings" are broadly appealing
because they offer the promise of improvement without serious inquiry,
study, or effort; if participating in the cult of Oprah is gratifying, the
gratification is superficial, solipsistic, and transient rather than lastingly
meaningful.

Oprah was an active participant in her church throughout most of
her youth, attended public services regularly into her early thirties,
and still seems to hold Christian beliefs.[24] Whatever her private beliefs
may be, in her most public roles as host of her talk show and editor of
her magazine, she is careful to downplay affiliation with any particular
belief system, focusing instead on "spirituality." Taylor points out that
Oprah's brand of spirituality meets many needs amongst her U.S.
audience: Americans. As Taylor argues, Americans desire a spiritual
practice that is pragmatic and hopeful. At the same time, American
society has a long history of "dabbl[ing] in a variety of belief systems."[25] Exhorting viewers to "remember their spirit" and to nurture
their spirituality through meditation and introspection allows Oprah
to include the widest possible audience; if she does not endorse any
specific religion, she can make viewers of any religion feel included.

The problem for religious observers is that being inclusive of all
beliefs waters down the import of one belief and allows people to congratulate themselves on being "spiritual" without making the commitment and sacrifices associated with devout faith. Taylor cites the
criticism of one former pastor, Reverend Jeremiah Wright, who felt that
Oprah, "now has this sort of 'God is everywhere, God is in me, I don't
need to go to church, I don't need to be a part of a body of believers,
I can meditate, I can do positive thinking' spirituality. It's a strange
gospel. It has nothing to do with the church Jesus Christ founded."[26]
Though Oprah does not explicitly reject orthodoxy, her flexible
approach to spirituality is inevitably heterodox. Thus, if Oprah has
come to occupy the place of a cult—as system of belief—in people's
lives, it threatens, at worst, to be a distraction from other cults like
Christianity. At the very least, the Oprah cult may have illusory goals:
as Taylor suggests, Oprah's "brand of spirituality is ultimately unsatisfying. Perhaps the most telling thing about Oprah's role as a spiritual
leader to the seeking masses is that she herself is such an ambitious
seeker. Indeed, the smorgasbord of religions and ideas that make up

her belief system suggest that she still has not found what she's looking for."[27]

This last criticism from a Christian perspective overlaps with the concerns of more secular critics about Oprah's potential status as a cult figure: that the teachings and advice people rely on her for are, in fact, part of a *brand*; that "Oprah" is an uncomfortable mix of truth seeking and product marketing, where the imperatives of the latter undermine the potential of the former for critical inquiry and transformative action; and finally, that Oprah's own restlessness, combined with her accumulated social influence, makes viewers susceptible to the ebbing and flowing of her interests, regardless of what their own best interests may be.

When we encounter criticism of Oprah-as-cult, her detractors almost always make an effort to point out the genuine good that Oprah does: the fact of her considerable philanthropy is not in dispute, and much of the advice she and her chosen experts dispense is, at worst, noncontroversial and, at best, necessary and beneficial. If viewers are inspired by Oprah to volunteer time and money to help their neighbors, to conserve resources to help the planet, to eat more vegetables, pay down their credit-card debt, declutter the family room, and develop greater overall self-efficacy, surely the world is a better place as a result. But, as with so many other products in the larger self-help industry—books, magazines, seminars—what is most appealing about Oprah's message is also potentially most limiting: the focus on the individual and on shopping. As Kathryn Lofton has pointed out, the practice of the cult of Oprah can be expressed with this formula: "here's what to do, here's some sage testimony as to the utility of your newly chosen habit, here's where to go to get it done, and here are some smart products to assist and decorate your process of self-realization."[28]

Oprah insists that we have the power to live our best lives—that all of us, as individuals, have the right to make changes for the better, and that all of us have the obligation to do so. We find this message of personal responsibility compelling—it is an essential element of our larger cultural identity and our notions of democracy. Nevertheless, if we focus on the rights and duties of the individual alone, then only the individual can be held responsible for the outcome, overlooking the possibility that some outcomes are unavoidable consequences of larger forces of inequality or injustice in our society.

As one example, much of Oprah's advice has to do with achieving and maintaining a healthy and attractive weight; indeed, Oprah's celebrity is significantly dependent on the fact that despite constant effort, she has never been able to achieve celebrity thinness, a failing that her audience embraces as a sign of how much "like us" she is. In January 2009, Oprah dedicated a full episode of her program and a feature in her magazine, to her confession that she had fallen into a complete backslide, going from 160 pounds to 200 in the last several months. She portrayed this problem, typically, as *her* problem: the weight was partly due to a hormonal problem, but she also had come to see it as a symptom of unhappiness; she had lost sight of her values and needs. Her life, she concluded, had come out of balance and it was up to her to set it back in alignment—through a program of diet, exercise, spiritual work, and medical treatment that she would be sharing with her audience over the coming weeks in all of her associated media. As has been the case many times before, Oprah has identified a problem in her life that she believes she has the power to solve—when she succeeds, she can regard it as a personal triumph; but when the solutions do not work, it is her responsibility, her fault.

What we see Oprah doing to set things right, as only she can, is consulting experts, expending resources, consuming products—the solutions are commodities. Even the essential component of remembering one's spirit depends on a certain degree of materialism: Oprah has spiritual guidance from a changing roster of experts, all of whom profit enormously from their association with her (she does not pay them, and does not have to). Additionally, she has the ability to create a tranquil and harmonious environment for spiritual practice in any one of several homes she maintains around the country. What we do *not* see Oprah doing is challenging the social structures that make it so difficult for individuals to live "balanced" lives, the institutional injustices that might weigh a woman down with the burdens of racism, poverty, sexism, and sexual assault. Oprah—as an individual, and in the form of her various media products—does address injustice; for example, she works to combat child exploitation, her magazine ties poor self-esteem amongst women to "unrealistic expectations" by society. But these wrongs are cast as perpetuated by individuals against individuals or as problems that simply exist, the response to which can only be a change in individual mindset or habits.

Moreover, for every special investigation into a shocking abuse, Oprah does broadcasts or print features on figure-flattering clothes; for every occasion to remember one's spirit, there is an interview with a celebrity (who often has a cause to promote). On a January 2009 episode devoted to decluttering one's house, Oprah and her organizing guru, Peter Walsh, emphasized that clutter is "never about the stuff"—that a messy house is a reflection of a life out of balance, of misplaced or lost priorities, of the individual losing touch with what matters most to her. Then, Walsh and an army of assistants descended on the apartments of three lucky New York women, removed the clutter, and left each unit redecorated with "affordable" accents from Pottery Barn (Edison Chandelier, $399). The conflation of the deep and the superficial pervades Oprah's message: while Oprah does offer meaningful insight into serious issues, the information is blended in with such a mix of other topics and products that the import of one gets crowded out by the others. A viewer might be moved by a story about poverty to go to Oprah.com and click on the Web link to donate to a charity; while on the website, she can also check out the "Clean Up Your Messy House" plan and take advantage of the special discount the Container Store is giving only to Oprah viewers by spending $1,207.69 for an Elfa Freestanding Closet.[29]

Of course, what I am describing here about the Oprah industry is no different than any other well-run media enterprise, especially the variety that promotes self-improvement. Wellness magazines such as *Men's Health* simultaneously promote the building of character, muscle, and wealth; we read about problems of national and global concern, then turn the page to learn about the newest trends in business attire; the individual reader is promised on every cover that he will learn, and can then buy, "tons of useful stuff" that will make his individual life better. The Oprah industry is simply applying (and indeed was part of developing) a very successful formula that obviously appeals to large numbers of people: we want the world to be a better place, but we cannot help but feel that we are best able to influence our own lives first. We may genuinely believe that such change starts within, on the psychological and spiritual level—but material change tends to be more gratifyingly observable and seems more attainable if, instead of making over our psyches, we go shopping to make over our closets.

Thus, if the Oprah industry capitalizes on a perhaps-inevitable degree of self-absorption and materialism among its consumer/audience, then we can shrug an academic-feminist-socialist shrug and console ourselves with a new lip gloss. But if Oprah does occupy the status of cult for even a portion of her millions of readers, viewers, and listeners, the capitalist excuse will not suffice. Her audience trusts her, as a charismatic leader, to help them, to give them good and reliable advice, whether on matters as trivial as which crisp-bread to buy (Wasa) or as important as their spiritual development. Because Oprah is not a fringe, subculture leader, because she actively promotes herself as an advocate for her audience who wants to help them lead better— not more difficult or marginalized—lives, does her audience not have a reasonable expectation that their leader can be counted on?

I certainly do not mean to accuse Oprah of misleading her followers; I see no evidence that she is trying to exploit or deceive her audience for her own benefit. However, what I have noticed is that Oprah is *restless*—her attention moves from one issue to another, from one cause or solution to another. In just the last few years, she has promoted such fringe "philosophies" as the Secret and has provided a powerful forum for people who might have good intentions but questionable claims to authority, such as Ekhart Tolle or Suzanne Somers. When she features new insights, new experts, on her show or in her magazine, she seems to endorse them sincerely and whole-heartedly—these people are the ones with the answers! But within a few months, they have faded into the background, Oprah has set out on some new path— and with every change of direction, she takes many of her trusting audience with her.

In spiritual matters, if Oprah moves restlessly from one guru to the next, what harm might she do to those of her audience who move with her? Oprah never suggests that anyone adopt a particular new philosophy instead of adhering to the tenets of an established religion; and these new ideas have little potential to overthrow an individual's beliefs, as they are usually fairly banal. As we saw earlier, religious observers are critical of Oprah's spiritualism precisely because it is shallow rather than deep. Nevertheless, the self-appointed gurus who promulgate the "secret" or the "power of now" also have books and associated products to sell; at the very least, viewers who may be as spiritually restless as Oprah may invest time and money in these products with questionable returns. More problematic, however, is that viewers who may be experiencing some serious confusion and uncertainty in their lives may be frustrated—trusting Oprah, they follow her as she skims the surface of spiritual practices that are themselves superficial. When they most need something, they may not get it.

Worst of all, because Oprah tends to adopt new spiritual trends that focus on the individual as the start and end of all problems, she is missing an opportunity to direct people's attention to larger questions of moral or spiritual obligation and social activism, instead reinforcing a practice of self-absorption and, potentially, self-blame instead. As I have argued elsewhere, the industries of wellness and self-improvement that operate in our popular culture "seem to give [their audience] choices," but instead create "an anxious feeling of obligation to choose and act, but only within a prescribed set of options that never provide fulfillment;" the result is that the audience dutifully following the example of their wellness leaders ends up doggedly trying to "improve their selves as a means to power instead of challenging the definition of, and definers of, that power."[30] If the Oprah industry is no more than that, a part of the larger wellness and self-improvement business, then anxiety, frustration, and solipsism in place of activism are desirable effects to have on its audience. If Oprah functions in people's lives as or in place of a cult—a system of beliefs, a guideline for living—the effect on viewers is not without some problems.

Finally, one definition of the term *cult* we must consider in relation to the Oprah industry has to do with "a system for the cure of disease based on dogma set forth by its promulgator."[31] This might be the realm in which Oprah has the most power to influence her audience, with potentially beneficial, potentially very harmful results. Some of the most popular elements in her media products have to do with health. She regularly features medical experts such as Doctor Oz, whose advice on fitness, nutrition, and overall wellness is clearly explained; he is usually careful also to frame his advice within the context of evidence-based medicine. In general, this sort of health advice is in keeping with mainstream medical thinking; Oprah seems to be doing a service by providing her audience with the time and attention to worrisome or embarrassing problems that our health-care system may not address very well. But as always, there is the flip side to the beneficial aspect: as we have seen, Oprah is restless; like her audience, she has problems that do not lend themselves to any easy solution, but she cannot help but be curious about the promise of something new that will—this time, finally—target the problem and fix it.

For example, in January 2009, Oprah took up the problem of hormones: on the show and website, the focus was on the "promise" of bioidentical hormone therapy for the relief of menopausal symptoms. The featured expert in this case was not Doctor Oz but Suzanne Somers, the one-time sit-com actress, successful businesswoman, and now self-styled hormone therapy prophet. The episodes featuring Somers did include physicians with specialized knowledge of hormone research and women's health issues, but they were seated in the audience and only called upon to comment occasionally; Somers had the floor, summarizing the treatment plan she describes in her latest book, which recommends large doses of bioidentical hormones, "customized" for the individual woman. As several observers promptly pointed out, this particular program offered a very one-sided platform for a drug regimen that has little basis in scientific research, and that, in fact, has been linked to increased risk for diseases such as heart disease and cancer.[32]

The feature in *O* was more balanced but still biased toward the bio-identical option, a bias emphasized by Oprah herself in her regular column, "What I Know for Sure." Oprah does not tell her readers what to do, saying "I share my story in hopes of opening the door to restoration and balance to women (and men) everywhere. I do so knowing that bioidentical hormone therapy is controversial, and, to many people, confusing." Nevertheless, her description of her recent own experiences leaves no doubt about her views on the subject of hormone therapy. Oprah explains that she suffered from physical and mental malaise for months: "Anxiety. Fatigue . . . Lack of confidence, curiosity, drive, ambition. A sense of being overwhelmed." She suspected the problem might be hormonal but found that "not enough doctors know or care enough about women's hormonal issues." Finally, she found a doctor who confirmed her self-diagnosis and prescribed a custom-blended formula of bioidentical hormones; almost immediately, Oprah says, "the sky was bluer."[33]

The corresponding material on Oprah's website was similarly skewed in favor of bioidenticals—though an FDA statement warning of the possible risks of Somers's recommendations was available, though the website text did not explicitly endorse her plan, and though both program and website (and Oprah) did encourage viewers to discuss their options with their doctors—it would be very possible for audience members to assume that, as with Oprah's other recommended products and solution, the advice is safe and reliable. And even though Oprah does not tell her audience what to do, the mere fact of her adopting a particular practice may be endorsement enough for many. Scrolling through reader comments on the bioidentical issue on the "community" discussion board, we can see that many viewers had promptly bought Somers's book after watching the show and had embarked on a search for doctors and compounding pharmacies who would follow Somers's plan. Many of these postings are poignant expressions of individuals who describe themselves as very unwell in both body and mind—for what complex assortment of medical, emotional, and social reasons it is impossible to tell, but that certainly, in the posters' minds, seem to boil down to problems with their bodies, for which they are desperate to find a "cure." And yet, what immediately struck me in reading these posts was the obstacles these readers encountered as they tried to implement Somers's advice—in postings ranging from eloquent to grammatically broken, posters complained that they could not find doctors or pharmacies that would follow the plan; if they did, their insurance companies would not cover the cost (from $300 to $1,000). What remains to be studied is what some of these women will end up paying to follow this advice, in terms of both money and possible health consequences.[34] It is one thing to feel like one *might* buy the soy milk or chandelier Oprah likes; it is another thing to invest in a treatment regimen that one feels one *must* follow if one wants to feel as well as Oprah does.

According to the National Endowment for the Arts, as of 2003, only 13 percent of adults read at a "proficient" level; even among adults with bachelor's degrees, only 30 percent are at the proficient level—at least 70 percent of the adult population in the United States, in other words, is not capable of understanding language at a very sophisticated level.[35] Also in 2003, the National Assessment of Adult Literacy surveyed more than 19,000 adults in the United States on their levels of general and health literary. The NAAL found that 38 percent of American adults had limited health literacy—they might be able to follow basic instructions about medical care, but in general, "they struggle with drawing appropriate inferences from the written material, and they may apply text using irrelevant information."[36] If Oprah's American audience is a fairly broad cross-section of the population, these data on health literacy suggest that a similar proportion of Oprah viewers do not have the literacy and critical thinking skills to evaluate the information they receive from the show. These are the individuals who are most susceptible to the power of a charismatic leader, who might be most likely to rely on Oprah, even venerate her, and who would invest her with cult status; they are also the ones most likely to be led from one of Oprah's enthusiasms to another, possibly spending money and other resources on commodities that may not give them the results they crave.

Semantically speaking, it is difficult to pin Oprah—as individual, industry, phenomenon—down; there is something about her position in our culture that is more than "popular," not exactly "cult." Pragmatically speaking, however, Oprah's effect on the lives of many of us is certainly that of a charismatic leader. She has not (yet) put those leadership skills to the test in a political setting but certainly does perform the role of leader in many aspects of our lives. For spiritual and material guidance, instruction and encouragement, she seems to offer something that we do not easily find elsewhere in modern culture.

Religion, medicine, government—all are abstract, distant, and seem disinterested, whereas Oprah is like us, cares about us, and provides us with a justification to care for ourselves. She makes recommendations, and though she does not order us to obey them, though we are not under any obligation of faith or ideology to follow her, follow we often do. If Oprah has, if not by intention, then nevertheless by effect, come to occupy the status of a cult within popular culture, her followers have a right to demand accountability of her: her audience must call on her to be careful and responsible in the advice she dispenses, in the stances she takes, in the causes she endorses, in the way she involves us in all things Oprah. The best thing Oprah could do is to use her influence more than she does to explicitly teach her audience to be less dependent on and more skeptical of her own teachings. She has invited us to trust her, usually to our benefit; it would benefit us even more if she encouraged us to trust her a little bit less.

Notes

1. "Oprah Winfrey's Biography," *Oprah.com*, www.oprah.com (accessed February 23, 2009); LaTonya Taylor, "The Church of O," *Christianity Today*, April 2002, www.christianitytoday.com, (accessed February 23, 2009). "Oprah Winfrey," *Wikipedia*, http://en.wikipedia.org/wiki/Oprah_Winfrey (accessed February 15, 2009).

2. Patricia Sellers, "The Business of Being Oprah," *Fortune*, 145.7 (1 April, 2002), 7.

3. Taylor.

4. Cecilia Konchar Farr, *Reading Oprah: How Oprah's Book Club Changed the Way America Reads* (Albany: State University of New York Press, 2005), 2. Farr has calculated that in the first four years of the Book Club, Oprah's choices were responsible for average book sales of 1.2 million copies per year.

5. Bret Lott, "Toward Humility," *The Pushcart Prize 2001 XXV* (New York: W. W. Norton, 2001), 54.

6. "Bret Lott Profile," *LSU Profiles*, September 2004, www.lsu.edu (accessed February 27, 2009).

7. "Oprah: 'Free Speech Rocks,'" CNN.com, February 26, 1998, www.cnn.com (accessed February 27, 2009).

8. "Oprah Winfrey's Biography," Oprah.com.

9. "Oprah.com Facts," *Oprah.com*, www.oprah.com (accessed February 23, 2009); Alleyne, Sonia, "Oprah Means Business," *Black Enterprise*, 38.11 (June 2008), 116 (8).

10. "Oprah's Angel Network Fact Sheet," *Oprah.com*, www.oprah.com (accessed February 23, 2009).

11. Aswini Anburajan, "Breaking Down Oprah's Numbers," *MSNBC First-Read*, December 7, 2007, www.MSNBC.com (accessed February 23, 2009).

12. "Oprah.com: Demographics," Quantcast, www.quantcast.com (accessed February 27, 2009).

13. Taylor.

14. "Cult Following," *Wikipedia*, http://en.wikipedia.org/wiki/Cult _following (accessed February 13, 2009). What better source for definition of cult pop culture products than such a product itself?

15. "Sub-Culture," *Wikipedia*, http://en.wikipedia.org/wiki/Sub_Culture (accessed February 13, 2009); "Counter-Culture," *A Dictionary of Sociology* (Oxford, UK: Oxford University Press, 2009).

16. "Counter-Culture."

17. Eva Illouz, *Oprah Winfrey and the Glamour of Misery: An Essay on Popular Culture* (New York: Columbia University Press, 2003), 64.

18. Illouz, 62.

19. Katherine Zoepf, "Saudi Women Find an Unlikely Role Model: Oprah," *New York Times* (September 19, 2008).

20. "Cults," *Dictionary of the Social Sciences* (Oxford, UK: Oxford University Press, 2002).

21. Charles D. Laughlin, "Cults and the Body," In Colin Blakemore and Sheila Jennett, eds., *The Oxford Companion to the Body* (Oxford, UK: Oxford University Press, 2001).

22. Catherine Donaldson-Evans, "The Cult of Oprah," *Fox News*, August 2, 2001, www.foxnews.com (accessed February 13, 2009): "The definition of 'cult' as 'harmful group' doesn't apply to Oprah," said Joe Szimhart, a cult-information specialist and former exit counselor. "But certainly 'cult' as 'devotional activity surrounding a charismatic person' does."

23. Maximilian Weber, *The Theory of Social and Economic Organization*, A. R. Anderson and Talcott Parsons, trans. (New York: The Free Press, 1947); Illouz, 43.

24. Taylor.

25. Taylor.

26. Taylor.

27. Taylor.

28. Kathryn Lofton, "Practicing Oprah; or the Prescriptive Compulsion of a Spiritual Capitalism," *Journal of Popular Culture*, 39.4 (August 2006), 608.

29. "Oprah's Clean Up Your Messy House Tour," *Oprah.com*, www.oprah.com (accessed February 23, 2009).

30. Carol-Ann Farkas, "Well or Weak? The Construction of Knowledge, Agency, and Competence in Women's Wellness Magazines," in Margaret C. Wiley, ed., *Women, Wellness, and the Media* (Newcastle, UK: Cambridge Scholars Publishing, 2008), 136. Also see: Shari L. Dworkin and Michael Messner,

"Just Do . . . What? Sport, Bodies, Gender," in Pamela J. Creedon ed., *Women, Media, and Sport: Challenging Gender Values* (Thousand Oaks, CA: Sage Publications, 1994) 341–61.

31. "Cult," Merriam Webster Dictionary, www.merriam-webster.com (accessed February 23, 2009).

32. Pat Wingert and Barbara Kantrowitz, "Uh, O! Why Medical Experts Were Shocked by Oprah Winfrey's Take on Hormone Replacement and Suzanne Somers's Controversial Theories on Aging," *Newsweek*, www.newsweek.com (accessed February 17, 2009). As this article's authors report, "major medical organizations, like the National Instititutes of Health, the FDA, the American College of Obstetricians and Gynecologists, the Endocrine Society, and the North American Menopause Society now recommend taking the lowest effective doses for no more than a few years" because of the health risks associated with taking high and sustained doses of hormones, "bioidentical" or otherwise.

33. Oprah Winfrey, "What I Know for Sure," *O, The Oprah Magazine*, February 2009, 220.

34. In fact, Chicago artist Robyn Okrant is doing just this, in a project called Living Oprah. She dedicated 2008 to following all of Oprah's advice to "live your best life;" her goal was to find out if "the costs of living as Oprah prescribes (financial, energy, time spent) [would] be worth the results." She has blogged about her experiences at "Living Oprah" (http://www.livingoprah.com). Okran't book *Living Oprah: My One-Year Experiment to Walk the Walk of the Queen of Talk* appeared in 2010. No doubt, she hoped to appear on Oprah's show, but was never invited prior to the final episode on May 25, 2011.

35. "Executive Summary," *To Read or Not to Read: A Question of National Consequence* (Washington: National Endowment for the Arts, 2007), 12.

36. Sheida White, *Assessing the Nation's Health Literacy: Key Concepts and Findings of the National Assessment of Adult Literacy* (Chicago: AMA Foundation, 2008).

Bibliography

Alleyne, Sonia. "Oprah Means Business." *Black Enterprise*. 38.11 (June 2008), 116 (8).

Anburajan, Aswini. "Breaking Down Oprah's Numbers." *MSNBC FirstRead.* December, 7, 2007. http://www.MSNBC.com (accessed February 23, 2009).

"Bret Lott Profile." *LSU Profiles.* September 2004. http://www.lsu.edu (accessed February 27, 2009).

"Counter-Culture." *A Dictionary of Sociology.* Oxford, UK: Oxford University Press, 2009.

"Cult." Merriam Webster Dictionary. http://www.merriam-webster .com (accessed February 23, 2009).

"Cults." *Dictionary of the Social Sciences.* Oxford UK: Oxford University Press, 2002.

"Cult Following." *Wikipedia.* http://en.wikipedia.org/wiki/Cult _following (accessed February 13, 2009).

Donaldson-Evans, Catherine. "The Cult of Oprah." *Fox News.* August 2, 2001. http://www.foxnews.com (accessed February 13, 2009).

Dworkin, Sheri L. and Michael Messner. "Just Do ... What? Sport, Bodies, Gender." In Pamela J. Creedon, ed., *Women, Media, and Sport: Challenging Gender Values.* Thousand Oaks, CA: Sage Publications, 1994, 341–61.

"Executive Summary." *To Read or Not to Read: A Question of National Consequence.* Washington, DC: National Endowment for the Arts, 2007, 12.

Farkas, Carol-Ann. "Well or Weak? The Construction of Knowledge, Agency, and Competence in Women's Wellness Magazines." In Margaret C. Wiley, ed., *Women, Wellness, and the Media.* Newcastle, UK: Cambridge Scholars, 2008, 136.

Farr, Cecilia Konchar. *Reading Oprah: How Oprah's Book Club Changed the Way America Reads.* Albany: State University of New York Press, 2005, 2.

Illouz, Eva. *Oprah Winfrey and the Glamour of Misery: An Essay on Popular Culture.* New York: Columbia University, 2003.

Laughlin, Charles D. "Cults and the Body." In Colin Blakemore and Sheila Jennett, eds., *The Oxford Companion to the Body.* Oxford, UK: Oxford University Press, 2001.

Lofton, Kathryn. "Practicing Oprah; or the Prescriptive Compulsion of a Spiritual Capitalism." *Journal of Popular Culture* 39.4 (2006), 599–620.

Lott, Bret. "Toward Humility." *The Pushcart Prize 2001 XXV.* New York: W. W. Norton, 2001, 52–71.

Okrant, Robyn. *Living Oprah.* http://www.livingoprah.com (accessed February 27, 2009).

"Oprah's Angel Network Fact Sheet." *Oprah.com.* http://www .oprah.com (accessed February 23, 2009).

"Oprah.com Facts." *Oprah.com.* http://www.oprah.com (accessed February 23, 2009).

"Oprah.com: Demographics." *Quantcast.* http://www.quantcast.com (accessed February 27, 2009).

"Oprah: 'Free Speech Rocks.'" *CNN.com.* 26 February 1998. http:// www.cnn.com (accessed February 27, 2009).

"Oprah Winfrey." *Wikipedia.* http://en.wikipedia.org/wiki/Oprah _Winfrey (accessed February 15, 2009).

"Oprah Winfrey's Biography." *Oprah.com.* http://www.oprah.com (accessed February 23, 2009).

"Oprah's Clean Up Your Messy House Tour." *Oprah.com.* http:// www.oprah.com (accessed February 23, 2009).

Sellers, Patricia. "The Business of Being Oprah." *Fortune.* 145.7 (April 1, 2002), 50.

"Sub-Culture." *Wikipedia.* http://en.wikipedia.org/wiki/Sub_Culture (accessed February 13, 2009).

Taylor, LaTonya. "The Church of O." *Christianity Today.* April 2002. http://www.christianitytoday.com/ct/2002/april1/1.38.html (accessed February 23, 2009).

Weber, Maximilian. *The Theory of Social and Economic Organization.* A. R. Anderson and Talcott Parsons, trans. New York: The Free Press, 1947.

White, Sheida. *Assessing the Nation's Health Literacy: Key Concepts and Findings of the National Assessment of Adult Literacy.* Chicago: AMA Foundation, 2008.

Winfrey, Oprah. "What I Know for Sure: Hormones!" *O, The Oprah Magazine* (February 2009), 220.

Wingert, Pat, and Barbara Kantrowitz. "Uh, O! Why Medical Experts Were Shocked by Oprah Winfrey's Take on Hormone Replacement and Suzanne Somers's Controversial Theories on Aging." *Newsweek.* http://www.newsweek.com (accessed February 17, 2009).

Zoepf, Katherine. "Saudi Women Find an Unlikely Role Model: Oprah." *New York Times* (September 19, 2008).

CHAPTER 11

What Would Tony Soprano Do? A Cult of Immorality

Deborah McLeod

They are violent, racist, adulterous, greedy, and hypocritical. They lie constantly and, what is even more annoying, they whine all the time. They are, as Tony himself points out, "fucking murderers, for Chrissakes!"[1] But the characters of HBO's hit series *The Sopranos* (1999–2007) maintain a cult following that has aroused Internet debates, scholarly critiques, parodies, and continuing reruns on A&E.[2] Mixing gangster myth with domestic drama, existential angst with gluttonous sex, and dreamscapes with postmodernist pastiche, *The Sopranos* provides an intelligent and blunt portrayal of the Mafia underworld and its uncomfortable relation to our own lives.

Not long after HBO aired the last episode of the series, I saw a bumper sticker asking, "What Would Tony Soprano Do?" The slogan is, of course, an irreverent twist on the popular Christian motto, "What Would Jesus do?" As such, it suggests a disturbing alternative to moral authority that anyone who sincerely cares about humanity must reject. But it is, nevertheless, an intriguing question. Numerous authors have analyzed why audiences love Tony Soprano. We identify with Tony's domestic troubles. He seems like such a child sometimes. We have sympathy for the devil. Tony's vigilantism provides wish fulfillment for those who feel powerless. Tony is sexy, fun loving, and embraces life. He takes care of his own. There are in real life, to use Carmela Soprano's (Edie Falco's) words, "far bigger crooks than [her] husband."[3] All of those reasons are undeniably true.

Personally, I hate Tony Soprano. I hate his phallic cigar and utter disregard for anyone's feelings but his own. I hate his smug narcissism and cruelty toward those he claims to love. For me, the show's attraction lies in its combination of excellent writing, acting, directing, and unflinching portrayal of the dark side of human nature. And the fact that Tony is not merely a monster but is, instead, all too human only makes his character more chilling. *The Sopranos* portrays an immoral universe, but it does so in a way that is complex and provocative and always entertaining. By examining several aspects of the series, I hope to gain some insight into what makes the Tony Sopranos of the world so fascinating.

"Gary Cooper, the Real Gary Cooper, or Anybody Named Cooper, Never Suffered Like the Italians."

The mobsters themselves primarily look to their Italian heritage as the source of their own moral, or immoral, authority. The pasta dinners, designer suits, *goomahs*, and Mafia traditions all reflect the characters' (mis)perceptions of what it means to be an Italian American. They use but keep a safe distance from all ethnic outsiders, such as employing African Americans to steal cars and allowing the Jewish Hesh Rabkin (Jerry Adler) to earn money and offer advice. But Tony balks when his daughter begins dating an African American, and Hesh is never allowed to become a "made guy." The paradox is that, while the mobsters are blatantly racist, the series as a whole essentially treats all ethnic groups the same, that is, as equally corrupt.[4] It is a Caucasian soccer coach who has sex with a student, Hasidic Jews turn to the gangsters when they need muscle, and an African American preacher encourages a protest against discrimination before profiting from the work stoppage.

In a society pervaded with corruption, these Italian Americans stand out naturally because they are the main characters, and it is their ethnicity that has drawn the most complaints. Among other incidents, Columbus Day Parade organizers criticized New York City mayor Michael Bloomberg for inviting Dominic Chianese (Uncle Junior) to attend,[5] the American Italian Defense Association sued Time Warner claiming the show violated the "individual dignity" clause of the Illinois Constitution,[6] and Representative Marge Roukema, a New Jersey Republican, sponsored a Congressional resolution against the show.[7] Series creator and producer David Chase, himself the grandson of Italian immigrants, strongly rejects such criticism:

I think the Italian-American experience is an advertisement for America, for the democratic experiment. It's hard for me to think of a group who has come from so little who has done so well. [. . .] If your self-esteem is that shallow, and you have a problem with the fact that this tiny minority called "gangsters" make it tough for the rest of us, I think you should take your case to them.[8]

Indeed, not only does the series present its characters as atypical, it also has them debate media portrayals of Italian Americans. Its moral center, Dr. Jennifer Melfi (Lorraine Bracco), also shares the group's ethnic background.

Tony, however, repeatedly defends his crimes as a result of his family's immigrant background, as he does in this exchange with Melfi:

tony: When America opened the floodgates and let all us Italians in, what do you think they were doing it for? Because they were trying to save us from poverty? No, they did it because they needed us. They needed us to build their cities and dig their subways and to make them richer. The Carnegies and the Rockefellers, they needed worker bees and there we were. But some of us didn't want to swarm around their hive and lose who we were. We wanted to stay Italian and preserve the things that meant something to us: honor and family and loyalty. And some of us wanted a piece of the action. We weren't educated like the Americans. But we had the balls to take what we wanted. And those other fucks, those other . . . the J. P. Morgans, they were crooks and killers too, but that was a business, right? The American way.

melfi: That might all be true. But what do poor Italian immigrants have to do with you and what happens every morning you step out of bed?[9]

Although Melfi accepts Tony's reasoning in order to make a more significant point—that whatever happened to those immigrants has nothing to do with the mobster's current actions—Tony is characteristically cherry-picking his argument. Tony's logic links his criminal behavior to the immigrants' need to establish status against a dominant culture, to "stay Italian." But he moves quickly from an appeal to "honor and family and loyalty," all noble values, to having "the balls to take what we wanted." From one sentence to the next, he is ready to assimilate, to become the "crooks and killers" that the American powermongers were, rather than acknowledge that his crimes are morally wrong.

Ironically, Tony is also asserting the immigrants' status as victims, "worker bees" for the rich, a position he normally rejects. He takes a similar stance with daughter Meadow (Jamie-Lynn Sigler) when she asks if he is in the Mafia: "You know there was a time, Mead, when the Italian people didn't have a lot of options."[10] But in his argument with Consigliere Silvio Dante (Steven Van Zandt) about the Columbus Day parade, Tony repeats Melfi's point that the immigrants' predicament has no relation to these men's lives now:

silvio: Hey, people suffered.
tony: Did you? Except for maybe the Feds?
silvio: My grandparents got spit on because they were from Calabria.
tony: Let me ask you a question, all the good things you got in your life, did they come to you cause you're Calabrese? I'll tell you the answer. The answer is no. [...] You got it 'cause you're you, 'cause you're smart. [...] Where the fuck is our self-esteem? That shit doesn't come from Columbus, or *The Godfather*, or Chef-fucking-Boyardee.[11]

As Christopher Kocela points out, Tony's "conclusion that self-esteem does not derive from these master signifiers contradicts everything we know about Tony, his friends, and his family. It is *precisely* through reference to Columbus and *The Godfather* in particular that Tony [and the others] derive their sense of themselves as Italian Americans and *Mafioso*."[12] Ever the hypocrite, Tony even rejects ethnic pride when it serves his purpose.

Meadow does a better job of defending crime as a result of Italian tradition: "The truth is they [her father's associates] bring certain modes of conflict resolution from all the way back in the old country, from the poverty of the Mezzogiorno, where all higher authority was corrupt."[13] Meadow's comments come in response to her boyfriend's description of mob violence. But she too is being dishonest. Meadow once railed against her father's hypocrisy until he forced her to acknowledge that she enjoyed the fruits of his crimes.[14] Now, having learned to accept and defend her father's way of life, Meadow simply refuses to face the brutality it involves.

Part of the mobsters' ethical uncertainty arises from their confusion between reality and fiction. As numerous commentators have pointed out, the series is rife with intertextual allusions, both to its crime film ancestors and various other cultural images. Indeed, much of the humor in the show comes from the characters' awareness of their own position in popular culture. For example, when Christopher shoots a bakery clerk in the foot, the actor, Michael Imperioli, is getting revenge for his being shot in the foot in his earlier role as Spider in *Goodfellas*.

Thus, just as the slogan "What Would Tony Soprano Do?" appeals to the authority of a fictional character, so Tony turns to Gary Cooper as his primary role model. Tony, however, is thinking of Cooper's cowboy persona in such films as *High Noon*, and in the argument over Columbus Day, Silvio calls him on the discrepancy:

tony: Whatever the fuck happened to Gary Cooper? That's what I'd like to know. [...] Gary Cooper, now there was an American. A strong, silent type. He did what he had to do. [...] And did he complain? Did he say, "Oh, I come from this poor, Texas-Irish illiterate fucking background, or whatever the fuck, so leave me the fuck out of it because my people got fucked over"?

silvio: T, not for nothing, but [...] that was the movies.

tony: What the fuck difference does that make? Columbus was so long ago he might as well been a fucking movie! [...]

silvio: The point is that Gary Cooper, the real Gary Cooper, or anybody named Cooper, never suffered like the Italians.[15]

Silvio almost has a valid point about the suffering of immigrant groups under a dominant White culture, but Tony's reference to Cooper as part Irish invalidates it. Irish Americans, of course, were immigrants, too, and endured their own struggle. More significantly, Tony is acknowledging a lack of discernment between real life and "the movies;" indeed, for him as for many Americans, the distinction does not matter because Columbus lived so long ago that the historical reality has become merely a matter of perception.

The confusion between reality and art hits home most profoundly when Tony's son, Anthony, Jr., known as A. J. (Robert Iler), seeks revenge on his uncle for shooting his father. After the boy fails in his attempt to stab Uncle Junior (Dominic Chianese), A. J. defends his act to Tony by referencing *The Godfather*:

a.j.: Because everytime we watch *Godfather*, when Michael Corleone shoots those guys in the restaurant, those assholes who tried to kill his dad, [...] you say it's your favorite scene of all time.

tony: Jesus Christ, A. J. You make me want to cry. That's a movie. You gotta grow up.[16]

By his own standards, Tony has never grown up, either, as indicated by his praise of Gary Cooper. Ironically, though, in the world of *The Sopranos*, A. J.'s act is consistent with Tony's code of conduct. Tony frequently obtains revenge on an enemy by committing murder, and the characters constantly refer to the *Godfather* films. A. J. is wrong only because his father does not want the boy to follow in his footsteps, as Tony tells him: "It's not in your nature. [...] You're a good guy. I'm very grateful."[17] Since he began the rebuke by castigating

A. J.'s failure, though, one wonders how Tony would have felt had his son succeeded.

As these scenes demonstrate, Tony's attempt to rationalize his crimes by recalling his immigrant ancestors is no more valid than appealing to the actions of Gary Cooper or Michael Corleone. Neither the Italian Mafia, the Italian American Mafia, nor Tony's fictional heroes provide an excuse for his crimes. But, at the same time, glimpses of truth appear in their discussions of immigrant struggles, government corruption, and even the moral fortitude of Cooper's cowboy heroes.

"I Already Took His Horse"

Aside from family quarrels and mobster violence, the activity most often depicted on *The Sopranos* is probably sex, and here, the series presents a tableau of sexuality that is deceptive in its moral complexity. The married gangsters spend much of their time at Silvio's strip club, the Bada Bing!, both eyeing topless dancers and engaging with prostitutes; thus, the club functions as a symbol of both their objectification of women and serial adultery. Other provocative scenes include Tony relieving his boredom through doggie-style sex with a "born-again Christian,"[18] and sister Janice (Aida Turturro) indulging either the masochistic preferences of Ralph Cifaretto (Joe Pantoliano) or the gun-toting, he-usually-takes-the-clip-out, sexual violence of Richie Aprile (David Proval). Through skillfully written portrayals, the show itself refrains from making moral judgments about any consensual sexual activity, with the exception of the soccer coach and high school student. Indeed, Debbie (Karen Sillas), the brothel owner, appears to be one of the more ethical characters in the series. Instead, the sexual encounters illustrate the cruelty inherent in the characters' self-centeredness.

In one particularly trenchant plotline, Tony's wife, Carmela (Edie Falco), has a close encounter with her priest. Although he ultimately backs down, he is guilty of both hypocrisy and manipulation, as she points out when he begins discussing Tony's soul:

> Father, he doesn't give a flying fuck. You know it and I know it. [...]
> He's a sinner, Father. And you come up here, and you eat his steaks, and you use his home entertainment center. [...] You know what I think, Father? I think that you like the, I don't even know what to call it, the, uh, whiff of sexuality, that never goes anyplace. [...] I think you have this M.O. where you manipulate spiritually thirsty women, and

I think a lot of it is tied up with food somehow, as well as the sexual-tension game.

Carmela's description of the priest's behavior is blunt and accurate; he is not only enjoying the profits of Tony's crimes but also using his role as spiritual advisor to fulfill his own sexual needs. But what is Carmela doing? She was ready to have sex with her priest and is only angry now out of jealousy over his attentions to another woman.

The character development of Capo Vito Spatafore (Joe Gannascoli) is equally intriguing. Vito turns out to be gay, and, for macho viewers used to ogling the strippers, the series surprises by having the camera push in on a male–male kiss. The show presents Vito's homosexuality sympathetically, but we still must question his behavior; although his gay relationship is a sincere one, he is betraying his wife and children, and he ultimately chooses the Mafia life over the man who loves him.

Another plotline that illustrates how the gangsters' sexual ethics intertwine with their overall immorality occurs when Ralph beats a young "hoo-er" (whore) to death. The progression of incidents reveals much of the hypocrisy in the gangsters' codes of conduct, as well as the mobsters' basic separation of women into two classes, respected family member or whore. Like most of the crew, Ralph has a *goomah*, in this case, a young topless dancer, Tracee (Ariel Kiley). When the girl slaps Ralph during an argument, the gangster responds by beating her to death in the Bada Bing!'s parking lot. Because Tracee reminds Tony of his daughter, however, the boss becomes enraged over Ralph's act and attacks him. Ralph cannot fight back; no one hits the boss. But Tony has broken a well-known rule; no "made guy" is supposed to hit another, and, as Ralph whines, "Rules are rules."[19] Further, Ralph knows that he is allowed to kill outsiders at whim: "All this over some dead whore?"[20] Tony, to retain his status, cannot admit that he felt sympathy for the girl, and so he characterizes Ralph's mistake with the absurd "He disrespected the Bing."[21] Tony eventually allows Ralph to apologize, but the boss never admits being angry with Ralph for murdering an innocent young woman, who, moreover, is pregnant with Ralph's child. Instead, personal slights and the offender's choice of locations become a sign of disrespect not to the woman but to the Mafia family.

Tony and Ralph's disharmony recurs when a new *goomah* enters the scene, Valentina La Paz (Leslie Bega). Valentina is Ralph's mistress, but Tony quickly breaks another rule by having sex with her himself. After the first encounter, though, Tony dismisses her with the blunt

"I already took his horse."[22] Tony had, indeed, usurped Ralph's owner-ship of a prize-winning racehorse, but the line pointedly describes her status in his eyes: a commodity on par with the horse. Further, when Tony dreams about reuniting with Carmela, he sits atop the racehorse while she insists, "You can't have your horse in here."[23] Whether she actually says "horse" or "whores" is unclear, but the analogy is obvious. The show makes a final connection between Valentina and the racehorse by having them both become victims of a fire. The inci-dents are doubly horrific; not only does Ralph cause the animal to be burned alive, but Tony's intense distress over the horse contrasts markedly with the little concern he shows for Valentina's injuries. In the world of *The Sopranos*, one is better off as a horse than a whore.

But the objectification of women is only one aspect of the show's sexual immorality. Sex in *The Sopranos* is ultimately about self-indulgence. Love or concern for others' feelings is rarely part of the equation, and betrayal is a constant factor. Further, Tony appeals sex-ually to women because of his association with violence and money, major attractions even for Carmela. And what about viewers? Isn't the combination of nudity and danger, our "Knight in White Satin Armor," what attracts so many of us?[24]

"Comfortably Numb"

The character who most tries to follow the "What Would Tony Soprano Do" philosophy is Christopher Moltisanti (Michael Imperioli), who progresses (or descends) over the course of the series from newbie gangster to Capo. As a young wiseguy anxious to make a name for him-self, Christopher eagerly becomes Tony's personal protégé, and he remains at Tony's side despite continual moments of doubt.

Through Christopher's experience, viewers witness a formal initia-tion into the Mafia, and the episode, "Fortunate Son," illustrates both the mobsters' conception of the Mafia as a sacred and noble tradition and its hypocrisy. At the induction ceremony for Christopher and Eugene Pontecorvo (Robert Funaro), Tony explains the rules for membership in their new "family": "There's no getting out. [. . .] This family comes before everything else, everything. Before your wife or your children and your mother and your father."[25] (So much for the concept of family that Tony argued to Melfi.) Christopher and Eugene take a sacred blood oath, in which Tony pricks their fingers and has them light a picture of St. Peter on fire between their palms.[26] The pair then repeats the phrase "May I burn in Hell if I betray my friends." Christopher tries to believe in the sacredness of his oath, even claiming it as his version of AA's "higher power."[27] Ultimately, though, Christopher realizes the truth of mob ethics: "Fuck family. Fuck loyalty. It cost [Tony] a dime, you're a fucking pariah."[28]

The murder of Christopher's fiancée, Adriana La Cerva (Drea de Matteo), becomes the breaking point for Christopher's relationship with Tony. After being arrested for drug use, Adriana is forced to co-operate with the FBI, the primary sin in the gangsters' world. When Christopher finds out, he briefly considers leaving with her to join a witness protection program. But a glimpse of a man his age, bogged down with wife and kids, sends the young gangster back to Tony, knowing that Adriana must be killed. Years later, Christopher actually thanks Tony for not making him handle the murder. As the scene flashes back to Christopher's revelation about Adriana, he proclaims to Tony, "You always had my back [. . .]. I love you, man."[29] In an audio commentary to the episode, writer Terence Winter points out the chilling irony of the dialogue: "When you listen to this conversation, what they're ultimately bonding over is the murder of his fiancée, and it's really horrible [. . .] that this is the intimate connection that these guys have."

Earlier in the same episode, Christopher arrives at the Bada Bing! to announce his marriage to Kelli (Cara Buono), and here, too, the younger gangster praises his mentor: "I tell you, T, with the example you set, plus the wisdom I learned from AA, it's an inspiration. Building blocks: home, family."[30] As Winter points out though, while Christopher is praising Tony as a role mode, the camera is positioned to show a stripper sliding down a pole in the background. The meaning is clear; Tony's values are dubious at best, and "home" and "family" become ignored when it is convenient.

Fans know, too, though, that the moment of bonding is a brief one. When Christopher finally makes his long-planned film, *Cleaver*, it depicts a young wiseguy killing the overbearing boss who slept with his fiancée. Tony is initially impressed with the portrayal, praising his film counterpart as "a tough prick."[31] But when Carmela points out that the film is a "revenge fantasy," based on Christopher's belief that Tony had sex with Adriana, Tony must face up to what his nephew really thinks of him. With tears in his eyes, Tony tells Melfi that he tried to be "a friend, a fucking guy you could look up to," but that, now, "All I am to him is some asshole bully. [. . .] All I did for this fucking kid, and he fucking hates me so much."[32]

What Tony has mostly done for Christopher is constantly berate the young man, cast him aside when convenient, use his nephew to isolate himself from the FBI, and alternately encourage then castigate Christopher's alcohol and drug use. While Christopher is driving his boss home one night, the young wiseguy finally pays the ultimate price for worshipping the wrong idol. As the scene begins, Christopher once again extols Tony's leadership, repeating the boss's new mantra that "Each day is a gift," and asserting, "Every time I look at my kid, that's what I realize."[33] By this point, Christopher has become a husband and father, and he is genuinely moved by the experience of having a child. But remaining in the Mafia proves incompatible with the true fulfillment of domestic life. The constant insults, "breaking balls," and degradation leads Christopher back to drugs to numb his feelings. In the car, he slips a CD into the stereo, commenting, "This *Departed* soundtrack, it's a fucking killer." The words "departed" and "killer" produce a brief moment of chilling dramatic irony as the audience realizes before Tony does that Christopher is high and anticipates the consequences. As the song "Comfortably Numb" begins to play, its tranquilizing melody and lyrics amplify both Christopher's mental stupor and Tony's growing awareness. The lyrics we hear, "The child is grown, the dream is gone," seem to be a poignant reflection of Tony's thoughts; Christopher is not the loyal subordinate that Tony had hoped he would be. Then, when the incipient crash finally comes, Tony notices the crushed child seat and hears Christopher admitting, through a bloody cough, "I'll never pass the drug test." Christopher's paternal love has not overcome his desire to remain with Tony and, thus, his need to feel "numb" endangers his child as well as his boss. The actual murder is eerily quiet, as Tony slowly ends Christopher's life rather than dialing 911, and the silence signals Tony's transformation into the cold-hearted killer he really is. Incapable of admitting loss or his own complicity in Christopher's behavior, Tony responds only with irritation at having to appear sad. In a dream, he confesses to feeling that "The biggest blunder of my career is now gone, and I don't have to be confronted by that fact no more."[34] Unable to experience remorse, Tony becomes the one who is "comfortably numb."

"My Son Is Talking Suicide, So Now I'm Trapped Here Forever"

Tony's ability to shut off emotion comes primarily from his mother, a cold-hearted, domineering shrew he once called "the real gangster."[35] Indeed, the impetus for *The Sopranos* was a story about the relationship between a mob boss and his mother, and how the man's psychiatrist realizes before he does that the mother is the real danger in his life.[36] Thus, the first two seasons follow Tony's therapeutic insights, or attempts at insights, into the consequences of being Livia Soprano's (Nancy Marchand's) son. Livia is impossible to please, unceasingly critical, and the one who manipulates Uncle Junior into attempting to murder her own son. As usual, though, *The Sopranos* portrays her as (at least slightly) more human than beast. Tony comes to realize the effects of his own father's adultery on his mother, including the father's absence when she is hospitalized for a miscarriage. Further, when we meet Livia, she is old and losing all control over her life. She remains overall, however, almost impossible to sympathize with. Livia's legacy, through Marchand's brilliant performance, is to be one of the most original and provocative villains in literary history, and, within the show's diegesis, the instigator of Tony's panic attacks and of A. J.'s existential angst. Her nihilistic declaration to A. J.—"It's all a big nothing. What makes you think you're so special?"—has become one of the series' most famous and discussed lines.[37]

Janice Soprano almost steals the show as Tony's scheming, drama-queen sister. Always out to make a profit, Janice bullies her way back into the Soprano family world by feigning concern for her aging mother and remains to annoy Tony by exploiting his sense of familial duty. Through the course of the series, she changes religions as often as she does men, hungry for both spiritual guidance and love. But she is capable of ruthless manipulation. When she steals the prosthetic leg of her mother's nurse, she is punished by the woman's Russian gangster friends and their beating leads her, briefly, to feel "born again in the Lord."[38] But when she realizes that Tony has settled the score, Janice is overcome with adoration for her violent defender. It is hard to fault Janice, though, for her worst (in the legal sense) crime. When fiancé Ritchie hits her, Janice simply grabs a gun and kills him. Audiences cannot help but applaud the woman's refusal to be abused, even as they are forced to question their own moral relativism.

Carmela Soprano is also an impressively strong female character, a Catholic who truly believes in both God and Hell but knowingly makes a deal with the devil. Carmela stands up to her mob boss husband, oversees the traditions that keep the family together, and is willing to use blackmail to help her children (she threatens an acquaintance into writing a letter of recommendation to get Meadow into college). But though she continually seeks spiritual guidance from her priest, she ultimately admits,

The minute I met Tony, I knew who that guy was. [...] I don't know if I loved him in spite of it or because of it. [...] I knew, whether consciously or not, that behind [the gifts he brought], there was probably some guy with a broken arm, you know, or worse. [...] I would go to my priest, and I would cry and say how bad I felt about how my husband made his money, but that was bullshit because there are far bigger crooks than my husband.[39]

Carmela's confession is interesting for two reasons. First, she admits being insensate to the suffering of Tony's victims. The fact that Tony may break someone's arms "or worse" in order to buy her a gift is an appalling notion, but she is not only unconcerned, she is actually attracted by his violence. Secondly, Carmela has not had a change of heart but rather feels guilty over involving the children. As she tells Melfi, "They don't decide who they're born to. [...] It's all out in the open now, the whole thing. They're not in grade school anymore, they've become, the longer they stay with us, ...," and Melfi supplies the difficult word, "complicit."[40]

Carmela is paying the cost for her own complicity in Tony's crimes, something she was warned about in one of the series' most memorable scenes. Years earlier, feeling ill used by both Tony and her children, Carmela sought the advice of a psychiatrist, only to hear his blunt instruction to leave her husband: "Take only the children, what's left of them, and go. [...] I'm not charging you because I won't take blood money, and you can't either."[41] Carmela's problem is just that, though; she has been knowingly living on "blood money" since she married Tony and is not willing to give it up. Indeed, when Carmela and Tony come near divorce, she retreats again over money; her price for reconciliation is $600,000; the cost is an investment she hopes will secure her future.

The astute Meadow Soprano finds her own way of living the lie. As a teenager, Meadow was disrespectful and openly critical of her parents' hypocrisy. But she, too, likes the money—the Ivy League college, the trips to salons, the clothes. And, though she suspects her father or his crew of murdering an ex-boyfriend, Jackie Aprile, Jr., (Jason Cerbone), she continues to defend her father against outsiders. At the end of the series, Meadow is set to marry the son of one of Tony's gang members, and, more significantly, to turn the FBI's treatment of her father into a reason to study law, that is, to protect minorities (such as her family) against government oppression. Thus, although she never clearly states this view, she seems prepared to defend criminal activity as a result of corrupt governmental authority.

Young Anthony Soprano, Jr., known as "A. J.," first attracts audience attention in the series' pilot episode when the thirteen-year-old complains, "What, no fucking ziti?" In that one sentence, *The Sopranos* ushered in a new version of television teenager, one who mimics his parents' profanity, talks back, and rarely gets his voice heard within the home. In interviews, David Chase has explained that the Soprano family environment is similar to the one he grew up in, except that there was no cursing in his home. But, mainly, he wanted to create teenage characters who seemed realistic: "So many movies now deal with empowered kids, [...] and that's not my recollection of being a teenager, that you triumph over anything."[42]

A. J. stumbles his way toward maturity, getting expelled from school, using drugs, enjoying the reputation of being Tony Soprano's son, and even suffering his own panic attacks. But he also participates in violent acts, and it is only his weakness that prevents him from becoming like his father. By the end of the series, though, as Chase points out, "Anthony, Jr., is not going to be a killer of men."[43] He will earn some level of financial success through his father's connections, but he will not be a killer, thus forging a path of ambiguous moral compromise.

Tony's parenting skills are best illustrated, though, in his reaction to A. J.'s suicidal drive. When A. J. finally finds and then loses real love in his life, through his affair with Blanca (Dania Ramirez), he becomes severely depressed. He eventually fails in his suicide attempt, and his father is sincerely distraught. But Tony's primary response to all problems is to think of himself first. As he exclaims to Dr. Melfi, "My son is talking suicide, so now I'm trapped here forever."[44] Though A. J. needs serious help, Tony is mainly frustrated at how his son's problems affect himself.

"A Highly Moral Affair"

Vladimir Nabokov once called his controversial novel *Lolita*, "a highly moral affair." The same can be said of *The Sopranos*. By refraining from didacticism or censorship, and, instead, presenting consistently entertaining and provocative art of the highest quality, *The Sopranos* invites us to make our own judgments about the thin line between morality and immorality. Then again, if we ask seriously ourselves "What Would Tony Do?," we may not want to know the answer.

Notes

1. "Chasing It," *The Sopranos*, Season 6, Part 2, Episode 4, first broadcast April 29, 2007, by HBO. Directed by Tim Van Patten and written by Matthew Weiner.

2. As part of the package *The Sopranos: The Complete Series*, a Bonus Features disc includes three parodies of the series from *The Simpsons, Saturday Night Live*, and *MadTV*.

3. "Mayham," *The Sopranos*, Season 6, Episode, first broadcast March 26, 2006, by HBO. Directed by Jack Bender and written by Matthew Weiner.

4. For insight into other aspects of the show's racial issues, see Brian Gibson, "'Black Guys, My Ass': Uncovering the Queerness of Racism in *The Sopranos*," and Christopher Kocela, "From Columbus to Gary Cooper: Mourning the Lost White Father in *The Sopranos*," both in *Reading the Sopranos: Hit TV from HBO* (New York: I. B. Tauris, 2006).

5. Jennifer Steinhauer and Robert F. Worth, "*Sopranos* Uninvited, Mayor Finds a Parade He Can Refuse," *New York Times*, B.1. October 12, 2002.

6. "Italian-American group sues makers of *The Sopranos*," The Associated Press. April 6, 2001. http://www.freedomforum.org (accessed March 31, 2009).

7. "Congresswoman asks House to Rap *Sopranos* for Stereotyping," The Associated Press. May 24, 2001. http://www.freedomforum.org (accessed March 31, 2009).

8. "Exclusive Interview with David Chase by Peter Bogdanovich," *The Sopranos*. Season one, disc four, 1999.

9. "From Where to Eternity," *The Sopranos*, Season 2, Episode 9, first broadcast March 12, 2000, by HBO. Directed by Henry J. Bronchtein and written by Michael Imperioli.

10. "College," *The Sopranos*. Season 1, Episode 5, first broadcast February 7, 1999, by HBO. Directed by Allen Coulter and written by James Manos, Jr., and David Chase.

11. "Christopher," *The Sopranos*. Season 4, Episode 3, first broadcast September 29, 2002, by HBO. Directed by Tim Van Patten; teleplay by Michael Imperioli, story by Michael Imperioli and Maria Laurino.

12. Christopher Kocela, "From Columbus to Gary Cooper: Mourning the Lost White Father in *The Sopranos*," in *Reading* The Sopranos: *Hit TV from HBO*. Ed. David Lavery (New York: I. B. Tauris, 2006), 104–17.

13. "Unidentified Black Males," *The Sopranos*. Season 5, Episode 9, first broadcast May 2, 2004, by HBO. Directed by Tim Van Patten and written by Matthew Weiner and Terence Winter.

14. In the episode "Full Leather Jacket," Tony gives Meadow a car that had belonged to a friend of hers. The friend's father gave the car to Tony to repay a debt, and Tony admits that he "must have known" that she would recognize the car, that "I want to rub her nose in it"; that is, Tony wants Meadow to

face the fact that the family's material success, which she clearly enjoys, comes from his crimes. "Full Leather Jacket," *The Sopranos*, Season 2, Episode 8, first broadcast March 5, 2000, by HBO. Directed by Allen Coulter and written by Robin Green and Mitchell Burgess.

15. "Christopher."

16. "Johnny Cakes," *The Sopranos*, Season 6, Episode 8, first broadcast April 30, 2006, by HBO. Directed by Tim Van Patten and written by Diane Frolov and Andrew Schneider.

17. Ibid.

18. "House Arrest," *The Sopranos*, Season 2, Episode 11, first broadcast March 26, 2000 by HBO. Directed by Tim Van Patten and written by Terence Winter.

19. "He is Risen," *The Sopranos*, Season 3, Episode 8, first broadcast April 15, 2001, by HBO. Directed by Allen Coulter and written by Robin Green, Mitchell Burgess, and Todd A. Kessler.

20. Ibid.

21. Ibid.

22. "Mergers and Acquisitions," *The Sopranos*, Season 4, Episode 8, first broadcast November 3, 2002 by HBO. Directed by Daniel Attias; teleplay by Lawrence Konner; story by David Chase, Robin Green, Mitchell Burgess, and Terence Winter.

23. "The Test Dream," *The Sopranos*, Season 5, Episode 11, first broadcast May 16, 2004, by HBO. Directed by Allen Coulter and written by David Chase and Matthew Weiner.

24. "Knight in White Satin Armor" is the title of Season 2, Episode 12, first broadcast April 2, 2000, by HBO. Directed by Allen Coulter and written by Robin Green and Mitchell Burgess.

25. "Fortunate Son," *The Sopranos*, Season 3, Episode 3, first broadcast March 11, 2001, by HBO. Directed by Henry J. Bronchtein and written by Todd A. Kessler.

26. Although based on real Mafia tradition, these induction rituals have apparently grown slack. Mobster "Little Joe" D'Angelo testified in March 2006, that, in his induction ceremony, attended by "Junior" Gotti, the mob bosses simply wrote "saint" on a piece of paper and drew a cross (Richard Willing, "The Mafia is on Shaky Ground," *USA Today*, March 9, 2006).

27. "Kaisha," *The Sopranos*, Season 6, Part 1, Episode 12, first broadcast June 4, 2006, by HBO. Directed by Alan Taylor and written by Terence Winter.

28. "Long Term Parking," *The Sopranos*, Season 5, Episode 12, first broadcast May 23, 2004, by HBO. Directed by Tim Van Patten and written by Terence Winter.

29. "The Ride," *The Sopranos*, Season 6, Part 1, Episode 9, first broadcast May 7, 2006, by HBO. Directed by Alan Taylor and written by Terence Winter.

30. Ibid.

31. "Stage 5," *The Sopranos*, Season 6, Part 2, Episode 2, first broadcast April 15, 2007, by HBO. Directed by Alan Taylor and written by Terence Winter.

32. Ibid.

33. "Kennedy and Heidi," *The Sopranos*, Season 6, Part 2, Episode 6, first broadcast May 13, 2007, by HBO. Directed by Alan Taylor and written by Matthew Weiner and David Chase.

34. Ibid.

35. "Down Neck," *The Sopranos*, Season 1, Episode 7, first broadcast February 21, 1999, by HBO. Directed by Lorraine Senna and written by Mitchell Burgess and Robin Green.

36. "Exclusive Interview with David Chase by Peter Bogdanovich."

37. See, for example, Kevin L. Stoehr's article "'It's All a Big Nothing': The Nihilistic Vision of *The Sopranos*." *The Sopranos and Philosophy: I Kill Therefore I Am* (Chicago: Open Court, 2004).

38. "Employee of the Month," *The Sopranos*, Season 3, Episode 4, first broadcast March 18, 2001, by HBO. Directed by John Patterson and written by Robin Green and Mitchell Burgess.

39. "Mayham."

40. Ibid.

41. "Second Opinion," *The Sopranos*, Season 3, Episode 7, first broadcast April 8, 2001, by HBO. Directed by Tim Van Patten and written by Lawrence Konner.

42. "Exclusive Interview with David Chase by Peter Bogdanovich."

43. "Supper with *The Sopranos* II," *The Sopranos: The Complete Series*, Bonus Features, 2007.

44. "Walk Like a Man," *The Sopranos*, Season 6, Part 2, Episode 5, first broadcast May 6, 2007, by HBO. Written and directed by Terence Winter.

Bibliography

"Cast and Crew: Christopher Moltisanti." *The Sopranos*. HBO.com, http://www.hbo.com/sopranos/cast/character/christopher_moltisanti.shtml.

Greene, Richard, and Peter Vernezze, eds. *The Sopranos and Philosophy: I Kill Therefore I Am*. Chicago: Open Court, 2004.

"Italian-American Group Sues Makers of *The Sopranos*." The Associated Press. April 6, 2001. http://www.freedomforum.org.

Lavery, David, ed. *Reading the Sopranos: Hit TV from HBO*. New York: I. B. Tauris, 2006.

The Sopranos. HBO. 1999–2007.

Steinhauer, Jennifer and Robert F. Worth. *"Sopranos* Uninvited, Mayor Finds a Parade He Can Refuse." *New York Times*. B.1. October 12, 2002.

Willing, Richard. "The Mafia Is on Shaky Ground." *USA Today*. March 9, 2006.

CHAPTER 12

"If It Sucks, It's Your Fault": Joss Whedon and the Empowerment of Fans

Aaron Barlow

"If it sucks, it's your fault." Or so Joss Whedon claims in a filmed intro-duction for preview audiences to the rough cut of his 2005 movie *Serenity*. Whedon's point? That the movie would not exist if it had not been for fans: they had raised the money that paid for an ad that ran in *Variety* on December 9, 2002, asking that the Fox TV show *Firefly* not be can-celled; they had peppered a rival network with postcards, asking that it pick up the show, and then later bought DVDs in large numbers. Though the fans' efforts ultimately failed, their persistence convinced Universal Studios that a movie based on the series could be a success. Thus, *Serenity* was born—and a new bond between creator and fans made its power clear.

Whedon, in his introduction, encapsulates what had occurred:

> The people who made the show, and people who saw the show, which is roughly the same number of people, fell in love with it a little bit too much to let it go. . . . In Hollywood, people like that are called "unrealis-tic, quixotic, obsessive." In my world, they are called "Browncoats." . . . Failed TV shows don't get made into major motion pictures unless the creator, the cast, and the fans believe beyond reason.

The nickname Browncoats has been adopted by the fans of *Firefly*, especially those involved in the movement to save it. Their evident passion extended beyond the movie and continues today through fund-raising activities associated with the movie and with causes Whedon endorses. Whedon, recognizing their impact, honors them by claiming membership (and not leadership) himself in the Browncoat movement.

Though the movie did not live up to financial expectations, it certainly has had an afterlife, too, living on through DVD sales and fundraising showings, demonstrating that a new, dynamic, and effective partnership between fans (or fan cults) and creators is beginning to become less rare and more than wishful thinking. They are proving that the barriers between artist and audience that were erected through electronic media in the twentieth century are beginning to fall in the twenty-first.

There are actually three related barriers, two even older than that electronic one that grew through the nature of the "new" media of the time. Whedon and his fans, along with a growing number of others, are beginning to overcome all three.

One of the barriers descends from the "fourth wall" of the proscenium stage that came into vogue during the nineteenth century. It was later compounded by the separation created by electronic reproduction, whether it took place in radio, film, television, or other types of recording or broadcast, but it rests on a tacit understanding between actors and audience and not on factors of media.

For a long time—actually starting in late-eighteenth-century theaters and concert halls—sight and sound during performances were considered to be appropriate only when going one way, from the performers to the audience, though with certain restrictions and exceptions. Performers, for example, were expected never to acknowledge the presence of the audience except when the performance was over. The separation, however, was rarely complete or as formal as it would seem on the surface: audience members had multiple ways of conveying their reactions, and performers found plenty of methods for communicating with their audiences beyond the work itself. And though it was frowned upon, performers did occasionally ignore the imaginary wall to communicate directly with the audience, a practice common to earlier drama. However, the general conceit was that the relationship was one of active offering (while ignoring the audience) and passive accepting (while ignoring the possibility of participation). The decorum of nineteenth-century audiences is still particularly apparent in the conventions adhered to by classical music audiences.

The second barrier, one of ownership, is even a little older, evolving from the first copyright laws (in the Anglo-American tradition, the Copyright Act of 1709) placing control of written works (and, later, other artifacts and even performance rights) in the hands of authors or their agents for specified periods of time, removing such creations from the "commons" so that creators could benefit financially from their works. Though such laws were meant to circumvent unauthorized or "pirate" editions, they also served to limit how the work could be used subsequently both by other artists and by fans.

During the twentieth century, these two barriers were compounded by a third, the one erected by the nature of electronic media themselves. In this era of media development, creative works were mainly presented via one-way media (ignoring the telephone and a few other two-way communications devices). The medium itself created a barrier that disallowed immediate audience interaction with the performance. While a device like the television hoped to spur viewers into buying products advertised by a network's sponsors, for example, the medium itself demanded one-way communication.

As a result of these three barriers, the more intricate interactions today between the creators of those media properties that have become the focus of fan cults and those very fans are problematic because the media environment is undergoing a nearly complete transformation. Given new interactivity and multiplicity, both sides (creators and fans) now feel ownership over the works in question, the creators by virtue of origin and fans because success rests with them (more clearly than ever)—and neither wants the other to dictate how proprietorship should be utilized. The contemporary results of this phenomenon have often been something like an impasse, the creators having copyright and trademark law on their side, the fans having sheer numbers and pliable, evolving technology much more under their own control than anything seen in the last century.

The divide created between the two has become, at times, acrimonious. Whedon, going against the common assumptions of ownership, however, refuses to see a separation at all. Instead, he views the new relationship between his work and fans as a partnership. He is showing that what could be problematic can be turned productive.

For a variety of reasons, it generally falls on the creators to break the impasse between proprietor and fan when such an instance develops. Given the structure of the American (and most other) legal systems, where creative output is regarded as property, this would be expected to be the case. As we have seen, it has long been established both in law and in custom that it is with the creator that real power over the work lies. The situation is not simple, though. Purchaser (fan) rights and the power of the cultural commons pertain as well—though for generations some creators have tried to limit and control these.

The legal situation remains ambiguous. The "fair use" doctrine for scholarship and classroom, for example, is ill defined in American law, often leading to publishers (and others) to err on the side of caution. Failing to adequately clarify their own rights through law, some creators have tried to control fan (and professional) interactions and utilizations of the works simply through threat of legal action or through selective prosecution aimed less at courtroom victory than at intimidation. The Recording Industry Association of America (RIAA) famously has tried to limit the downloading of music, and the 1991 Biz Markie case (*Grand Upright Music, Ltd v. Warner Bros. Records Inc.*), where sampling of an earlier song was deemed willful infringement of copyright by a federal court, led to severe curtailment of the practice in commercial situations—and to a limit on what even fans are willing to present publicly of their own amateur, derivative compositions. In these cases, distribution of the art is seen simply and only as a commercial transaction and not as something with intangible but real cultural and artistic value beyond simple gain.

Other creators, like George Lucas of *Star Wars*, have worked to control use of their creations through a carrot-and-stick approach, inviting fans and their fan art (and other manipulations of his characters, themes, etc.) into the fold, so to speak, while implicitly threatening action against those who don't come in. They see that what they have made becomes more than simply something that can be bought and sold and recognize that future sales depend on a content audience.

Still others, like the rock bands the Grateful Dead and Pearl Jam, have allowed fans to make the art their own on the theory that the fan base will thereby grow and that returns to the creators will grow as well—perhaps not as quickly, but with greater impact over the long run. I call this the Grateful Dead Effect. The Effect rests on an expansive economic model in which the simple transaction is only one part of a dynamic relationship and a growing cultural whole. What the Grateful Dead did was to actively encourage the taping of their shows and the trading of those tapes. This increased interest in their live performances, eventually making them a top draw for two decades. By giving up a part of their creative content, the Dead realized that a fervent, growing fan base would reward it in other ways. Some critics make a similar case when arguing for allowing fans to illegally download music: by giving away some content, a group can build a fan base that is more loyal and committed to the group's long-term success.

Clearly, different people and different organizations have reacted to fans, fan art, and "sampling" (in its most expansive sense) in diverse ways, leading to a general situation of uncertainty, especially as fan art (extension from the primary work by fans and not for commercial purposes) has grown as a public movement apace with the Internet itself and as fans increasingly find new ways for utilizing the commonalities they had earlier discovered.

Whedon, perhaps best known as creator and screenwriter for *Buffy the Vampire Slayer* (Fran Rubel Kuzui, 1992) and as creator of the spin-off *Angel* (which ran from 1997 to 2003, the first five seasons on the WB network, the final two on UPN), follows the Grateful Dead pattern, at least to some degree. To use the Grateful Dead Effect efficiently, one must be focused not on a quick return but on long-term confidence in the product and in the probability of fan base growth. Whedon has shown this confidence consistently throughout his career, even though Fox did not share his certainty when it came to *Firefly*. Whedon says:

> At one point, I was asked, "Why should we keep this show?" and my answer was, "You're going to have a fanbase that loves it like they don't love other things . . . and I believe it'll grow—if you ever air it." The kind of shows I make start out this way and then the word spreads and they become part of people's lives—people who are more dedicated than anything—but the network was interested in opening-weekend mentality and they weren't going to listen to that.[1]

Other artists and their corporate sponsors may still be stuck in what could soon be seen as an antique sensibility centered on those old conceptions of unidirectional media and silent viewers. Not Whedon. He recognizes that his fans are more than simply passive receptors for his art or voyeurs restricted by that fourth wall, a recognition that Fox—in 2002, at least—did not share. Like many of those in contemporary creative media arts, Fox seems to have imagined audience members as empty vessels requiring immediate fulfillment and to have accounted financial return based on the number it could reach immediately—still the standard for television (and even for film) as we enter the second decade of the new century. Whedon saw, and sees, the audience much more as his immediate partners for future gain, an entirely different (and much more twenty-first-century) mindset.

Just so, Jane Espenson, a writer for Whedon on a number of his shows (including *Firefly*), someone who has seen up close how he works, writes that Whedon has a "secret ingredient" to his success, which is:

> Joss's attitude toward the viewers. I don't recall Joss ever talking about "the audience" as a separate identity with an agenda separate or lesser (or greater, for that matter) than his own. He writes what interests

him, what he would want to see. This is why when Joss writes a surprise it genuinely surprises, why his shocking revelations shock us, why his jokes make us laugh. It's not just that he assumes that you, the viewers, are as smart as him. He assumes, in a way, that you *are* him. And that he is you.[2]

This is quite a different attitude from that of the Fox network, which still was adhering to "the persistent cliché," as Murray Hasknecht called it more than 50 years ago, "that television brings the world into our living room."[3] Whedon's attitude sidesteps the old view of separation between media and audience and of television as the "doer" or "bringer," a view that carries the assumption that the creator (television) is the giver and the source of all that is dynamic, the audience (completely distinct from the creator) merely receiving what is offered. This hierarchical conception centers all motion within the creator and is at odds with Whedon's vision of a collaborative approach bringing audience into the creative process, an approach necessarily vested in growth and not on immediate return.

The history of the ill-fated *Firefly* demonstrates Whedon's under-standing of the importance and impact of fans in other ways as well, especially through the "life after death" of the series. Not only did *Serenity* get funded, but the stories of the *Firefly* world continue in other media (comic books, in particular). Of separate but real impact has been the subsequent Can't Stop the Serenity (CSTS) project (from a line in *Serenity*, "can't stop the signal") that raises money for Equality Now, a charity Whedon supports, through showings of the movie. The project demonstrated, in particular, what the power and effect of a fan cult can be when it is given freedom to act on its own, espe-cially when given a sense of ownership over the original creation.

The success of the project certifies Whedon's faith in the power and discernment within audiences and demonstrates that fans needn't be seen merely as adoring followers but, given the leeway, can take the original concept and purpose and sail in new directions of their own charting. At the very least, fans can take on a much more substantial and overt role (though one that has always existed to some degree, even if *sub rosa*) as partners with the creators.

To reiterate, when the series was clearly in danger of cancellation in the fall of 2002, fans, who had begun to coalesce into those self-styled Browncoats (after the losing side that two of the main characters of the show had fought for in a recent war), began a campaign to keep the series going. They failed, but their dedication led to quick release of the series on DVD and to the decision by Universal Studios to back *Serenity*—and fans began to seek other avenues for demonstrating their love for the show. Even before CSTS, fans (through the website fireflyfans.net) raised money so that, in conjunction with Whedon's Mutant Enemy, Inc., copies of the series DVDs could be donated for viewing on U.S. Navy ships at sea. Asked about the effort, Whedon responded, "I'm very lucky to have such generous fans . . . who have always used their community to serve the community at large."[4]

In addition to demonstrating his rejection of the passive-audience model, Whedon's simple statement in response to the Navy project is perhaps a key to understanding his relation to the fan cults that have built up around his works and to his view of his own (and his fans') responsibilities to the broader world around them. He doesn't see himself as simply giving works to audiences but to active fans, to people who he hopes will be interacting with him through the art itself and (again) not simply viewing his works passively, people who are already leading active and productive lives.

The passivity, then, of audience implied by descriptors, such as *viewer* and *listener*, is no longer even an accepted myth, not to artists like Whedon, nor is the distinction between *audience* and the once much more pejorative *fan*. As Will Brooker and Deborah Jermyn wrote about evolving media relationships in 2003, "the experience of being part of an audience will change, and will perhaps, in the shift towards greater participation, become similar in some ways to what we are used to thinking of as fandom: a pattern of engagement characterized by detection, discussion, interaction and community."[5] Whedon recognized this long ago, as *Buffy* demonstrates, and he also must have asked himself if he could avail himself of the new dynamic for other purposes. His answer, we find, is "yes."

Once more showing that his is no simple "academic" belief, on May 20, 2007, Whedon posted the following on the fan blog Whedonesque:

All I ask is this: Do something. Try something. Speaking out, showing up, writing a letter, a check, a strongly worded e-mail. Pick a cause—there are few unworthy ones. And nudge yourself past the brink of tacit support to action. Once a month, once a year, or just once. If you can't think of what to do, there is this handy link. Even just learning enough about a subject so you can speak against an opponent eloquently makes you an unusual personage. Start with that. Any one of you would have cried out, would have intervened, had you been in that crowd in Bashiqa. Well thanks to digital technology, you're all in it now.

I have never had any faith in humanity. But I will give us props on this: if we can evolve, invent and theorize our way into the technologically magical, culturally diverse and artistically magnificent race we are and still get people to buy the idiotic idea that half of us are inferior, we're pretty amazing. Let our next sleight of hand be to make that myth disappear.[6]

Whedon was responding to the stoning death of a 17-year-old girl, Du'a Khalil Aswad, in Bashika, Iraq, a death caught on cell-phone video and widely seen via the Internet. Consistent with his attitude toward his fans, Whedon also sees the world as one whole and so asks others to help him break down barriers between people. His fans took his words seriously and still do.

One of their responses came through CSTS specifically, which had already begun to raise money for Equality Now. Since inception, it has raised more than $250,000, well more than $100,000 in 2009 alone. Early in that year, Anne Barringer, Global Organizer for CSTS, started a series of posts on the group's website entitled "Why We Are Here" that provide a continuing explanation of the purposes of the group:

> Many of us participate in CSTS events and other Browncoat related activities for a number of reasons. We join together to make a difference in the world because we've been rallied by Joss's words to do something, anything. We meet up so that we can share our love of the Serenity/Firefly/Whedonverse, and because we are like-minded folk who want to share other aspects of our lives with our fellow Fireflyians. These are just a few of the reasons we come together in this fellowship.
>
> And they are all, very good reasons.
>
> The main focus of Can't Stop the Serenity has always been to help Equality Now keep the signal going. EN seeks to let the voices of abused women the world over, cry out and be heard. Humanity can listen and come together, seeking to end all suffering and abuse—one voice at a time.[7]

The "About" section of the CSTS website describes the genesis of the organization, recapping the reaction of many fans to Fox decisions about "their" show:

> When his [Joss Whedon's] newest baby, *Firefly* was prematurely cancelled, fans of the show sprang into action to get the series back on. While we are still working for the return of the TV series, we DID manage to make enough noise to get our beloved Serenity to the big screen. Along the way, we discovered another worthwhile cause: **Equality Now**....
>
> So, once a year, we join together around the globe and host charity screenings of *Serenity* as well as many other festive events. We raise money to give to Equality Now and other worthy causes. Basically, we convene to watch a movie. Not a bad way to support charity, huh?[8]

Not a bad way to celebrate a common passion, either.

In many ways, what Whedon is doing is nothing new but simply a demonstration of his respect for the reality that has always been with us, yet a reality obscured for a century by the nature of electronic media and an even older cultural conceit establishing audiences as unnoted observers and not participants in the art—and not even qualified judges of the art. Ultimately, however, as Whedon understands, it has always been the audience that has determined the art (in partnership with the creator), not the other way around—though this view was (and is) hotly contested. Not only that, but it frightens many of those with ownership over art. Writing in 1946, Clement Greenberg claimed that "any resentment ⌈towards art not corresponding to audience 'reality'⌉ the common man may feel is silenced by the awe in which he stands of the patrons of this art. Only when he becomes dissatisfied with the social order they administer does he begin to criticize their culture. Then the plebian finds courage for the first time to voice his opinions openly."[9] Greenberg, like many of the corporate controllers of electronic media today, argues that audiences need to be shown what to "want." They are not partners but possible rivals, possibly dangerous and revolutionary rivals vying for the central position as controlling "patron" but lacking artistic discernment.

To those wedded to the older style of artistic ownership, possible *hoi polloi* involvement represents encroachment on a protected domain. To Whedon and those like him, it is freeing instead, not threatening. After all, he doesn't have to take the blame alone. As he says, "If it sucks, it's your fault."

Notes

1. Joss Whedon, in "Still Flying: An Interview with Joss Whedon," Abbie Bernstein, Bryan Cairns, Karl Derrick, and Tara DiLullo, *Firefly: The Official Companion, Vol. 2* (London: Titan Books, 2007), 12.

2. Jane Espenson, "Introduction," *Serenity Found: More Unauthorized Essays on Joss Whedon's* Firefly *Universe* (Dallas: Benbella, 2007), 3–4.

3. Murray Hasknecht, "The Mike in the Bosom," in Bernard Rosenberg and David Manning White, eds., *Mass Culture: The Popular Arts in America* (Glencoe, IL: Free Press, 1957), 375.

4. Joss Whedon, quoted in Ingrid Mueller, "Sci-Fi Series 'Firefly' Available through Navy's Afloat Library Program," Navy.mil, http://www.news.navy.mil/search/display.asp?story_id=12580, March 31, 2004.

5. Will Brooker and Deborah Jermyn, "Conclusion: Overflow and Audience," in *The Audience Studies Reader*, Will Brooker and Deborah Jermyn, eds. (London: Routledge, 2003), 333.

6. Joss Whedon, "Let's Watch A Girl Get Beaten To Death," Whedon-esque Blog, http://whedonesque.com/comments/13271, May 20, 2007.

7. Anne Barringer, "Why We Are Here (Part I)," Can't Stop the Serenity, http://www.cantstoptheserenity.com/wwah/wwah1/, May 4, 2009.

8. Can't Stop the Serenity, "About," http://www.cantstoptheserenity.com/about/.

9. Clement Greenberg, "Avant-Garde and Kitsch," *Partisan Review*, 1946, rpt. in Bernard Rosenberg and David Manning White, eds., *Mass Culture: The Popular Arts in America* (Glencoe, IL: Free Press, 1957), 107.

CHAPTER 13

WHO KILLED LAURA PALMER? PERHAPS WE ALL DID: *TWIN PEAKS* AND THE AMERICAN FASCINATION WITH THE MYSTERY OF WHO KILLED LAURA PALMER

Brian Cogan

When David Lynch's offbeat and groundbreaking television show *Twin Peaks* debuted on ABC on April 8, 1990, it was unlike anything audiences had seen before on American network television. The show, a *dramedy* (a term used to describe a mixture between a comedy and a drama) or prime-time soap opera, was a continuation of its creator/director David Lynch's dystopian view of suburbia.

In his 1986 film *Blue Velvet*, he had explored the seething underbelly below the surface of suburban life and won acclaim for the film's quirky and daring use of European art-house sensibility as well as a sort of down-home, "aw shucks" Boy Scout vision of a Norman Rockwell-esque version of America. Lynch, along with cocreator and former *Hill Street Blues* writer Mark Frost, attempted to see if this sensibility could be worked into a weekly television series. The results were startling.

The show starred *Blue Velvet* star and Lynchian surrogate Kyle MacLachlan as FBI agent Dale Cooper, exploring a murder mystery in a small town populated by strange and eccentric characters, each of whom seemed to have a secret or multiple secrets simmering just below the surface. The town, populated by a log lady, a mysterious giant, a dancing dwarf (or man from another world) who spoke backward, secret societies, and possibly a conduit to another dimension, was nonetheless obsessed with something that would soon consume the imagination of the American public—the central mystery of a murdered prom queen. This seemingly routine murder case, investigated by the FBI, led to the quintessential question that took American by storm in 1990: who killed Laura Palmer? The answer was initially unclear, but what was not uncertain was the fact that many Americans (more than 35 million watched the pilot) wanted desperately to know the answer. Within a few short weeks, the mystery of who killed Laura Palmer became an American television obsession.

Not since the television show *Dallas* had successfully gripped the television watching public with its mystery of "who Shot J. R.?" in 1980 had a show's central murder mystery taken on a life of its own. To many, the show's central mystery was the driving force around which the series worked, unlike television shows that came after it, such as *The X-Files* and *Lost*, which prolonged the mythology of the program for several years or even close to a decade. Instead, *Twin Peaks* eventually felt the pressure of fans and network executives to solve the mystery. Yet the culmination of events leading to the reveal of that famous question also led to the demise of the show. Network executives cancelled *Twin Peaks* after only two seasons. However, for a brief period, much of America buzzed over the beautiful blonde teenager who had been killed—and, of course, the dancing dwarf and the mysteries of the perfect cherry pie.

Twin Peaks and Laura Palmer as a Phenomenon

The initial *Twin Peaks* pilot captured the imagination of much of the viewing public who had, quite literally, never seen anything like it before on network television. The show, much more in the sensibility of an art film, with moody atmospheric music by composer Angelo Badalamenti and a young, mostly attractive—yet beguiling cast— was both a tribute to classic soap operas and shows such as *Peyton Place* and a unique presentation of Lynch's mixture of innocence and subversion. It was also a program that rewarded close viewing, which served as a boon for those who owned a VCR and could watch the program multiple times. The series abounded in coded clues and hints regarding many of the show's (multiple) central mysteries.

Critics raved and showered *Twin Peaks* with accolades, sensing that the ossified rules of prime-time television were finally being eroded. As one writer in the *New York Times* noted, "This is event television given a memorably wicked spin. Nothing like it has ever been seen on network prime time."[1] He further noted that Lynch "adds his own peculiar touches, small passing details that suddenly and often hilariously, thrust the commonplace out of kilter."[2] The attention to detail was striking in a sea of remarkable faceless network programs. *Twin Peaks* and its late lamented beauty queen Laura Palmer served as the subject of endless water-cooler speculation. As O'Connor wryly observed, "Mr. Lynch was soon proving that it pays to be weird and even a bit creepy."[3]

Laura Palmer fever was soon becoming a "commodifiable" product. Her face was emblazoned on t-shirts, some with just her picture, others simply stating: "I know who killed Laura Palmer." But for all the speculation, precious few fans actually knew what was going on, but they did know that they wanted to learn more. As a *New York Times* writer put it, "Offices buzzed with jokey inside references. In supermarket bakery departments, puzzled employees pushed record numbers of cherry pies across the counter on Thursday nights."[4] Like fans of science fiction programs, such as *Star Trek*, or movies like *Star Wars*, Lynch inspired a cult audience—one that grew larger than the typical smaller cult following of televised science fiction programs. As Grimes described, Lynch had "developed what might be called a mass cult following."[5]

Lynch's show was paradoxically a cult show and one that reached a mass audience, one in which "highly motivated fans were watching in groups, maintaining disciplined silence until the last credit rolled, then in an orgy of interpretation, analyzing the obscure visual symbols in the show."[6] It is rare for an American prime-time show, ostensibly one that combined numerous elements of the evening soap opera genre, to be so beloved and so closely followed, even if for a relatively short period of time.

Twin Peaks embodied both characteristics of the prototypical cult show and a mass culture phenomenon. As Grimes explained, "For an intoxicating few months, '*Twin Peaks*' seemed to be crackling away on every synapse in the collective American brain."[7] And if *Twin Peaks* was on everyone's brain, the center of the obsession revolved around the question of its central but largely absent character as seemingly all of America wondered in unison, "Who killed Laura Palmer?"

The Life (and Death and Life and Death) of Laura Palmer

Twin Peaks cocreator Mark Frost was quoted as saying "we want people to realize there is more to the show then Laura Palmer."[8] However, for many viewers and fans, Laura Palmer was *Twin Peaks*. In the complex mythology of *Twin Peaks*, Laura Palmer in some ways was the ultimate embodiment of the Madonna/whore complex. She was to some in town the virginal, innocent doting daddy's little girl, faithful to her boyfriend, and the ultimate virtuous small-town girl. But, as viewers soon realized, there was a much darker side to Laura Palmer. She was haunted, not just by the dark undercurrent of her life, that is, in stripping, prostitution, and drugs, but also literally haunted by the malevolent spirits of the Black Lodge (a place where fear is the only currency and where malevolent spirits and other malicious entities dwell, waiting for the chance to escape and corrupt the innocent), and in particular the embodiment of evil, Killer Bob.

Killer Bob, a spirit, or perhaps a person who had haunted Laura, represented the single most horrific dynamic in her life, one that turned her from hometown beauty queen to cocaine-addled prostitute. Laura's unfolding story, told through tantalizing bits of information, a diary entry here, a picture or snippet of video there, was the central glue that held *Twin Peaks* together and the single most compelling reason to watch—and obsess—over the show.

Twin Peaks used multiple platforms long before the advent of the Internet. To truly understand the series and the character of Laura Palmer, hardcore fans needed to not only read the companion book to the series, *The Secret Diary of Laura Palmer* (written by David Lynch's daughter, Jennifer Lynch), but also to watch the show's filmic prequel, *Twin Peaks: Fire, Walk With Me*, released after the television series left the airwaves. To understand Laura was to understand innocence despoiled but somehow maintained, to understand the dark undercurrent of the doting daughter and the Elektra myth, and to understand other mythology of the butterfly in a constant state of metamorphosis.

When viewers are first introduced to Laura Palmer, she is already dead, presumably stabbed to death, wrapped in plastic sheeting, and covered in sand. Her body is discovered on the shore of a river by local lumberjack and fisherman Pete Martell. This sets into motion the mystery that brings FBI agent Dale Cooper to Twin Peaks to find out who killed this representation of small-town America. Unsettling secrets start to unravel around Laura's friends' attempts at secrecy (she is soon found to have been cheating on her boyfriend Bobby Briggs with another friend, the gentle but mysterious motorcycle riding James Hurley); but this is just the tip of an iceberg composed almost entirely of black ice. Laura is quickly discovered to be the antithesis of the all-American girl; instead, she is a cocaine-abusing, sometime-prostitute at One Eyed Jack's Casino. Laura is haunted by the malevolent spirit Bob, who has been abusing her at night for years.

Her secrets are revealed to Agent Cooper at the same time they are revealed to the audience, and Cooper acts as a symbolic surrogate for how we the audience love, sometimes fear, and mourn Laura.

Although the actress Sheryl Lee was only supposed to play Laura as a murder victim, and appear on screen in video, photos, and brief flashbacks, her skill as an actress inspired to Lynch to cast her as her own cousin—the sweet and (actually) innocent Maddy Ferguson, who tries to solve the mystery of the death of Laura Palmer. Through Maddy, the audience is given a chance to view a more innocent, less world-weary Laura Palmer, one that is haunted only by the question of which boy to kiss as she tries to help solve the murder.

But the murder mystery dragged on, far into the second season and far too long for most ardent viewers. Eventually, after several delays in the first season (as a *New York Times* writer noted, by the time the killer was revealed, it was the "third time that *ABC* promised to solve the murder plot"), Lynch and Frost realized they needed to end the anticipation.[9] After much suspense, the killer was revealed to be Laura Palmer's father, Leland Palmer, who was possessed by the evil spirit Bob. The audience was shocked to discover this, since Leland then killed Laura a symbolic second time by brutally beating and then savagely killing Maddy. After a contrite Leland, now left alone by Bob, dies at the police station, Laura Palmer's ghost appears to him to forgive him for his actions while being possessed by Bob.

Although this was the end of the tenure of Sheryl Lee playing Laura Palmer or Maddy Ferguson on the program, the character had already appeared in *The Secret Diary of Laura Palmer*, a seeming must for any obsessed fan. The diary itself contains valuable but sometimes misleading, clues regarding Laura's past and her eventual fate. In her review of the Laura Palmer diary, Alessandra Stanley of the *New York Times* wrote that the book "reads like a twisted variation on *"The Diary of Anne Frank"*[10]

This is an apt comparison, since Laura Palmer's diary reveals an ingenuous young girl also struggling to maintain her innocence and even her sanity in an increasingly dark world. As Laura writes in the last page in her diary: "I am so afraid of death, I am so afraid that no one will believe me until after I have taken the seat that I fear has been saved for me in the darkness. Please don't hate me. I never meant to see the small hills and the fire. I never meant to see him or let him in."[11]

The film *Twin Peaks: Fire Walk With Me* (1992) further fleshed out details of Laura's life, revealing that when Bob/Leland Palmer attacked her for the last time, Bob had wanted to posses Laura, but upon her refusal, he stabbed her to death. Later, Laura's spirit appeared in the waiting room between the Black Lodge and the White Lodge, where the imprisoned Agent Cooper helped her to enter the White Lodge and finally find peace. While the mythology was complex and did indeed lead to numerous academic journals and popular blog speculation as to its meaning (even to this day), the story of the murdered Laura Palmer had to have an end, even if the ending was unsatisfying to many.

While the actual television show *Twin Peaks* went on after the resolution to the mystery of who killed Laura Palmer, the show did not last long without her. After the famous question received an answer, the series still contained mysterious elements and plotlines that needed to be solved, but without Laura Palmer, something, some essential life force seemed to leave *Twin Peaks.*

Who Killed Laura Palmer? Who Cares?

Whether it was the show that killed itself, the network that killed the show, or the fans, who were tired of waiting for resolution was the culprit, one thing was for certain: *Twin Peaks* was dead—murdered—with plenty of suspects to go around. As Grimes wrote, by the time of *Twin Peaks* went into its second season, "the doughnuts turned stale awhile ago."[12]

What went wrong was the question on the mind of many fans, academics, and television critics, who had all predicted a long life for the latest cult phenomenon. Although *Twin Peaks* had solved the problem of killing off one of the most beguiling characters on the show before the program actually began, it had solved it by bringing back the same actress Sheryl Lee as Laura's cousin Maddy Ferguson (only to kill her off again). However, it waited too long to do so, allowing critics to gripe that "it is now apparent that the central mystery of the show, which became last season's television phenomena, has become an albatross to the program this season."[13] It might have not helped much that Lynch and Frost deliberately toyed with the linear notions of television, hoping that fans had the patience to keep up with them. Cocreator Mark Frost was quoted as saying: "We try to play with time and space and dimension. Why can't films and television be more like real life? Real life is really weird."[14]

In reality, life may be strange and filled with multiple odd bumps, but Lynch and Frost frustrated television viewers by building a scenario in which viewers were ravenous for a resolution, but one that

Lynch and Frost did not seem eager to provide. In addition, the show also never seemed to solve a riddle before moving on to the next one.

Some critics thought it was the fault of the writers, who seemed more concerned with adding new and weird elements to the show than anything else. As Grimes wrote, "The show lost sight of two things: story and character."[15] As John O'Connor noted in the *New York Times*: " . . . fans lost interest due to changing and never resolved plot lines the "breathless 'who killed Laura Palmer?' headlines became 'who cares who killed Laura Palmer?'"[16]

Another factor that caused fan consternation was ABC shuffling the program around on the schedule, as if the network had no real idea where best to land the program. In addition, it did not help that director Lynch also put the show on the back burner, seeming to give other projects priority status. He seemed in no hurry to resolve the story, which contributed to fan dismay. As O'Connor explained, "Unable, or unwilling to devise an appropriate end to Laura's story, the *Twin Peaks* producers have fallen back on riffing and vamping."[17]

Twin Peaks was also too much too soon. Perhaps there was no way for a show to survive as a mass-market cult show at that point in television history. Playing on a major network, the series had to deal with everything from ratings to the often-fickle nature of the typical American television viewer. As Dennis Lim noted more than a decade after the show's demise, *Twin Peaks* "had to deal with the tricky contradictions of a cult phenomenon that briefly achieved mass popularity."[18] But there were limits, even when a show purposely attempted experimentation.

American audiences were weaned on dramas that delivered plot resolution within an hour's timeframe. Most viewers had no real experience with the surreal, especially on television, leading one critic to snipe that Lynch was being merely arty for the sake of being arty, and asked, "What do you do after breaking the rules of television? You go on breaking the same rules and hope that your fans, not noticing, will continue to compare you with Luis Bunuel, Jean Cocteau and Federico Fellini."[19]

Something was clearly wrong when British fans, much more used to daring television programs, such as *The Prisoner*, were not amused. *The Times* of London quoted critic Annie Leibovitz as saying, "the smart set who analyze the meaning of *Twin Peaks* are falling into his trap . . . the only 'meaning' is the coherence of the Lynch-shifted-logic that keeps the series going."[20]

Ultimately, the love affair America had with the exquisite corpse of Laura Palmer could not last. After all, she was dead and the fans had to keep on going, even after the demise of *Twin Peaks* itself. Perhaps

Denis Lim summed it up best when he noted, "at its best, the show achieved a crazy cosmic harmony, setting the comforts of the everyday against the terror of the void."[21] If the death, rebirth, death, and eventual resolution to the story of Laura Palmer taught the viewer anything, it is of the capacity of well-written and conceived television to capture the imagination. And as the other great deceased blonde icon of the twentieth century, Marilyn Monroe, has also taught us, an idea is transitory—an image, even of a beautiful dead women wrapped in plastic, may be far more enduring.

Notes

1. John O'Connor, "Time to Let Go of Laura Palmer," *New York Times*, October 2 1990, http://www.nytimes.com (accessed March 5, 2009).

2. Ibid.

3. Ibid.

4. William Grimes, "Television; Welcome to Twin Peaks and Valleys," *New York Times*, May 5, 1991, http://www.nytimes.com (accessed March 5, 2009).

5. Ibid.

6. Ibid.

7. Ibid.

8. Bill Carter, "Twin Peaks Splash on Both Sides of Atlantic; Who killed Laura Palmer? Stay tuned!" *New York Times*, November 8, 1990, http://www.nytimes.com (accessed March 5, 2009).

9. Ibid.

10. Alessandra Stanley, "Are the Owls What They Seem?" *New York Times*, October 28, 1990, http://www.nytimes.com (accessed March 5, 2009).

11. Jennifer Lynch, *The Secret Diary of Laura Palmer* (New York: Pocket Books, 1990).

12. Grimes.

13. Carter.

14. Quoted in Carter.

15. Grimes.

16. O'Connor.

17. Ibid.

18. Dennis Lim, "The Year the Pie and Coffee Ran Out," *New York Times*, April 8, 2007, http://www.nytimes.com (accessed March 5, 2009).

19. O'Connor.

20. Craig Whitney, "'Twin Peaks': Splash on Both Sides of the Atlantic; In Britain It's All Just Beginning," *New York Times*, November 8, 1990, http://www.nytimes.com (accessed March 5, 2009).

21. Lim.

Bibliography

Carter, Bill. "*Twin Peaks* Splash on Both Sides of Atlantic; Who killed Laura Palmer? Stay tuned!" *New York Times*, November 8, 1990, accessed March 5, 2009, from http://www.nytimes.com.

Grimes, William. "Television; Welcome to Twin Peaks and Valleys." *New York Times*, May 5, 1991. Accessed March 5, 2009, from http://www.nytimes.com.

Lim, Dennis. "The Year the Pie and Coffee Ran Out." *New York Times*. April 8, 2007. Accessed March 5, 2009, from http://www.nytimes.com.

Lynch, Jennifer. *The Secret Diary of Laura Palmer*. New York: Pocket Books, 1990.

O'Connor, John. "A Skewed Vision of a Small Town in 'Twin Peaks.'" *New York Times*. April 6, 1990. Accessed March 5, 2009, from http://www.nytimes.com.

O'Connor, John. "Time to Let Go of Laura Palmer." *New York Times*. October 2, 1990. Accessed March 5, 2009, from http://www.nytimes.com.

Stanley, Alessandra. "Are the Owls What They Seem? *New York Times*. October 28, 1990. Accessed March 5, 2009, from http://www.nytimes.com.

Whitney, Craig. "'Twin Peaks': Splash on Both Sides of the Atlantic; In Britain It's All Just Beginning." *New York Times*. November 8, 1990. Accessed March 5, 2009, from http://www.nytimes.com.

CHAPTER 14

SYNDICATION OF BROADCAST TELEVISION PROGRAMS

Carmen Stitt

Most Americans spend the majority of their leisure time watching television. Plenty of research over the years indicates that all the while they are being cultivated by a pattern of stereotypes, omni-celebrity, and gilded ways of living seemingly so commonplace nowadays that it almost defies perception. Whether it is a frequent water-cooler conversation at work, catching up with friends, or following a blog about one's favorite television program, chances are that within those discussions about television comes a reference to a favorite program that lives on into seeming infinity in syndication. The cultural and social effects of syndication per se are not well studied, but from research on the effects of media use, there is ample data from which to draw conclusions on the effects of repeated exposure to television programs that have become a part of cult pop culture.

Ever since broadcast television became popular with mass audiences in the late 1940s and 1950s, audiences have developed an affinity not only for the programs themselves but also for the ritual of watching television itself. As creatures of habit, Americans find solace in the predictable nature of watching their favorite characters become entangled in a predicament and then try to work themselves out of it. Viewers are somehow comforted by seeing their favorite programs and characters, even if they have seen them a hundred times before. Whatever genre is preferred, the odds are that aside from news and sports, one's favorite program has made its way into syndication.

This essay provides an overview of the syndicated world of broadcast television, particularly examining TV shows that could now be considered part of cult popular culture. It does so by explaining the background of syndicated television programs from a historic, economic, and global perspective based on factual information. Highlights will be provided of popular broadcast television programs from the peak of broadcast television in the 1970s to the present day. This is intended to offer points of interest regarding some of the most watched programs, but it is in no way an exhaustive review. The impact of popular syndicated television programs will also be explored. This analysis is based on selected studies of exposure to television programs over time and is followed by a more general discussion of effects.

Background of Syndicated Television

In the early days of broadcast television, no one would have predicted audiences would watch a television program more than once. Like motion pictures, the thinking was that once people saw a show, that would be the end of it. However, that projection was incorrect. Syndication caught on after reruns of *I Love Lucy* were aired and soon found a growing audience.[1]

Prior to the 1970s, the three television networks (ABC, CBS, and NBC) fed the production of programs for television. The cost-effective strategy was for the networks to pay Hollywood for the use of its studios to create programs. This was a lucrative means for the networks, given that they might pay half of what they would accrue in advertising revenue from the airing of a single one-hour episode.[2] This all changed, however, when regulations were passed allowing Hollywood to gain more control over profits of its productions.

Executives from Hollywood realized that the real money was to be made in licensing reruns and that the networks were a step behind in planning to exploit this new source of revenue. Hollywood had already exerted its power when it began to successfully apply pressure to then-President Nixon to adopt laws favoring Hollywood rights to the syndication business.

To set a backdrop for these legal changes, some background is in order. As a general principle, Nixon disdained the media because of journalists' coverage of him, which he thought biased and inaccurate.[3] So in 1971, when Lew Wasserman of MCA (Music Corporation of America), a multifunction talent agency and owner of music, television, and film production facilities, approached Nixon to adopt laws that made it easier for Hollywood to gain control over the network television programming, Nixon did not hesitate. The president approved the financial interest-syndication rules (which came to be known as "fin-syn rules") that remained in effect until the 1980s. The fin-syn rules prohibited the networks from any rights to a program beyond its initial run, including those produced prior to 1971. After that, rights to a program reverted to the production company, typically a Hollywood studio, and all profits went into its coffers. The rule excluded news and sports.[4]

While publicly, these laws were designed to promote diversity of programs among the networks by preventing them from owning more than first-run rights to any television program, they largely benefitted the Hollywood studios that gained ownership of these video libraries. The intended effect of these laws, however, was to spread the wealth of television programs and effectively hand over a huge cash cow to Hollywood.

Syndicated Broadcast Television Programming

Early syndication hits on broadcast television began in the 1950s with *Sea Hunt* and *Highway Patrol* as first-run syndications (programs produced for a first airing in syndication), and *The Adventures of Superman, Mr. Ed., Firing Line,* and *I Love Lucy* all followed.[5] Through several decades of television, audiences became accustomed to viewing reruns of their favorite television shows. By the 1970s and 1980s, syndication hit its peak. Here is a look at the top-rated television programs, their lives in syndication, and consequent cultural impact:

Syndicated Television during Boom-time in the 1970s

There are a number of ways to select programs for analyzing syndicated programs. The method used in this chapter is to review the top-rated television programs by viewership as reported by Nielsen Media Research and then discuss their history in syndication and pop culture influence. Of all the television programs making the Nielsen top TV ratings during the 1970s, seven programs were in the Nielsen top ten four or more times. *All in the Family* and *M*A*S*H* appeared in the Nielsen top TV ratings six times each during the 1970s, more than any other program.[6] Each of them is equally famous and influential in its own right.

Norman Lear produced a number of situation comedies (sitcoms) during the 1970s and 1980s, but he is probably best known for *All in the Family*. The program ran on CBS from 1971 to 1979. It tied with two other programs (*60 Minutes* and *The Cosby Show*) to be the number one-rated program five consecutive years in a row (1971–1976).[7] Modeling it somewhat after his own family, Lear created *All in the Family* to tackle social issues of the time such as racism, politics, feminism, and women's rights. The infamous protagonist of the show is Archie Bunker, the bigoted, blue-collar patriarch of a Brooklyn family of three. The blatant racial epithets and stereotypical references made by Archie along with the ensuing philosophical debates initiated by his liberal, peacenik son-in-law (referred to by him as "Meathead") set off a national controversy.

In defense of regular plotlines surrounding sensitive topics, Lear is quoted as saying that the program "brings bigotry out in the open and has people talking about it."[8] However, a study using both adolescents and adults as participants during that era demonstrated that viewers did not take issue with Archie's use of racial slurs.[9] Moreover, participants in the study reported Archie to be a more likeable character than his son-in-law, Mike. This, coupled with other studies, suggests that while under the guise of satire, the media may have subtly endorsed people's stereotyped assumptions about minorities in the 1970s, making it acceptable to support racist opinions. The series was commemorated when Archie and Edith's chairs were inducted in the Smithsonian Institutes' National Museum of American History[10] and the U.S. Post Office issued a stamp honoring the program.[11]

The actor, Carroll O'Connor, was immortalized as Archie Bunker. Perhaps a secondary aspect of his legacy was his antidrug public service announcements admonishing parents to talk with their kids about drugs. His own personal testimonies about his unsuccessful battles with his son's drug use and his ultimate death were both inspiring and a sad footnote to his career.[12] Rob Reiner, a.k.a. Meathead, shook off his on-screen persona and went on to an illustrious career as an actor-writer-director-producer of such movies as *The Princess Bride*, *When Harry Met Sally*, and *This is Spinal Tap*.

The program itself inspired two other noteworthy Lear productions. *Maude* was a sitcom that originally aired from 1972 to 1978. The show topped out at number four on the Nielsen ratings in 1972–1973.[13] Another famous spin-off was *The Jeffersons*. George and Weezie were African-American and former neighbors of Archie and Edith who became successful chain dry cleaners and moved up to Upper Eastside Manhattan. The show carried on themes of bigotry dressed in satire, but the twist was that the remarks were coming from George, a member of a minority group. It was also one of the first prime-time shows to portray interracial marriage. It too became a hit with audiences and is shown internationally in syndication. The show aired on CBS from 1975 to 1985.[14]

The other top-rated program of the 1970s was *M*A*S*H*, running from 1972 until its record-breaking season finale in 1983, when 106 million viewers tuned in to see the final episode, making it the most-watched episode in American broadcast television history.[15] The plot centered on a mobile surgical hospital military staff during the Korean War. Although the war depicted is the Korean War, many of the sentiments and symbolism paralleled the Vietnam War, which weighed heavily on a generation's conscience when the program was first broadcast. Its satire, the wit of the characters when faced with life-or-death situations and coping with human emotions and frailties, captured audiences' attention worldwide.

Syndication of the series began while the regular series was still being originally broadcast and continues today around the globe. In 1983, as the series ended, syndicated episodes of *M*A*S*H* were already earning the production company $200 million.[16] The program airs to this date on channels such as ION and the Hallmark Channel, with TVLand hosting a recent *M*A*S*H* marathon.

Happy Days directed audience attention to a romanticized malt shop era two decades prior to its original airtime. From 1973 to 1983, ABC aired the program that followed a Midwestern, middle-class, suburban Milwaukee family and the circle of friends surrounding their children.[17] Primarily the focus was on their two children, Richie (played by Ron Howard) and Joanie (played by Erin Moran), and their friends. The setting for the show was two decades earlier, during the height of popularity of malt shops, poodle skirts, fishtails, and men's hair slathered with Brylcreem, but the overriding theme of the show hit home with audiences: a wholesome family with a father running a hardware store and a stay-at-home mom. Though not originally intended as a central figure, the show's center of attention became Fonzie (played by Henry Winkler), a social misfit in a leather jacket who defined "cool." Lunch boxes, mugs, posters, and now mouse pads can be found easily to this day with a familiar black leather jacket-clad man holding "thumbs up" and echoing the "Ehh!" that so indelibly etched the Fonz in our memories.

A spin-off of *Happy Days, Laverne and Shirley*, followed the ups and downs of Milwaukee brewery workers by the same names. The lead characters were played by Penny Marshall and Cindy Williams. The program ran from 1976 to 1983 and was rated number one for two years in a row (1977–1979).[18] Mego created lookalike characters for not only Laverne and Shirley but also their inopportunely timed visits from friends, Lenny and Squiggy, as well as a model of the Shotz brewery where the characters worked. Recorded albums featuring the Laverne and Shirley characters singing were also distributed in 1976 by Atlantic, and three years later, and an album by Lenny and Squiggy was distributed by Casablanca.[19]

There are other broadcast television programs that did not make the Nielsen top TV ratings during the 1970s; however, their popularity soared in syndication. *The Brady Bunch* never cracked the top ten rated programs, but its place in pop culture history is remarkable. The program aired on ABC from 1969 to 1974.[20] The series portrayed a husband and wife married with three children each from previous marriages, and an affable housekeeper. Perhaps it was the innocent mistakes of the children and the inevitable learning of life's lessons with attentive parents that was a draw for young audiences. But, unlike Norman Lear, producers of *The Brady Bunch* avoided plots that smacked of controversy. Instead, the stories hearkened back to the halcyon days of television with programs like *My Three Sons* and *Leave it to Beaver.*

Syndication of the program began in 1976 after the series went off the air and from there, the program enjoyed ever-increasing audiences. By 1985, the program was rated number one on TBS.[21] This may be due in part to the after-school time slot allocated to the program when children were most likely to be watching, thereby giving it a new audience. Merchandising for the show furthered increased the fame of the actors with actions figures and dolls resembling the characters, as well as made-for-TV movies and motion pictures carrying on the Brady tradition.[22] The original show remains in syndication to this day.

Along with other "feminist" programs of the 1970s like *Alice* and *One Day At a Time, The Mary Tyler Moore Show* was in the Nielsen top ten ratings three times, and its impact swelled after syndication. The program originally aired on CBS from 1970 to 1977. For that time period, the program was unique because it was the first program depicting a single, career-minded woman in a lead role. Mary Richards (played by Mary Tyler Moore) visibly felt the pain of dealing with sexism, criticisms from peers for her tenacity in the face of strife, and dating woes.

That sentiment struck a chord with audiences in an era of rising feminism. Perhaps it was her exposed vulnerabilities and the occasional triumph that led to her popularity with audiences. In the pre-Internet boom, two decades later, during the early 1990s when America was feeling the weight lifting from a recession of the late 1980s, young audiences still found Mary's character attractive. Young adults were still delaying marriage compared to previous eras and could watch Mary exposed to the travails of career and dating and yet be encouraged.[23]

"To boldly go where no man has gone before," or should we say where no other program has gone before? *Star Trek* was a science fiction television program that never saw the glory of the top ten rated TV programs, yet it is a chart-topper by any stretch of the imagination with its cult-like following. With William Shatner as Captain Kirk and Leonard Nimoy as Mr. Spock, the concept for *Star Trek* was created by Gene Roddenberry in 1966 and has since become a multibillion-dollar franchise. It includes six individual television series (in chronological order: *The Original Series, The Animated Series, The Next Generation, Deep Space Nine, Voyager,* and *Enterprise*). *The Original Series* inspired books, motion pictures films, comics, toys, and untold other *Star Trek* products.

Syndication of the television series began in off-network syndication rather than on a major network (reruns of a program aired on a network other than its original airing)[24] and was eventually distributed in 48 countries.[25] From trading cards, action figures, films, DVDs, to toy spacecraft, the iconic television show has a continually mushrooming merchandising fleet. In 2009, CBS Consumer Products, the owners of the *Star Trek* television enterprise (pun intended) expanded its line of Trekkie products to include a line of Barbie Collector dolls, die-cast vehicles, radio-controlled vehicles, cobranded games (with Monopoly and Uno, for example), and videos.[26] From a cultural influence, scores of Trekkies make the voyage to conventions held throughout the world each year. Software applications for iPhones are also available so that Trekkies can watch original episodes on tv.com.

The 1980s Syndicated Programs

The 1980s ushered in a new political era, and that meant change for the distribution of media profits from syndicated television programs. With many rules on the limits of conglomerate growth loosened during the 1980s, media companies could swell into mega-corporations that handled production, distribution, and exhibition segments of the industry.[27] For one period, in a strange twist of fate, this allowed broadcast television networks to reach a broader audience than its rival cable television. Previous limits on network ownership of the number of affiliate stations were gone. The result was that networks could charge advertisers higher rates for delivering their advertisements to larger audiences because of the many network affiliate stations. What is more, advertising limits during prime time were relaxed, giving advertisers unprecedented airtime on broadcast TV.[28] Moreover, it forced the television industry to rely more formulaic scripting and plots rather than cash-intensive creative endeavors requiring the craft of gifted writers.[29] Financial and legal wrangling aside, what was going on in programs that people watched?

The 1980s meant not only new rules but also new types of programming. Stars were demanding higher salaries, coupled with rising production and personnel costs and increasingly fierce competition from satellite and cable TV stations. This placed a strain on the networks. Moreover, women were entering the workforce faster than ever before and networks could no longer rely on profitable daytime soap opera advertising (targeting women) to carry them.[30] The big three networks sought to broaden their audiences by going for prime-time soap opera formats. Aiming for a more balanced distribution of male and female audience members would increase the networks' chances for mass audiences.

Like makers of the original TV soap operas of the 1940s and 1950s, producers of prime-time soap operas attempted to capitalize on audiences that possessed an increasing disposable income, lavish wardrobes, and real estate—what the 1980s era of conspicuous consumption came to be.[31] By focusing on these aspects of lifestyle, producers not only brought potential customers to the doorstep of advertisers that could deliver the coveted lifestyle during those programs but also had characters of the programs model the standard of living that characterized the 1980s with products advertised during the commercial breaks.

Dallas and *Dynasty* were two top earners in Nielsen ratings. *Dallas* followed the adult Ewing children in a wealthy Texas oil ranch. Leading the cast of morally challenged characters was J.R., along with his brothers Gary and Bobby. It later became known that there was a fourth illegitimate son, Ray, who had been the ranch foreman. The infighting, affairs, and drinking problems that kept the series going were all popular with audiences.

Each season the show ended in a cliffhanger. It was an episode with J.R. being left for dead that spawned a generation of "Who Shot J.R.?" t-shirts and rocketed the program to number one in the ratings for the two subsequent years (the 1980–1981 and 1981–1982 seasons).[32] The original series ran from 1978 through 1991 on CBS, and it was not until 2003 that it reappeared in syndication on SOAPNet when the cable channel gained rights to all 13 seasons. In 2008, however, SOAP-Net lost its rights to the program and it has not yet been rebroadcast.

Building on a formula that worked with audiences, a competing program called *Dynasty* was created. *Dynasty* was a prime-time soap opera sensation that ran on ABC from 1981 to 1989.[33] It was the number one-rated show during the 1984–1985 season and appeared four times in the top ten. Like *Dallas*, this over-the-top outlandish program featured a wealthy oil family living in Denver, Colorado, with each character trying to outdo the others in immoral turpitude.

A rarity among top-rated programs during the 1980s was *Murder, She Wrote*, a one-hour mystery drama on CBS that aired from 1984 to 1996. The program made it into the Nielsen top ten programs nine years of its run on broadcast television.[34] The lead character was Jessica Fletcher (played by Angela Lansbury), a widowed and retired teacher who became a successful mystery writer who becomes somehow involved in unfolding murder mysteries. Although the program topped out at the number-three slot during the 1985–1986 season, the show was wildly successful abroad, being syndicated in more than 40 countries, and continues in syndication to this day.

Another enduring program that catered to more mature audiences is *Golden Girls*, a sitcom about four older women living together in south Florida. It originally aired on NBC from 1985 to 1992.[35] The show's highest rating was at number four, but, as with many shows, its payoff lay in syndication. Reruns of the program began in 1990, two years before the original broadcasts ended. It remains a syndication sensation for Disney/ABC, which distributes the program.

A number of researchers have examined the show's potential impact on stereotyping. Studies have found that the program's use of humor to address age issues is associated with audiences' being more likely to endorse stereotypical assumptions about their elders and to be less likely to address elder concerns seriously.[36] Nonetheless, the humor and perhaps familiarity and talent of the actresses Bea Arthur (the lead character from *Maude*), Rue McClanahan, Estelle Getty, and Betty White (from the *Mary Tyler Moore Show*) kept audiences wanting more. Indeed, today the program is finding new life with younger audiences in syndication.[37]

Cheers aired on NBC from 1982–1993. The setting was a local bar in Boston "where everybody knows your name." The show was in the Nielsen top ten ranks five out of 10 years during its original airing.[38] The plot was driven by Sam (played by Ted Danson), a recovering alcoholic and former professional baseball player, who ran the bar. He had a highly anticipated love affair with one of the waitresses, Diane (played by Shelley Long), and another later with the bar's new manager, Rebecca (played by Kirstie Alley). Yet it was the entire cast of colorful bar characters that audiences could identify with.

When NBC ended the program in 1993, it was syndicated in 38 different countries and 179 markets in the United States. The show continued to grow in popularity even after the initial run ended. It ran in syndication on Nick At Nite from the time it ended, until 2004 and entered into an agreement with TVLand until 2008. The Hallmark channel now has plans to pick up the syndication, and plans for additional syndication contracts are in the works.[39] The *Cheers* bar scene itself is so recognizable and marketable that hospitality giant Host Marriott mounted *Cheers* lookalike bars and life-like characters in its hotel and airport facilities.[40]

A spin-off from *Cheers* was another long-running program that enjoyed phenomenal success in syndication, *Frasier*. From the *Cheers* cast came the title character (played by Kelsey Grammer), a divorced psychiatrist living in Seattle with his competing-for-neuroses brother, Niles (played by David Hyde Pierce) and his smart-aleck father, Martin, who was forced into retirement from a law enforcement career due to an injury attained while in the line of duty. Rounding out the cast was Daphne, a live-in British caretaker for Martin. The show ran for 11 seasons on NBC from 1993 to 2004. It continues today in syndication in the United States and abroad. It has been cited as the most successful spin-off in history and was rated the number-one comedy by a British poll.[41]

By far one of the most successful sitcoms on broadcast television during the 1980s was *The Cosby Show*. It aired 1984 to 1992 and was rated number one five out of ten years in a row (tied for number one in 1989–1990 with *Roseanne*).[42] Starring Bill Cosby as physician Cliff Huxtable, head-of-household, a position he shared with his successful attorney wife, Clair (played by Phylicia Rashad), the program followed the lives of the successful Brooklyn couple and their five children. The show was studied closely under a microscope for its portrayals of an idyllic African American family who rarely mentioned their "Blackness" and who floated through life overcoming problems with ease. The concern with the program was not its rosy way of life but the potential effects on audience members' beliefs about African Americans.

In academic debate, the differences boiled down into a dichotomy of those who thought the program would be a prototype for contemporary

African American families, role-modeling an ideal lifestyle, and those who believed if African Americans were not living the Huxtable way of life, they had failed to work hard enough for their fortune. *The Cosby Show* was the most popular show among Whites, but for Blacks, while the show was still popular, feelings were mixed. Some studies suggest African Americans may have liked the show but felt it sided more with White values and, therefore, did not encourage a Black society.[43]

The program was wildly successful with American audiences and also abroad. From 1985 to 1995, *The Cosby Show* was rated in the top 10 programs in Norway, the Philippines, Lebanon, and Australia.[44] The show was also a hit in South Africa, but popularity differed along racial lines. One report claims that by 1991, the show had made $1 billion from syndication alone.[45] The show also spun off another popular program entitled *A Different World* that followed the life of elder daughter Denise as she left the Huxtable nest to attend college.

As part of the successful television lineup following *The Cosby Show*, *Family Ties* enjoyed a healthy syndication history. The program aired on NBC from 1982 to 1989 and made the Nielsen top ten three times.[46] Unlike *The Cosby Show*, *Family Ties* quite pointedly addressed politics as former liberal hippie parents (Elyse and Steven played by Meredith Baxter Birney and Michael Gross) addressed the ideology of their ultraconservative son, Alex (played by Michael J. Fox). The clash between parents and child paralleled the Democratic reign during the Carter administration and the about-face policies when Reagan was elected into office in 1980. The program went into syndication after it went off the air and has remained in syndication, most recently on FamilyNet, and also on such channels as Nick At Nite, TVLand, and WGN.

Nearing the end of the 1980s, television witnessed a new breed of character, literally and figuratively, when the program *Roseanne* rose up the ratings. *Roseanne* aired from 1988 to 1997 on ABC. The title character, played by stand-up comedienne Roseanne Barr, was a sarcastic, overworked mother of three who, along with her loving husband, Dan (played by John Goodman), tried their best to guide their children while holding down steady jobs. Stylistically, this was in stark contrast to the more harmonious family relationships dominating television on *The Cosby Show* and *Family Matters*. Not since *The Honeymooners* had American audiences experienced such sarcastic wit and candor in a female lead role. Its appeal to audiences became apparent when, in only its second season, it catapulted to number one during 1989–1990.[47] Starting in 1992, the program went into off-network syndication and has been in syndication on TVLand, TBS, Oxygen, and Nick at Nite ever since.

The 1990s Syndicated Programs

The 1990s continued to see the successes of such programs as *Cheers, Roseanne, Cosby, Frasier,* and *Murder, She Wrote.* And a newcomer on the scene arrived with *Home Improvement.* Concomitant with or perhaps a catalyst for America's obsession with renovating and improving one's home, *Home Improvement* was a refreshing comedy. Here, Tim (played by Tim Allen), a father of three boys in suburban Detroit, haphazardly hosts a home-improvement television program alongside his deadpan sidekick (played by Richard Karn). His sharp homemaker wife (played by Patricia Richardson) manages to stay one step ahead of him to avert disaster and improve their home lives as well. The show aired on ABC from 1991 until its final episode in 1999. It scored in the top ten ratings seven times and was number one during the 1993–1994 season.[48] Off-network syndication began in the mid-1990s and continues to the present day.

A trend of the networks was to group a series of programs together that essentially captured a certain demographic group, thereby making it more appealing to advertisers. Advertisers not only were buying space for a program but also had the attention of audiences for what was typically a two-hour block, thus increasing audience exposure. Thursday-night lineups on NBC became "Must See TV." Airing on Thursday nights was the sitcom *Friends,* which aired from 1994 to 2003, earning a spot in the top ten rankings seven times.[49] Syndication of the program began abroad in the United Kingdom as early as 1994. The program featured the lives of six young adult friends in New York as they dealt with frank discussions about their fears, personal relationships, careers, dreams, and quirks.

An episode of *Friends* is one of many instances in media where health information was incorporated into the screenplay and has been cited as "edutainment." The episode dealt with a pregnancy scare between Rachel (played by Jennifer Aniston) and Ross (played by David Schwimmer). After Rachel discloses her pregnancy to Ross, an indignant Ross wonders aloud how it could have happened given that they used a condom. Rachel explains that condoms are only effective "like 97% of the time." Viewers' reaction to this subtext of the plot was incorporated into a larger study of adolescents. An impromptu study revealed that after watching the program, viewers who recalled the condom information were more likely to have learned about condom efficacy than before seeing the program. More importantly, regular viewers of the program were significantly more likely to recall the condom efficacy information six month later compared to nonregular viewers. Given the number of times that an episode may be seen over its syndication life, viewers have increased likelihood to learn health information.[50]

Part of the NBC Must See TV nights was another hit, *ER*, a one-hour medical drama chronicling the work and lives of doctors in a hospital emergency room in inner-city Chicago. The program aired in 1994, on the same network and year as *Friends*, and it broadcast its last episode in April 2009. The program ranked in the top ten Nielsen ratings for six years and was number one three times in the 1990s.[51]

The most prominent show in NBC's former Must See TV lineup is *Seinfeld*. Based on the stand-up comedy by the actor of the same name, *Seinfeld* centers around "nothing," as one of its characters explained mid-plot. The characters are Jerry (played by Jerry Seinfeld), Jerry's one-time girlfriend and now platonic friend Elaine (played by Julia Louis-Dreyfus), his best friend George (played by Jason Alexander), and a neighbor from across the hall, Kramer (played by Michael Richards). The program aired on NBC from 1989 to 1998 and ranked number one twice during its nine-season run. The program's meteoric rise to stardom endures to this day not only in syndication but in the catchphrases it left behind. "Sponge-worthy," "serenity now," "yada, yada, yada," and "festivus" made their way into everyday vernacular. Since it began syndication, *Seinfeld* has been among the top-rated syndicated programs.[52]

The 2000s Syndicated Programs

The 2000s saw ever-increasing competition to capture and retain audiences and a need to cut expenditures. A method for dealing with this quandary was for the networks to rely on unscripted programs and hire unknown "actors," including staged competitions. A number of programs fit this format (dubbed "reality TV"), among them, *Survivor*, *The Amazing Race*, and, most notably, *American Idol*. *American Idol* was a spin-off from the British *Pop Idol*, and it became a pop culture phenomenon in the United States. It first aired on Fox network in 2002 and has been ranked number one in five of its eight seasons.[53]

Contestants arrive at auditions throughout the United States in order to battle to become the next big pop singing sensation. The final contestants come to a televised audition where four judges (music and talent brass) assess their potential as singers and give them feedback. The feedback, of course, is part of the entertainment, as contestants face humiliating but oftentimes constructive criticism about their talent. Audiences at home participate in the program by voting for their favorite singers by phone.

American Idol aired in 2000, with Kelly Clarkson emerging as the first *American Idol* winner. It took several years for the program to reach its peak, topping the Nielsen charts in 2003–2004 and remaining there at present. There is, however, an interesting paradox with *Idol's* success. Despite its number-one spot in watched television programs, viewership has slowly eroded since 2006, dropping from 30 million viewers to an average of 25 million viewers. All the while, the profit margin during that same period increased from a mere 69 percent ($67 million) to 77 percent ($96 million). To what can this increase be attributed? The answer lies in astute marketing and licensing agreements with international broadcasting, airing off-network reruns on TV Guide Network, and music sales. Combined, these brought the revenue for *Idol's* production company, 19 Entertainment, to $223 million in 2008. Moreover, 64 million people voted for their favorite contestant, the highest ever for a nonfinale episode.[54] Regardless of its diminishing audience on any given day, *Idol* and its marketing packages, along with its participatory audience model, seem to show no signs of slowing down. American audiences are enthralled and have now increasingly been acculturated to believe that everybody can become a celebrity.

The Cult of Syndication

The sample of programs discussed here is a testament to the potential cultural and economic forces that drive television as a medium. In many ways, television is an escape that audiences seek out without much forethought, only giving attention to programs that match their needs for drama, comedy, or action. However, there are more enduring qualities of programs that speak to generations beyond what the program was intended for. What similarities can audiences identify within an episode of *I Love Lucy* from over 50 years ago? Likewise, in our so-called "enlightened" society, why might audiences continually tune in to watch Archie hurl racial slurs at a vaguely defined ethnic minority group?

Perhaps there are more general and timeless themes than what are overtly portrayed. Audiences who seek out television as a release from everyday concerns might initially be attracted to the satire brought to them in *All in the Family* or *M*A*S*H*. They then become immersed in the world in which the characters find themselves, although perhaps removed from any sense of modern reality. However, themes that transcend time are evident and viewers relate to them.

For example, people may have interacted with bigoted elders while growing up and a program could remind them of their relatives, not of the controversial aspects of the series. In that way, the show feels familiar. In another instance, viewers may have served in the military, and watching reruns of *M*A*S*H* replaces otherwise unpleasant memories with a humorous perspective. Connecting past parts of our lives through television (whether socially desirable or not) in a way that is somewhat detached allows viewers to "try on" other ways of being (e.g., you may not perceive yourself as racist, but you can vicariously experience it through watching a television character) and to connect with feelings that they know. As a current example, *The Simpsons* has experienced an unprecedented success as an animated series on broadcast TV running 18 years and counting. Few would admit that they agree with Bart's behavior or Homer's reasoning, yet the family themes and tensions have obviously resonated with contemporary audiences.

By the same token, do we take seriously that audiences believe in *Star Trek* adventures or that people can actually become stars of stratospheric proportions as we watch in *American Idol?* While these programs have broad appeal for quite different reasons, an explanation for sustained viewership could possibly be reduced to the notion of escapism. Audiences seek out other ways of living and the prospect that there is some other "universe" than the more mundane existence that occurs in our daily lives.

If we were to be removed from the world as we know it, what challenges might we face and how would people come to solve problems? The act of pondering these questions serves a purpose for audiences. Television gives audiences a contrived sense of universe, one that is prefabricated and a one-stop shop. For those looking for extraction from otherwise boring or mundane lives, television programs fulfill that need. And whatever genre we prefer, we can watch our favorite programs live on in infinity in syndication.

Notes

1. Douglas Gomery, *A History of Broadcast in the United States* (Oxford: Blackwell, 2008), 127–28.

2. Ibid., 15.

3. Anthony Fellow, *American Media History* (Boston, MA: Wadsworth Publishing, 2010), 335–38.

4. Gomery, 189.

5. Ibid.

6. Nielsen TV Ratings Data: 2005. Nielsen Media Research, Inc.

7. Ibid.

8. Lear quoted in Neil Vidmar and Milton Rokeach, "Archie Bunker's Bigotry: A Study in Selective Perception and Exposure," *Journal of Communication.* Winter 24, no. 1 (1974), 36.

9. Ibid.

10. "The Bunkers' Chairs," http://americanhistory.si.edu/news/factsheet.cfm?key=30&newskey=54.

11. *"All in the Family* stamp at National Postal Museum," Smithsonian Institution,http://arago.si.edu/index.asp?con=2&cmd=1&id=74776&img=1&mode=2&pg=1&tid=2043993.

12. "Carroll O' Connor's Son Kills Himself at 33," *The New York Times*, March 30, 1995, http://www.nytimes.com/1995/03/30/us/carroll-o-connor-s-son-kills-himself-at-33.html (accessed July 8, 2009).

13. Nielsen TV Ratings Data: 2005 Nielsen Media Research, Inc.

14. Ibid.

15. "Broadcast TV Faces Struggle to Stay Viable," *The New York Times*, February 27, 2009, http://www.nytimes.com/2009/02/28/business/media/28network.html?pagewanted=all (accessed July 8, 2009).

16. Denise Worrell and Richard Corliss, "M*A*S*H, You Were a Smash," *Time*, February 28, 1983, http://www.time.com/time/magazine/article/0,9171,955150,00.html (accessed July 8, 2009).

17. Nielsen TV Ratings Data: 2005 Nielsen Media Research, Inc.

18. Ibid.

19. *"Laverne & Shirley* Catalog Library," http://www.megomuseum.com/catalog/1978/happydays_001.shtml.

20. Nielsen TV Ratings Data: 2005 Nielsen Media Research, Inc.

21. Mimi Marinucci, "Television, Generation X, and Third Wave Feminism: A Contextual Analysis of *The Brady Bunch*," *The Journal of Popular Culture* 38 (2005), 505–24.

22. Sean Griffin, "The Brady Bunch," The Museum of Broadcast Communications, http://www.museum.tv/eotvsection.php?entrycode=bradybunch (accessed July 8, 2009).

23. Jib Fowles, *Why Viewers Watch: A Reappraisal of Television's Effects* (Thousand Oaks, CA: Sage, 1992), 121–26.

24. David Alexander, *Star Trek Creator: The Authorized Biography of Gene Roddenberry* (New York: Roc, 1994), 546.

25. "Star Trek," http://topics.nytimes.com/top/reference/timestopics/subjects/s/star_trek/index.html?scp=1&sq=revenue%20from%20star%20trek%20franchise&st=cse.

26. "CBS Consumer Products Beams Up New Partners for Merchandising Program," http://www.bhimpact.com/consumer_productspress_releasescbs_consumer_products_beams_up_new_partners_for_star_trek_merchandising_program.html.

27. Chris Jordan, "Who Shot J. R.'s Ratings?: The Rise and Fall of the 1980s Prime-time Soap Opera," *Television & New Media* 8, no. 1 (February 2007), 68–87.

28. Tino Balio, "Introduction to Part II," in Tino Balio, ed. *Hollywood in the Age of Television* (Boston: Unwin Hyman, 1990), 259–96.

29. Nick Browne, "The Political Economy of the Television (Super) Text," in Horace Newcomb, ed. *Television: The Critical View* (New York: Oxford University Press, 1987), 69–80.

30. Jordan, 79.

31. Jostein Gripsrud, *The Dynasty Years: Hollywood and Television Critical Media Studies* (New York: Routledge, 1985), 88.

32. Nielsen TV Ratings Data: 2005 Nielsen Media Research, Inc.

33. Ibid.

34. Ibid.

35. Ibid.

36. Howard Giles and Jake Harwood, "Don't Make Me Laugh: Age Representations in Humorous Context," *Discourse & Society* (1992), 203–36.

37. Jake Harwood, "Sharp!: Lurking Incoherence in Television Portrayals of Older Adults," *Journal of Language and Social Psychology* (2000), 110–40.

38. Nielsen TV Ratings Data: 2005 Nielsen Media Research, Inc.

39. "Cheers," http://www.museum.tv/archives/etv/C/htmlC/cheers/cheers.htm.

40. Dennis Bjorklund, *Toasting Cheers: An Episode Guide to the 1982–1993 Comedy Series, with Cast Biographies and Character Profiles* (Jefferson, NC: McFarland, 1996), 19.

41. Channel 4' Ultimate Sitcom. http://www.listology.com/content_show.cfm/content_id.22029.

42. Nielsen TV Ratings Data: 2005. Nielsen Media Research, Inc.

43. Timothy Havens, " 'The Biggest Show in the World': Race and the Global Popularity of *The Cosby Show*," *Media Culture & Society* 22, no. 4 (2000): 371–90.

44. Ibid., 375.

45. Bill Carter, "Making a Difference: For Cosby It's No Secret the Word is Syndication," *The New York Times*, November 3, 1991, http://www.nytimes.com/1991/11/03/business/making-a-difference-for-cosby-it-s-no-secret-the-word-is-syndication.html (accessed July 8, 2009).

46. Nielsen Media Research.

47. Ibid.

48. Ibid.

49. Ibid.

50. Rebecca Collins, Marc Elliott, Sandra Berry, David Kanouse, and Sarah Hunter, "Entertainment Television as a Healthy Sex Educator: The Impact of Condom-efficacy Information in an Episode of *Friends*," *Pediatrics* 112 (2003), 1115–21.

51. Nielsen Media Research.

52. Ibid.

53. Ibid.

54. Edward Wyatt, "Despite Lower Ratings, Cash Flow Rises for *Idol*," *The New York Times*, May 10, 2009, http://www.nytimes.com/2009/05/11/business/media/11idol.html?scp=1&sq=Despite%20Lower%20Ratings,%20Cash%20Flow%20rises%20for%20Idol&st=cse (accessed July 8, 2009).

CHAPTER 15

FIGHTING CRIME: *CSI* AND *LAW & ORDER* REDEFINE TV

Donna Waller Harper

Competition drives the current television market. Producers must attract a broad audience because competition is much more stringent than in the advent of television in the mid-twentieth century. In contrast, in the earliest days of television, the president could ask for and almost guarantee time on all major channels if he had an important announcement. However, in today's environment, the networks choose whether to broadcast a particular event. Gone are the days of coverage of virtually every moment of a national political convention. The changing dynamic between TV and its advertisers has changed the contemporary television landscape.

Today, advertising agencies and corporate sponsors stay with those shows that attract a consistent viewing audience or that have a special attraction. Television producers would love to have a crystal ball to advise advertisers on the possible success of a particular show. Sometimes shows become popular because they are unique versus traditional programs; sometimes the opposite occurs, and programs gain popularity because they mirror the current times.

During the 1950s, shows like *The Adventures of Ozzie and Harriet* (1952–1966) and *Leave It to Beaver* (1957–1963) portrayed idyllic American life: father working at a profession with life in suburbia, where the wife stays home and takes care of the home and children. These were the ideals to which America evidently aspired in the 1950s, but another very popular and long-running program appealed to America's sense of western adventure and justice. *Gunsmoke* (1955–1975) brought a tough lawman whose values were those of the frontier and the justice that needed to be imposed. While *The Adventures of Ozzie and Harriet, Leave It to Beaver*, and *Gunsmoke* portrayed an idealized version of American life, programs like *All in the Family* (1968–1979) and *M*A*S*H** (1972–1983) satirized issues of American society, calling into closer scrutiny issues facing America at the time, like racism, war, rape, menopause, and abortion.

Mark Kurlanksy argues in *1968: The Year That Rocked the World* that Robert Kennedy assessed the power of television and utilized it in his brother's bid for the White House in 1960. Historical texts and biographies of John Kennedy and Richard Nixon attest to the power that television played in the 1960s election. As television gained power, it portrayed issues previously masked by the idealism of the 1950s, particularly in dramas and situation comedies. *The Mary Tyler Moore Show* (1970–1977) featured an independent woman facing the problems of professional, single women of the 1970s. Yet experts acknowledge that programmers concerned themselves with whether the public would confuse the character of Mary Richards in *The Mary Tyler Moore Show* with Laura Petrie of *The Dick Van Dyke Show*. By the 1990s programs like *Friends* (1994–2004) examined not only friendship among six New Yorkers but also the ever-changing social mores of the decades—a far cry from the asexual images of earlier comedies. After all, Lucille Ball and Desi Arnaz (who were married to each other in real life) were portrayed in *I Love Lucy* (1951–1957) and *The Lucy Desi Comedy Hour* (1957–1960) sleeping in separate beds.

A unique feature of many successful programs in television history is the special chemistry of cast members. *Law & Order* (1990–present), a Dick Wolf franchise, and *CSI* (2000–present), a Jerry Bruckheimer franchise, are cases in point. *Law & Order* and its various offshoots have experienced significant character turnover but still maintain a high level of popularity and critical acclaim. The series even received a special Edgar Award, a literary award for mystery writers, in 2002.

Other parts of the franchise, *Law & Order: Special Victims Unit* and *Law & Order: Criminal Intent*, have witnessed fewer character changes. In contrast, the *CSI* shows set in Las Vegas, Miami, and New York have shown mixed cast stability. In most cases, the supporting stars change, but the main characters stick around. The most notable exception to this rule is William Petersen from the original *CSI*, who chose to leave the program in 2008. The interaction of the characters is important to the success of these programs. Not only does an actor have to create a unique character, but that character's interaction with others also needs to have a special chemistry.

Law & Order and Its Sister Series

Law & Order has stayed true to its original format by dividing the program, with the first part dedicated to the police investigation of a crime and the second half to the prosecution. Within the first year of *Law & Order*, the cast began to change. George Dzundza, who played Max Greevey for 23 episodes from 1990–1991, was only the first of many characters to leave the shows. In "Confession," the men he is investigating execute him while he is off duty. Chris Noth as Mike Logan showed the loyalty and temper that became synonymous with his character. Mike Logan's new partner was Paul Sorvino (who plays Phil Cerreta), who lasted only 31 episodes from 1991–1992. Noth found himself replaced in 1995. The infamous Logan temper prevailed when a city councilman on trial for killing his gay lover becomes involved in homophobic comments. Logan hits him; however, Noth reprised the character in *Law & Order: Criminal Intent* from 2005 to 2008. Jerry Orbach replaced Sorvino and played Lennie Briscoe from 1991 to 2004. His character is a recovering alcoholic who is gruff but experienced and dedicated. Briscoe is given to comments about his drinking, his divorces, and his poor performance as a father. Orbach's character also appears in each of the other *Law & Order* franchises, including the less-than-stellar *Law & Order: Trial by Jury* (2005–2006), where he appeared mere months before his death. This portrayal saw him listed on Bravo's "100 Most Memorable Television Characters," a list that left many commentators questioning the choices, especially in the top 10. In "COD," Briscoe chooses retirement after helping convict two women who arranged the murders of each other's husbands in Hitchcockian fashion.

After Orbach's arrival, he is the steady character for several years working with Benjamin Bratt (1995–1999), who, as Rey Curtis, brings the use of technology to the series. Curtis is familiar with the Internet and computer programming, which is totally different from the way Briscoe has been used to working cases. As a matter of fact, in early shows, the detectives seek out pay phones for some of their interchanges with the office.

With the arrival of Curtis, technology is much more significant, and the young officer contrasts to Briscoe as he initially does with his happy marriage in comparison to Briscoe's multiple divorces.

In "Aftershock," Curtis strays from his marital vows and struggles with an effort to reconcile with his wife, who suffers from a degenerative illness. He eventually resigns to spend more time with her and help with his daughters. His replacement is the suave, debonair Ed Green, portrayed by Jesse L. Martin until 2008. Green's character has the experience of his father's foreign placement in diplomatic circles; he enjoys gambling, cigars, and fine clothes. His upbringing has him at odds with many of the ethnic criminals, since he is much more sophisticated.

After Orbach's death, Ed Green is paired with Dennis Farina, playing Joe Fontana from 2004–2006, and then Jeremy Sisto beginning in 2007. Fontana is a match for Green in that he too is quite suave and sophisticated but, like Briscoe, brings much experience to the office. Sisto's character, Cyrus Lupo, returns to police work from the military to find his brother's killer.

After Martin left the series, Anthony Anderson stepped in as his replacement. Interestingly, however, even with the frequent change of characters in the police department, including Dann Florek's replacement by S. Epatha Merkerson, the program depicts the reality of adaptation, which many people experience in the workplace. The characters also find themselves contemplating change and its consequences. Logan resists liking Briscoe because he hopes Cerreta will return. Briscoe and Curtis are initially uncomfortable with each other but eventually bond, as do Briscoe and Green. The importance of their investigative work proves more significant than personalities. They learn to trust each other.

From its inception, *Law & Order* provided what the public enjoyed with its ripped-from-the-headlines storylines and characters that held strong beliefs and unique personalities. Ben Stone, played by Michael Moriarity, was the executive district attorney whose values were intact and who sought to do that which was right. Such was the case in "Subterranean Homeboy Blues," the story of a ballerina who shoots teenagers in the subway, allegedly after an assault that destroyed her dancing career; the plotline was similar to that of subway vigilante Bernie Goetz. Moriarity's sense of justice and his role as a prosecutor comes to a head in "Old Friends" when he presses a witness to testify against the mob who had infiltrated her business; her death after testifying causes him to resign his post. His replacement was Sam Waterston, who plays heavy drinking, occasionally bellicose Jack McCoy, who also has a reputation for having had intimate relations with many of the female assistant district attorneys who worked with him. McCoy's character also has a strong sense of right and wrong but is more willing to twist and reinterpret the laws of justice, as he does when he prosecutes a gun manufacturer in "Gunshow" after a young man shoots several female students in Central Park, a case similar to that of Marc Lepine of Canada, who killed female engineering students.

McCoy also took a strong stand in prosecuting a drunk driver who had excessively imbibed during an international trip in "Under the Influence." In this case, he also withheld the information about the flight attendant from the defense, causing him to be called before the ethics committee. In 2007, McCoy moved from his work as an assistant district attorney to district attorney when Fred Dalton Thompson resigned his role as Arthur Branch to make an unsuccessful attempt for the Republican nomination for president.

For the first 10 years of the program, Steven Hill played Adam Schiff, district attorney. His character was gruff politician who oversaw his office but allowed his executive and assistants as much leeway as possible before stepping in. Hill's replacement was Academy Award-winning actress Dianne Wiest, who played district attorney Nora Lewin for two seasons. She seemed much more ambivalent in her role and was more tenuous in her position concerning the death penalty and more liberal in her political views than Fred Thompson, who played Arthur Branch. The character's political views appeared similar to those of Thompson himself. He regaled the executive and assistants with stories of his life as a law student and with folksy Southern stories. He also appeared in *Law & Order: Special Victims Unit*, questioning the behavior of the prosecutors of certain cases.

Of the many prosecutorial positions, the one with the most turnover is the assistant district attorneys. Michael Moriarity worked with Paul Robinette (played by Richard Brooks from 1990–1993). However, Robinette's character later returned as a defense attorney, taking cases involving racial discrimination.

Brook's replacement was Jill Hennessey (who played Claire Kincaid from 1993–1996), a well-educated woman who occasionally makes minor mistakes, as in "Discord," the case of a heavy metal artist accused of raping a young woman. Kincaid fails to prepare the victim well enough to learn that the young woman and her father have filed a civil suit against the artist. Stone threatens to fire her but relents after he attains a guilty verdict and recounts a similar mistake he made. A similar omission occurs in "Censure" when she fails to relate her own relationship with a judge who is under indictment. Here, she faces a personal censure. Even though she initially chastises

Jack McCoy when she learns of his previous relationships with assistants working with him, she herself develops a relationship. In "Aftershock," she, McCoy, and the detectives experience an execution. Her opposition to the death penalty surfaces again, as does her desire to quit the district attorney's office. She goes to a bar to find McCoy but misses him and is killed while driving Lennie Briscoe home. Her death at the hands of a drunk driver resurfaces in "Under the Influence."

Subsequent assistant district attorneys have all been female. Few that have followed have developed the quiet serenity, and security of Kincaid. Carey Lowell (who portrays Jamie Ross) adds the insight of a woman who has practiced corporate law but wants to aid justice by prosecuting. She also provides insight as a woman who is a single parent; she will return to private practice and reappear in the series as did Richard Brooks. Angie Harmon advocates the death penalty and maximum punishment. Elizabeth Rohm as Serena Southerly provides the more liberal counterpart, especially in light of working with Thompson's Branch. Annie Parisi as Alexandra Borgia, and Alana de la Graza as Connie Rubirosa made minimal contributions in characterization.

Even though the program revolves around the interaction of police and prosecution, some other characters recur. Both Carolyn McCormick as Dr. Elizabeth Olivet and J. K. Simmons as Emil Skoda made numerous appearances as psychiatrists who offer insight into the minds of killers or the possible reasoning behind crimes. Their tenure with the department appears to overlap to some extent. Leslie Hendrix has recurred as Dr. Elizabeth Rodger, the medical examiner. Tovah Fedshuh has made many appearances from 1991–2007 as lawyer Danielle Melnick, a major advocate for constitutional protection for the accused to the point of violating the judge's rulings if she can help her clients. She clashed with both Ben Stone and Jack McCoy, but both admire her immensely. Lorraine Toussaint appeared only in the first three seasons, always providing representation for clients, many of whom were minorities. She appeared to be a thorn in Ben Stone's side and yet he recognized her commitment to her clients.

Other TV veterans had recurring roles, such as Ron McLarty (playing Judge William Wright). His character appears to go out of his way to antagonize and rule against McCoy, even overturning a jury verdict that he deems unfair. Paul Hecht appeared as both defendant and lawyer. Hecht is the doctor who rapes Elizabeth Olivet in "Helpless," but shows up later as a lawyer for a defendant. Actress

S. Epatha Merkerson is the mother of the victim in "Mushrooms" before she begins her stint as Lt. Anita Van Buren.

Wolf's other *Law & Order* franchises have been more stable in their casts. Mariska Hargitay (Olivia Benson) and Christopher Meloni (Eliot Stabler) have been consistent on *Law & Order: Special Victims Unit*. Their partnership and the closeness of their relationship has been a program staple. Like Noth's Logan, Benson is a troubled soul who was a product of her mother's rape and who also dealt with her mother's alcoholism. She appears to have a unique empathy and connection to victims, especially those raped. She may be tough and determined, but she is also committed to the ultimate truth and protection for the victim, as is her partner, Stabler, who suffers from a temper.

Like Logan, he pushes the barrier of interaction with perpetrators. He is also given to outbursts of violence, whether it is against an unfair verdict or the inability to prove a case against a particular perpetrator. Dann Florek's Captain Cragen is usually able to act as buffer when Benson and Stabler clash with the public or when they occasionally clash with one other. Their friendship is intensely personal. Benson frequently refers to Stabler as her best friend, and they do all they can to protect each other.

Their colleagues in investigation are Fin Tutuola, played since 2000 by Ice-T, and comedian Richard Belzer, who reprises a role he created in *Homicide: Life on the Streets* as John Munch. Despite Tutuola's rough exterior and his life as an undercover in vice, he occasionally tires of the rants of Munch, who sees the conspiracy of the government to know the coming and going of its citizens. Tutuola claims to be Republican, while Munch is very left of center and highly critical of the government. Yet these two pair with each other more than they do with either Benson or Stabler.

This series, more than the original, shows the dependence on the good relationship and interaction of the police with the prosecutors. In the case of *Special Victims Unit*, the prosecutor frequently tells whether or not the case is able to go to court—which happens occasionally on the original—but is more likely to occur in *Special Victims*. Stephanie March played Alexandra Cabot who was cooler, calmer, and more reserved than Rohm's Serena Southerly. She interacted with the unit to bring criminals to justice while maintaining a stoic exterior and a calm professionalism.

She was replaced by Diane Neal's Casey Novak. Neal, like S. Epatha Merkerson, had made an appearance in an earlier episode, but Neal's character was a defendant. Neal appears to have tried to recreate the stoic distancing and elegance as Cabot, but comes across as a mere copy. Tamara Tunie began her recurring role as medical examiner Dr. Melinda Warner; she is efficient and deeply concerned about the dead and the evidence they are able to provide to help find their killers. She also takes special interest when Olivia might have been exposed to HIV. Also significant to the series is a tough bureau chief, Elizabeth Donnelly, played by Judith Light. Her appearance serves much for the prosecution side as does Cragen for the police; Donnelly eventually becomes a judge and relinquishes her supervision of Novak.

This part of the *Law & Order* programming has seen little replacement and more additions. In 2007, Adam Beach came on as Chester Lake, but he appears to work with either Munch or Tutuola. During Hargitay's pregnancy, Connie Neilson added to the show as Dani Beck, a policewoman who had lost a husband to violence and who appeared to have great difficulty hiding her temper—even Stabler appeared more balanced. She also had a strong attraction to Stabler, which they appeared to suppress once she became his partner. People like J. K. Simmon as Skoda, Elizabeth McCormick as Olivet, Thompson as Branch, and Orbach as Briscoe made appearances on the *Special Victims* program. Other well-known actresses, such as Beverly D'Angelo, Marlo Thomas, and Mariette Hartley made appearances in several episodes. Thomas played a judge who shared a special relationship with Neal's Novak.

While *Law & Order* and *Law & Order: Special Victims Unit* tend to expend energy toward the crime and the apprehension with occasional twists and turns as to the perpetrator and the conviction, *Law & Order: Criminal Intent* (2001–present) examines the crime from the viewpoint of the criminal and the development of the crime. Vincent D'Onofrio develops a quirky and intense portrayal of Detective Robert Goren, partnered with Kathryn Erbe (Alexandra Eames).

Eames is initially uncomfortable with Goren's style, which has him portraying what is in effect a psychological Sherlock Holmes. His keen observation and intense questioning help him solve many of the cases. He rarely meets anyone who is his intellectual equal. The series has provided him with a nemesis in Olivia d'Abo, who appears more than five times during the program's run as Nicole Wallace, always avoiding prosecution. Her first appearance in "Anti-thesis" brings to light her lurid background, which Goren uses against her, and she turns the tables on him in "A Person of Interest."

Until 2006, Captain James Deakins, played by Jamey Sheridan, oversees Goren and Eames, and ADA Ron Carver, played by Courtney

B. Vance, handles the prosecution. In *Criminal Intent*, few of the cases go to the courtroom; Carver merely provides insight regarding the legalities if the case were to go to trial.

When Sheridan and Vance left the series in 2006, Eric Bogosian replaced Sheridan, playing Captain Danny Ross, who is less congenial with Goren's hunches and weird interrogations. In 2005, D'Onofrio himself faced some personal difficulties and asked for time away from the series. As a remedy, Chris Noth returned to the franchise, reprising his Mike Logan role for Major Case rather than homicide; his partner was initially Annabella Sciorra, who seemed to be a female version of Goren. Julienne Nicholson replaced Sciorra after one year as Megan Wheeler. When Noth left the series in 2008, his replacement was Jeff Goldblum.

As with the other *Law & Order* franchises, some cast members cross over, with appearances by Briscoe, Green, and medical examiner Elizabeth Rodgers. In backstory involving Goren's life, Tony Goldwyn appeared in four episodes as Goren's brother and Rita Moreno appeared in three episodes as his mother. Dominick Dunne's son Griffin also appears in numerous episodes as a variety of characters. Even though *Criminal Intent* and *Special Victims Unit* appear to have more stable casts, there is no question that the public likes the premise of law and order and likes seeing the how justice is either served or how it is thwarted.

Searching for Clues: CSI and Its Offshoots

In Jerry Bruckheimer's successful *CSI*, crime is still at the center, but with a slightly different focus. In this series, science rules the day. The crime scene unit appears more actively involved in cases, accompanying police, carrying weapons, shooting suspects, and helping make arrests, but the real issue revolves around detailed scientific examination.

Beginning in 2000, William Peterson (Gil Grissom) and Marg Helgenberger (Catherine Willows) begin to work crime scenes in Las Vegas. Grissom is very much the scholar and scientist of the two but suffers from some hearing loss, while Willows is a divorced mother who worked as an exotic dancer while training for the crime scene unit. Like Benson and Stabler of *Special Victims Unit*, Grissom and Willows are extremely close and serve as supervisors and surrogates to the others in the unit. Until 2008, the stability of the cast was similar to that of *Special Victims Unit* and *Criminal Intent*, with little change. George Eads (Nick Stokes), Jorga Fox (Sara Sidle), and Gary Dourdan (Warrick Brown) rounded out the crime investigators for the science lab, and veteran actor, Paul Guilfoyle (Lt. Jim Brass) handled the actual police investigation.

One of the reasons the show gained so much popularity was that it revolved around the concept of science being fun. Special attention was paid to techniques of the crime scene investigators, with Robert David Hall coming into the show as the permanent medical examiner, Dr. Al Rollins. The team chemistry appealed to viewers, as did the humanity of the characters, each seeming to have real-life flaws to overcome. For example, Warrick Brown joined the team with a serious gambling problem that he later overcame. Sara Sidle seemed perpetually silent and unlucky in love, haunted by a past that was never completely revealed but appeared to have involved time in foster homes.

The cast included, from the very beginning, an eccentric character in the lab, a young technician who appeared to be flighty but scientific and looked perpetually disheveled. Eventually Eric Szamanda's Greg Sanders moves from the lab to field experience. The focus of his replacement in the lab is Wallace Langham's David Hodges, a much more stodgy and pretentious character. The cast chemistry is pertinent to the success of the series, but more important is science: chemistry, DNA, trace evidence, and fingerprints. With *CSI*, science became trendy and attractive. These were not mad scientists creating monsters in their labs. The characters were highly educated and used that knowledge and experience to serve society.

The task is not always easy for the investigators. From early episodes, Grissom encounters difficulty with several cases—discounting his own personal issue with processing crime scenes as his hearing diminished. In "Anonymous," he encounters Paul Millander, who will continue to appear and thwart Grissom and his crew; Grissom does notice that Millander's victims all have the same birthday as he. Grissom is also called to reinvestigate a crime in "Fahrenheit 932" when the convicted arson-murderer asks Grissom to recheck the evidence. Grissom becomes convinced of the man's innocence for the arson crime and helps exonerate him.

Grissom's peculiar interest in entomology helps solve the case of "Sex, Lies, and Larvae." Grissom is himself convinced that the estimation of time of death is inaccurate and reenacts the crime scene to prove his point. Science is also the basis of his proving what might have otherwise been considered a random killing by a wilderness creature in "Justice Is Served." Yet Grissom's investigation proves that the culprit needs the enzymes from the victims to fight her degenerative disease, porphyria, which is the same disease that supposedly haunted King George III at the time of the American Revolution.

Yet Grissom, with his unique knowledge, is not the only one involved in solving cases. Graphologists, at the request of the investigators, help in solving the I-15 murders by proving that the abductor-killer is a woman. This information is determined by the handwritten notes—not only the handwriting style but also the syntax of the notes. A forensic sculptor helps in several cases, including "Face Life," by helping with the reproduction of the skull to give a sense of what the victim looked like before massive decomposition. The same is true in the case of a body found imbedded in cement in "Who Are You?"

The forensic science in the cases appears to be accurate, if slightly misleading, to the untrained public. On many occasions, the investigators send tests to the laboratory, and by the time they walk back past the room, the tests results are ready so that they can proceed to find the criminal. Yet even students in high school biology are aware that tests for DNA may take months. However, the program rests on its heroes finding resolution within the one-hour time slot. Even given that exaggeration, procedures for the various tests appear to be accurate. After all, the program has its scientific consultants to insure the accuracy or legitimacy of the various techniques and procedures.

Not all the investigations center on mere forensic evidence. In five episodes to date, Melinda Clark portrayed Lady Heather, a woman who oversees a sadism-masochism enterprise. Her knowledge of her trade and the preferences for certain types of clients come into play in "Slaves in Las Vegas," while "Pirates of the Third Reich" reveals more intimate details of her life. Her daughter's murder has her interested in the pursuit of the sadistic killer and her own vigilantism, which Grissom stops. As Peterson chooses to leave the agency and turn supervision over to Catherine, he revisits Lady Heather and discusses with her his relationship with Sara Sidle and its demise. Despite the disparity between Lady Heather and the highly intellectual, private, and almost reclusive Grissom, the two appear to have a special bond. He goes to some lengths to protect her and acknowledges her psychological insight into certain aspects of the human psyche.

The interaction between the various characters on *CSI*, like that of the *Law & Order* franchises, is a critical attraction to the show. Even though Grissom could fire rookie Warrick Brown for his abandonment of a crime scene to place a bet, Grissom gives him a second chance. The team is so dedicated and interpersonal even with the variety of personalities that when Warrick is killed on the job, Sara

returns to help process the scene and find his killer. Warrick had himself looked up Brass's daughter just as Grissom himself does when
Brass lay near death in one of the season-ending episodes. Grissom
had also taken special interest in Greg Sanders as he became a field-
operative rather than working in the laboratory.

Yet despite the fundamental importance of character chemistry, *CSI*
proves time and time again that the investigation is more important
than the prosecution. Only on occasion does the viewer see the results
of the courtroom and the prosecution. Instead, the series offers the satisfaction that science helped find the killer by showing the culprit con-
fessing or being led away in handcuffs. Grissom's appeal is his astute
knowledge and deep intellect, which is not unlike that of D'Onofrio's
Goren. People are also drawn to a beauty like Willows who, despite
her experience in the glitzy, stereotypical Vegas life, has abandoned
that lifestyle for science and helping keep the city safe.

The personal lives of the Las Vegas characters are more closely scru-
tinized than in the *Law & Order* franchise or even other *CSI* shows.
Grissom becomes intimate with Sara, but despite their feelings,
she leaves to learn more about herself and feel more comfortable. For
several episodes, romance appears to bloom between Warrick and
Catherine, but he marries someone else—even if the results are less
than successful. This combination of science and personal romantic
intrigue is part of the series' allure.

Warrick and Catherine travel to Miami in pursuit of a killer;
this creates the *CSI: Miami* series, which, like the many spin-offs of
Law & Order, has seen a certain stability of characters. Having quit
the very popular *NYPD Blue* to launch a film career (perhaps one of
the biggest mistakes a topflight actor ever made), David Caruso
returned to television as Horatio Caine. His character appears to have
an incredible empathy with crime victims and a special affinity with
children in whatever capacity they find themselves involved in the
investigation. Scenes with children frequently show him sitting at
their level, removing the ubiquitous sunglasses and talking to them
about what is being done or can be done.

Just as the Las Vegas team has a good interaction, so does the one in
Miami. Caine supervises Calleigh Duquesne (played by Emily Procter)
as well as Eric Delko (played by Adam Rodriquez). Rory Cochrane's
early character, Tim Speedle, is the first casualty on the show, dying
due to sloppy maintenance of his sidearm. His replacement is a former
patrolman, Ryan Wolfe (played by Jonathan Togo).

As with most contemporary serial dramas, backstory is an important element in storytelling. Caine, for example, is deeply troubled by the death of his brother; Duquesne has to deal with an alcoholic father; Delko's sister has cancer. Just as is the case with the original *CSI*, the team of criminal investigators is more hands on than might be true of real crime scene investigators. Certainly on *Law & Order*, the crime scene unit is not usually involved in the interrogation of suspects.

Like its predecessor, *CSI: Miami* does have the crime scene unit present and involved in autopsies. Khandi Alexander is Dr. Alexx Wood who, like Horatio, has a special connection to the victims. Rex Linn is Detective Frank Tripp, who assists in the literal police aspects of the crimes.

In all the *CSI* and *Law & Order* programs, the setting is as important as the crime itself, becoming an additional character within the storylines. While Las Vegas and the trappings of gambling are important to *CSI*, Miami and its allure of drug trafficking and tourists feature prominently in the very essence of the series. The same is true of *CSI: NY* (the only of the series franchises not to win an Emmy). Just as Horatio Caine shows great empathy for victims, Mac Taylor (played by producer Gary Sinise) is more akin to Gil Grissom in his dedication to science, but unlike Grissom, he appears to have a stronger supervisory nature to his crime laboratory.

Where Grissom finds himself more drawn to the investigation, Taylor seems to be able to balance both with equal ease, supervising Stella Bonasera (played by Melina Kanakaredes), as well as Danny Messer (played by Carmine Giovinazzo) and Lindsay Monroe (Anna Belknap). This crime scene unit has its own physician scientist, Dr. Sheldon Hawkes (Hill Harper).

As with the cases in Las Vegas and Miami, the city of New York becomes an additional character, providing the audience with an understood context for the action that takes place in the Big Apple. The crimes feature Holly Golightly characters, killers of cab drivers, Russian mobs, and immigrants.

As with the other series, chemistry exists with characters. Although nothing more than friendship has surfaced, chemistry exists between Taylor and Bonasera. Messer and Monroe have acted on their chemistry, with Monroe giving birth. As with the tortured souls—similar to Sidle in Las Vegas and Caine in Miami—Taylor is tortured by the death of his wife during the attacks on the World Trade Center in 2001 and discovers her child, whom he begins to mentor.

Detective Shows as Cult Programming

Detective programs have served as a staple of the television/
entertainment industry since its inception. Many of those programs
have enjoyed long-term success, but in contemporary TV history,
Law & Order has carved out its space as one of the most important
shows ever created. The ripped-from-the-headlines format has worked
well in distinguishing the show from its predecessors and contemporaries. Observers of the news, whether Internet, print media, or otherwise, cannot help but notice the connection between cases like that of
Tawana Brawley, who said she was assaulted by six white men and
whose defense became a cause célèbre for Al Sharpton, or the alleged
relationship between an married female FBI agent and a famed female
novelist. Similar stories have appeared on *Law & Order*. The program
itself now rivals *Gunsmoke* as one of the longest-running primetime
television shows. Of the programs discussed in this format, it has seen
the most cast changes, yet it still draws a successful rating and has
survived threats to its programming.

The public appears captivated by its format of capture and prosecution—whether prosecution is successful or not. Likewise, the viewing
audience is also captivated by pursuit of criminals using scientific technology. *Law & Order* rarely makes use of mentions of the laboratory
work involved in capturing and prosecuting. Most of the action
revolves around street-smart police and savvy prosecutors, in stark
contrast to the allure of *CSI*. Contemporary TV viewers find the use
of science in bringing criminals to justice captivating, which reveals
how ingrained these procedures are in American popular culture.

Bibliography

"Aftershock," *Law & Order*. Dick Wolf Productions, May 26, 1996.
"Anonymous," *CSI*. Jerry Bruckheimer, producer, November 24, 2000.
"Anti-thesis," *Law & Order: Criminal Intent*. Dick Wolf Productions, October 13,
    2002.
"Censure," *Law & Order*. Dick Wolf Productions, February 2, 1994.
"COD," *Law & Order*. Dick Wolf Productions, May 19, 2004.
"Confession," *Law & Order*. Dick Wolf Productions, September 17, 1991.
"Discord," *Law & Order*. Dick Wolf Productions, October 6, 1993.
Dwyer, Kevin and Fiorillo, Jure. *True Stories of Law and Order*. New York:
    Berkley Boulevard, 2006.
"Face Lift," *CSI*. Jerry Bruckheimer, producer, March 8, 2001.
"Fahrenheit 932," *CSI*. Jerry Bruckheimer, producer, December 22, 2000.

"Gunshow," *Law & Order*. Dick Wolf Productions, September 22, 1999.

"Helpless, *Law & Order*. Dick Wolf Productions, November 11, 1992.

"I-15 Murders," *CSI*. Jerry Bruckheimer, Producer, January 12, 2001.

"Justice Is Served," *CSI*. Jerry Bruckheimer, Producer, April 26, 2001.

Kurlansky, Mark. *1968: The Year That Rocked the World*. New York: Ballantine, 2004.

"Leave Out All the Rest," *CSI*. Jerry Bruckheimer, Producer, November 6, 2008.

"Mushrooms," *Law & Order*. Dick Wolf Productions, February 26, 1991.

"Old Friends," *Law & Order*. Dick Wolf Productions, May 25, 1994.

"Person of Interest," *Law & Order: Criminal Intent*. Dick Wolf Productions, May 18, 2003.

"Pirates of the Third Reich," *CSI*. Jerry Bruckheimer, Producer, February 9, 2006.

"Pride," *Law & Order*. Dick Wolf Productions, May 24, 1995.

Ramsland, Katherine. *The C.S.I. Effect*. New York: Berkley Boulevard Books, 2006.

Ramsland, Katherine. *The Forensic Science of C.S.I*. New York: Berkley Boulevard Books, 2001.

"Slaves in Las Vegas," *CSI*. Jerry Bruckheimer, Producer, November 15, 2001.

"Subterranean Homeboy Blues," *Law & Order*. Dick Wolf Productions, September 20, 1990.

"Under the Influence," *Law & Order*. Dick Wolf Productions, January 1, 1998.

"Who Are You?" *CSI*. Jerry Bruckheimer, Producer, November 10, 2000.

CHAPTER 16

WE'RE ALL FAMOUS NOW: REALITY TV AND THE MEANING OF FAME

Larry Z. Leslie

Mark Burnett was sure he had a hit show. Although he tirelessly lobbied executives representing the major networks and a cable channel, the response was less than enthusiastic. The Discovery Channel turned him down. He also struck out at FOX, CBS, ABC, and NBC. But Burnett, the successful producer of several shows in Europe (as well as Discovery's *Eco-Challenge*), was not the sort of man to give up easily. He tinkered a bit with the show's name and format and pitched it to CBS again. Although CBS president Les Moonves had some reservations about the show, as did the CBS legal department, those issues were resolved, and CBS agreed to the program. *Survivor* aired in the summer of 2000. By that time, Moonves was fully on board. He emphasized the network's bold step into the world of reality television, noting that CBS was not willing to stand for the same old programming anymore.

Despite the upbeat attitude from CBS, the network apparently was not all that confident the show would be a success. It was scheduled for a summer run. It is common knowledge in the television world that the summer season is a dumping ground for shows that either were withdrawn from network schedules earlier in the season before their full runs, were ordered, shelved, and never aired, or were authorized specifically for a limited summer run. The networks don't expect much during the summer season. After all, viewers are more likely to be outside enjoying the daylight, warm weather, and any number of summer activities than they are to be sitting in front of their televisions. Still, a summer program could capture viewers' interest. It is not unheard of.

Although *Survivor* was beaten in the ratings during its first outing (by ABC's *Who Wants to Be a Millionaire?*), the program's viewership increased by almost 20 percent in the second week. The show's popularity continued to build through the summer. The buzz surrounding the season finale was as intense as the excitement generated by the finales of two other popular shows: *Seinfeld* and *M*A*S*H*. It was fairly clear to television program executives everywhere that reality television was becoming a force to be reckoned with. Although several networks were considering other sorts of reality programming, CBS is usually credited with launching the genre and *Survivor* is usually considered the first successful program in the genre. It could be argued that MTV's *Real World*, which aired in 1992, was the first reality show, but it was cable only and had a younger target audience than today's network reality shows. Back in the early days of television, Allen Funt's *Candid Camera* would probably qualify as a reality show.

Today, no one really knows exactly how many reality shows have aired on the networks and on cable. They come and go so quickly they are often lost or forgotten in the overwhelming variety of channels and choices available to the viewer. A website devoted to tracking reality television shows listed 239, from *1 versus 100* to *Work Out*. That list did not include such popular favorites as Bravo's *Real Housewives of Orange County* or Discovery's *Deadliest Catch*, among others. Some of the more popular shows include *The Amazing Race, American Idol, Big Brother, The Biggest Loser, Dancing with the Stars, Hell's Kitchen, The Bachelor,* and *Top Chef.*

It is obvious that television executives have become quite fond of reality television. Reality shows often get good ratings, and they are fairly inexpensive to produce. As Michael Hirschorn notes in *The Atlantic*, "reality shows steal the structure and pacing of scripted television, but leave behind the canned plots and characters." This is an important point. Reality shows do not require scriptwriters. "Reality shows cost anywhere from a quarter to half as much to produce as scripted shows," says Hirschorn. They don't require traditional sets, rehearsals, or large salaries for the actors involved.

Reality shows are, however, not as "natural" or "real" as they appear. As Hirschorn suggests, "reality TV can place real people in artificial surroundings designed for maximum emotional impact." For example, the island Palau Tiga is in the South China Sea. It was the location of the first *Survivor* show and is clearly a real island with natural flora and fauna, but the program that resulted from the interactions of Richard Hatch, Susan Hawk, Rudy Boesch, and the others was not necessarily "natural." None of the contestants would likely have visited the island had they not been taken there for the program, so we can't say that their time on the island was part of any "real" lifestyle they could have expected. So while the island was real, it wasn't a part of the contestants' reality until they arrived there. Thus, one could argue that the program was actually *realistic art*, that is, an artistic representation of a reality that would not normally be a part of anyone's life unless physical and social elements were manipulated and arranged for effect.

Moreover, *Survivor* is heavily edited; all reality shows are edited with a view toward the anticipated emotional reactions of the viewer. In other words, the show does not always proceed in a linear fashion, that is, one event after another. An afternoon conversation between two contestants can be edited and placed before a morning conversation by the same two (or two other) contestants. More than a few reality show participants who were not around to claim the final prize have complained that the program presented them in a negative light. "That wasn't the real me," one of them said. Nevertheless, as David S. Escoffery writes, reality television "shows us social interaction, group dynamics, interpersonal struggles, the process of voting, and even, perhaps, the workings of power itself."

CBS's Emmy-winning *The Amazing Race* provides another example of how realistic art is used to represent the real. The show sends American teams of two around the world. The teams visit a number of different countries and are asked to perform certain tasks before arriving at a "pit stop" at the end of each day. The last team to arrive at the pit stop is usually eliminated. The team that wins the final leg of the race gets the million dollars. But Jordan Harvey notes that the "race sites trivialize foreign cultures by focusing on their food, alcohol of choice, or methods of labor." There is much more to a culture than food, alcohol, and work. Most cultures have a history of artistic and/ or literary accomplishments. Cultures have different political, social, and economic climates. The show does not give the viewer any real picture of the cultures that race participants visit. The show's producers manipulate selected elements of a culture to fit their needs. In other words, they use cultural elements as an artistic representation of a culture that is far more complex than viewers are led to believe.

Reality shows are now a recognized and widely accepted staple of television programming. Most networks and many cable channels

have one or more. It is clear that reality television has changed the face
of prime-time programming. Networks still air cop shows, dramas,
and situation comedies, but those alone will not bring networks the
ratings they need and desire. However, although reality television
has changed network profits, the viewing habits of the audience, and
the lives of the shows' participants, reality television has not much
changed the meaning of *fame*.

Like most words in the English language, the meaning of *fame* has
evolved down through the years. Its archaic meaning was "rumor."
Well, of course, that is not what it means today. The word has been
used to identify a musical, a song, a comedy tour, a talent competition
for a television series, and a recording studio. These identifications,
while interesting, are important only insofar as they indicate the multiple meanings and uses to which a word can be put. If you were to stop
100 people on the street and ask each to give you a brief definition of
fame, you might get responses like "famous," or "well-known," perhaps
even "rich." Writers of dictionaries, naturally, are somewhat more specific, if a bit less clear, when they say fame means "great renown." Try
getting your 100 people to define that term! Dictionaries are on more
predictable ground with terms such as *distinction, prestige, prominence,*
and *great reputation.* In short, the word *fame,* like many other words in
our language, can mean whatever we want it to mean at a given time.
The meaning of a word, often its primary meaning, can change rather
quickly. Take, for example, the word *gay.* In your grandmother's time,
the word meant "happy," "carefree," "joyous." Today the word *gay* is
used to refer to sexual orientation. Happy, carefree, and joyous are not
the first words that come to mind when one hears the word in reference
to another person. Language and meaning change.

Do you consider yourself famous? Many people do simply because
they are good at their jobs, have received some recognition for something they have done, or have spoken out publicly and widely on some
current issue. Others may consider themselves famous for something
as simple as having written a letter to the editor of their local newspaper that got published. It is easy to be famous these days.

Pseudo-intellectuals might say that being famous is not only easy but
also expected. They'd quote pop art icon Andy Warhol, who said, "The
day will come when everyone will be famous for fifteen minutes." You'll
get your fifteen minutes; I'll get mine. Case closed, right? Well, not
exactly. The pseudo-intellectuals are wrong here, as they often are.
Warhol actually said, "In the future everybody will be world famous
for fifteen minutes." The difference between those two quotations is

important. The Warhol paraphrase leaves out the qualifying phrase *world famous*. Nevertheless, both quotations are useful because they show us that our fifteen minutes of fame may be seen in several possible contexts. It might be useful to develop a taxonomy, that is, a classification, of individuals who are—or consider themselves—famous.

A Taxonomy of Fame

Level	Description
1	Not famous; not known to many coworkers, neighbors, or family members
2	Not famous, but known to coworkers, neighbors, family, and a few outsiders
3	Famous, but recognition limited to a city, state, region, or country; recognized perhaps in a neighboring country
4	Famous as a celebrity—by birth or deed—usually inspired by circumstances of birth or work
5	Famous via significant and longstanding accomplishments in a truly important area of life. An individual at this level is recognized and appreciated worldwide, holding a top-notch reputation.

Take a look at the taxonomy chart. It classifies individuals, placing them on one of five levels of fame. The higher the level, the greater the fame. Let's add some detail to each level.

Believe it or not, there are a lot of people on Level 1. Individuals on this level live isolated lives. They may be separated from others by geography or economic circumstances. Some are on this level by temperament, that is, they wish to be alone, avoiding the sort of contact with others that often results in friendship or, at least, general acquaintance. Others may have health or other issues that force them into isolation. If you are on this level, you are obviously not famous.

Most of us are on Level 2. We are close to our families, are well acquainted with our neighbors, and are widely known at work, school, or church. We may be known by a few others outside the circles of family and work. For example, your barber or hair stylist, your doctor or dentist, your banker, and others with whom you do business may know you by name and greet you warmly when you enter their establishments. But this does not mean you are famous. It simply means you are known within the framework of your lifestyle.

Many of those on Level 2 aspire to Level 3. They'd like to be better known than they are; they'd like to achieve even a small amount of fame. For example, tens of thousands regularly fill out the long *Survivor* questionnaire and provide the short videotape explaining why they want to be on the show. Other reality shows have open casting calls. This often results in a deluge of potential contestants, many of whom, Richard M. Huff says, have little talent but have a willingness to make fools of themselves. This is especially true of those who wish to appear on *American Idol*. Surely many of those who try out know they can't sing a note, but they show up anyway and proceed to shriek out their songs. Thankfully, we never see these people again; no fame for them!

Individuals on Level 3 have limited fame because the recognition that propelled them to this level is usually restricted to a local, regional, state, or national environment. A few might be recognized in a nearby country. It is in this category that we find most of the winners (and some participants) of the various television reality shows. There are a couple of interesting examples here. Omarosa Manigault-Stallworth was an irascible young woman who regularly stirred things up on Donald Trump's *The Apprentice*. Regular viewers of the show became well acquainted with her, and reports of her behavior—both during and after the show—in newspapers and magazines and on the Internet led to her fame. But her fame was limited and probably did not extend beyond the borders of the United States, if it extended even that far.

On *Survivor*, Johnny Fairplay was known as a master manipulator. Through a series of lies and half-truths, he attempted to manage the game so that he would be the million-dollar winner. When he received news from home (as the castaways often do as a reward for winning a competition), he told the show's host and the other contestants that his grandmother had died. She had not. The lie was intended to engender sympathy from other contestants and perhaps endear him to some of the more emotional so that he would not be voted out of the game. Fairplay was well known to *Survivor* fans, individuals in his hometown, and perhaps a few others in the United States, but his fame did not extend much beyond that. Thus, the small amount of fame enjoyed by those who play important roles in television reality shows is fleeting. Having spent only a brief time on Level 3, many drop back to Level 2.

True celebrity status arrives on Level 4. You can land on this level either by birth or by deed. If by birth, you have to be born into a wealthy, well-known family. Paris Hilton, for example, is a celebrity by birth. As a socialite, model, and actress, she has no significant accomplishments other than a few B movies, a silly television show, and an Internet sex tape. But she is the granddaughter of Conrad Hilton, founder of the Hilton hotel chain. Her father is a wealthy real estate broker who deals primarily in high-end properties. Had she not been born into the Hilton family, it is doubtful Paris would be a celebrity. She is a perfect fit for the definition of *celebrity* provided by the historian Daniel Boorstin: she is famous for being well known. Her fame may extend to some foreign countries, but a starving teenager in a third-world country probably doesn't know or care who Paris Hilton is.

If you are on Level 4 due to your deeds, that is, your actions or performance, it is likely that those accomplishments are related to the worlds of media, entertainment, sports, or politics. Most movie stars, television performers, recording artists, heads of state, prominent world politicians, and the like are on Level 4. People such as Oprah Winfrey, former presidents George W. Bush and Bill Clinton, the male vocal group The Three Tenors, and even late terrorist leader Osama Bin Laden are residents of Level 4. International recognition is more common for individuals whose actions and accomplishments go beyond those who achieve this level by virtue of their birth.

Level 5? Good luck getting there. This level requires individuals to have significant and longstanding accomplishments in some truly important area of life. If you are on this level, you are recognized and appreciated worldwide, and you have a top-notch reputation. Three people come to mind at this level, and all three are dead. Pope John Paul II, Mother Teresa, and Princess Diana can be said to have reached Level 5. All three worked for worthy causes, usually at the expense of their personal lives.

Of course, these five levels are not absolute, nor are they mutually exclusive. There is likely to be some variation and movement from one level to another. Nevertheless, the taxonomy provides a useful approach to understanding the meaning of fame, particularly as it relates to television reality shows.

But wait! What about the Internet? Surely it plays a role in one's being famous. After all, scenes from some reality shows are often uploaded to YouTube. Well, sure, that's true, and there is likely some attention paid to reality show stars on MySpace and Facebook. But this essay is not about the influence of the Internet on fame. Still, the author would argue that the fame taxonomy that applies to reality television could just as easily be applied to Internet content.

Perhaps it is time for us to forget Warhol's take on fame, especially since it is obvious few of us will ever become world famous. We might be better off to quote American poet Emily Dickinson, who wrote:

How dreary to be somebody!
How public, like a frog

To tell your name the livelong day
To an admiring bog!

Has reality television changed the meaning of fame? No, not much. It has enabled a few individuals to enjoy some temporary fame, but such fame does not last. It is merely a candle flame guttering in the wind and soon extinguished.

Bibliography

Escoffery, David S. "Introduction: The Role of Representation in Reality Television." In David S. Escoffery (Ed.), *How Real Is Reality TV?* Jefferson, NC: McFarland, 2006.

Harvey, Jordan. "*The Amazing Race*: Discovering a True American." In David S. Escoffery (Ed.), *How Real Is Reality TV?* Jefferson, NC: McFarland, 2006.

Hirschorn, Michael. "The Case for Reality TV." *The Atlantic Online*, May 2007.

Huff, Richard M. *Reality Television.* Westport, CT: Praeger, 2006.

Other Sources

Carter, Bill. *Desperate Networks.* New York: Doubleday, 2006.

"Fame." http://www.answers.com/topic/fame.

"Fifteen Minutes of Fame." http://www.phrases.org.uk/meanings/fifteen-minutes -of-fame.html.

"Top Reality Shows." http://www.realitytvmagazine.com.

CHAPTER 17

How *Family Guy* Changed Television Forever

Jodee Hammond and Bob Batchelor

Traditionally, cartoons were created for children and focused on themes that kids would find appealing. Jodee remembers Saturday morning at her house devoted to cartoons. *Scooby Doo* and *The Rugrats* were some of her favorites. Growing up a generation earlier, Bob watched *Bugs Bunny*, *The Flintstones*, and other 1970s animated reruns. Later, at Jodee's house, the family gathered on Sunday evenings to watch *The Simpsons* (1989–present) when the program debuted on Fox. "My dad would let my siblings and me watch it even though my mom disapproved," she recalls. "I remember it was one of my dad's favorite shows." Jodee remembers thinking: cartoons that adults loved just seemed unnatural.

The Simpsons, however, ushered in a new era that allowed adults to enjoy animation again. The show's success led to a number of other primetime, animated sitcoms, from *King of the Hill* (1997–2010) and *South Park* (1997–present) to *American Dad!* (2005–present). As a result, what constituted animated programming would change forever. One journalist explained, "Cartoons used to be just kids' stuff."[1] This essay examines the cult-like preoccupation viewers have for animated television shows, using *Family Guy* (1999–2002, 2005–present) as a case study in revealing how powerful a cult following can become—in essence, changing the very face of television.

***

Before the late 1980s boom ushered in by *The Simpsons,* many television viewers disparaged animation because the content was not real or based in reality. Old standards, such as the *Looney Tunes'* Wile E. Coyote and Bugs Bunny's long-time nemesis Daffy Duck have little connection to reality.[2] They often plunge thousands of feet off cliffs or get blown up by mountains of dynamite and appear in subsequent frames with no damage. It's these types of cartoons that are meant for children, although current cartoons are less violent and more education-based than the popular ones from the past. For example, *Dora the Explorer* or *The Backyardigans* (Bob's 6-year-old daughter Kassie's current favorite) provide loving environments that nurture today's children (and enable their high-stress parents to feel good about the shows), rather than older cartoons that centered on violence, such as poor Wile E.'s near-constant horror via explosions, crumbling mountains collapsing on him, and a sea of hardware smashed over his skull.

In contrast, writers, from shows like *The Simpsons* and *Family Guy,* purposely created shows that would attract an adult audience, while also being curiously attractive to children. Rather than completely suspend reality on these animated series, the writers and producers hoped to appeal to viewers via the presentation of scenarios that they faced. Obviously, the animated families are designed to be hyper versions of real people, thus Homer Simpson is a little less intelligent and able to attend to daily life than most real-world viewers. In the end, shows like *The Simpsons* and *Family Guy* wanted viewers to forget that they were watching a cartoon, but still have the ability to use animated tropes, such as violence and exaggerated satire that live actors could not perform without physical or moral outrage.

Airing on ABC from 1960 to 1966, *The Flintstones* followed the prehistoric antics of Fred and Wilma Flintstone, their daughter Pebbles, and the Barney and Betty Rubble family (later to include adopted son Bamm-Bamm), as well as each family's pets. Like the highly popular sitcom *The Honeymooners,* which ran for 39 episodes in the mid-1950s, the animated series examined the working-class lives of the two families.

The Flintstones is recognized as laying the foundation that changed the stigma of cartoons, serving as the first to combine the animation and sitcom formats.[3] By incorporating a sense of realism, the show changed viewers' perceptions of television animation. The combination of realism, animation, and sitcom laughs appealed to a wide audience. *The Flintstones* opened the door for adult cartoons and, subsequently, cartoons for adults caught on, though it would take 20 years for the next major animated series to stick with the viewing audience.

The Simpsons, created by Matt Groening, began as an animated short airing on the fledgling Fox Network's *Tracey Ullman Show*. Despite its parent show's mediocre ratings, viewers gravitated toward the snippets. Eventually spinning off as a half-hour show, *The Simpsons* blossomed into one of television's most important franchises and currently stands as the longest-running sitcom in TV history.

Although the early seasons of *The Simpsons* capitalized on the chaos of 10-year old Bart Simpson and "Bart-mania" that ensued in the real world, gradually the family patriarch Homer J. Simpson developed into the show's driving force. Homer's antics at work (as a bumbling safety inspector at the local nuclear power plant), at Moe's Tavern (his nightly haunt with friends), and at home with his family drew on the traditional live-action family-based sitcom.

Airing in 1989, *The Simpsons*, like other sitcoms, tried to create a sense of realism by focusing on the family's financial problems.[4] The first episode involved Marge spending all their year-end, holiday savings to have a tattoo removed from Bart's arm only to find out Homer was not going to receive a Christmas bonus. Groening said he wanted the show to be realistic as possible. In addition to financial stress, the streets of Springfield are portrayed as full of trash and display imperfections in the pavement, which adds to its realistic approach.

The Simpsons currently stands as the longest running American primetime entertainment series in television history. Its longevity and popularity turned the show into a cash cow for Fox. In 2009, *USA Today* reported that the previous year saw consumers spend more than $750 million on Simpsons-related licensed merchandise (half from the United States) and advertisers forked out $315 million on news episodes and reruns.[5] In addition, the 2007 big screen film *The Simpsons Movie* brought in $183 million in the United States and totaled more than $527 million when including international revenue.[6]

Due to the success of *The Simpsons*, networks recognized the financial potential of animated shows.[7] Although Fox was leery about producing another cartoon for fear of getting labeled an animated network, the outcome of *The Simpsons* was the "show that won't die," better known as *Family Guy*.[8] Seth MacFarlane created the show in 1999. At 25-years-old, he managed to land a $2.5 million-a-year production deal with the network.[9] But equally important, the show won a premiere slot—it debuted in January after Super Bowl XXXIII.[10] The prime place in the schedule, getting a lead-in from the most-watched, annual sporting event seemed destined to ensure success, but a meager 12.6 million viewers watched.

Even though Fox initially recognized its potential by giving it a post–Super Bowl debut, the network apparently doubted the show's success. The show bounced around the weekly schedule,[11] inheriting a total of nine different time slots.[12] Its unstable airing time contributed to the show's continual decrease in ratings.

Fox cancelled *Family Guy* in 2002, which at the time certainly looked like the end of the line for the show. However, if there were a silver lining in its demise, the cancellation marked the launch of *Family Guy's* standing as a cult phenomenon. Hearing news of the show getting dropped, fans went ballistic. They began online petition campaigns to bring the show back.[13] More importantly, they proved their love for the show by supporting it by spending their disposable income, not only on the *Family Guy* DVD, but also on other add-ons like video games and ringtones.[14] *The Family Guy: Season One* DVD ended up selling 2.2 million copies, making it one of the bestselling TV series DVDs of all-time. In Hollywood, this kind of fan revolt, followed by tremendous sales, causes studio executives to turn their heads.

After *Family Guy* got cancelled, Time Warner's Cartoon Network picked up the show on a trial basis.[15] It aired the series during its popular Adult Swim block of animated programming designed for young adults. The fans followed. As one journalist explained, "Adult Swim, Cartoon's late-night block ... draws young viewers with its edge animation from 11 PM to 6 AM It was the number four cable network for ages 18 to 49."[16]

The show's young male demographic group, targets for Cartoon Network and *Family Guy*, made a difference in the life of the show. Given the show's edgy material and indie slot on Adult Swim, young viewers built a cult around Peter Griffin and his family, which proved the power of fans to invigorate a show. According to Josh Wolk, "They [Adult Swim fans] watched the same 50 reruns over and over again ... until the show regularly beat out Jay Leno and David Letterman."[17] The two prime comedians getting beat by an animated toy-factory worker from Rhode Island seems nearly beyond comprehension.[18] All in all, *Family Guy* brought about 2 million viewers a night to Adult Swim.[19]

Examining the show's success on Cartoon Network and the subsequent resurrection on Fox, Peter Staddon, executive vice president of Fox Home Entertainment said, "This is the first time I've seen something like this happen. We were surprised at how insatiable the demand was."[20] After these staggering DVD sales, the chairman of 20th Century Fox said it was the first show of the DVD age to benefit from such sales. And *Family Guy* indeed benefited; the sales, thanks to its obsessed fans and new viewers who obsessed over every detail of the show on Adult Swim and continued watching rerun after rerun, brought the show back to life.

For the first time in television history, a show was brought back into production, and two years after its cancellation at that. At least Fox admitted its mistake, but it had no choice; it couldn't argue with DVD sales. The network recognized that it missed an opportunity to increase its core audience. A budding magazine founder told one journalist, "The self-described 20-something Gen X-ers say this audience has been overlooked and underappreciated by Hollywood."[21] The top-selling DVDs of a canceled show prove it.

The second time around with *Family Guy*, Fox was determined to unveil the show properly. The network revived the show in 2005. *Family Guy* aired on Sunday nights at 9 p.m., opposite ABC's popular *Desperate Housewives*. Ironically, given the show's competition, the new time slot garnered attention not only from its traditional fan base of males between 18 and 34 years old, but also among women.

The first time around with Fox, there is a great deal of evidence supporting the notion that the producers and writers of *Family Guy* immediately put it on a fast track to nowhere based on its nontraditional humor. One journalist describes MacFarlane's humor as "planting tactless humor bombs."[22]

In a strictly, traditional narrative sense, *Family Guy* is so nonlinear and random, with no real story line, that it can be hard to digest, particularly for mainstream audiences (the kind shows need to break out in primetime programming). Kool-Aid Man, for example, is one of the show's most random interruptions. One writer explains, "The Kool-Aid Man is a gigantic frosty pitcher filled with the red liquid and marked with a smiley face, as seen in advertisements for Kool-Aid." He is known for bursting through walls and yelling "Oh, yeah!" He first appeared in the episode titled "When Death Has a Shadow." Peter was in court for committing fraud. He pleaded innocent but was found guilty. After each family member shouted, "Oh, no!" in the courtroom, the Kool-Aid Man busted through the wall and yelled, "Oh, yeah!" Executive producer David Zuckerman had to fight for Kool-Aid Man because the network thought that the transgression would "totally alienate the audience." It's a good thing Zuckerman won the fight, because "the Kool-Aid Man . . . has become one of the 'most popular' and 'most often-cited' gags on the show."[23]

The chaotic appearance of characters like Kool-Aid Man and others in the midst of unrelated storylines provides the basis for the show's non-sequiturs. Simultaneously, these snippets give *Family Guy* added character and also a hipster aesthetic that asks the audience to goof with nostalgic figures, brands, or characters. They provide, according to one commentator, "even more drama, cutting away from the main story to another place or time, as the plot is interrupted and segues into unrelated, self-contained sketches of variable length. These are often introduced when a character refers to a past event, using such phrases as 'I haven't felt like this since . . . ,' 'This is worse than the time . . . ,' or 'Like that time when . . . ' "[24]

Peter dominates in this area. He usually takes the lead in using those phrases. For example, in one episode, he said, "This sucks worse than that time I went to that museum." It then flashes back to his childhood when he's standing in the museum looking at a dinosaur. In another episode, Peter is going to get a prostate exam, and he says, "This sucks worse than the time I forgot how to sit down." Peter's famous phrases offer a nice transition to regress to content that has no logic.

In another running gag on *Family Guy*, Ernie the Giant Chicken, a human-sized fowl appears out of nowhere and confronts Peter. The two engage in ultra-violent, graphic fight scenes that have nothing to do with the story arc. The skirmishes could be viewed as a skewering of the over-the-top fight scenes that dominate action films. Often resulting from a simple misunderstanding, like the first fight that took place because the chicken gave Peter an expired grocery coupon, the carnage leaves Peter broken, but able to hobble on.

Kool-Aid Man and the non-sequiturs are just a couple examples of the show's wackiness that its fans love. But viewers also enjoy the other characters that contribute to its out-of-this-world content. The youngest Griffin offspring, toddler Stewie, epitomizes the campy nature of *Family Guy*. The irony that a baby is hell bent on controlling the world, killing his mother, all the while acting like an infant, reveals MacFarlane's bizarre sense of humor, but fans can't get enough. Included in the over-the-top *Family Guy* universe is family dog, Brian, who is Peter's best friend and serves as the only bit of class incorporated into the show. Viewers are supposed to understand this point because the dog speaks in a more educated manner than the rest of the family, reads left-leaning magazines and literature, and loves martinis.[25] This all makes it apparent that *Family Guy* has a "fractured approach" to content.[26] Obviously, the show does not place much value on traditional storylines with linear plots and logical outcomes.

Although the lack of a storyline is what attracts many viewers, the show gets a lot of criticism for it, including from rival cartoons. Comedy

Network's *South Park* produced a two-part storyline around *Family Guy*.[27] The first episode involved a "war" over the show; Kyle loves *Family Guy*, while Cartman hates it. Cartman calls the show "poorly written" and complains about the jokes that have nothing to do with the plot. In the second episode, Peter Griffin goes on a date in Mexico with Gary Coleman. But all the *Family Guy* bashing garnered some attention. Apparently, producers from *The Simpsons* and *King of the Hill* supported the episodes of *South Park*, but it's difficult to say just how intense the cartoon wars are in reality. According to scholar Alison Crawford, such "criticism is a fertile source of satire for MacFarlane and the *Family Guy* writers."[28] In the high-stakes world of television programming, one could argue that a cartoon war among these popular animated shows actually helps drive higher ratings and buzz, particularly given the intensity and love fans have for these particular shows.

There's no rule for what constitutes a good cartoon—or entertainment for that matter. No one said a show had to possess a storyline in order to be successful. As a matter of fact, many viewers enjoy programs that enable them to escape from their lives, if only for a little while, regardless of narrative style. The long history of alternative forms of entertainment, from nonlinear science fiction to the technical use of flashbacks across channels, reveals the pervasiveness and popularity of experimental programming. Social scientist Harold Mendelsohn suggests that television offers a form of escapism from everyday life and serves as a way of alleviating tensions viewers feel in confronting life's issues.[29] Rather than challenge the quality of TV programming, Mendelsohn recognizes the audience's desire for entertainment. He explains, "Mass entertainment theory asserts that television and other mass media, because they relax or otherwise entertain average people, perform a vital function."

Dolf Zillman later developed a contemporary version of entertainment theory. He seeks to differentiate entertainment processes from information, education, and persuasion. Zillman views entertainment as an information-processing theory. From Zillman's perspective, audiences control their selection of entertainment content, but people also hold underlying psychological processes that influences their selection. Entertainment theory, according to Zillman, coordinates with mood management, a subtheory of entertainment theory that focuses on psychological processes and potentially explains why people desire entertainment.[30]

It is obvious that the vital function of entertainment is to enable people to relax, to have fun, and do what they enjoy; it affects one's frame of mind. Mood management theory "argues that a predominant motivation for using entertainment media is to moderate or control our moods."[31] With the increasing amounts of entertainment available, especially those involving senselessness, it's easy to regulate one's mood. The wacky nature of *Family Guy* is uplifting. For example, when people stress out after a busy day at the office, they turn to comedy to take a break and calm them down. Individuals often find it nice to turn to mindless humor. As discussed, viewers of *Family Guy* can rely on it for just that, and that is what its fans love about it.[32]

Fans also love its risqué humor. Crawford explains, "*Family Guy* has been accused of all the crimes of blank parody: meaninglessness, plagiarism, banality, laziness, and being formulaic."[33] Despite criticisms from those who do not appreciate *Family Guy*'s irreverent humor— often bordering on disgust—the show maintains its popularity and cult-like devotion. Perhaps it's the "I can't believe they just did that" feeling that keeps viewers intrigued. MacFarlane and his team of writers explores the seedy underbelly of society and a myriad of topics often considered over the line, such as pedophilia, spousal abuse, venereal disease, and extreme racism. The show's creator rarely thinks anything is over the line. Fox is also a willing partner, which shows in its continued support of the show, despite facing potential criticism.[34] There is also a kind of equal opportunity in the way *Family Guy* attacks every political, cultural, and societal norm, which lends the program authenticity and respect among fans. Viewers know everyone is going to be singled out at some point or another, which only makes it fair.

Not everyone, though, is willing to accept *Family Guy*'s humor in a good-natured manner. A highly publicized dispute occurred with former governor of Alaska and Republican vice president nominee Sarah Palin, who has a son with Down syndrome. In one episode, Chris courts a girl from his class named Ellen with Down syndrome. When asked about her family, Ellen responds that her mother is the former governor of Alaska. Palin took the joke as a jab to her young son, Trig, and later voiced her frustration by saying some things just aren't funny. The popularity of the show, however, backfired on Palin. Media critic James Poniewozik explains:

> Palin posted on Facebook that the scene was "another punch in the gut." . . . Palin's outrage prompted not an apology but a smackdown, from Andrea Fay Friedman, a *Family Guy* voice actress—who actually has Down. "My parents raised me to have a sense of humor," she said. "My mother did not carry me around under her arm like a loaf of French bread the way former governor Palin carries her son Trig around looking for sympathy and

votes." Ouch. Cartoon 1, Politician 0. The *Family Guy* scene was a personal shot—but at Palin, not Trig. Friedman's character was assertive, intelligent and confident (and a young woman, not an infant boy). Palin seemed to be defending neither her son nor the disabled generally but herself, a public figure whom a cartoon had the temerity to poke fun at.[35]

Microsoft also believes the jokes on *Family Guy* aren't funny.[36] The company announced it was going to be a sponsor of a special episode of the show, but when it learned of its content, Microsoft backed down. The company reported that the show was "not a fit with the Windows brand." The episode contained jokes about the Holocaust, feminine hygiene, and incest. It makes sense that a highly regarded company would not want to associate with such humor, but maybe the company should have recognized the show's offensiveness before agreeing to be a sponsor.

Critical acclaim has also followed in the wake of the show's intense popularity. In 2009, *Family Guy* received an Emmy nomination for Outstanding Comedy Series.[37] It was the first cartoon show to do so since *The Flintstones*. Although *Family Guy* did not snag the win, it's obvious the show deserved a nomination. Because *Family Guy* is unique in that no other show has ever come back from cancellation,[38] some sort of recognition should be achieved. *The Simpsons*, the gold standard of animation as previous mentioned, has never received an Emmy. MacFarlane hopes the nomination of *Family Guy* will "promote a new Emmy world order, in which animated shows routinely compete again live-action ones."[39]

Overall, *Family Guy* is one of a kind with its "bathroom humor" and "staccato punch lines style."[40] And since its resurgence, its random style has spiraled out of control, bringing in more avid fans. Its revival has sparked an air of cockiness and complacency; non-sequiturs and pop culture references are more and more frequent in the storylines.[41] But because its fans have spoken, it can get away with practically anything it desires. It's the power of the fans that helps it get away with its inappropriate content, which additionally demonstrates the power of its cult. In 2007, Dana Walden, chairman of 20th Century Fox TV, said, "I cringe sometimes while watching it. But that's really part of the formula for any comedy that reaches the status of cultural phenomenon, as this one has. If the creators aren't constantly pushing the limit and sometimes stepping over the line, they won't be part of the zeitgeist."[42]

The cult-inspired power of *Family Guy* fans has changed television forever. The death and rebirth of the animated series revealed that fans have power (particularly if they are willing to put up money to prove their love). The resurrection of the show surprised not only the network itself but MacFarlane too. The show was cancelled for three years, so the revival was unexpected.[43] MacFarlane noted that it is easier to bring back an animated show for many reasons. Actors in live-action programs have moved onto other things, making it difficult to recreate. In addition, animation characters don't age; so it is less problematic to pick up where the show left off. *Family Guy* proves a show can have a life of its own, as MacFarlane pointed out.

In addition to achieving two afterlives, rebirth, and release into syndication, the *Family Guy* cult has also inspired a spinoff show.[44] *The Cleveland Show* focuses on *Family Guy* secondary character Cleveland Brown, one of Peter's friends. The show is meant to be a "kinder, gentler *Family Guy.*" The premise of the show is that Cleveland, the Griffins' African American neighbor, moved to his hometown to start his life over again after marrying his soul mate. The show quickly drifted from this and picked up characteristics of *Family Guy*. It, too, obviously possess MacFarlane's random humor with cutaway jokes and pop culture references. While the show's producers may have wanted to deviate from the success of *Family Guy* with *The Cleveland Show*, obviously fans wanted more of the former, which further proves the fans' obsession with *Family Guy.*

Overall, *The Simpsons* and *The Flintstones* changed viewers' perceptions of cartoons. They opened the door for shows, such as *Family Guy*, to make it on air due to its appeal to a broad audience.[45] *Family Guy* features jokes for all ages, all mindsets, and all intellectual levels. Because the show is a series of jokes, one right after the other, it is bound to get everyone laughing at one point; that is the key to the show's success. Its edgier content also attracts young viewers, even though it offers sophisticated content and carries parental advisory warnings.[46] It is this aspect, the scatological, adult humor, which helped the show come back to life, survive numerous challenges from the Federal Communications Commission, receive an Emmy nomination, and get an afterlife in syndication. *Family Guy* is proof that adults can love cartoons, too.

Notes

1. Oldenburg, Ann. "Younger viewers tune in to 'toons aimed at adults." *USA Today*, July 12, 2005. *Academic Search Complete, EBSCOhost* (accessed April 1, 2011).

2. Alison Crawford, "'Oh Yeah!': *Family Guy* as Magical Realism?" *Journal of Film & Video*, 61:2 (Summer 2009): 52–69. http://search.ebscohost.com/login.aspx?direct=true&db=a9h&AN=37564157&site=ehost-live (accessed June 1, 2011).

3. Ibid.

4. Ibid.

5. David Lieberman, "Pressure is on 'The Simpsons' to Capitalize on Merchandise, *USA Today*, May 15, 2009.

6. "The Simpsons Movie," Box Office Mojo, n.d., http://boxofficemojo.com/movies/?id=simpsons.htm (accessed March 30, 2010).

7. T. L. Stanley, "All Kidding Aside, Here Comes a Family Guy Beer," *Brandweek* 48, 42 (November 19, 2007): 9. *Academic Search Complete, EBSCOhost* (accessed January 24, 2011).

8. Ray Richmond, "CULT CLASSIC," *Brandweek* 48, no. 39 (October 29, 2007): S-2-S-6. *Academic Search Complete, EBSCOhost* (accessed November 15, 2011).

9. Tom Russo, "The Go-to-Guy." *Entertainment Weekly* 466 (January 8, 1999): 39. *Academic Search Complete, EBSCOhost* (accessed Feb 15, 2011).

10. Stanley.

11. Ibid.

12. Richmond.

13. Gloria Goodale, "Cult Fans Bring 'The Family Guy' Back to TV." *Christian Science Monitor*, April 22, 2005. 13, *Academic Search Complete, EBSCOhost* (accessed August 29, 2010).

14. Stanley.

15. Ibid.

16. Oldenburg.

17. Josh Wolk, "RETURN OF FAMILY VALUES." *Entertainment Weekly* 816 (April 22, 2005): 36–39. *Academic Search Complete, EBSCOhost* (accessed June 30, 2011).

18. Devin Gordon, "Suddenly, 'Family Guy.'" *Newsweek*, 142:2(2003): 11. http://search.ebscohost.com/login.aspx?direct=true&db=a9h&AN=10187464&site=ehost-live.

19. Richmond.

20. Qtd. in Goodale.

21. Ibid.

22. Richmond.

23. Crawford.

24. Ibid.

25. Stanley.

26. Crawford.

27. Brioux.

28. Crawford.

29. Baran & Davis.

30. Ibid.
31. Ibid.
32. Poniewozik, 2009.
33. Crawford, 2009.
34. Poniewozik, 2009.
35. James Poniewozik, *"Family Guy* Defeats Palin." *Time* 175, no. 9 (March 8, 2010): 20. *Academic Search Complete, EBSCOhost* (accessed June 30, 2011).
36. Stelter.
37. Snierson.
38. Stanley.
39. Snierson.
40. Richmond.
41. Crawford.
42. Richmond.
43. Goodale, 2005.
44. Poniewozik, 2009.
45. Richmond.
46. Oldenburg.

Bibliography

Baran, Stanley, & Dennis K. Davis. *Mass Communication Theory: Foundations, Ferment, and Future, Fifth Edition.* Boston, MA: Wadsworth Cengage, 2008.
Brioux, B. "Battle of the Animation Stars; *Family Guy* in Crosshairs of 'Toon Wars." *Toronto Sun,* November 3, 2006. http://www.lexisnexis.com/.
Crawford, Alison. "'Oh Yeah!': *Family Guy* as Magical Realism?" *Journal of Film & Video.* 61:2 (Summer 2009): 52–69. http://search.ebscohost.com/login.aspx?direct=true&db=a9h&AN=37564157&site=ehost-live (accessed June 1, 2011).
Goodale, Gloria. "Cult Fans Bring 'The Family Guy' Back to TV." *Christian Science Monitor,* April 22, 2005. 13, *Academic Search Complete, EBSCOhost* (accessed August 29, 2010).
Gordon, Devin. "Suddenly, 'Family Guy.'" *Newsweek, 142*:2 (2003): 11. http://search.ebscohost.com/login.aspx?direct=true&db=a9h&AN=10187464&site=ehost-live.
Greenwood, D. "Of Sad Men and Dark Comedies: Mood and Gender Effects on Entertainment Media Preferences." *Mass Communication & Society,* 13:3 (2010): 232–249. http://search.ebscohost.com/login.aspx?direct=true&db=a9h&AN=51174589&site=ehost-live.
Oldenburg, Ann. "Younger viewers tune in to 'toons aimed at adults." *USA Today,* July 12, 2005. *Academic Search Complete, EBSCOhost* (accessed April 1, 2011).
Poniewozik, James. "Family Guy Defeats Palin." *Time* 175:9 (March 8, 2010): 20. Academic Search Complete, EBSCOhost (accessed September 15, 2011).

Poniewozik, James. "Hyper Animation." *Time*, 174:16 (2009): 61. http://search .ebscohost.com/login.aspx?direct=true&db=a9h&AN=44714758&site =ehost-live.

Richmond, Ray. "CULT CLASSIC." *Brandweek* 48:39 (October 29, 2007): S-2-S-6. *Academic Search Complete, EBSCOhost* (accessed November 15, 2011).

Russo, Tom. "The Go-to-Guy." *Entertainment Weekly* 466 (January 8, 1999): 39. *Academic Search Complete, EBSCOhost* (accessed Feb 15, 2011).

Snierson, D. "Emmys: Animated Series Get Some Love." *Entertainment Weekly*, 1058 (2009): 12. http://search.ebscohost.com/login.aspx?direct=true &db=a9h&AN=43464759&site=ehost-live.

Stanley, T. L. "All Kidding Aside, Here Comes a Family Guy Beer." *Brandweek* 48, 42 (November 19, 2007): 9. *Academic Search Complete, EBSCOhost* (accessed January 24, 2011).

Stelter, B. "Window Closes On 'Family Guy' Special." *New York Times*, October 28, 2009, 3. http://search.ebscohost.com/login.aspx?direct=true&db =a9h&AN=44851036&site=ehost-live.

"The Simpsons Movie." Box Office Mojo. n.d., http://boxofficemojo.com/ movies/?id=simpsons.htm (accessed March 30, 2010).

Wolk, Josh. "RETURN OF FAMILY VALUES." *Entertainment Weekly* 816 (April 22, 2005): 36–39. *Academic Search Complete, EBSCOhost* (accessed June 30, 2011).

CHAPTER 18

IT's FUNNY BECAUSE IT's TRUE: *THE OFFICE* AND OUR INNER MICHAEL

Joseph Darowski

> What is the most important thing for a company? Is it the cash flow? Is it the inventory? Nuh-uh. It's the people. The people. My proudest moment here . . . was a young Guatemalan guy, first job in the country, hardly spoke a word of English, but he came to me, and said, "Mr. Scott, will you be, the Godfather to my child?" Wow . . . wow. Didn't work out in the end. We had to let him go. He sucked.
> —Michael Scott, "Pilot" (Original air date March 24, 2005)

Rumors of downsizing drive conversations among workers at a mid-size paper company. That is about all that happens. Oh, and a temp begins working at the office. The plot is not very memorable.

The idea is that a documentary film crew is recording all of this, leading to many awkward pauses that stretch to uncomfortable lengths and meaningful looks directly into the camera. Characters address the audience directly to explain their thoughts and motivations yet are clearly awkward being filmed. The camera, in essence, becomes an unseen character. The whole thing is laughably absurd yet features uncomfortably familiar characters.

These are the elements of "Pilot," the first episode of *The Office*, NBC's Americanized adaptation of a popular British series of the same name. The temp worker, Ryan, creates the opportunity for characters to introduce themselves to the new guy and the audience at the same time. These wonderful characters include the egomaniacal yet tender boss Michael, who just wants to be loved; the sycophantic, power-mad

Dwight Schrute, who longs for authority; Jim, who is bored with his job but secretly in love; and Pam, the receptionist and Jim's love interest, who is engaged; and many other secondary characters, who later develop into primetime players as the series progressed. Over time, *The Office* became one of NBC's most important shows, eventually anchoring its famed "Must See TV" Thursday night schedule and scoring well in the coveted 18-to-49 viewer age demographic. In addition, the series received multiple award nominations and wins each season and became the network's highest rated show.[1]

One might ask why exactly a hit sitcom like *The Office* has a chapter in a book on cult pop culture. After all, *The Office* is one of the most popular shows on NBC's schedule and is a key part of NBC's Thursday night schedule. For decades, NBC's Thursday night television lineup stood as the most highly rated block of programming on television. There was a time when the four sitcoms and one hour-long drama that NBC aired on Thursday nights were the five highest-rated shows on television.[2] And now *The Office* is one of the anchors for NBC's Thursday night lineup of sitcoms, the same role that *Cheers* had in the 1980s and *Seinfeld* had in the 1990s. Nobody would consider *Cheers* or *Seinfeld* as having merely cult followings, since they were pop culture phenomena.

The Office, however, is a much different show than the traditional NBC Thursday-night sitcom and has built its audience in different ways. Without the original cult popularity of *The Office* that NBC nurtured, the show may not have lasted long enough to become as popular as has been over the years.

To better understand how unlikely it seemed when *The Office* first premiered that it would become a key part of NBC's Thursday night lineup, an understanding of the importance of that night on that network is necessary. NBC structured Thursday night with its most popular half-hour sitcoms at 8:00 PM and 9:00 PM, followed by an hour-long drama at 10:00 PM. In between, at 8:30 and 9:30 PM, NBC aired sitcoms that it hoped would become hits, then gradually able to establish an audience of their own, which would follow the show to a new time slot. Shows airing at 8:30 and 9:30 often had fantastic ratings when sandwiched between the anchor shows of the night but would later struggle to retain the audience when moved to a new night. In 1999, it was reported that Thursday night's ad sales were responsible for 38 percent of NBC's revenues.[3]

The Thursday night schedule launched this format in 1984 with *The Cosby Show* and *Cheers* at 8:00 and 9:00 and *Hill Street Blues* at 10:00. *The Cosby Show* was the number one-rated show on television its first five years, causing Thursday night to became the most important night of NBC's schedule. Following the combination of *The Cosby Show* and *Cheers* as the anchor sitcoms of the 1980s, *Friends* and *Seinfeld* were the most significant anchor shows of the 1990s.

Friends and *Seinfeld* each averaged more than 20 million viewers at the peak of their popularity.[4] In between the hit anchor shows on Thursday night, NBC would air sitcoms it hoped would gain their own popular followings independent of the lead-in audience. Because these sitcoms aired between shows that had more than 20 million viewers, they often retained significant portions of their audiences. However, if the drop were significant enough, NBC would cancel them. For example, in 2000, NBC canceled both shows that aired in between the Thursday night anchor slots, *Jesse*, which averaged 16.7 million viewers and was the tenth-most-watched show on television, and *Stark Raving Mad*, which averaged 15.5 million viewers and was the fifteenth-most-watched show on television that year.[5]

In 2000, NBC was cancelling shows with more than 15 million viewers, but its fortunes had changed significantly when *The Office* premiered that same year as a mid-season replacement that would only air six episodes. No longer the most-watched network on television, NBC was pleased when the series premiere drew 11 million viewers.[6] However, the second episode of the season lost almost half the audience and only had 5.9 million viewers.[7] At the end of the first season, *Media Life Magazine* reported, "The network's one worry was whether the show would connect with viewers used to broad humor and a predictable laugh-tracked pace . . . NBC's one worry was a big one. The show did not connect with viewers, and it connected less and less over its short lifespan."[8] This prediction of demise was understandable; the first season only ranked as the 102nd-most-watched show of the season.[9]

Why did *The Office* struggle to find an audience? One likely reason is that the show was markedly different from the sitcoms NBC traditionally aired. NBC had a very specific style for its sitcoms, which it had been following for decades by the time *The Office* premiered. The quirky workplace mockumentary camera style did not conform to these standards. Nancy San Martin identified the many of the stereotypical elements of traditional NBC sitcoms:

> The "must see" fictions are typically set in metropolises that index the larger nation—*Friends, Just Shoot Me* and *Will & Grace*'s New York, *Frasier*'s Seattle, *ER*'s Chicago. Resisting ambiguous, fictional, isolated, or fantastical settings, "must see TV" codifies urban centres as microcosms of the USA.[10]

Martin goes on to argue that NBC is pursuing a viewer that resembles the characters who typically populate their sitcoms: White, straight, employed, and affluent enough to have cash to spend. This is descriptive of the majority of NBC's Thursday night sitcoms, with some notable exceptions such as *The Cosby Show*, which featured an African American cast, and *Will and Grace*, which prominently featured homosexual characters. NBC's Thursday sitcoms have also featured similar production styles, including three- or four-camera shooting styles, a studio audience, and laugh tracks.

This chapter will consider why *The Office* began with such low ratings, including discussions of the ways in which *The Office* departed from the dominant trends in NBC's sitcoms. The setting is Scranton, Pennsylvania, rather than a metropolis on either coast. Also, the series is shot in a mockumentary style, with a single camera, no laugh track, and frequent "talking head" shots. Some distinct aspects of *The Office* that will be considered are the nonglamorous cast members and the culturally diverse characters. Despite being in a small-town setting, the cast includes an African American, a Mexican American, and an Indian American rather than a strictly WASPish cast. These aspects stand out, especially when compared to NBC's previous comedy series, which generally featured White actors with classic movie star looks and body types.

Many of these facets of the show create a sense that the show could exist in the real everyday lives of the viewers, a sense that never existed with the photogenic beauties of *Friends* or the absurd intertwining narratives of *Seinfeld*. These aspects of the show were perhaps so different from what viewers were accustomed to encountering on NBC's Thursday-night schedule that a period of adjustment was needed before the show was embraced as widely as it has come to be.

This paper will also examine how NBC nurtured a cult following, thus allowing the series to grow in popularity. More specifically, the network used the Internet and new media channels to help create a group of core fans. The small cult following the show initially had prevented the network from cancelling the show despite poor early ratings.

"Hot Girl" (Original Air Date April 26, 2005)

The purse girl hits everything on my checklist. Creamy skin. Straight teeth. Curly hair. Amazing breasts. Not for me, for my children. The Schrutes produce very thirsty babies.

—Dwight Schrute

In the season 1 episode "Hot Girl," an attractive saleswoman named Katy comes to the Dunder Mifflin office in the hopes of selling purses. Michael tells her that he usually does not allow salespeople to solicit the office, ostensibly to prevent disruption. However, he makes an exception for Katy because he is so attracted to her. Her beauty disrupts the office more than her attempts to sell purses, as Michael, Dwight, and Jim vie for her attention. In the end, Jim, who has been the least aggressive of the males pursuing Katy, gives her a ride home and takes her out for drinks.

Very early on in the episode, the theme of attraction and impulse is established. Michael has the opportunity to purchase an incentive for employees from the sales department. He asks what motivates people, and Dwight immediately answers, "Sex!" This foreshadows the plot of the episode, as physical attraction motivates the men in the office as they pursue Katy. A desire to date Katy makes Dwight and Michael act particularly foolish. Dwight buys a purse from Katy, convinced it can double as a mini-briefcase, and carries his belongings in it. Michael, who can purchase a prize for the top employee on his sales force, buys a $1,000 espresso machine from Starbucks because Katy says she would like a cup of coffee. Dwight's statement that sex motivates people has been proven.

In entertainment production, a common maxim is that "sex sells," and often the hope is that the sex appeal of the actors in movies or on television will bring viewers in. "Hot Girl" drew explicit attention to, for lack of a better term, the deliberate plainness of the cast of *The Office*. In contrast, the casts of many NBC sitcoms, most notably *Friends*, were known for their glamorous good looks, and likely to be chased by the paparazzi. Jennifer Aniston even created a national hairstyle craze called "the Rachel," named after her character on *Friends*.[11]

The cast of *The Office* is meant to consist of people who could be found in any office in the country, not walking the streets of Hollywood with packs of photographers following them. In the commentary to "Pilot," Jenna Fischer, who plays Pam, the object of desire for many men in the office, explained:

> When I got my first call to go in and audition I spoke with her, and she said that her notes were to really downplay my looks. Like, don't at all try to be pretty, don't put on any make up. And I said, "Really?" Because casting directors always say, "OK, so be really hot. I mean really hot and sexy. Hotter and sexier than you think you need to be." And so she said, "Really, be as plain as possible." And then she said, "Dare to bore me." And I said, "Really? Bore you?" And she said, "Don't try to be funny.

Please, please don't come in here and do a bunch of shtick and try to be funny." So that was my goal.[12]

In the same commentary, executive producer Greg Daniels discussed the character in the original British series that Pam was based on and the attributes that they hoped to translate over to the American show:

> The thing that made her so appealing in England is that she was the opposite of glamorous, and how glamorous is very off-putting, and the fact that since she was just this real person with kind of low self-esteem, all these people were attracted to her who don't like the normal glamour thing.[13]

The most attractive character, Pam, was meant to be more of a girl-next-door than to have movie star good looks.

In a celebrity-obsessed culture that typically values tall and skinny, many of the characters are notably short or stout. In "Women's Appreciation," Angela is said to stand only 5'1" and wear child's size 10 clothing.[14] Kevin, Stanley, and Phyllis are all overweight. The size and shape of the cast of *The Office* is very different than what was seen in the sitcoms NBC aired from the mid-1980s to the mid-2000s.

One reason several of the actors may not have classic movie star looks is that they are not primarily Hollywood actors but, rather, work behind the scenes and have been given roles in front of the camera on *The Office*. The primary characters, Michael, Jim, Pam, and Dwight, are played by actors who have worked on other shows. However, BJ Novak, who plays Ryan ("the temp"), was a producer and writer on the show before being cast, as were Mindy Kaling (Kelly Kapoor) and Paul Lieberstein (who plays Toby Flenderson). Phyllis Lapin worked in the casting department on *The Office*, and the producers liked her work so much when she read with potential cast members that she was given the role of Phyllis Smith on the show.[15]

Also, the cast of *The Office* is older than the young stars that were generally featured on NBC's hit sitcoms. The fact that *The Office* featured older, larger, and less classically attractive people than what NBC had trained audiences to expect may have been a contributing factor in the difficulty the network had in attracting an audience. NBC, which for years produced sitcoms with very specific looks to the cast, was airing a show with a much more diverse group of actors as far as age and body type, as well as ethnicity.

"Diversity Day" (Original Air Date March 29, 2005)

Let me ask you, is there a term besides Mexican you'd prefer? Something less offensive?

—Michael Scott

In "Diversity Day," Michael's bosses send a representative from Diversity Today to train the Scranton office in racial tolerance. The seminar is in response to Michael's offensive imitation of a controversial Chris Rock comedy skit. Michael attempts to help teach the seminar but ends up disrupting it. After the seminar, Michael calls the staff together for another round of diversity training. He has the staff put index cards with various ethnicities written on them onto their foreheads and tells everyone to treat others as though they were the minority written on their cards. Michael's goal is to raise awareness by having everyone use offensive stereotypes in their interactions with one another.

A common criticism of NBC's programming following the end of *The Cosby Show*, and indeed most programming on major networks, is the lack of minority representation. In 2001, the NAACP threatened boycotts of networks because of the lack of diversity in original prime-time programming.[16] It is especially striking that in NBC shows set in New York City, such *Seinfeld, Friends, Just Shoot Me, Will and Grace*, or *Mad About You*, the primary casts were entirely White. The casts of other hit shows such as *Cheers* and *Frasier* were similarly overwhelmingly Caucasian.

The Office features regular appearances by Stanley, an African American; Oscar, a Mexican American; Darryl, African American; and Kelly, an Indian American. Oscar is also openly gay (after being involuntarily outed by Michael). The show is also progressive in its portrayals of interracial relationships. In "The Dundies," Stanley is revealed to be married to a Caucasian woman. Kelly dates both Ryan (White) and Darryl (African American) in the course of the series. Oscar is in a relationship with a Caucasian man.

Though the cast is diverse, it should be noted that Michael is constantly insensitive to ethnic groups and sexual orientation. There is obviously a high level of ignorance in Michael's understanding of different social groups, but there is also some self-deception involved, as Michael seems convinced that he is an open and understanding individual. As Jonathan Evans and Peter Murphy note in their essay

"Authenticity or Happiness?: Michael Scott and the Ethics of Self-Deception,"

> In spite of the continuing feedback that he is racially insensitive and unsophisticated, Michael is able to hang on to the illusory self-image of being progressive. And at the end of the day he seems quite satisfied with himself. . . .By projecting and sustaining this false self-image, Michael seems happy—or at least happier than he would be without it.[17]

Michael does not want to be bigoted or prejudiced, but he is constantly tripped by his own actions. Once Michael realizes he has done something insensitive, he often tries to make it better, though his efforts almost always backfire.

For example, Dunder Mifflin's corporate office orders the diversity seminar because Michael offended his coworkers with a racist impression of Chris Rock. When Michael tries to make matters better by having his own improved diversity seminar (sponsored by Diversity Tomorrow rather than Diversity Today, because "today is almost over") he pushes the limits until getting slapped by Kelly for making fun of Indian stereotypes.

In "The Fight," Michael has a much quicker reaction to a prejudiced expression. When Jim explains that he will not punch Michael in the stomach because he just got a manicure, Michael yells, "Oh, queer!" Michael then looks at the camera and obviously recognizes that he has said something inappropriate, and then says, " . . . eye. *Queer Eye for the Straight Guy.* That's a good show. Important show."[18]

In "The Return," Oscar arrives back from his three-month paid vacation (a payoff he received in return for not suing Dunder Mifflin in retaliation for Michael outing him) and wants to throw Oscar a party to make amends. Michael explains:

> Your gayness is not what defines you. Your Mexicanness is what defines you. To me. And I think we should celebrate Oscar's Mexicannity. So Phyllis, I want you to go find firecrackers and a chihuahua.[19]

It should be noted that the humor the audience is supposed to find in these situations is not reinforcing stereotypes. Viewers are not meant to agree with Michael's understanding of Mexican culture; rather, the comedy comes from the audience being appalled. This kind of comedy actually subverts stereotypes in a complex interaction between Michael's intents, his actions, and the audience's interpretation. Viewers should be horrified by Michael's use of existing stereotypes and therefore question the validity of those stereotypes. This is one instance where the use of stereotypes is meant to weaken their influence for the discerning viewer.

"The Accountants" (Webisodes Released Online, Summer 2006)

> Idiot. Now we don't have the element of surprise. It's impossible to trap her . . .
>
> —Angela

Despite, or perhaps to a certain level because of, its progressive portrayal of race, *The Office* struggled in the ratings, so much so that many did not expect it to get renewed. It is always difficult to analyze why exactly a series struggles to find an audience. If analysts knew what audiences wanted to watch and why, every show that was produced would be a hit. Perhaps the combination of the single-camera mockumentary style, the lack of a laugh track, and the nonglamorous cast that featured more diversity made the show different enough to make it difficult for viewers to quickly get comfortable. It should be noted that NBC had many struggles finding an audience for *Scrubs* a show with similar a single camera, no laugh track, and diverse cast. Perhaps NBC had so trained audiences to expect a specific product that audiences were not receptive to variation.

Despite those early struggles, *The Office* is now a hit. How did the quirky show get so popular? Viewers fell by the wayside through the abbreviated six-episode run in the first season, when the show lost almost half of its audience between the first and second episodes. In addition, the final episode of the first season was the lowest in series history. Timing played a role in the show getting a reprieve. NBC, which had few high-rated shows on its schedule at this point, believed in the creative forces behind the show and renewed it. Then, using the Internet, NBC nurtured a cult fan base.

NBC took a chance on *The Office* and used innovative marketing to gain viewers, such as signing on with Apple as one of the first shows to be available for purchase on iTunes. Angela Bromstad, the president of NBC Universal Television Studio, identified iTunes as one of the reasons the show rebounded in the second season:

> In December, NBC started selling episodes of "The Office" on iTunes, and on that platform, the show has been a runaway success—at press time, it occupied 17 slots on iTunes' top 100 downloads chart. Bromstad

said Apple executives were the first to identify *The Office* as a perfect iTunes show. The show's success on iTunes, though, caught everyone off guard. "It was just unbelievable," Bromstad said. "That helped it get a full-season order."[20]

Selling the show online, a new method at the time that many observers doubted would help, actually significantly increased the audience. Greg Daniels, the creator of the American version of the show, credits the iTunes sales with helping fans spread the show to their friends:

> "If you're trying to talk to someone about this show you saw, and you actually have the ability to whip something out of your pocket and show them a scene, it helps word of mouth spread," Daniels said. Still, he said the show's success on iTunes wasn't a complete shock. "Last year, one of the reasons we got picked up I think, in addition to all the creative [momentum] and Steve's great movie career, was that the sales department was pleased with our demographics, they were sort of young and affluent. And maybe that overlaps well with the iPod-buying audience," Daniels said.[21]

One can't help but wonder if that is why a video iPod was featured so prominently in the second season episode "Christmas Party," despite Apple not paying for product placement in the show.[22] Perhaps the writers were offering a thank-you to Apple.

Following the second season, *The Office* offered more online content, this time for free. A series of Webisodes, two- to three-minute-long episodes available online, followed the accounting staff as they tried to track down $3,000 that disappeared. "The Accountants" allowed fans to stay connected to the characters in the break between seasons and also served as a special feature on the second-season DVD.

Two years later, NBC.com again hosted a batch of Webisodes between seasons, this time called "Kevin's Loan." Television critic Ed Bark said that the online series made "NBC look visionary in times of trouble for its conventional prime-time lineup."[23]

NBC also increased audience interaction by pioneering online content for the show. Character blogs, written by Dwight and Creed, for example, have been popular destinations online for fans. Also, merchandise inspired by the show enables fans to announce their allegiance to the series. Particularly items that were used in the show, such as a Dwight Schrute Bobblehead or Star Mugs, have more direct ties to *The Office* itself than to the actors who play parts on the show.

NBC cultivated a fan following for *The Office* by allowing the audience to interact with the universe of the show online. This provided fans with easy links to send to friends, family, or coworkers and thus create new viewers. Also, such involved interaction online created a sense of ownership or personal connection, which is important for a sustained cult following. Such investment makes the show's success a point of personal pride for fans.

"The Dundies" (Original Air Date September 20, 2005)

> Was this year's Dundies a success? Well, let me see. I made Pam laugh so hard that she fell out of her chair and she almost broke her neck. So I killed. Almost.
>
> —Michael Scott

In the second season premiere, "The Dundies," the staff is invited to Chili's for the annual Dundy awards. Michael invents an award for each worker, such as "hottest in the office," which Michael awards to Ryan. Michael emcees the event, much to the embarrassment and shame of all. However, when a group of strangers makes fun of Michael as he ends the award presentation, the staff rallies around their crestfallen boss and supports the Dundies.

The key moment in this episode is when the staff bands together after strangers mock Michael. In the DVD commentary, Jenna Fischer explains, "This is the sort of idea where you can make fun of your family, but somebody else can't. The office really rallies for him."[24] The cult followers of *The Office* felt the same family-like relationship with the show. Their interactions with the online content and the ready availability of clips and episodes for viewing allowed the fan base to grow more attached to the series. There was a possessiveness and protectiveness in the relationship between the fans and the show itself, which has allowed the show to grow in popularity each season.

Notes

1. During March sweeps this year, it was reported that *The Office* was NBC's top-rated show (Hibberd, "Fox Leading").

2. For example, in 1996, the AP reported, "The five shows in NBC's Thursday prime time lineup were the top five rated shows for the week of Dec. 9–15, Nielsen Media Research said." At the time, the shows were the classics *ER*, *Seinfeld*, and *Friends*, and the less memorable *Suddenly Susan* and *Single Guy* (Bauder, "NBC Triumphs").

3. "Frasier vs.," 1999.

4. *Friends* was the number 1 show in 2002 and had an average of 24.5 million viewers ("How Did"). *Seinfeld* was the number 1 show in 1998 and had an average of 21.2 million ("TV Ratings").

5. Brian Lowry, "ABC, UPN."

6. The premiere did not air in *The Office*'s regular time slot for that year but was helped by airing after the popular series *The Apprentice*, which inflated the number of viewers for the first episode (Dominic Timms, "US Version").

7. The move from the post-*Apprentice* time slot to a Tuesday-night slot hurt *The Office*'s ratings considerably (Jason Deans, "US Remake").

8. "Lower the Lights."

9. The first season of *The Office* averaged 5.4 million viewers, but that included the inflated numbers from the premiere's *The Apprentice* lead-in ("Primetime Series").

10. Nancy San Martin, "Must See TV," 33.

11. "Aniston Gives."

12. Krasinski et al., "Pilot Commentary."

13. Ibid.

14. "Women's Appreciation."

15. There are two separate commentaries provided to "Pilot" on the first season's DVD set (Carell et al., "Pilot Commentary").

16. "NAACP Sees Scant Progress on TV." http://speakout.com/activism/apstories/10083-1.html.

17. Evans et al., 101.

18. "The Fight"

19. "The Return"

20. Ryan, "*Office* Promotion."

21. Ibid.

22. Goo, "Apple."

23. Bark, "*The Office* Punches In."

24. Krasinski et al., "The Dundies Commentary."

Bibliography

"Aniston Gives Hairstylist the Cut." *Daily Express*, March 29, 2009, http://www.express.co.uk/posts/view/91941/Aniston-gives-hairstylist-the-cut (accessed March 30, 2009).

Bark, Ed. "The Office Punches in Early—with Four New 'Webisodes.'" *Uncle Barky's Bytes*, July 9, 2008, http://www.unclebarky.com/reviews_files/9071e2884a518f5a2410674de7eeaf3e-448.html (accessed March 31, 2009).

Bauder, David. "NBC Triumphs in Ratings Race." *Deseret News*, December 19, 1996, http://archive.deseretnews.com/archive/531506/NBC-TRIUMPHS-IN-RATINGS-RACE.html (accessed March 21, 2009).

Carell, Steve, John Krasinski, Rainn Wilson, and BJ Novak. "Pilot Commentary." *The Office: Season One*, DVD. Directed by Ken Kwapis. Universal City, CA: Universal Studios, 2005.

Deans, Jason. "US remake of *The Office* loses half its audience." *Guardian Unlimited*, March 31, 2005, http://www.guardian.co.uk/media/2005/mar/31/broadcasting1 (accessed March 21, 2009).

Evans, Jonathan and Peter Murphy. "Authenticity or Happiness? Michael Scott and the Ethics of Self-Deception," in The Office *and Philosophy: Scenes from the Unexamined Life*, ed. J. Jeremy Wisnewski (Malden, MA: Blackwell Publishing, 2008), 101.

"The Fight." *The Office: Season Two*, DVD, directed by Ken Kwapis (Universal City, CA: Universal Studios, 2006).

"Frasier vs. 'Stone Cold' Steve? Let's Get It On!" *Business Week*, September 6, 1999, http://www.businessweek.com/archives/1999/b3645071.arc.htm (accessed March 28, 2009).

Goo, Sara Kehaulani. "Apple Gets a Big Slice of Product-Placement Pie." *Washington Post*, April 15, 2006, http://www.washingtonpost.com/wp-dyn/content/article/2006/04/14/AR2006041401670.html (accessed March 31, 2009).

Hibberd, James. "Fox leading March sweep." *The Hollywood Reporter*, March 31, 2009, http://www.hollywoodreporter.com/hr/content_display/news/e3i19ba8a8fc75ea904cde04bee9be514ab (accessed March 31, 2009).

"How did your Favorite Show Rate?" *USA Today*, May 28, 2002, http://www.usatoday.com/life/television/2002/2002-05-28-year-end-chart.htm (accessed March 30, 2009).

Krasinski, John, Jenna Fischer, BJ Novak, Mindy Kaling, Paul Lieberstein, David Denman, Editor Dave Rogers, and Executive Producer Greg Daniels. "The Dundies Commentary." *The Office: Season Two*, DVD. Directed by Greg Daniels. Universal City, CA: Universal Studios, 2005.

Krasinski, John, Rainn Wilson, Jenna Fischer, BJ Novak, and Executive Producers Greg Daniels and Ken Kwapis. "Pilot Commentary." *The Office: Season One*, DVD. Directed by Ken Kwapis. Universal City, CA: Universal Studios, 2005.

"Lower the Lights for NBC's *The Office*," *Media Life Magazine*, April 27, 2005, http://www.medialifemagazine.com/News2005/april05/apr25/3_wed/news2wednesday.html (accessed March 21, 2009).

Lowry, Brian. "ABC, UPN Find the Answer to Stop Drop." *Los Angeles Times*, May 26, 2000, http://articles.latimes.com/2000/may/26/entertainment/ca-34093 (accessed March 30, 2009).

"Primetime Series." *The Hollywood Reporter*, May 27, 2005.

"The Return." *The Office: Season Three*, DVD, directed by Greg Daniels (Universal City, CA: Universal Studios, 2007).

Ryan, Maureen. "'Office' promotions pay off in a big way." *Chicago Tribune*, February 23, 2006, http://featuresblogs.chicagotribune.com/entertainment _tv/2006/02/office_workers_.html (accessed March 31, 2009).

San Martin, Nancy. "'Must See TV': Programming Identity on NBC Thursdays." In *Quality Popular Television: Cult TV, the Industry and Fans*, ed. Mark Jancovich and James Lyons (London: British Film Institute, 2003), 32–48.

Timms, Dominic. "US version of *The Office* scores ratings victory." *Guardian Unlimited*, March 29, 2005, http://www.guardian.co.uk/media/2005/ mar/29/broadcasting (accessed March 21, 2009).

"TV Ratings: 1997–1998." *ClassicTVhits.com*. http://www.classictvhits.com/ tvratings/1997.htm (accessed March 30, 2009).

"Women's Appreciation." *The Office: Season Three*, DVD, directed by Tucker Gates (Universal City, CA: Universal Studios, 2007).

CHAPTER 19

DOCTOR *WHO*: A GLOBAL CULT PHENOMENON

Brian Cogan

Doctor Who is a long-running British science fiction program that originally ran from 1963 to 1989 on BBC television (reruns also ran on many PBS stations in America from the mid-1970s until the late 1980s; there was also an American television movie pilot in 1996) and was recently successfully revived in 2005 and continues to the present, with greater worldwide popularity than in its heyday. The program was originally created by Sydney Newman, C. E. Weber, and Donald Wilson for the BBC, although many other producers worked on the program during its original run, particularly John Nathan Turner, who ran the show for most of the 1980s run until the show ended. After years of trying to revive the program, in 2003, it was announced that British writer/producer Russell T. Davies (creator of *Queer as Folk*) would reboot the program. After its relaunch in 2005, Davies's innovative reimagining of iconic characters such as the Daleks, Cybermen, and the Master brought the show back to the heights of popularity it had not seen in England and America for several decades. Davies left in 2009, and the show is now produced by Steve Moffat, one of the key writers of the new series.

Doctor Who is one of the few worldwide cult classics that seems to appeal to varied audiences despite the particularly British nature of the program. The Doctor is one of the most iconic science fiction characters of the twentieth century and is a major part of British popular culture. He is also the subject of a sizable cult following in America.

Although there is a broad canon of British science fiction heroes (such as Dan Dare), the Doctor, especially his fourth incarnation (played by Tom Baker) and the tenth and eleventh doctors (David Tennant and Matt Smith, respectively) have proven worldwide appeal that transcends nationality.

"Hello, I'm the Doctor"

Despite the longevity of the main character and the program, one of the main misconceptions that nonfans have about the show is that there is a character called Doctor Who. While that is the title of the program, the main character has never been called Doctor Who during the history of the series. Since the inception of the series, the character has always referred to himself primarily as The Doctor, and the show's title Doctor Who is a play on people wondering what the character's real name is (although on some occasions, he has used the alias John Smith when too many questions are being asked about his identity).

The central premise of the program is that the Doctor is a time traveler (known mostly as a Time Lord) from the planet Gallifrey. In the original series, his race, the Time Lords, were featured prominently in many episodes. However, in the new series, all of the Gallifreyans were killed or exiled into other dimensions during a terrible Time War with the Daleks. But even in the new version of *Doctor Who*, the same essential concepts have been maintained. In the original series, the Doctor had "borrowed" a Tardis (the Time Lords' machines that travel through time and space), and, after traveling through time had settled down on Earth with his granddaughter Susan. After two of Susan's teachers had become suspicious of the young girl's vast knowledge of multiple subjects, they accompanied her back to her home, which turned out to be a British police box in a junkyard. After entering the Tardis and meeting the Doctor, the two became the first of the doctor's companions in a series of adventures that continued throughout the course of the series.

Companions

The Doctor has almost always traveled with (mostly) human companions over the course of the series. Originally, the Doctor traveled with his granddaughter and her teachers, but he eventually moved on to travel with varying companions over the course of the series.

Few companions stayed more than a year before being replaced by various other characters. The main function of a companion is to advance the story by asking the Doctor to explain situations (particularly involving complex references to time and space) and to occasionally act as a stand-in for the audience. Several characters have proven to be particularly popular over the years—particularly the robot dog K-9, Sarah Jane Smith, Captain Jack Harkness, and Rose Tyler—and K-9, Sarah Jane Smith, and Captain Jack Harkness were all spun off into their own television shows.

Music

One of the key innovations of the original series was the electronic music of the opening and closing themes, as well as the incidental music used during the program. While many BBC shows relied on canned or orchestral music, the series featured cutting-edge, avant garde electronic music as imagined by Ron Grainer of the BBC Radiophonic Workshop and realized by Delia Derbyshire, who did not receive proper credit for her innovations until years later. The *Doctor Who* theme, although reimagined, continues to be one of the most recognizable musical themes for any science fiction program.

Regenerations

The central premise of the program is that the doctor is a time traveler from the planet Gallifrey, where the two-hearted Gallifreyans are the most advanced and powerful race in the universe. In the original series, his race, the Time Lords were featured prominently in many episodes, however in the new series, all of the Gallifreyans were killed or exiled into other dimensions during a terrible "Time War" with the Daleks. The Doctor (and his fellow Time Lord, the Master) alone have survived and have maintained the powers of the Time Lords, which includes not only power over time and space but also the ability to regenerate in times of extreme bodily injury or trauma. The function of regeneration also helps to advance the plot when the actor portraying the Doctor moves on and a new actor takes over. The Doctor has regenerated ten times over the course of the series, and each regeneration was portrayed as difficult, with the Doctor needing time to recover for the first day after regeneration. Often, the Doctor has to discover what kinds of food he now likes, what kinds of clothing he finds comfortable, and even what kind of personality he now has.

During the course of the series, many companions were surprised to see the Doctor's new incarnation except for a returning Sarah Jane Smith, who recognized the doctor again after seeing the Tardis.

The Tardis

The Tardis (Time and Relative Dimensions in Space) is a time machine the Doctor uses to travel in space and time. It is equipped with a chameleon circuit that allows it to change into anything in the area in order to blend in, but since the start of the series, has remained stuck looking like a vintage 1950s-era British police box. The Tardis, due to its nature, is also much larger on the inside then it is on the outside (it contains an uncountable number of rooms, including several levels and perhaps even a swimming pool). Although the Doctor has been using the Tardis for several centuries, he has yet to master all of its functions and has suggested on several occasions that he actually had "borrowed" the Tardis, acknowledging his relative unfamiliarity with how it functions. Although numerous other Time Lords have been shown using a Tardis over the course of the series, the nature of the Tardis has yet to be fully explained, and the Doctor on one occasion suggested that a Tardis is "grown" instead of manufactured. The Tardis is also one the most powerful forces in the universe, possessing immense energy. When the Doctor's Tardis was destroyed by a mysterious entity, it formed a crack in time and space that almost destroyed the universe (the Doctor was able to "reboot" time and space, restarting the Tardis).

Popularity

One constant thing about *Doctor Who*, which started out as a children's show, is how devoted its adult following is after nearly fifty years. As one British writer put it, the show resonates with the British audience because "The people working on it have a passion for it, unlike any other show on Earth. It is as thrilling and as loved as *Jolene*, or bread and cheese, or honeysuckle, or Friday. It's quintessential to being British" (Moran, 2007).

The show has also been a staple of British television in general, with references to the Tardis or the Doctor popping up in numerous songs, television shows and advertisements. The *Doctor Who* theme music was even used by the electronic group KLF (under the name the Timelords) in a top-ten song, "Doctoring the Tardis," which married Garry Glitter's

"Rock and Roll Part Two" with the *Doctor Who* theme music. The song went to number one on the UK charts in 1988.

While *Doctor Who* has always been a huge cultural phenomenon in Britain, but not nearly as popular in the United States, the reimagined program has become a minor sensation over the last decade. *Doctor Who* seems to have a resonance with many long-term fans, particularly for people who watched the initial series. As one critic noted,

> It is hard to overstate *Doctor Who*'s significance for Britons of a certain age. First broadcast in 1963, when many households here were just getting used to that novel new device, the television set, it was a triumph of family viewing, a science fiction show that (unlike, say, *Star Trek*, with its particular audience) parents and children stayed home to watch together. (Lyall)

Don't Call It a Comeback! The Doctor Returns

While enormously popular in England, the show was always a cult classic in the United States during its initial run and was this was not helped by the fact that in the United States, it was not available in many cities during its initial run. However, the revival in 2005 proved to be enormously popular with American fans as well, and when BBC America started running the show in 2008, even more Americans became part of the *Doctor Who* phenomenon. While the inherent Britishness of the show might have proved daunting to some, the much-improved production values and more sophisticated plot lines brought science fiction fans from all over the world to embrace the new version of the show. On April 11, 2011, a New York Premiere of the sixth season was held at a theater on the Lower East Side in New York City and was attended by more than 650 eager fans, most of whom slept overnight in order to see not only the première but also stars Matt Snyder and Karen Gillan in person. According to one fan interviewed by the *New York Times*, " 'I haven't eaten today,' says Ms. Whitton, 19. Through last night's mist, she and her friends slept on the sidewalk. 'But it was worth it'" (Maalouf).

Main Villains

The Daleks are a race of evil aliens from the planet Skaros who reduced themselves to protoplasmic forms with larger robot bodies in order to survive a long-term war. The Daleks are genocidal and, feeling that all races are inferior to them, they strive to exterminate any species that are not of direct use to them. Despite their lack of mobility (initially, Daleks could not climbs stairs), they soon become the key villains of the program.

The Master is essentially the Professor Moriarty character to the Doctor's Sherlock Holmes. The Master, first introduced in 1971, is a fellow Time Lord who dedicates his time to trying to conquer the universe instead of aiding it. Although the Doctor has been forced to work with the Master at times, they are usually antagonistic, and the Master, on occasion has caused the Doctor's death and regeneration. The Master, like the Doctor, also has twelve regenerations and at one point was at the end of his cycle, when he was granted new life by the Time Lords in exchange for aid during the Time War. The Master returned in the new series and has died twice since then.

List of the Doctors

The Doctor has been played by twelve actors over the last fifty years, with most actors staying in the role for three to four years, with the exception of the fourth Doctor, Tom Baker, who remained in the role for seven years. The Doctor was also portrayed by Peter Cushing in two *Doctor Who* movies that are not considered part of the canon by most fans.

    First Doctor (William Hartnell)

    Second Doctor (Patrick Troughton)

    Third Doctor (Jon Pertwee)

    Fourth Doctor (Tom Baker)

    Fifth Doctor (Peter Davidson)

    Sixth Doctor (Colin Baker)

    Seventh Doctor (Sylvester McCoy)

    Eighth Doctor (Paul McGann)

    Ninth Doctor (Christopher Eccleston)

    Tenth Doctor (David Tennant)

    Eleventh Doctor (Matt Smith)

Spin-Offs

Several programs featuring characters from the television show were spun off. In 2007, actress Elisabeth Sladen revisited her character Sarah Jane Smith in *The Sarah Jane Adventures*, K-9 was featured in a program geared more toward children in *K-9 and Company*, and Captain Jack Harkness was spun off into the more adult-oriented *Torchwood.*

Newfound Popularity

While the program was always popular in Britain, by the time the series ended, it was considered by many critics to be past its prime and a bit of a relic. However, the reboot of the program proved extremely popular with younger audiences. As a British critic noted in 2008, "This season's opening episode of *Doctor Who* drew 9.14 million viewers—more than one-seventh of the population of Britain" (Lyall). In addition, many fans were impressed by the way in which the new program was not just faithful to the original series but also contemporary. A British television critic noted,

> Mr. Davies's *Doctor Who* has examined the bonds that tie us to even annoying family members. It has plumbed the mysteries and possibilities of chaste love. It has made the case against slavery and violence, played with existential questions about past, present and future and explored what happens when everyone is about to be annihilated by poison gas spewing from automotive exhaust pipes. (Lyall)

In short, despite its sabbatical, *Doctor Who* remained one of the quintessential science fiction programs of the twentieth century.

Bibliography

Lyall, Sarah. "Who Altered British TV? 'Who' Indeed." *New York Times,* June 15, 2008. Accessed April 12, 2011, at http://www.nytimes.com/2008/06/15/arts/television/15lyal.html?scp=9&sq=doctor%20who&st=cse.

Maalouf, Grace. "At Village East, Waiting for the Doctor." *New York Times The Local: East Village.* April 11, 2011. Accessed April 13, 2011, from http://eastvillage.thelocal.nytimes.com/2011/04/11/at-village-east-waiting-for-the-doctor/?scp=1&sq=doctor%20who&st=cse.

Moran, Caitlin. *"Doctor Who* is Simply Masterful: So Farewell then Doctor Who, Conqueror of Space, Time, and our Correspondent's Heart. The Sofa will be Cold Without You." *The Sunday Times.* June 30, 2007. Accessed April 12, 2011, from http://entertainment.timesonline.co.uk/tol/arts_and_entertainment/tv_and_radio/article1989181.ece.

CHAPTER 20

REALITY TV AND THE NEW AMERICAN FAMILY

Leigh H. Edwards

Reality television has become a cult phenomenon over the past two decades. It inspires significant fan devotion, media attention, heated public debate, and a high level of identification between viewers and participants. There are so many reality programs and formats that the genre, once seen as a passing fad, is now a television staple. Reality television programming reached a notable level of influence when Fox launched an all-reality channel in 2005, and shows ranging from *American Idol* to earlier powerhouses like *Survivor* have enjoyed top ratings. It would not be too far fetched to say that as the genre continues to evolve, many viewers will know someone who has been on a reality program, turning a slew of average Joes into reality TV "celebrities."

Three key factors could have contributed to reality TV's appeal and its cult phenomenon status. Most important is the fact that it reflects so powerfully the concerns and anxieties of our current cultural moment, specifically the collective fears and adjustments brought on by the digital age. A second factor in the genre's cult status is how it popularizes new variations on older models of fame and stardom. Finally, a third factor is the degree to which the genre utilizes familiar narrative codes, specifically the way it turns real people's lives into media stories. As I will discuss more fully in what follows, these three elements are instrumental in generating reality TV's vast appeal and in garnering devoted followings for cult shows and for the genre as a whole.

Digital Anxieties

In capturing the Zeitgeist of our digital era, reality shows capitalize on an underlying sense of cultural change. More and more people are living parts of their lives on camera for audience consumption, while viewers question what is true about what they see on screen. What does it mean to put yourself on camera for others to see? What does it mean to feel you "know" the "real person" you are seeing on screen? These questions are complicated by the fact that the range of cameras and screens on which we see other people and ourselves is proliferating—spanning from surveillance footage or satellite feeds, such as Google Earth, to personal digital photos on Facebook or videos on YouTube, to broadcast or cable reality shows.

Watching a reality TV show and parsing out what seems more genuine and what seems more manipulated can be a way of practicing one's survival skills in our digital age. Critics such as Jon Dovey and Arild Feitveit think reality TV meditates on how digital technology has led to greater manipulation of images and more questioning of truth claims, because audiences are trying to understand what "reality" means now that any image can be seamlessly altered.[1] I would agree with this line of argumentation and believe that reality TV's popularity reflects our current fascination with the status of "truth" and "reality" in a digital context, in which it can be harder to distinguish between "real" and "fake." While any act of representation is an act of mediation, digital texts amplify some of these issues. On reality TV, this problem of truthfulness is present in the visual image as well as in the loose scripting that leads cast members to "perform" versions of themselves for the audience.

Audiences in search of media literacy need to know how to tell the difference between, for example, corporate advertisements masquerading as content versus user-generated content on YouTube. It can be a challenge to distinguish between the two. Moving from social networking and user-generated content sites to reality TV, we might ask, for example, just how scripted is MTV's hit *The Hills* and to what extent is that part of the show's appeal, since most audiences will be aware of that dynamic from extensive media reports about it. We all know reality TV is "fake," as even reality celebutante Paris Hilton tells us (meaning it is edited, manipulated, and often lightly scripted). Yet one audience study found that viewers see reality programming as at least "moderately" real.[2]

Even if the difference is one of degree, these shows are presented as something "realer" than scripted television. Often that sense of "reality" involves cast members performing their emotions or identities, explicitly drawing on the idea that "being themselves" as fully as possible on reality TV is the most "authentic" thing they can do and will garner viewers' sympathy (and even gain cult legions of devoted fans). Indeed, even though they know reality TV is highly edited, many viewers still look for what Ien Ang would term moments of "emotional realism," or psychological accuracy in the program.[3] Critic Annette Hill, in a large audience study, has documented how audiences seek out moments of "authenticity" while watching reality TV.[4] It is no mistake that the climactic moment of *Extreme Makeover: Home Edition* is the shot of the family weeping at the "reveal" of its palatial new home—courtesy of ABC. Fan devotion is evidenced by the show's high ratings, but also by the thousands who volunteer to help build a home in their local neighborhood. Through such practices, reality TV spectacularly captures the opportunities and anxieties of the digital age.

Industry Context

In order to establish the context for reality TV as a cult phenomenon and how its versions of fame and narrative power have also contributed to its status, it is useful to outline how reality TV has evolved in the TV industry and built on existing norms and conventions. The emergence of reality TV as a genre and marketing category involves a movement from a fad to a growing critical mass of devoted fans to broad incorporation into television programming. This success has often been the result of cult followings for particular reality franchises, as when *Survivor*'s summer 2000 high ratings sparked a reality boom.

Most critics date the current genre's full emergence to MTV's *The Real World* (1991), although related forerunners like police and emergency nonfiction series appeared in the late 1980s and factual programming has been around since the medium's origins, as television has always marketed the ability to convey "liveness."[5] The term *reality TV* refers to factual programming with key generic and marketing characteristics, such as unscripted, low-cost, edited formats featuring a documentary and fiction genre mix. Its hybrid genre mix includes the "docusoap" mixture of documentary and soap opera narrative and visual conventions, or the incorporation of classic sitcom storylines into observational documentaries, such as in the "reality sitcom" *The Osbournes*.[6] The documentary form allows reality TV to make a sociological claim to document the people portrayed, while the conventions of fictional TV genres encourage audiences' emotional investment in the real people portrayed as characters onscreen.

Once considered an ephemeral trend, reality TV is now recognized as a staple of television that has thoroughly altered writing, production, and distribution practices.[7] It has swept across the major networks and a large number of cable channels, combining many genres, including the sitcom, prime-time drama, talk show, game show, travelogue, soap opera, and variety show. Several tentpole franchises have enjoyed record Nielsen ratings, notably Fox's *American Idol*, with each season averaging around 20 million viewers through 2009, and CBS's *Survivor*, whose first season finale in 2000 netted 52 million.[8] With reality formats booming since, some industry executives see the genre maturing and achieving permanency, with one *Los Angeles Times* article arguing it has "mushroomed from a marginal trend to the brightest hope of the beleaguered broadcast TV business."[9] It has received Emmy categories from the Academy of Television Arts & Sciences, which indicates a sign of industry acceptance.

Examples of how this programming has changed industry practices abound. The success of unscripted fare prompted television writers to worry about their jobs and to argue for writing credits on loosely scripted shows.[10] Networks and production companies have pirated formats and sued unsuccessfully over copyright infringement.[11] Responding to summer reality hits, the schedule for network programming changed to more flexibly defined seasons, deemphasizing the old model of September premieres and thirty-five-week seasons with summer reruns in favor of year-round, fifty-two-week new programming. Instead of twenty-two episodes over a September-to-May season, they frequently feature eight to thirteen episodes in successive weeks as short-run series. In the summer of 2004, Fox and NBC began moving to year-round programming. Fox's parent company, News Corp., then launched its reality cable channel in 2005.[12] The Fox Reality Channel has further institutionalized the genre, exemplifying the narrowcasting trend in which cable channels, as Graeme Turner has established, adopt a genre identity to promote viewer loyalty.[13]

Many critics have noted how the industry's political economy in the 1980s and 1990s, especially deregulation, contributed to the genre's rise. Chad Raphael notes that cable competition, fewer financial resources, the 1988 writers' strike, and other union battles initially sparked network interest in nonfiction formats such as *Cops*.[14] This trend of broadcast networks and cable channels turning to reality programming during a writers' strike or labor disputes continued with the 2007 Writers Guild of America strike.[15]

Reality TV's formal elements and industry context have crucial ramifications for its content. Because reality TV can be produced and edited in weeks while scripted programs can take months, it can respond more quickly to socio-cultural changes. Even though reality programs have "story editors" who cull storylines from hours of raw footage and some have light scripting and staged situations, the amount of scripting is much less than in fictional series.

Scholars have been eagerly discussing key issues reality TV raises, including voyeurism, surveillance and social control, identity shaped through the media, the role of mass media in democracy, and the possibilities and limits for audience access and agency offered by new media forms.[16] This critical attention to reality TV is important given not only the high number of viewers but also the passion of fan devotion. Witness the screaming fans jamming phone lines to vote for *American Idol, Survivor* viewing parties, or fans watching live Internet feeds of *Big Brother* or *The Real World* and flooding Internet forums.

Reality Fame

As the reality genre both responds to and shapes the television industry, the way it alters the normative categories of fame and narrative is central to the success of reality formats. On the issue of fame, what does it mean to make people famous for being themselves on TV? How does celebrities' fame change when they let viewers see their "private" home lives, behind closed doors? Will everyone eventually have his or her own reality show, whether self-broadcast it on YouTube or as part of a reality TV program? The way reality TV offers the prospect of fame to everyday viewers contributes greatly to it garnering a cult following with legions of devoted followers (who express their enthusiasm on websites such as realitytvworld.com).

Reality programs provide more people access to fame and audiences more access to the inner workings of stars. Critics have long argued that the rhetoric of "stardom" involves a split between the public and the private and a relationship between what critic John Ellis calls the ordinary and the extraordinary.[17] Stars must be extraordinary (some talent or quality makes them exceptional, unreachable, thus seen in glamorous, larger-than-life surroundings). Yet they must also be ordinary (relatable, in close proximity to the viewer because they want the same things everyday people want, often described in terms of the personal: home, family, marriage, happiness for their kids).[18]

Reality TV puts the interaction of the public and private and the ordinary and extraordinary on greater display than ever before. When a noncelebrity becomes famous simply for performing a version of him- or herself on reality TV, the genre offers us the spectacle of an ordinary person being placed in extraordinary circumstances. A program like MTV's long-running franchise *The Real World* masterfully places 18- to 24-year-old cast members on display as they perform on the lifestyle programming MTV uses to sell products to its target audience. While they are "extraordinary" for being on TV and gaining reality stardom, these cast members retain their "ordinary" connection to the viewers at home, because viewers could audition to be on the show's next season. Meanwhile, when a celebrity has a reality show, he or she offers audiences greater access to the private person or his or her ordinary life behind the extraordinary stardom. MTV's *The Osbournes* (starring heavy metal icon Ozzy Osbourne) and *Run's House* (featuring Joseph "Reverend Run" Simmons from pioneering rap group Run-DMC) publicize the stars' relatable family life.

I would argue that as reality programming becomes ubiquitous, reality formats place more pressure on the "ordinary" side of the extraordinary–ordinary balance in the rhetoric of stardom. If an average person becomes famous for being him- or herself on TV but then begins to behave pretentiously, insert the "celebrity" status too aggressively into the reality show, or become too obvious in the search for fame, audiences can turn against the person for leaving the relatable "ordinary" too far behind. Or if a celebrity suffers a scandal that makes her or his private life impossible to appear "ordinary," the reality show narrative breaks down (as when famous bounty hunter Duane "Dog" Chapman, of A&E's *Dog the Bounty Hunter*, had his show suspended briefly after he made racist comments in 2007 and then tried to renovate his public image).

Indeed, for either celeb-reality shows or programs about noncelebrities, abandoning the "ordinary" seems to violate the conventions of reality TV fame. A spectacular case in point is the backlash against Jon and Kate Gosselin, stars of TLC's *Jon & Kate Plus 8*. The program enjoyed ratings success as it followed the couple raising their two sets of multiples, twin girls and sextuplets. While the premise of raising such a large family and the unusual situation of two multiples provided an "extraordinary" setting, the show's narrative focused on how "ordinary" this family really was, as they tried to replicate a stereotypical modern nuclear family unit of breadwinner father and dependent mother and children.

Yet in 2008, the show's fourth season began focusing on product placement tie-ins and lavish vacations provided gratis by resorts looking for advertising. This dynamic created a narrative tension that escalated in the program's fifth season in 2009, when tabloids accused Jon of cheating on Kate and Kate of desperately seeking fame and fortune, with the children caught in the middle. In response to a media firestorm, the couple actually addressed the rumors in one episode, announcing their divorce and decrying the toll the media scrutiny had taken on them, while insisting that they never put fame or fortune above their family.[19] The fact that they found it necessary to respond to media allegations directly, within the narrative of their show (in direct-address interviews and in shots of paparazzi camped outside their home), indicates the degree to which they were perceived as violating codes of fame as well as the normative family codes they had earlier reproduced.

Celebrity reality programs in particular invite audiences to see the star's authentic personality even in the midst of a mediated show where stars could be understood as playing the role of themselves. Richard Dyer and Richard deCordova have shown that in Hollywood film, when a star gives media access to her or his "private" life, that supporting material actually reinforces the "public" star persona. The star's publicly available private life—splashed across tabloids and promotional materials—and her or his film roles mutually inform each other, as if a star's performance in a film appears to reveal something about the individual's personality (even though the film scenario has nothing to do with her or his actual life).[20] The process of manufacturing the star image glamorously becomes part of the image itself, as Dyer puts it, "like a conjuror showing you how a trick is done."[21] Yet audiences continually look for traces of the star's authentic self in her or his performances.

Reality television twists this formula. As noted earlier, Annette Hill observes that reality audiences know people act differently when a camera is watching, yet they still look for authentic moments of self beneath the performance,[22] just as in society more generally, we still search for some version of an authentic self even while knowing most identity is constant performance. On reality programs about celebrities, we see multiple layers of performance, as the stars navigate their public personas, their private personas, and different kinds of selfhood. Viewers are encouraged to parse out which moments are "authentic."

If, as Dyer argued, the classic Hollywood film star served as an exemplar of individualism in a capitalist society, an exceptional person who becomes famous for some quality or talent, what does it mean if anyone can be a star now for being him- or herself on reality TV?[23] Critic Su Holmes argues persuasively that reality stars who "play" themselves on camera speak to an anxiety about changing models of selfhood—a postmodern view of identity as constantly changing performance versus an older, premodern notion of stable identity. Holmes insists that the fear now is about how to have an authentic selfhood in an era in which identity is mass mediated.[24] If a star's performances are in a feedback loop with supporting media (fanzines, biographies), reality series redefine stardom by trying to be all encompassing, covering all aspects of stars through Web tie-ins, material incorporated into the program, and even behind-the-scenes specials.[25]

MTV's *The Osbournes* is a prime example of a program that achieved ratings success by ironically juxtaposing Ozzy's domestic life with his bat-biting Prince of Darkness public rock star image. Looking at the raw footage of Ozzy's family life, producers saw typical domestic sitcom plotlines and edited them as such in a "reality sitcom."[26] Ozzy, his manager wife Sharon, and two of their children who agreed to participate, Jack and Kelly, embody the sitcom types of doddering dad, caring mom, and rebellious teens. Critics have argued that the point of the show is to highlight the ordinary underneath the extraordinary.[27] But for me, the emphasis in the show is on the difficulty of maintaining the ordinary–extraordinary balance of stardom.

The Osbourne kids in particular are aware of this problem. The show's distinctive merger of fame versus domestic life emerges in moments such as when Kelly hits Jack. He points to the camera, breaking the invisibility conceit that had been operating in the scene, and says in direct address, "That's on camera, Kelly!" Like the typical sitcom teen, he wants to complain to his mother. Unlike the standard sitcom brother, Jack can plead his case by showing MTV's footage to his mother as visual proof.[28]

One controversial surveillance camera scene in season one features a "family meeting" Sharon calls so the parents can urge Jack and Kelly to curb their partying and drug use. Both teens eventually went to drug rehabilitation clinics. MTV later aired a special with Jack urging viewers to avoid drugs. The teens respond to this by highlighting the difficult ordinary–extraordinary mix in their star family life. Kelly details the hardships of fame, such as a childhood raised on the road during rock tours and being ridiculed at school. Taped in black and white with a stationary unattended camera, the scene's surveillance visual style implies that viewers have been allowed into a private family meeting in an upstairs room not usually shown to the public. Jack and Kelly later claimed they did not know the planted camera was there and that MTV staged the scene, while Sharon insisted MTV did not stage it. The fact that Sharon knows the cameras are there while the teenagers claim they did not suggests that she and the producers tried to get a less mediated reaction from the kids. The scene is a direct cinema-style long take uninterrupted by cuts, lending it grainy realism compared to other scenes.

As it offers a supposedly more authentic moment, the program insists that it gives access to the Osbournes' real lives, yet it suggests there is purer entrée to be had. The family meeting scene undercuts the authenticity of other scenes and reinforces the idea that this scene is less mediated than others, when, of course, it is all mediated and edited. Here we get the ever-vanishing real, the promise of newer vistas of reality to be consumed. Even in this supposedly more authentic moment, the star image is still the prevailing rhetoric, the private/public, ordinary/extraordinary mix Kelly bemoans.

In response to criticism about this scene, the Osbournes and producers made a season-three finale mockumentary. The family pretends Jack had accidentally killed Sharon's favorite dog and Sharon had left the family.[29] The episode ends with a "man behind the curtain" shot of the Osbournes gathered laughing with the camera crew in the kitchen, the dog safely there. Sharon wanted to ridicule press reports that MTV contrived events, so they orchestrated a parody of that charge. But as in Dyer's formulation of film, once we see how the conjuror performs the trick, we do not have any less fascination with the performance of that trick. Indeed, Internet message boards lit up with viewers debating whether to appreciate the self-reflexive joke or feel betrayed by it, with some fans so invested in the show's truth claims that even after hearing it was a hoax, they still worried about whether the dog was actually alive.[30]

Other celebrity family programs similarly struggle to maintain a delicate ordinary/extraordinary mix. In MTV's *Run's House*, Reverend Run, like Ozzy before him, markets his domesticom through ironic juxtaposition: the rapper lives the star life but has a normal family life and is even a minister.[31] Deeply intertwining commerce and family, Run presides over a growing business empire that includes his music, clothing lines with his mogul brother, Russell Simmons, and various media and business endeavors his children launch. While the program follows their jetsetter lifestyles, it must balance that dynamic with domestic scenes of Run and his second wife Justine parenting their blended family of six kids.

Similarly, A&E's *Gene Simmons Family Jewels* balances the extraordinary with the ordinary in depicting KISS rock star Simmons's "normal" family life, marketed as a "real-life A&E family series."[32] While Simmons and his partner, model Shannon Tweed, question family norms by emphasizing their unmarried state, the program nevertheless applies a modern nuclear family framework. Using *The Osbournes'* blueprint, the show implies savvy audiences steeped in rock marketing practices will be fascinated to see Simmons the domesticated father behind the fire-breathing image. Since his rock star image is so iconic, so immediately recognizable, and so incessantly consumed by fans eager for more (or nostalgic for their favorite band's heyday), the next logical step in branding that image is to give fans behind-the-scenes access to Simmons's daily life.

Far from undercutting his "rocker demon" stage persona, the "reality sitcom" account of Simmons out of his black leather and puttering around the house only fuels his media image. Fans see the extraordinary rock star living a glamorous life, but they see that balanced with footage of the ordinary, goofy father overly invested in his kids' lives. They are encouraged to envy the star yet identify with the man behind the curtain, maintaining an equilibrium lest the star seem too remote or the ordinary man seem too familiar.

Reality Narrative

In addition to such thematic complexity around stardom, a third factor that contributes to reality TV's appeal and cult following is how the genre utilizes narrative, specifically the way it turns real people's lives into media stories. While the use of stock tropes, such as hero or villain, girl next door or relatable "everyman" is prevalent, some shows take this narrative process one step further. In turning a cast member into a narrative trope, some reality formats actually allow people to perform TV narratives as if they are their own lives (witness *My Life is a Sitcom*, where families pitched their lives as TV sitcoms, or *Scream Play*, where participants reenacted popular movie stunt scenes). The genre more generally pictures people enacting media fantasies in various ways; some programs have fans become contestants on the series they have just been watching (*Paradise Hotel*), some have casts enact new versions of old TV sitcoms (*The New Partridge Family*,

The Real Gilligan's Island), while others have experts transform people into their favorite fictional characters or media celebrities, like movie character Rocky Balboa or country singer Loretta Lynn (*In Character*). Thus, reality shows often push for a collapse between a viewer at home and a character on the screen, because any of those viewers could become the character on television.

As reality series illuminate the process of identity formation through narrative, they raise larger issues about turning real people into characters or fashioning their real lives into stories for entertainment. Many of these programs imply that one can learn to find one's true self through media narratives. One result of this dynamic is that these series imply that social identity is an arbitrary performance—one can switch places with someone else and inhabit that person's social identity or choose to change who oneself is. The reality genre speaks to the appeal of storytelling, which in this case purports to make people's daily lives as compelling as fictional plotlines.

Indeed, reality TV appears as something "new" because it launches, in fuller form than ever before, the idea that viewers can not only interact with television series through connectivity such as Internet tie-ins and call-on voting shows, but also by literally entering into the stories and events pictured on the screen. It meditates on the role of television as a medium in the sense that it as it lets audiences watch "people just like them" enact their lives on shows structured like television plotlines. It speaks to some desire to live out TV scripts—for audiences to have their lives more closely resemble their favorite television tropes. Reality television reverses classic narrative; instead of trying to make characters seem real, it tries to turn real people into characters, using predictable and repetitive narrative frames. Likewise, it is important to analyze the dynamics through which individuals choose to embrace or reject their character narratives.

Big Brother has a striking example of a participant interacting with the show's narrative conventions. Cast member Will Kirby's strategy to win CBS's *Big Brother 2* implies fictional narratives can be more compelling than supposedly real life stories. Kirby created a persona, an obnoxious puppetmaster. Later describing the fictional characters he drew from to play this "role," Kirby notes the plan he and his brother Ian developed:

> We pulled from Christian Bale's character in *American Psycho* and Tyler Durden (Brad Pitt's character) from *Fight Club*. . . . We developed a character who was to be hated by everyone. He would appear weak at first

and not considered a threat while he let everyone else pick each other
apart. Then he would become a threat, doing anything he had to do to
win.... By the end I was just making up lies right and left. It was
crazy.[33]

Kirby dubs himself "the P.T. Barnum of reality TV."[34] He used his persona to win the gamedoc (and $500,000) and to garner spots on *Big
Brother All-Stars* and *Dr. 90210*. His self-consciously produced literary
persona becomes another level of narrative reality on these reality
shows.

However, participant's efforts to control their own reality narratives
often lead to frustration and ambivalent results. Reality programs that
have home viewers join shows "already in progress" constitute an
extreme example. *Paradise Hotel* turned fans into contestants. The
host selected several viewers from the studio audience, and producers
flew them to the tropical location where the dating gamedoc was
occurring. The new cast members mistakenly believed they would be
able to control how they were represented on television and win the
game because they had just been watching the events unfolding from
the TV camera's omniscient point of view. They responded with irritation when they realized that they did not have complete control over
their entrance into the TV narratives they had been watching. As
many reality TV producers insist, they cannot turn people into something they are not or create events out of whole cloth, but they can
choose to amplify events or emphasize existing character traits.[35]
Reality cast members sometimes bemoan the TV characters they
become, illuminating the vacillating pull of TV narratives (witness
Survivor All-Star cast member Jerri Manthey, who fled a studio audience interview, crying "we're real people too!" when hundreds of fans
booed her for being the villain).[36]

Consequently, the way reality TV shapes identity through narrative
is also fluctuating and ambivalent. One program has contestants live
out a romance prewritten for them. In *The Dating Experiment*, adapted
from a hit Japanese show, each episode followed two strangers who go
on a series of blind dates together; they read a diary that details what
they will do each day, describes their unfolding love story, and even
says how they should be feeling. After the diary finishes its narrative,
the two participants decide whether or not to continue dating. The
story was supposed to induce "real" love between the daters, with
varying degrees of success.[37] The program implied that the act of
living out a media romance narrative generates "true" emotions.

While not all reality programs take this narrative dynamic that far, most turn people into characters using common TV narrative tropes, like Osbourne as sitcom dad. In so doing, they illuminate the appeal of TV narratives and the depth of audience identification with them. Likewise, reality TV's cult following speaks to how the genre successfully updates ideas of fame now that anyone can become famous for playing him- or herself as a character on a reality show. But perhaps more powerfully, the genre captures the anxieties that come with this level of media interaction and with the idea that our lives are now lived digitally, on a range of cameras (whether on someone else's Facebook page or on a major network reality show), in images and stories that may circulate beyond our control.

Notes

1. Arild Fetveit, "Reality TV in the Digital Era: A Paradox in Visual Culture?" in *Reality Squared: Televisual Discourse on the Real*, ed. James Friedman (New Brunswick: Rutgers University Press, 2002), 119–37. Jon Dovey, "Reality TV," in *The Television Genre Book*, ed. Glen Creeber (London: British Film Institute, 2001), 134–137.

2. Robin L. Naby, Erica N. Biely, Sara J. Morgan, and Carmen R. Stitt, "Reality Based Television Programming and the Psychology of Its Appeal," *Media Psychology* 5 (2003): 303–30.

3. Ien Ang, *Watching Dallas: Television and the Melodramatic Imagination* (London: Routledge, 1985), 47.

4. Annette Hill, *Reality TV Audiences and Popular Factual Television* (London: Routledge, 2005).

5. Though we know unscripted programming has been around since television's earliest days, the date of the current reality trend's onset is a matter of critical debate. To cite representative examples, Kilborn dubs *America's Unsolved Mysteries* (1987) the original impetus for current reality TV, while Jermyn points to *Crimewatch UK* (1984–). Richard Kilborn, "How Real Can You Get?: Recent Developments in 'Reality' Television," *European Journal of Communications* 9 (1994): 421–39. Deborah Jermyn, "'This *Is* About Real People!': Video Technologies, Actuality, and Affect in the Television Crime Appeal," *Understanding Reality Television*, ed. Su Holmes and Deborah Jermyn (London: Routledge, 2004): 75.

6. For an excellent discussion of reality TV and genre, see John Caldwell, "Prime-Time Fiction Theorizes the Docu-Real," in *Reality Squared: Televisual Discourse on the Real*, ed. James Friedman (New Brunswick: Rutgers University Press, 2002), 259–92. See also Caldwell, *Televisuality: Style, Crisis, and Authority in American Television* (New Brunswick: Rutgers University Press, 1995).

7. Bill Carter, "Reality TV Alters the Way TV Does Business," *New York Times*, January 25, 2003, A1.

8. Carter, A1. *Survivor*'s high ratings spawned other reality successes, with a number of reality programs reaching the top ten shows for each year; during both the 2002–2003 and 2003–2004 seasons, five of the top ten network shows were reality formats. Alex Strachan, "Reality Check: Conventional Television Wisdom Turned on Its Ear," *The Star Phoenix* [Saskatoon, Saskatchewan], July 17, 2004, E1, final edition.

9. Scott Collins and Maria Elena Fernandez, "Life Imitates Reality TV When Execs Square Off," *Los Angeles Times: Electronic Edition*, July 16, 2004, http://articles.latimes.com/2004/jul/16/entertainment/et-tvwar16.

10. Statistics like networks running 14 percent of their schedules as reality shows in early 2003 prompted television writer Stephen Godchaux to state apocalyptically: "Scripted television is actually in peril," though that has not proven to be the case. Jenny Hontz, "Reality Is Harsh on TV's Creative Teams," *New York Times on the Web*, February 9, 2003, http://www.nytimes.com/2003/02/09/business/yourmoney/09TVTV.html?ex=1047286669&ei=1&en=7f296d3686edbd6a.

11. In 2003, CBS failed to convince judges that ABC's *I'm a Celebrity... Get Me Out of Here!* infringed on *Survivor*, and NBC aired another season of that franchise in 2009. Meanwhile, in 2004, ABC accused Fox of shoplifting the wife swap and nanny formats ABC acquired the rights to from British originals, while NBC accused Fox of scooping their boxing gamedoc format. Collins and Fernandez.

12. There was an earlier, as yet unrealized, plan by former reality stars to create a channel called Reality Central. Lynn Elber, "All-Reality TV Channel Planned for 2004," *Yahoo! News*, April 28, 2004, http://old.chronicle.augusta.com/stories/2003/04/29/tel_371151.shtml.

13. Graeme Turner, "The Uses and Limitations of Genre," in *The Television Genre Book*, ed. Glenn Creeber (London: British Film Institute, 2001), 4–6.

14. Chad Raphael, "The Political Economic Origins of Reali-TV," in *Reality TV: Remaking Television Culture*, ed. Susan Murray and Laurie Ouellette (New York: New York University Press, 2004), 119–136.

15. When production on some scripted shows was suspended during the strike, networks rushed new seasons of reality franchises to air, such as CBS's *Big Brother* and *The Amazing Race*.

16. For solid overviews of the field, see: Laurie Ouellette and James Hay, *Better Living through Reality TV: Television and Post-welfare Citizenship* (Malden, MA: Blackwell, 2008); Jonathan Bignell, *Big Brother: Reality TV in the Twenty-First Century* (New York: Palgrave Macmillan, 2005); Susan Murray and Laurie Ouellette, eds., *Reality TV: Remaking Television Culture* (New York: New York University Press, 2004); Richard Kilborn, *Staging the Real: Factual TV Programming in the Age of Big Brother* (Manchester: Manchester University Press, 2003); Su Holmes and Deborah Jermyn, eds., *Understanding Reality*

Television (London: Routledge, 2004); James Friedman, ed., *Reality Squared: Televisual Discourse on the Real* (New Brunswick: Rutgers University Press, 2002).

17. John Ellis, *Visible Fictions: Cinema, Television, Video*, 2nd ed. (London: Routledge, 1992).

18. In my arguments here, I am agreeing with media studies scholars who have argued for a nuanced application of star theory to TV in general and reality TV in particular, asserting, contra Ellis, that his film paradigm is applicable to television.

19. "Houses and Changes," *Jon & Kate Plus 8*, TLC, 22 June 2009.

20. Richard Dyer, *Stars* (London: British Film Institute, 1998); Dyer, *Heavenly Bodies: Film Stars and Society* (Basingstoke, UK: Macmillan, 1986); Richard deCordova, *Personalities: The Emergence of the Star System in America* (Urbana: University of Illinois Press, 1990).

21. Richard Dyer, "Four Films of Lana Turner," in *Star Texts: Image and Performance in Film and Television*, ed. Jeremy G. Butler (Detroit: Wayne State University Press, 1991), 228.

22. Hill, *"Big Brother," Reality TV*.

23. Richard Dyer, "Four Films of Lana Turner," in *Star Texts: Image and Performance in Film and Television*, ed. Jeremy G. Butler (Detroit: Wayne State University Press, 1991), 226–28.

24. Su Holmes, "'All You've Got to Worry About Is the Task, Having a Cup of Tea, and Doing a Bit of Sunbathing': Approaching Celebrity in Big Brother," in *Understanding Reality Television*, ed. Su Holmes and Deborah Jermyn (London: Routledge, 2004), 128, 132.

25. John Ellis, "Stars as a Cinematic Phenomenon," in *Star Texts: Image and Performance in Film and Television*, ed. Jeremy G. Butler (Detroit: Wayne State University Press, 1991), 302.

26. Nancy Miller, "American Goth: How the Osbournes, a Simple, Head-banging British Family, Became Our Nation's Latest Reality-TV Addiction," *Entertainment Weekly*, April 19, 2002, 25.

27. Jennifer Gillan, "From Ozzie Nelson to Ozzy Osbourne: The Genesis and Development of the Reality (Star) Sitcom," in *Understanding Reality Television*, ed. Su Holmes and Deborah Jermyn (London: Routledge, 2004), 54–70. Derek Kompare, "Extraordinarily Ordinary: *The Osbournes* as 'An American Family,'" in *Reality TV: Remaking Television Culture*, ed. Susan Murray and Laurie Ouellette (New York: New York University Press, 2004), 97–116.

28. "A House Divided," *The Osbournes*, MTV, March 5, 2002.

29. "Ozz Well That Ends Well," *The Osbournes*, MTV, August 12, 2003.

30. Jeannette Walls, "*The Osbournes* Goes to the Dogs: Some Fans of *The Osbournes* Are Not Amused by the Latest Episode," *Jeannette Walls Delivers the Scoop, MSNBC.com*, August 16, 2003, http://today.msnbc.msn.com/id/3076379/ns/today-today_entertainment/t/osbournes-goes-dogs/.

31. *Run's House: Complete Seasons 1 & 2*, DVD, Paramount, 2007.

32. *Gene Simmons Family Jewels: The Complete Season 1*, DVD, A&E 2006.

33. Mark Hinson, "What You Don't Know About the Good Doctor. Really, He's Not So Bad. It Was All An Act, You See," *Tallahassee Democrat*, September 30, 2001, D1.

34. Lynette Rice, "The Q&A: 9021-Oh, Snap!," EW.com, August 2, 2007, http://www.ew.com/ew/article/0,,20049601,00.html (accessed August 2, 2007).

35. *Reality of Reality*, Bravo, September 8–11, 2003. Obviously, the edited narrative is collaborative in a complex way, since producers take footage of the cast's actions and create story arcs.

36. *Survivor: All-Stars*, CBS, May 9, 2004.

37. ABC described the concept for the show as follows: "Complete strangers give up all control of their lives to be ruled by a mysterious diary, all in the hopes of finding true love, in a unique new reality romance series! The idea behind *The Dating Experiment*: If actors and actresses on movie sets fall in love because of heightened circumstances, can the same happen if real people are put in a similar situation?" For more information, please see Amber Grapestain, "The Dating Experiment Experiment," Blogcritics.org, June 26, 2003, http://blogcritics.org/video/article/the-dating-experiment-experiment/

ABOUT THE EDITOR AND CONTRIBUTORS

The Editor

BOB BATCHELOR is an assistant professor in the School of Journalism and Mass Communication at Kent State University and academic coordinator of the school's online master's degree program concentrated in public relations. He received his undergraduate degree in history, philosophy, and political science at the University of Pittsburgh and earned a master's degree in history at Kent State University. Bob earned his doctorate in English literature at the University of South Florida, where he studied with Phillip Sipiora.

A noted expert on contemporary American popular culture, Bob is the author or editor of 10 books: *The 1900s; Kotex, Kleenex, and Huggies: Kimberly-Clark and the Consumer Revolution in American Business; Basketball in America: From the Playgrounds to Jordan's Game and Beyond; Literary Cash: Unauthorized Writings Inspired by the Legendary Johnny Cash; The 1980s; The 2000s;* and the four-volume *American Pop: Popular Culture Decade by Decade.*

Bob has published more than 500 articles and essays in magazines, websites, and reference works, including *Radical History Review, The Journal of American Culture, The Mailer Review,* the *Dictionary of American History, PopMatters.com, The American Prospect Online,* and *Public Relations Review.* He is a member of the editorial advisory board of *The Journal of Popular Culture* and on the editorial board of *Pop Culture*

Universe: Icons, Idols, Ideas (ABC-CLIO). He also pens book reviews for *The Journal of American Culture.*

Bob's current research includes books on John Updike, Bob Dylan, and the role of the rubber industry in the Allied World War II victory. In addition, Bob is co-editing two collections with colleague Danielle Coombs for Praeger: *We Are What We Sell: How Advertising Shapes American Life . . . And Always Has* (3 volumes) and *American History through American Sports* (3 volumes).

The Contributors

AARON BARLOW teaches writing at New York City College of Technology of the City University of New York. He focuses his scholarship on film and on the intersection of technology and culture. His latest books are *Quentin Tarantino: Life at the Extremes* (Praeger, 2010) and *Blogging America: The New Public Sphere* (Praeger, 2008).

ADAM G. CAPITANIO is a Ph.D. candidate in American Studies at Michigan State University. He holds an M.A. from the Cinema Studies department at New York University. His current dissertation project is on the depiction of space and the transformation of public and private spheres as manifested in home movies and videos. Other research topics he engages in include technological and aesthetic histories of film and media, cult and exploitation film, digital media, and comic books.

BRIAN COGAN is an associate professor and chair of the Department of Communication Arts and Sciences at Molloy College in Long Island, New York. He is the author, co-author and co-editor of numerous books, articles, and anthologies on popular culture, music, and the media. His specific areas of research interest are punk rock, comic books, and the intersection of politics and popular culture. He is the author of *The Punk Rock Encyclopedia* (Sterling, 2008), co-author with Tony Kelso of *The Encyclopedia of Popular Culture, Media and Politics* (Greenwood Press, 2009) as well as co-editor with Tony Kelso on *Mosh the Polls: Youth Voters, Popular Culture, and Democratic Engagement* (Lexington, 2008), which is about youth culture and political involvement. Cogan is also the co-author, along with William Phillips, of the *Encyclopedia of Heavy Metal Music and Culture* (Greenwood Press, 2009). He is on the editorial board of the *Journal of Popular Culture* and has written about these topics for publications such as the *New York Post, Chunklet,*

Go Metric, Punknews.org, and *Muze.com.* A native New Yorker, he has been a drummer/vocalist in the pop-punk band In-Crowd since 1987.

TOMÁS F. CROWDER-TARABORRELLI obtained his B.A. in journalism from San Francisco State University. He received his master's degree in comparative literature (SFSU) and his Ph.D. from the Department of Spanish and Portuguese at the University of California, Irvine (1996–2001). While teaching at the University of San Francisco, Crowder-Taraborrelli formed the Cine Campesino collective and made two documentaries in Honduras (2003–2004). He was a fellow in the humanities at Stanford University, where he researched the role of film in the prosecution of crimes against humanity, and founded the Stanford Film Lab (2004–2008). He studied scriptwriting, lighting, and directing at the Film Arts Foundation, San Francisco. He has taught courses and led workshops in film and is one of the editors of the forthcoming anthology *Film and Genocide* (University of Wisconsin Press, 2011). Dr. Crowder-Taraborrelli is currently a visiting professor of Latin American studies at Soka University of America in California, where he has begun work on a manuscript entitled *Documentary Film and Plan Condor.* He frequently publishes articles for film magazines and journals.

JOSEPH DAROWSKI is a Ph.D. student in American Studies at Michigan State University. He completed his bachelor's and master's degrees in English from Brigham Young University. His primary research area is comic books, and he makes frequent use of Michigan State's excellent resource, the National Comic Arts Collection.

LEIGH H. EDWARDS is associate professor of English at Florida State University. She is the author of *Johnny Cash and the Paradox of American Identity* (Indiana University Press, 2009). Her work in popular culture has been published in *The Journal of Popular Culture, Feminist Media Studies, Film & History: An Interdisciplinary Journal of Film and Television Studies, Narrative,* and *FLOW: A Critical Forum for Television and Media Culture.* She is on the editorial board of *Pop Culture Universe: Icons, Idols, Ideas* (ABC-CLIO) and is a staff writer for *PopMatters.* Writing on topics ranging from rockabillies to Twitter, she focuses in particular on constructions of gender in popular music, television, and new media.

CAROL-ANN FARKAS is an associate professor of English and the director of writing programs at Massachusetts College of Pharmacy and Health Sciences (MCPHS) in Boston. She received her doctorate from the University of Alberta in Edmonton Alberta, Canada; her dissertation examined the woman physician in late-nineteenth-century British and American fiction. At MCPHS, she teaches courses in first-year composition, nineteenth-century fiction, and literature and medicine. Her recent publications have examined portrayals of wellness in popular culture, ranging from fitness magazines to medical-mystery TV programs.

LINCOLN GERAGHTY is principal lecturer in film studies and subject leader for media studies in the School of Creative Arts, Film and Media at the University of Portsmouth. He received his Ph.D. in American studies from the University of Nottingham in 2005. He serves as editorial advisor for *The Journal of Popular Culture*, *Reconstruction*, and *Atlantis* with interests in science fiction film and television, fandom, and collecting in popular culture. He is the author of *Living with Star Trek: American Culture and the Star Trek Universe* (IB Tauris, 2007) and *American Science Fiction Film and Television* (Berg, 2009) and the editor of *The Influence of Star Trek on Television, Film and Culture* (McFarland, 2008), with Mark Jancovich *The Shifting Definitions of Genre: Essays on Labeling Film, Television Shows and Media* (McFarland, 2008), and *Channeling the Future: Essays on Science Fiction and Fantasy Television* (Scarecrow, 2009). He is currently serving as editor of the *Directory of World Cinema: American Hollywood*, an online and print publication from Intellect Books, and is working on a collection about the TV series *Smallville* to be published by Scarecrow.

JODEE HAMMOND grew up in Moundsville, West Virginia, the wild and wonderful state. She received a B.A. in public relations from Marshall University. While at MU, she served as president of the Public Relations Student Society of America. Jodee also was the performing arts/entertainment beat reporter for the student newspaper *The Parthenon*. She is currently a graduate student in the public relations master's degree program at Kent State University. She has worked in communications with a nonprofit called Southwestern Community Action Council, tourism at Oglebay Resort and Conference Center, and the Charleston Area Medical Center. Jodee won the Country Music Association *Close Up* Award of Merit that involved writing for CMA's blog for its annual music festival and awards show. She plans to move to Nashville to do PR in the country music entertainment industry.

DANIEL HARMON is an acquisitions editor at Praeger Publishers, where he oversees a large assortment of titles related to film, television, sports, media, literature, and American culture as a whole. He is also a contributing blogger at Brokelyn.com.

DONNA WALLER HARPER is a 35-year veteran of teaching. She currently adjuncts at Middle Tennessee State University in Murfreesboro, Tennessee. She has been active in the national Popular Culture/ American Culture Association and the Popular & American Culture Associations in the South serving as panel leader, area chair, and at the southern level on the advisory board. She is a contributor to Ray Browne's *Encyclopedia of Popular Culture*, as well as the *Dictionary of Literary Biography on Detectives* and Kathy Klein's Edgar-nominated *Great Women Mystery Writers*.

JEFFREY C. JACKSON teaches at NorthWest Arkansas Community College in Bentonville, Arkansas. He grew up in Carbondale, Illinois, and received his bachelor's degree from University of Illinois and master's from the University of Arkansas. Jeffrey taught English at the University of Arkansas for two years and has taught at NWACC since 2000. Jeffrey recently taught an honors course with an emphasis on popular culture. He is an avid reader and movie buff. Jeffrey saw *The Rocky Horror Picture Show* for the first time at the Southern Illinois University Student Center in 1987 (and hasn't been the same since).

LARRY Z. LESLIE (Ph.D., Tennessee, 1986) is associate professor emeritus in the School of Mass Communications at the University of South Florida, Tampa. He holds a bachelor's degree in English education from Eastern Illinois University and a master's degree in English from Austin Peay State University. He is the author three books: *Mass Communication Ethics: Decision Making in Postmodern Culture, Communication Research Methods in Postmodern Culture* and *Celebrity in the 21st Century: A Reference Handbook*, published in 2011 by ABC-CLIO.

DEBORAH MCLEOD is a doctoral candidate at the University of South Florida. She has been published in the *Journal of Modern Literature* and is currently working on her dissertation on disability and modernism.

PHILIP L. SIMPSON received his bachelor's and master's degrees in English from Eastern Illinois University in 1986 and 1989, respectively, and his doctorate in American literature from Southern Illinois University in 1996. He serves as associate provost at the Palm Bay campus of Brevard Community College in Florida. Before that, he was a professor of communications and humanities at the Palm Bay campus of Brevard Community College for eight years and department chair of Liberal Arts for five years. He also served as president of the Popular Culture Association and area chair of Horror for the Association. He received the Association's Felicia Campbell Area Chair Award in 2006. He sits on the editorial board of the *Journal of Popular Culture*. His first book, *Psycho Paths: Tracking the Serial Killer through Contemporary American Film and Fiction*, was published in 2000 by Southern Illinois University Press; his second book, *Making Murder: The Fiction of Thomas Harris*, was published in 2009 by Praeger Press. He is the author of numerous other essays on film, literature, popular culture, and horror.

CARMEN STITT (Ph.D., University of Arizona) is assistant professor of communication studies at California State University, Sacramento. She teaches such courses as Media Communication and Society, Mass Media Theory and Effects, Media History, Introduction to Research Methods, and Health Communication. Her research interests include social influence, persuasion, learning health information from media, and effects of processing television narratives. She has published works in *Health Communication, Media Psychology*, and *Encyclopedia of Children, Adolescents, and the Media*.

KRISTI M. WILSON is an assistant professor of rhetoric and humanities at Soka University. Dr. Wilson's research and teaching interests include classics, film studies, cultural studies, and rhetoric. She founded the Stanford Film Lab and taught at Stanford University for nine years before coming to Soka University. She is the co-editor of *Italian Neorealism and Global Cinema* (Wayne State University Press, 2007) and author of numerous publications in such journals as *Screen, Yearbook of Comparative and General Literature, Signs*, and *Literature/ Film Quarterly*. Her new anthology, *Film and Genocide*, will be published in 2011 (University of Wisconsin Press). In addition to teaching, she directs the writing program at Soka University of America and serves on the editorial board of *Latin American Perspectives* (SAGE Publications).

INDEX